Lynn Seymour was born in Canada in 1939 and joined the Sadler's Wells Ballet Company (now the Royal Ballet) in 1957. Among the roles she created are: the Bride in *Le Baiser de la Fée*, 1960: the Girl in *The Invitation*, 1960; Juliet in *Romeo and Juliet*, 1964; Anna-Anastasia in *Anastasia*, 1966; Natalia Petrovna in *A Month in the Country*, 1976; Mary Vetsera in *Mayerling*, 1978. In 1978–80 she was Artistic Director at the Ballet of the Bavarian State Opera, Munich. The ballets she has choreographed include *Rashomon* and *Intimate Letters*.

Paul Gardner was on the staff of the *New York Times* for seven years before moving to Europe as a freelance writer and following Lynn Seymour's career at Covent Garden. His reviews on the arts have appeared in *New York Magazine*, the *Financial Times*, *Art News* and *The Observer*.

Lynn

The autobiography of Lynn Seymour

with Paul Gardner

PANTHER
Granada Publishing

Panther Books
Granada Publishing Ltd
8 Grafton Street, London W1X 3LA

Published by Panther Books 1985

First published in Great Britain by
Granada Publishing 1984

Copyright © Lynn Seymour and Paul Gardner 1984

ISBN 0-583-13578-1

Printed and bound in Great Britain by
Collins, Glasgow

Set in Baskerville

Contents

List of Illustrations

The dress worn by Lynn Seymour in the jacket photograph is by Zoran from Browns, London; hair by Charlie of michaeljohn.

Acknowledgements

My thanks to the following without whom:
At the risk of omitting a few, in no particular order, I wish to thank the following for their time, insights, interest and assistance.

My husband Vanya Hackel, my mother Marjorie Springbett, the Hon. Jacob Rothschild and Rudolf Nureyev. Bruce and Pat Springbett. Dame Ninette de Valois. Sir Frederick Ashton. Clement Crisp, Sir John Tooley, and Lord Drogheda. Dame Margot Fonteyn de Arias, Sir Robert Helpmann, Fenella Fielding, Max and Ed Speight. Derek and Alison Smith.

Kenneth Barlow, Albrecht Widmann, Stephanie Rosenberg, Fran and Professor Irwin Corey, Chuck Green, Buzz Miller and Alan Groh, Connie Torey, Peg Buchanan, Fay Angus, Sarah Neece, Annie Russell, Clay Taliaferro, Peter Blake-Turner, James Herbert, David and Heather Springbett, Nicholas Hutchinson, Andrew Logan, Richard Selby, Joy and David Virgoe, and Sylvia Carson. Lord and Lady Rosehill.

Lord Goodman and his good offices. Those at Granada/ Collins, Alewyn Birch, Richard Johnson my attentive and supportive editor, Caroline Alcock who did the picture research and Mark Bonham Carter. Lord Weidenfeld for the initial suggestion.

Christopher Gable, Donald MacLeary, Betty Anderton, Vergie Derman, Brenda Bolton, Anne Whitelaw, Margaret

Lee, Roy Round and Georgina Parkinson, Dr Carl Lambert, Nigel and Maude Gosling, Nico Georgiadis. Henry Legerton, Peter Williams, Herbert and Nora Ross, Philip and Ellie Pace, Alvin Ailey, Colin Jones, John Field, Lady Sainsbury, Terry Southern, Peter Martins, Charles France, Nat Sherman, Richard Corey, Hal Lehrman, Glen Tetley and Scott Douglas, Peter Wright, Crazy Charlie, Robert North, Jeffrey Solomons and Kenneth MacMillan.

For their constant encouragement and support, Paul Gardner wishes to thank Lila and Paul Edwards, Caroline and Robert Blackman, Buzz Miller, Alan Groh, Lynn Bonsall, Grace Glueck, Adam Drewnowski and John Willenbecher.

TO MY REGAL MOTHER
and
the memory of
MY DEAR FATHER

A CITATION to My Darling Husband
For Conduct Above and Beyond
the Call of Duty

Part One
Leaps . . .

CHAPTER 1

In a Garden

When I looked up from my desk, a grey rabbit over five feet tall was staring at me. He sat very quietly on his haunches in the garden, his furry nose pressed against the glass doors. His eyes were grave and uncompromising. Neither of us moved. Then he winked at me.

It was twilight and the summer sky was streaked with purple and gold. From the living room, I have a clear view, across the snooker table, to the apple and pear trees, the rose bushes in full bloom and the honeysuckle vine creeping along a glass expanse that kept the rabbit out. But what if he became beastly and decided to pounce? Except for the obvious, I haven't a clue about the habits of rabbits. No one else was in the house which heightened the unease I felt. Usually at this hour before supper the big boys are doing their homework and my little one is playing upstairs. Now all the chaps were out, and I was not certain when they would return, a negligent bit of control on my part as I like to know their schedules. Then I am not stuck here alone confronting strange animals.

I had been poking around the kitchen wondering what to feed my brood, a housekeeping chore left up to nannies in earlier days. But when I stopped dancing, the nannies were dispensed with. For several months, while life was in a holding pattern, nothing was coming into the pot. A close inspection of the fridge yielded sausages, frozen fish fingers and a treacherous chunk of cheese. Some women, I know, buy all their groceries for the week in one omnivorous ecstasy. But I prefer not to plan the week's meals as meticulously as the repertory for the Royal Ballet. I always knew that I would be dancing *Giselle* on a given Monday and *A Month in the Country* on Thursday, but neither my family nor I want to know, for a fact, that we're doing mutton chops Tuesday, bangers-and-mash Wednesday, and so on. Eating should be like sex. You have what you want when you want it if you can get it.

The answering machine, Miss Brodie, is out of order, so, when the telephone rang, I forgot, quite happily, about a trip to the greengrocer in the Chiswick High Road and went to the phone, pulling shut the garden doors. I suspect the grey rabbit was hiding behind the hydrangeas watching every move. The house is a three-storey Norman Shaw building. The interior was completely gutted when we moved in ten years ago. The ground floor is essentially two rooms: a redbrick kitchen where we meet, eat and socialize around an enormous pine table, and the living room which runs the length of the house, front to back. I had the dividing walls knocked out, creating a vast area for the boys to play snooker, darts, run the electric train and horse around on heaps of pillows under the bay window. My desk, with the downstairs phone on a cobra-like cord, is between two fireplaces in the middle, floating into the space and separating the snooker table from the pillows. Guests who have no qualms about privacy frequently curl up on the pillows for weeks.

As soon as I heard Christopher Gable's voice, I settled down for a nice cosy chat. Christopher and I met yonks ago, in the late fifties, when we were students at the Royal Ballet School, and he became my favourite partner. With him I seldom made a wrong move onstage. We looked right together too. He was muscular and handsomely blond, I was supple and dark. We never lost eye contact when dancing. Christopher made me feel utterly beautiful. During our partnership, which lasted only four years, there was a claque, an audience at Covent Garden that came to see *us*. Christopher and I have been together through thick and thin. He asked what I was up to and I muttered, 'Trying to sort out what the press generously calls my "reckless, courageous, unpredictable life."' He had seen the recent headlines and replied sweetly with his tongue firmly in his cheek that I always did get the good reviews.

He began telling me about a television play he had just done and I was fishing for cigarettes amidst a clutter of letters, unopened bills, an encyclopedia-sized appointment book which I call the Talmud, two scripts which I could not finish, stubby pencils and the odd piece of jewellery. I looked up in frustration, realizing I had left the cigarettes in the kitchen, and that is when I spied the rabbit. I didn't know what to think. The creature winked. Then I sat frozen. My heart was doing the old curtain-time chest bumps. It was such an impertinent rabbit. Suppose it took a notion to plunge through the glass?

'Lynnie, Lynnie, are you playing possum,' Christopher asked, 'or have you gone to sleep? I'm getting no response.'

It took a moment to recharge my vocal cords. 'Christopher,' I whispered slowly, hardly daring to breathe and recalling that bears – or was it bulls – would not move until you did. Perhaps this applied to other animals as well. 'There's a rabbit outside the door and it's almost as tall as you.'

He burst out laughing. 'Are you sure it's not James Stewart's Harvey?'

I ignored his sportiveness. 'What am I going to do? I think it wants to come in.'

'Lynnie, are you feeling all right?' he asked, worried. Anyone who announces the appearance of a gigantic rabbit, particularly after a possum has been mentioned, is seldom taken seriously.

'Of course not,' I snapped. 'Aren't you listening?'

'Lynnie, rabbits, even wild rabbits, don't grow any

bigger than your average house pet,' he said. 'The hare is what you're thinking of. It has very long ears and legs.'

'In that case, the hare is here, my darling.' But where did it come from and how long did it plan to stay?

Silence from Christopher. Finally he asked suspiciously, 'What did you have for lunch?'

'A boiled egg.'

Christopher murmured soothing words but I did not hear them. For the hare suddenly turned away and leaped over the rose bushes. Even sitting down I felt wobbly, the same apprehension I experienced during every warm-up, before every performance. 'It's gone,' I said tightly. I am positive Christopher assumed I had gone too – completely crackers. He expressed relief that whatever I was seeing had passed and promised to come to the house soon for lunch. He always makes me feel better and we never lie to each other. After he rang off, I found my cigarettes in the kitchen and poured myself a glass of California white, with tons of ice. Had I conjured up that furry bogeyman out of fear? At the age of forty-two I brought my career to a halt, withdrew from the Royal Ballet three weeks before a performance at the Garden. The *Daily Telegraph* informed its readers that the sudden retirement 'shook the ballet world'. A dance historian estimated that more ballets were created for me than for any other dancers except Margot Fonteyn and Alicia Markova. My defection, to borrow one of Christopher's phrases, did not make me the Flavour of the Month. I was a moral misfit who collided with society. Some friends cared enough to write; others dropped me from their list. Today a letter came from the dance critic Richard Buckle. The message lodged inside me. 'You were our white hope,' he wrote. 'You seem to have thrown it all up . . . for what?' I once vowed I would never give up dancing; it would be like severing a limb. But sometimes a dancer must lose her life in order to find it.

I deliberately pushed open the glass doors and peered outside. Minutes had elapsed since I first saw the intruder. Moving watchfully on to the flagstone, in sweat pants and a black T-shirt, I dared the hare to accost me. I still had an uneasy sensation, but it was nowhere to be seen. The garden was quite tranquil. The grass smelt fresh and sweet. A breeze stirred the trees and vines but the sunflower plant wasn't doing anything. It was definitely squashed, trampled upon.

Returning to the desk, I lit a cigarette and, as my pulse raced, I remembered another disquieting episode. Shortly after breakfast, Demian, my youngest son, while rummaging through the armoire in the living room, came upon a batch of publicity stills of me with Christopher and Rudi. There were also clippings, old letters, limerick telegrams and well-thumbed diaries. I bought the marble-topped armoire at the Paris flea market and when it was uncrated here, I noticed the bottom drawer was lopsided, making it almost impossible to open. If you pull and press, the drawer eventually pops out at a pinched angle, looking like the peevish lip of a French concierge. Totally unusable, it became a convenient file-and-forget niche; and over the years I made frequent deposits. A corner of the lip is always askew. That morning Demi accidentally pitched a snooker ball inside. Somehow he coaxed the drawer out, whereupon it tango-dipped, dumping bits and bobs of my life on the floor.

He gazed upon the miscellaneous rubble as if he had discovered buried treasure. There were no secrets in the armoire. I've never hidden anything from the children. They know our home is somewhat different from that of their schoolmates, and so is the parade of people who come and go. They are equally comfortable with Rudolf Nureyev in mink and my hardcore Hell's Angel chum Crazy Charlie in black leather. Amazingly copable lads; they are not easily flummoxed.

Demian, who is seven, often saw me dance. He was

intrigued by a photograph of a petite twenty-year-old girl, with a relentlessly innocent face, in a white tutu, poised in flight. 'Is that you, Mum?' he asked, giving me one of his theatrically all-too-innocent glances.

'I suppose so,' I said, holding up the photograph for confirmation. I never had the finely sculptured face – or body – of the typical ballerina. My face reminds me of an upside down teacup and my body, instead of being stretched taut across acres of bones, is soft, curvy, rubbery. I grew up on Canada's western frontier, so my personality is not typically English either. The press described me as the logical successor to Margot Fonteyn and therein lies the rub. The Garden wanted me to fit an image exquisitely carved out by Fonteyn. I could not remake my body and would not remake my personality. The ballet is full of little Margots, but there *is* only one. I was different all over. And I insisted upon being me.

Always eager to hear a good yarn, Demian pressed on, wanting to know why the girl wore a tiara of white feathers. 'She's the Swan Queen,' I heard myself saying, 'in the power of a mysterious bloke – a magician, who only lets her become a woman for a few hours, in the moonlight.'

'Does the magician love her?' he asked.

'He's very secretive. But I think not. She'd like to break his potent spell, but this can only happen if a dashing prince swears that he'll love her for ever. Well now. The poor white bird struggles but she belongs to the sky and water. She's not very happy in the real world, you see. She's under a spell, Demi.'

He pulled a face. 'But she escapes from the magician?'

'Yes. After a fashion. She outwits him.' Envy, jealousy and sexual rivalry are the basis of this fantasy and so many others, with animals and sorcerers and fairy princesses; but, on the stage, the meanness is masked in a dazzling dream-like atmosphere of sumptuous palaces and heavenly forests.

The ballets are fantasies about our desires and wants, not what we are. The cruelty in these fables is usually glossed over. That is one reason why I tend to resist them.

Demian failed to put the photograph and papers away. Everything lay in a disorderly heap in front of the armoire. I carried an armful of letters and clippings back to the desk. Bloody hell. A most curious day, I reflected, downing the glass of wine. My mind refused to go forward. It fixed itself obstinately on the odd sequence of events. Dicky Buckle's note. A photograph of me as the Swan Queen. And the hare. Out of the blue, they jogged the old brain like some kind of signal that will help resolve the future. But first I must cut across circumstances to character, for I have made some mistakes out of sheer perversity and ignored them. I want to step outside myself, put my life in perspective, and take on Lynn Seymour with a dispassionate eye. My decision filled me with a gleam of cheerfulness, freeing me from any nostalgia of this acute anxiety hour when usually I would be in the underground barrelling along towards Covent Garden. I flicked an ash from my cigarette and stared into the violet darkness of the garden. As Dorothy Parker says, if you can get through the twilight, you'll live through the night.

CHAPTER 2

The North-west Corner

The stage is not magic for me. It never was.

I always felt the audience was waiting to see that first drop of blood. Before every performance, I deliberately drained myself with an hour or two of warm-up exercises; only then could I be relaxed enough to face the terrifying flood of shimmering white and blue and gold stage lights – an atmospheric prism that spiritually imprisons the spectacle with the spectators. My great pleasure was the rehearsal room where I was free to experiment and improvise, to seek perfection without two thousand sets of eyes. The rehearsal room transported me from the everyday world into the depths of a personal paradise in which I began to understand everything, including myself. For the performer whose artistic satisfaction is supposed to be consummated onstage, my reversal highlighted my loner instinct.

'Acting is a most natural thing,' says Ninette de Valois, who founded the Vic-Wells ballet in 1931. 'Ballet is not natural at all. It is an artificial use of the body for making a statement that can be more expressive than oral ranting and raving. And it exerts more physical strain on the body than anything an athlete endures.' Imagine a runner doing the hundred yards in ten seconds. A dancer exerts the same effort for five straight minutes in the second act of *Swan Lake*. When the physical strain collides with mental stress, you're in trouble. The prudent dancer is a stoic who embraces self-discipline as if it were a lover, whose personal life is often neglected. No one ever accused me of being prudent. You can't really do *everything*, I told myself. But for many years I tried. I broke the orthodox ballet rules, particularly about having children, and was in top form.

I am now sitting quite still at the long pine table in my farmhouse kitchen. Tacked along the redbrick wall above the open hearth are tidbits of my irregular past and present. A *Swan Lake* poster with Nureyev. A photograph of Christopher Gable as Romeo. A pair of white ballet slippers. A stuffed moose head from Canada. Snaps of my sons. Memorabilia and cards from friends around the world – a burgeoning collection that should go to the British Museum. Bawdy postcards I bought on Christopher Street in Greenwich Village. The cards would offend the carriage trade, but we don't get any, and all those incredible bums and bosoms lend a brio to the room. At the time of the power cuts my twins, Adrian and Jerszy, who were then tiny tots, had dinner by candlelight at a table *in* the hearth. Today it overflows, filled with three wicker laundry baskets.

The constant humming in the kitchen is not coming from me. It is the washing machine or dryer, either of which churns non-stop round the clock. At the moment we are five and last week there were guests from Rangoon and Islington. The rapidity with which the sheets and towels go in and out of the machines would suggest I was running a hotel. Anyway, I suppose all that activity at the tubs – a task once performed by nannies – is 'stage business' in my role as Mum. It gives me an opportunity to issue instructions to the cast on Woodstock Road, with a melodramatic push, shove or slap of wet garments and bedding from one machine to another. This is not a riotously glamorous image, but the job has to be done.

Yet subconsciously I know that something fresh and meaningful is happening with me as I roll out the mothballs of my life. I am rather like the child who insists upon building up again the house of blocks which just toppled over. I said earlier that I am loath to admit mistakes;

sometimes, like everyone else, I also refuse to face unpleasant truths. I have certainly not always benefited from experience.

My mother in Canada sent me a box of almost two thousand letters I wrote home over the years after I left to seek my fortune in London, which, incidentally, I am still seeking. 'Have you given up dancing completely or are you still keeping in shape?' she asked. 'I just can't imagine your retiring completely from performing after working all your life for that very thing and succeeding so well. There must be many places for you to use your talents even though you don't want to dance again. And why have you stopped writing? It would be so nice if you'd send a letter once in a while. It might make us both feel better.' Why does one usually stop writing home? Usually when one hasn't anything positive to say.

Tonight only the twins – the Big Boys, I call them – are with me for dinner. The twins are thirteen. They are not identical twins. They look like brothers. Jerszy is blond, Addie is dark. They are not interested in performing. Jers wants to be an architect, Addie intends to study marine biology. They are serious chaps, the kind you can count on. I must remind them to write to their grandmother in Canada. We planned a candlelit dinner together.

'Mum, I bought the chicken and the potatoes,' Jerszy said, closing the front door and coming straightaway into the kitchen.

Jers put his packages on the kitchen counter. We were going to roast the chicken. The twins could still live on tinned ravioli if I let them.

'We won't have dinner until nine.' Actually, we have no regular dinner hour. It falls anywhere from seven until eleven, depending on the demands of the day.

Addie strolled into the kitchen, a quirky grin on his face. 'That's quite a pile of letters in the other room,' he said.

'Did you have a look?'

'I really couldn't be bothered,' he said. Addie is the house detective. He hears and sees all and tells nothing.

'We're roasting the poulet,' I said, taking a package of onions and garlic from the fridge. 'We need a bit of seasoning.'

'Tons of garlic, Mum?'

'Tons of garlic. It keeps the vampires away.'

After the twins had written a letter to my Mom we three sat down to eat. Long ago they asked me to tell them about my family – storybook settlers in the North-west Territories – but there was never time for any childhood reminiscences when I was dancing. Now, feeling restlessly nostalgic in a high-backed rocker at the head of the table, with faint strains of laundry music in the opening allegros, this is what I told them.

Both sets of grandparents emigrated to Canada from Scotland in the mid-1800s when there was talk of gold in the Yukon and later a liquid gold called oil from north-west soil. They sailed with émigrés from England, Germany, France and the Ukraine. My parents grew up in the western province of Alberta. Mom's name was Marjorie McIvor and her father had his own pharmacy in Calgary where he sold smelling salts, ether, mercury, and cocaine for dental use. Mom rode to school on a buckskin pony. She was an expert horsewoman. She could handle the pony in pelting snowstorms and dusty prairie winds. The oldest of four children, she learned how to drive a tractor and a car when she was fourteen. She sewed, cooked, and could even bake in a woodstove. She was very striking with sculptured cheekbones, dark hair and a smooth complexion. Her enviable looks were passed on to my brother Bruce.

She longed to take dance lessons, but her parents – dour Scottish Protestants – considered dancing profane. Before I left for England when I was fifteen, Grandfather McIvor begged me not to go, warning that I would fall into a life of debauchery. My own dad urged me to stay home. He warned that I would meet a lot of homosexuals. I did not know what those words meant but since they caused heated rows, which Mom tolerantly ignored, I was resolved more than ever to cast aside the stiff corset of conventions that had shaped Mom's life, and find out for myself. Mom is an indomitable spirit, however. She substituted the upright piano for dancing and became a keyboard personality for at-home entertainments on freezing winter nights. Mom's family was closely knit, Dad's was not.

Edward Springbett was the last of seven children and unwanted by his mother. He hated her until he died, but worshipped his father who founded a town near a shallow crossing on the Red Deer River, used by trappers moving south. Grandfather Springbett was a blacksmith. He plunked himself down in the wilderness and opened a forge, befriending Blackfoot Indians who gave him furs in exchange for shoeing their horses so they could cross the ice. Dad spent boyhood hours wandering through the snow, his eyelashes covered with frost, setting traps for 'critters'. He unloaded banana crates that arrived on icy freight trains and saw frozen tarantulas, among the bananas, slowly thaw and stumble about like arthritic baby monsters. He once followed a circus troupe out of Red Deer, with dreams of becoming a high-wire artist, but he fed the animals for two days and returned home. During World War I, he fibbed about his age and enlisted in the Canadian Air Force. He was sixteen. He wanted to fly a plane and did. One day he crash-landed on the prairie and walked fifteen miles back to camp. The officers assumed he was dead and had already distributed his clothes. He was a rebel and a romantic. He was short and wiry, and had dark, unruly hair. 'Hang on to my hair and I'll pick you up,' he would say to me. I would cling to his thick curls and he would lift me into the air. As a child I grew up listening to stories of the snowbound west, of trapping foxes and wolves, of roving Blackfoot Indians, of cunning whisky-traders at Fort Whoop-up, and the stalwart Mounties in their red tunics, patrolling the lawless badlands. Stories of the Canadian frontier were more exciting than the lives of elves and sylphs in fairy tales.

Mom and Dad met in 1922 when they were both teaching at a four-room prairie schoolhouse. Ed Springbett was principal. He cut a bit of a dash. He had a roguish moustache. He wore a boater. He smoked. And he owned a radio. He courted Mom for six years. They played tennis, attended country folk dances, went horseback riding and speed-skating, hands clasped behind their backs. They were a handsome couple, entirely self-reliant, crackling with good humour and pioneer optimism. Dad did not want to spend his life in a prairie schoolhouse. He began studying dentistry at the University of Alberta in Edmonton and married Mom in 1928. Bruce was born there four years later. Their honeymoon was spent camping in the forests of the jagged green and brown and red Canadian Rockies, profuse with wild flowers, meadows, blue-purple lakes and white waterfalls. They drove a Model T Ford and were accompanied by a German shepherd dog named Mars who had a thick coat of sable-coloured fur. One day, after picking huckleberries, they returned to camp through leafy wooded trails and discovered a stray bear cub, brought up on bear's milk and honey, having a picnic in their bread box. Old Mama bear came shambling out of a thicket, looking for her missing cub, and slashed a seven-foot hole in their tent. Mars charged at the big brown she-bear making blood-curdling howls and frightening off the bears. Then Mom and Dad sat on a rock near a cascading stream and ate the huckleberries.

During the Great Depression, when thousands were unemployed, Dad set up his dental practice in the town of

Wainwright, about an hour from Edmonton. It was rolling prairie and farmland. Just as Grandfather Springbett traded with the Indians, Dad extracted molars and impacted wisdom teeth in exchange for fresh eggs, vegetables and chickens. I was born in Wainwright on 8 March 1939. My very first memory is one of disorientation. I was about three years old.

The world was at war again and Dad joined the Canadian army dental corps. He was being sent to a base in British Columbia. Two nights before Dad caught his train he and Mom went away for an overnight farewell. Bruce and I stayed with friends. I awoke at dawn in a strange room, feeling lost and frightened. I loved my dad. I did not understand why he was leaving us or why we were eventually moving. The continuity of our life was coming apart.

Mom sold the house and most of our furniture, packed our belongings and then drove, with Bruce and me, the 838 miles west to British Columbia where Dad was stationed in Victoria. I did not appreciate the 'Englishness' of Victoria on Vancouver Island until I finished my first season with the Royal Ballet touring company, dancing an adagio in Bournemouth and a bolero in Brighton. The provincial capital of British Columbia has tea shops, double-decker buses, pubs, neo-gothic buildings and Tudor homes with clipped green lawns. It is a seaside city of flowers and parks and beaches.

Victoria and Vancouver on the mainland, reachable by ferry, teemed with military men and their families. Vancouver was a jumping-off port for soldiers and sailors into the Pacific theatre. We lived on army bases, in rented rooms, apartments and shared flats. Bruce and I often shared the same bedroom. When Dad was transferred to Nova Scotia, we became fragmented. Bruce, who was growing into a lean, rugged youth, lived with friends in Victoria. Mom and I stayed with another family in Vancouver. I was rapidly becoming the Ugly Duckling, with crooked teeth and a crossed eye. A muscle was snipped to straighten out the crossed eye, but it required three operations and months of eye exercises. Later I wore braces on my teeth for almost two years. Finally I had the courage to stare into a mirror without flinching. The mirror on the bathroom wall never reflected Snow White. It did not reflect any facsimile of Shirley Temple either, who tap-danced her dimpled image across movie screens in the late thirties. I did, however, have my first dance class when I was six. A tall raw-boned British eccentric, straight out of the Mitfords, taught us both swimming and tap, with lots of clapping of hands and a ringing voice. 'Now kick!' or 'Now tap!' she would peal out. My public dance début was at a tap recital. I wore a blue dress, blue ribbons and glasses.

When Dad came home from the war I did not know him. He was a stranger. He took me down to the railroad station in Vancouver and we had our shoes polished together. I was wearing brown Oxfords. Then, holding hands, we walked back to our apartment. I was very proud. But he had changed and the insecurity I felt just before we moved from Wainwright returned. It has never gone away.

Dad had to begin his dental career all over again. His friends had prospered during the war. We still lived in tiny flats and shared houses. Dad was an embittered man. His youthful dreams had vanished; there were no more fantasies. He was middle-aged, with a wife, two children, no money and looking for a surgery to rent, trusting that the patients would gradually come. Mom had an inner strength and a curious calm amidst all the storms. She kept us glued together and relived her childhood dreams through Bruce and me. Bruce excelled in sports and Mom encouraged me to take dancing lessons, so I enrolled at the Rosemary Deveson Dance Studios in Vancouver. Dad seemed to push a sibling rivalry between us and was then jealous of our accomplishments. I know he bragged about Bruce's athletic prowess to his cronies, but what could he say about me? Dad did not know an entrechat from an entrecôte.

Bruce was the social and physical success. I was quiet, reserved and plain. I thought physical exercises which had nothing to do with dance class quite silly. Yet Dad made me feel that I must find a niche of my own, a specialty that would give me some kind of distinction even if he did not understand it, and, from the age of twelve onward, I began to concentrate on dance.

Dance class lifted me out of the humdrummery of home. It was a drug that I had to have for two hours every day after school. It was physically and sensually exciting, luring me into a world where I could imagine anything at all. I imagined far too much. I became totally hooked on dancing after Mom took me to a matinée of *Coppélia* by the Ballet Russe de Monte Carlo with Alexandra Danilova as the peasant maid who finds that her chap is in love with a doll and masquerades as the toy herself. And then I saw that classic 'art' film, *The Red Shoes*, and the ballet became a state of heart. I was enthralled by scenes in the rehearsal halls and at the practice barres; by the dancers' idealism and uncompromising standards of perfection in which no hardship was too severe or too demanding. The plot itself seemed absurd: a ruthless impresario discovers the planned marriage of his ballerina and forces her to choose between her lover and her career. Obviously, that conflict was contrived, thought I.

The Red Shoes was one of the revelatory experiences of my childhood. It was an updated overview of the eternal conflict between sacred and profane love, which forms the perennial theme for the majority of classical ballets. In my immature way I understood these polarities and set out to try and balance the equation. I was made to feel different, always. Sir Frederick Ashton, that extraordinary choreographer for the Royal Ballet, told a friend, 'Lynn was always having those babies, wasn't she?'

My Canadian ballet teachers, Jean Jepson and Nicholas Svetlanoff, were two stimulating, colourful characters. Jean had tremendous theatrical flair and costumed herself extravagantly for class, demonstrating in black fishnet tights how to bend and curve in perfect time to the music. She had danced with a small company in New York, done summer stock and performed in nightclubs. Mr Svetlanoff (as I always called him) taught me perseverance and the joy of slogging through an exercise even when you thought you'd drop. He had a striking Slavic face with high cheek-bones covered with finely-etched taut skin. His pale blue eyes inspired us and missed nothing. He was born in St Petersburg and fled during the revolution. His journey, by train, on sled and foot, took him across Asia to Manchuria and eventually, like many White Russians, he ended up in Shanghai. Here he found himself dancing in a cabaret with a woman named Vera Volkova. Their act was a series of acrobatic adagios. They had both studied ballet in Russia and Volkova eked out a living teaching dance in Shanghai. One of her students was the young Margot Fonteyn, whose father was an executive for a British cigarette company there. Volkova eventually reached London. Svetlanoff took a freighter to Vancouver. He it was who made me aware that dancing was not only synonymous with grace but also with sensuality. He taught me how to express unexpressed emotions spontaneously with the gesture of a hand, a raised foot, the half-turn of the head – and my eyes.

My days were spent at school, my evenings at dance class. I was not interested in dating and no one asked me out. The boys of my age were gangly, pimply and did not understand my dance addiction. Once on an ice-skating rink a high school boy held my hand and we kissed during the Couples Only Waltz, but I was more taken by the infinite refinement of the Russian courtship dances that we were discovering with Mr Svetlanoff – the dropped handkerchief and the knowing glance.

I won some prizes in dance festivals and competitions, playing a tulip, a faun and a fortune teller. The editor of *Dance News* said he would help me in New York if I moved east. But that would be years away. I was only fourteen. The Royal Ballet (then called Sadler's Wells) came to Vancouver in November 1953, and announced that auditions would be held for its school in London. An audition was set up. I remember feeling remarkably disembodied but not really nervous. Ailne Philips, Dame Ninette de Valois' trusty right arm, auditioned me. Then I spent about half an hour in a rehearsal room, performing as best I could, observed by the alert, blue-green eyes of Frederick Ashton, the company's associate director. It was a Friday morning. Mom then drove me to Kitsilano High School where I conjugated some irregular French verbs *mauvaise*ly and wrote a fanciful essay on Brobdingnags.

When I got home from school, Mom opened her arms and gave me a hug. My heart beat a little faster. 'The phone rang an hour ago. They want you to go to London in the fall. It's a kind of scholarship. They'll be writing about the financial arrangements.' Bruce was attending the University of Oregon on a track scholarship. I felt that, at last, I was catching up with him.

'Did you tell Dad?' I asked quickly.

She nodded. 'The *Vancouver Sun* telephoned. A reporter wants to interview you. It seems you were the only student accepted on the company's entire tour.' Her lips puckered with anxiety. 'If only you didn't have to go so soon.'

'Soon? It's almost a year away. I wish I could start for London tomorrow.'

On that afternoon my dreams of adventure became a reality without actually happening. I knew I would be stepping into another life, where I would be doing the only thing I wanted. In fables the magic genie offers three wishes. I had one wish and it had been granted. The next months were lived in a daze. Yet, at the same time, my excitement was marred by nervous tensions from Dad. He had started drinking heavily in the army. It was what macho men did when they got together. And, as he had to rebuild his life after the war, he drank to blot out memories of a boy who wanted to join the circus. His dental practice was all right. We lived on the top floor of a brown frame house near the sea. We had our own dining room where we played cribbage and a bay window that made the living room wonderfully airy and sunny. The big night of the week was Thursday when Mom and Dad and I went to the movies (*The Blue Grass of Wyoming*, *The Great Caruso*, *I Was a Communist for the FBI*, and *An American in Paris*). On Saturdays I often went for walks with Dad in Stanley Park, which covers one thousand acres in downtown Vancouver. We'd feed peanuts to the animals in the zoo and investigate the West Coast Indian canoes and totems.

But when the local papers found feature material in the Springbett children, Dad became morose. Bruce was a college track star. He ran in the 4×440 yards race at the British Empire Games that year and sparked the team to a gold medal. I had danced on Canadian television and was going to study ballet in London. We reminded Dad of his own frustrations and lost youth. He drank secretly. There were closed-door scenes with Mom, though I don't ever recall seeing her cry. She must have been dying inside. One night I was at the dining room table doing homework and he wandered in distractedly. He picked up a dictionary and hurled it at me. I looked at him stunned and screamed silently. It wasn't *him*, it wasn't the Dad who went hiking with me on winding trails to Point Atkinson Lighthouse. The person I loved was *someone else*. I ran out of the house, quite hysterical, wondering why Dad had the courage to express his rage only when his brain was released by alcohol.

I was very young then.

The dance classes went on, offering genuine security.

The live orchestra at the Ballet Russe performance demonstrated how classical music merged with the ballet, but I never fully grasped the greatness of music until one of the boys in dance class invited me to his home on a Saturday afternoon. Keith was nearly Bruce's age – a keen, intelligent young man with whom I could discuss dance history. He was well-built, with brown hair and large sad eyes. His schoolmates razed him because he went to dance class. He was a loner. I admired him because he was genuinely confident, willing to learn and unaffected by the gibes of his contemporaries. I am drawn to people with the daring to be themselves.

For the first time I heard the Beethoven symphonies. I was transported by the music. Those sublime masterpieces. Keith explained that this superb music, which I heard for the first time, was what one danced to. At home I heard Bing Crosby, the Modern Jazz Quartet and the Ink Spots. We listened to the records for hours and then walked silently in the forest which surrounded his house. I saw him before I flew to London, but when I visited Vancouver the following summer, his family had moved. I never saw him again.

That last summer, I spent entire days alone, wandering along wild isolated beaches. I had grown up by the sea, climbing rocks, untangling chains of salty seaweed and wrapping it around myself like delicate jewellery and dancing in the shallow waters. As a child I collected jellyfish and placed them on a piece of driftwood as if they were little cakes. I prowled the waters for sea anemones which look much like brightly coloured flowers. With a pail and shovel I dug for shells – periwinkles, tulip shells, fan shells and saucer shells which Mom and Dad used for ashtrays. I had two conch shells. When you hold them against your ear, you seem to hear the sea, but it's really just the air inside the twisted shell.

Tramping through the sand and searching for shells was my private pleasure. And so that last summer I returned to the sea again. My imminent departure was tying my stomach in knots, but the sea was quietening, even on cool days when puffs of wind pushed a line of breakers to the shore with a musical roar. I sat cross-legged on the sand, in jeans and a sweater, absorbed in the rolling waves, one after another, watching ripples become waves and then line up in swells moving together, building up energy like a demented dance corps wearing white caps, and then breaking and tumbling.

I walked idly on sloping beaches, picking up butterfly shells and tossing them into the air. I splashed through tide pools, gathering masses of seaweed and belting the dripping cords around my waist. On warm days when the sky was turquoise and the sun a ball of gold, I pretended the hard sand near the water's edge was an endless stage. Wearing a properly modest bathing suit I stepped on to this grainy stage exultantly, moving to the music of the waves, hands on hips, hands reaching for the sky and then spin, leap and run, run, run.

Eventually the waves washed over me, washing away the sweat and sand, and covering me with foamy wetness.

That was what I recalled for the Big Boys at dinner.

The candles still flicker. They have gone to their rooms and I remain at the table, which they cleared, except for my cigarettes and glass of wine. I must reply to Mom's letter, but she asked questions I cannot answer. Mom was the only constant female figure in my life. I do not have many girlfriends. I never did. I much prefer the company of men.

So many different kinds of men moulded my personality, urged me to transcend any limitation. Dad never dealt with me as a frilly feminine doll. He gave me a strong sense of drive and ambition and a desire to be physically noticed which I sought in dance as Bruce did in athletics. I am not sure I ever really pleased him. I adore Bruce. He has a strong, defined, manly beauty, and always respected my pursuits. He was the first man who ever treated me like a woman.

CHAPTER 3

Pulling Up the Old Socks

Little patches of farms and ribbons of roads seen through oceans of clouds from an airplane window – that was my first glimpse of England when I arrived in the fall of 1954. My farewell flowers, a bouquet of red roses, drooped lifelessly and I drooped with them, although the roses had been put on ice for part of the trip and Dad had given me a sleeping pill. I tried to remain very ladylike and calm, but I wished that I could have been put on ice with the roses. Midway over the Atlantic I had a nasty shock. The full realization hit that I was going to be dropped in a foreign country, without any relatives around for weekends or holiday visits. At the age of fifteen, I was not popping off three hours away by train from my parents. I was starting ballet school six thousand miles from home and I would be living with strangers. The night before I left Vancouver, Mom and Dad and I saw *Gone With the Wind* which now struck me as an awesomely prophetic title. I wanted to grab the roses and bail out. Instead I remained strapped in my seat, while the pubescent heart did flip-flops, clutching the flowers which I presented to my stand-in mom, Phyllis Fisher, of 28 Orsett Terrace, Paddington. I wore a new grey suit and red shoes, a silk scarf and white gloves. To fake a maturity I did not feel or have, I had boarded the plane carrying a hat shaped like a sponge cake, with a veil. A stewardess who chatted with me about my adventurous expedition gasped when she saw me adjusting the veil over my left eye. The British, it had been drilled into me, were quite proper, so what could be more proper than a hat, even though it made me look like a miscast dowager in a school play. 'I wouldn't wear that hat,' the stewardess said. 'You're not going to a funeral.' I left the grey velour sponge cake at Heathrow Airport.

A teacher from the Sadler's Wells School in Barons Court greeted me at the aircoach terminal, after a jittery bus ride into central London during which I stared straight ahead, forcing myself not to cry, and I was deposited at the Fishers' door in Paddington, a rather dreary area with faded houses and a few scraggly trees. London seemed so enormous and sprawling, with streams of people hurrying in every direction, and the streets clogged with buses, taxis and cars. There were no snow-capped mountains and sandy beaches. I was alone in the first big city I had ever seen, and there was no turning back. The lump in my throat was the size of a golf ball. Orsett Terrace was my new berth – the first of temporary boarding houses, bed-sits, flats, digs, lodgings and hotels for the next seventeen years of suitcase living, until I could afford to buy my own home in the suburb of Chiswick. When I stepped across the threshold and quiveringly gave Mrs Fisher the roses, I did not believe that I would ever remain long in London.

Phyllis Fisher was a small, rather shy woman with a pleasant face, in her late forties who constantly bustled. She had been a nurse during the war and continued hospital duties for a short time after her son Jeremy was born. Jeremy was eleven. She and her husband inherited a four-storey house and rented rooms to foreign students, usually teenage girls from France who were studying English for a year. There were always one or two English girls enrolled at the ballet school. Mrs Fisher did not take in boys, though that would have been more matey for Jeremy. Boys were mischievous and cheeky, she said, and did not like kitchen work. She provided breakfast, dinner and a room for four pounds four shillings a week. The girls set the table and washed up the dishes. We were also responsible for tidying our rooms. But Mrs Fisher did everything else. She shopped for a 'family' of seven or eight, trudging to markets and greengrocers four times a week; she planned her menus as carefully as a hospital cook. Rationing was only just over and it was difficult to satisfy French and Canadian palates. She also listened to the woes of her boarders and worried about them, which is why she preferred older girls, aged seventeen or eighteen: they had fewer adjustment problems. Sometimes, she remarked with a heavy sigh, it was easier being a nurse than running a boarding house, but she did not want to be on her feet all day tending grumbling patients and she had seen enough death during the war. She swapped the bedpan for the frying pan and pressed on with her lot in life. When boarders became tearful, she comforted them with the no-nonsense authority of a Head Nurse ordering a patient to gulp down his medicine: 'You simply have to pull up the old socks.' I was her youngest boarder. My scholarship gave me free instruction at the ballet school and two pounds a week towards my board. And Mrs Fisher was forever telling me to pull up the old socks.

When my son Addie commented on my huge box of letters, I jokingly asked if he read the juicy parts. There were no juicy parts, ever. The early letters were most often wet, as in full of tears. I repressed the dislocation of that first year. But the letters are vignettes of me, revealing far more than I could today of the young Berta Lynn Spring-bett, someone I tried to toss off later in a tumbler of sophistication.

Selected samples from those first months – candid verbal portraits of a girl I still remember:

September 5

Dear Mom,

I don't think I can stand it for a year. I miss you so much I could just fly home right now. It was childish of me, asking you to sleep with me the last night, but you calmed me down. Everything is Merrie in Olde England except me. The Fishers are trying to help me get over my homesickness and say I will feel lots better when the other girls arrive. Mr Fisher works for the government housing projects, listening to sob stories of homeless people. My first night here he had to listen to me. I explained how badly I felt and he consoled me no end. But, Mom, only me going home or your coming here can help me.

My room, on the top floor, is a little bigger than at home. I have a bed, a desk, a little dressing-table, a sink, an easy chair and a bureau. I gave Mrs Fisher my roses, but they were dead, and she put a vase of fresh daisies in my room. That was very sweet. For dinner the first night we had veal or something. Actually I am not sure what it was and did not want to ask. After dinner we watched TV, but each minute I got more homesick wanting you, till, by the time I was to go to bed, I was ready to die. I stood at the window a long time staring into the street. The houses in Orsett Terrace are all alike with thousands of chimneys on each roof. The district is not very pretty. I think we got Kensington mixed up with Paddington.

I heard the bells toll two. I don't know what time I finally dropped off. I had a terrible sleep. I am saving Dad's second sleeping pill for the Big Emergency, but I think it is here. Oh, Mom, please get me away. If you only knew how urgent I am.

All my love to you,
Lynn

September 8

Dearest Mom,

If you can't get me away before summer then I will have to stay but you must get me away or I will do something drastic. I receive piles of letters, but you must keep writing. The letters make me more homesick, but I feel so much closer to you. Do try to get me home with all your heart. I took Dad's second sleeping pill and that made me feel better. I dread going to bed at night because I get so lonely for you, but what is worse is waking up in the morning.

I am trying to accustom myself to London. On Saturday I went to the bank and got everything fixed up. Then I went to Cyril Beaumont's Book Shop where I bought a subscription to *Dance and Dancers* and a book on Sadler's Wells. Mr Beaumont signed the book for me. He is a dance historian and critic. I took a long bus ride. Mr Fisher said the way to see London is from the top of a double-decker bus. The problem is you just don't pay one fare. The conductor asks, 'Where are you getting off?' I told him I didn't know. He said I had to be going somewhere because my fare depended on that. So I said, 'Buckingham Palace,' and he said the bus didn't go there. Then I said, 'Piccadilly Circus,' and he answered that would be fine. I saw all the theatres and clubs and flashy restaurants in Piccadilly, where the traffic is wild, and walked to Trafalgar Square – you know, with all the pigeons and the fountain and the Lord Nelson column. I even walked past the Royal Opera House in Covent Garden and peeked in the stage door. Covent Garden itself is a marketplace. There is nothing around that makes you think of a theatre except the opera house. It is terribly grand. Then I bought some ballet cards. They were so lovely, in colour, I couldn't resist them. I stuck them into the frame of my bedroom mirror. I bought cards of Margot Fonteyn in *Swan Lake* and Svetlana Beriosova, also in *Swan Lake*. Beriosova is only twenty-two and began dancing at the Garden three years ago. She is very aristocratic-looking and I can hardly wait to see her dance. She was born in Lithuania. Just knowing that makes me feel less like a hick in London. I had to explain what a 'hick' was to Mr Fisher. He said, 'Oh, you mean country bumpkin.'

Leaving the card shop, I got a bit confused about where to go, so I went up to one of those British gentlemen with their handle-bar moustaches and asked him which way to Charing Cross Road. He then gave me a withering look and said, 'Madam, you are walking in the wrong direction.' Did I turn red! I bought some Kleenex and a roll of toilet paper. The kind the Fishers have is rather like paper for dress patterns. In fact the toilets themselves are so odd. You have to pull a little chain or string. It was dark when I got home to the Fishers and Jane had arrived. She studies at the Ballet school too, but her parents live only a few hours away in Birmingham. Her parents had just left and I suddenly felt a strange twinge. Mrs Fisher said she'd ring the school and get me passes for Covent Garden. Right now I would do anything to see you. If you only knew how urgent I am.

   All my love to you,
    Lynn

            September 15

Dearest Mom,

On Monday I trundled off to school full of excitement. Once I'm inside the school I am in a dancer's paradise. I am not homesick. For the first two weeks we have nothing but dancing. We were measured for our class uniform. We get a grey tunic and trunks, and pink knitted tights and a sort of wraparound sweater (we can buy them from the school). We received a dark red belt and headband. The headband makes my face as round as a billiard ball. Then we were given assigned places in the school dressing-rooms. I didn't know anyone. The girls are funny. 'Oh, darling!' and 'Jolly good!' are their favourite expressions.

I can't seem to do anything in dance class. I wobble all over the place. Everyone else is so good, I feel quite lost and inferior. After one class I worked about forty minutes by myself because I can't seem to get my head and body facing the right way at the same time. Then I found out we are not allowed to do any unsupervised practice. We had our first mime class. We're not supposed to put any feeling into it until we learn the complete vocabulary and do each movement-gesture correctly. My favourite expressions are fear and anger because they require subtlety without looking ridiculous. Mime is truly an art form – conveying all the emotions without words.

At the end of the day, we had foot inspection. We have to rub our feet with surgical spirit and powder them before and after class, and also powder our shoes. At night we have to bathe our feet in hot water, and rub them with surgical spirit and lanolin. Finally we must take a nail file and push down the cuticle of our toe nails and powder *them*. As soon as I return to the Fishers, I proceed to darn point shoes. We have to darn toes and all the little spots where the satin is likely to wear away. A tough linen thread is used on the heel and ball of the foot. Last night I struggled along and finally finished one shoe. The boys do not have to darn, because they are never on point. It seems as if I will spend my whole life darning shoes.

Two French girls are at the Fishers' now. They are twenty and learning English. They absolutely refuse to speak any English at the dinner table. They just talk to each other in French. The dining room and kitchen at the Fishers' are on the basement level and the shower is there too. It is the warmest part of the house. I have a little radiator in my room and it goes on after you insert a shilling and light a match. The heat stays on a couple of hours, then you must repeat the process. It is icy and pitch black outside when I wake and I must remember to keep the stack of shillings and little matchboxes on my bureau. I was preparing to get into bed and had just put a shilling in the radiator when, suddenly, I felt an odd little spasm again. Then I heard a huge wail, like a baby or lost child. It was so pitiful and I was sure someone was crying. I ran into the hall and looked around. Jane was coming out of the bathroom and she said that I had heard a 'London cat'. They are homeless and roam all over the city. She begged me not to worry. She came into my room and we talked about school. This is her third year. She is nice, but quite shy and the only boarder I can chat with. I said that I was very impressed with my dance teacher Winifred Edwards, a wonderful woman about sixty years old. Her hair is chalk white, parted in the middle and marcelled. She wears impeccable white shoes and her dresses are usually green and white, with flared skirts. She has lovely legs. Jane said that Winifred Edwards used to be known as Vera Fredova and, as a young girl, danced with the Anna Pavlova company. This was in the days when dancers had to have Russian names. The Russian impresario, Sergei Diaghilev, had many English girls in his troupe. Hilda Munnings changed her name to Lydia Sokolova and Lilian Alicia Marks became Alicia Markova. But that was years ago. Don't worry. I won't have to change my name. Winifred Edwards (Vera Fredova) met a Diaghilev dancer and his wife who formed a company back in 1917. She toured the United States with them and ended up in Hollywood where everything fell apart. Miss Edwards was told to hold on, there would be another tour, but there never was and she was stuck in Hollywood. Isn't that awful? She taught dancing there and one of her students was the choreographer Agnes de Mille. By the time Miss Edwards returned to England, it was too late for her to pursue a ballet career. I'm so lucky to have her for a teacher. I think she retires next year. She is very fierce at times but she has a marvellous dance history which I respect. When Jane left my room I lay in bed under mountains of blankets thinking of Miss Edwards. The story of her being stranded in California, yet still hopeful until the end, is so sad that it gave me the blubs. When she demonstrates a step I then see the lithesome young Vera Fredova. Jane says, 'People forget dancers, even the great ones, very quickly.' I don't think she expects to make it, but I want to. I just have to hold on, don't I?

All my love,
Lynn

September 16

Dear Dad,

I am gradually settling down (I think), though we won't have a regular routine until next week when we start academic subjects as well. The head-mistress asked what courses I wanted to take and I said, 'Everything.' I just finished a ballet class, which is what I look forward to. I am now five foot four inches and Winifred Edwards said, 'That is a good height, do not grow any taller.' When girls stand on point we gain about two inches and therefore it is best to be on the short side. It also makes it easier for the boys to fling us around. The boys have separate classes. They have to learn speed and strength like track stars. A difference is that when they leap, they're holding on to one of us instead of a pole vault, so they better know what they're doing.

You would like Mr Fisher. When I get the blues he is very patient. He is a bit on the portly side, wears thick glasses and has a moustache. He looks exactly like Groucho Marx. His opinion of the ballet is the same as yours. 'I like it all right,' he says, 'but I don't care if I see it or not.' He is interested in sports – cricket, soccer, rugby. Of course I lectured Mr Fisher and stressed that ballet gives boys stronger muscular development and body coordination than any sport.

Did I tell you what happened to my watch? Here's a 'London story'. I lost the crystal and one of the hands snapped off. Mr Fisher sent me to a wee little shop in Paddington. A strange fat lady was there seated at a rolltop desk. She must have weighed two hundred pounds and I wondered how she squeezed in and out of the doorway because it was so tiny. You have to go down several steps to get into the shop. Inside the shop were five yapping poodles, all with diamond-studded leather collars. I even saw one black poodle with a gold clip in its topknot. I thought perhaps I was in a weird kennel instead of a watch repair shop. Every five minutes different clocks would start chiming or ringing or going cuckoo-cuckoo. The fat lady wore several watches on her arms like bracelets and a diamond-studded collar around *her* neck. Mr Fisher said, 'She's quaint.' I think there are a lot of odd characters in London other than wailing London cats. Eccentricity is tolerated here far more than at home.

It was very reassuring that you wrote again that you are behind me all the time. It made me feel one hundred per cent better. Please remember, you are not just a 'bread-winner' to me. You are the most wonderful father anyone could have. You are working to keep me in London in order that I can do what I want with my life.

    All my love,
    Lynn

September 28

Dearest Mom,

We've started the full academic-dance schedule at
school. I have French three times a week and English,
Greek history, art appreciation, history of the ballet and
music once a week. The other classes are involved with
dance – pirouette, mime, point, character dancing, and
ballet every day with Winifred Edwards. We are learning
the corps de ballet sections of *Swan Lake*, Act 2. I'm up at
seven-thirty every morning to be at school by nine-fifteen
and we are finished at five o'clock. I'm not getting the
education I would at home, and this worries me, but I am
trying to make up for it by reading a lot. I have become
friendly with a Brazilian girl named Marcia Haydée
Pereira da Silva. She calls herself Marcia Haydée. She is
seventeen and began dancing when she was three, like all
well-bred girls in Rio. She had no interest in dolls or
games, something we have in common. And then she saw
The Red Shoes, and it changed her life. We talked about
The Red Shoes for hours. She met the director at a dinner
party given by her parents and he encouraged her to
attend our school. She knows that she won't be able to
graduate into the company because she is not a resident
of a Commonwealth country, but she is very determined
and works quite hard. I usually stand behind her when
we are doing our *pliés* at the barre, up-down, up-down,
bending our knees with our feet turned out. I wear woolly
tights but some mornings my cold bones make a crunch-
ing noise when I start the *pliés*. Marcia and I are
'outsiders', the other girls seldom notice us. Marcia has
long black hair and is about an inch shorter than me. She
has a long lovely neck, a swan neck, unlike me. I have to
concentrate on the use of my neck since I can't have it
stretched.

Marcia and I went for snacks in a very posh department

store. I worry about my expenses, but I did want to go with her so very much. A paunchy man, standing in a tail coat and pinstripe trousers with a carnation in his lapel, showed us to a table. The room had a red carpet and chandeliers. The waitresses wore white organdy aprons. I tried to be as nonchalant as Marcia. We had passes to Covent Garden. After coffee and sandwiches with olives and watercress, we took our passes to the stage door and exchanged them for a proper ticket. Then we went around to the front and dashed up to the Stalls Circle to get a decent place to stand without a pole in front of us. We saw *Les Sylphides* with Anne Heaton. She was marvellous. On the same programme was *Firebird*. Margot Fonteyn danced the firebird who helps the prince rescue an enchanted princess. It was a magnificent production with Fonteyn an exotic firebird and Svetlana Beriosova absolutely breathtaking as the princess. The other ballet was *La Boutique Fantasque*, about a bunch of toys that come to life, and I don't know why the Garden has it in the repertoire. We saw Winifred Edwards at the end of the performance and had a nice chat with her, although Marcia thought that I shouldn't have said the last ballet was dreadful. Miss Edwards just smiled. I suspect she agreed with me.

On Monday Miss Edwards sent me home after class. I developed a horrid cold and have a constantly runny nose. But I don't like to stay in bed by myself on the top floor because it is so lonely. I much prefer being around people, even if they don't talk to me, like the girls at school (not Marcia, of course!). It is also very chilly in my room. So the very next day I went to school again and Miss Edwards sent me home again. She phoned Mrs Fisher and urged her to make me stay in bed. My body aches and I have a burning head. Naturally I ran out of shillings for my little heater. I gave Jeremy Fisher a pound note and he sweetly left an envelope of shillings outside my door on a tray with hot tea and barley soup. Oh, Mom, I was expecting to hear you come to the door and make me feel better with a big hug. I wanted you so much.

All my love,
Lynn

P.S. Don't forget to send vitamins, instant coffee and Breck shampoo.

October 4

Dear Bruce,

I caught some kind of bug and was in bed for two days. The sky outside is very dark and the wind is howling. My windows rattle from the wind and rain. Mrs Fisher says, 'It's filthy,' meaning the weather. You teased me about adjusting to a foreign country where everyone speaks English! Just wait until you come over here and find that not only the money and manners are different but also the language. Quite different, old chap. Potato chips are called crisps, and French fries are chips. Crackers are biscuits, biscuits are scones, cookies are cakes, pies are tarts, rolls are buns and chocolates are sweets. Want to order?

The toilet is the loo, and if it's occupied the sign says Engaged. Mr Fisher ran through the Brit translations for me and we laughed so hard he tore his bloody pants. Bloody can mean almost anything, but it's close to damn, I think. Bleeding is stronger and considered quite rude. If you knock a girl up, she isn't preggers. You've simply called on her early in the morning. And pissed means Quite Intoxicated, not furiously angry.

'Want a fag, love?' I hear. So far I have resisted. Fags

are cigarettes. My linguistic education! Well, British-English is easier than Parisian French. When I come home next summer, I may have an accent, speak with a long a and ask for toMAHtoes. I could bring you a furled umbrella and a bowler hat. You'd stop traffic at the University of Oregon.

Please do me a heaping big favour. Send me a list of some of the books you read in literature class. I feel that I'm not learning enough and I don't want to be a dumb dancer. In geography class our poor little teacher was lecturing away and the kids were talking and sewing point shoes. I don't know how they expect to learn anything, or if they want to. Then, even in dance class, when I raise questions or ask the teacher to repeat a movement, the other girls look so disgusted, I don't understand their attitude. There are about fifty boys at the school, ranging in age from nine to twenty. I'm quite fond of one boy but we really do not 'talk'. He has your personality and looks – his name is Christopher Gable.

But it is almost impossible to get friendly with the students. After school they hurry home to their families scattered across London. I usually have lunch with my one friend Marcia Haydée. The problem is that I am blimping. When I see you I may look like a potAHto. We usually have sausages and piles of potatoes at the Fishers' because meat is so expensive. I dream of having a lean juicy steak. I asked Mom to send food parcels – anything that's not fattening. My life outside the school is spent reading, reading, reading, there is so much I want to know, and endlessly darning shoes and washing and mending tights. My fingers are quite swollen from pushing and pulling thread. Every tiny tear that appears on a point shoe must be fixed immediately.

I most enjoy my History of the Ballet class. We have been studying the influence of Diaghilev's famous 'Ballet

Russe'. Diaghilev was the first impresario to make dance a popular contemporary art form. Nijinsky was his great star. When Nijinsky got married he was banished from Diaghilev's company and eventually went bonkers – that is, mad – because he could not dance any more. My favourite movie, *The Red Shoes*, tells a similar story, but the Nijinsky character is played by a woman. Anything can happen in the movies, or real life too, I suppose. Diaghilev brought new choreographers together with designers and composers to create new ballets which seems the only creative way to work. The founder of the company here, Ninette de Valois, danced with his troupe. My orgy of dance classes are quite marvellous, although I stagger away every night stiff to the last muscle. I'm always sore and I'm always cold. The thing I miss most in London is having someone whom I really love and can depend on. But I am trying to be mature and I love you.
Lynn.

October 12

Dearest Mom and Dad,

Went to school wearing two sweaters and mufflers. It was freezing cold. I got so upset in dance class that I just about cried. I feel absolutely lost and so far behind everyone. After class I was walking toward the dressing-rooms and the tears started to flow, and who should come along but Miss Edwards. I was so embarrassed. I just told her the truth – my body is stubby and I am shaky. She said very curtly, 'Nonsense. You're doing quite well.' That made me feel better. She told me to get more sleep as I was looking pale. This was the first time I've had anybody express concern about me since I got here and that sure was nice.

I saw Margot Fonteyn take theatre class. I watched her at the barre. Fonteyn wore a great long-sleeved kind of pink sweater tied in the middle with a yellow cord, and pink tights. Her hair was pinned up. She was so graceful, so utterly lovely, I just gaped. There is nothing at all 'grand' about Fonteyn. She does not put on airs. Her grace is effortless, unaffected, without bravura. Her lively dark eyes are luminous. Her face is slightly heart-shaped and she has a light olive skin. Her total dedication is only noticed in the firmness of her mouth. Mine just quivers. The school has a big box of old point shoes that you can buy, for practising. I was rummaging through, found a pair my size and tried them on. They were fine. I turned them over and whose name should I see on them but Fonteyn's!

I love theatre class, but sometimes my body wants to do funny things and I'm afraid to 'let go'. We are learning that arm movements are just as important as what we do with our feet. The movements cannot be contrived posturings but rather part of a delicate, fluid 'line'. I like to put some flesh-and-blood into each detail and gesture.

Yesterday I was invited out by a girl at school I do not really like or admire, but accepted her invitation because it was so thoughtful of her to ask me. She lives at a Catholic hostel and she didn't introduce me to anybody. All she did was talk about how much she disliked the school and our dance teacher Miss Edwards. She called her a dictator! Anyway she put me in a dark mood, like the time I chased Bruce around the house with a knife for teasing me. I was angry with myself for having anything to do with a girl who said such hateful things, and, besides, she lived in a place where the older girls smoked!

I waited in the Standing Room line at the Garden for three hours on Saturday to buy a ticket (six shillings) for *Coppélia* with the radiant Svetlana Beriosova. During the intervals I wandered around the foyer and 'crush bar', a bit like an orphan at a palace party. I was so thirsty I ordered a glass of lemonade. I ran into Miss Edwards during the second interval. She noticed my sweaty brow and bought me an ice cream. She says I've got to relax more. I'm nervous because I am definitely gaining weight. Instead of filling up on an apple or pear, like I do at home, I fill up on bread. We don't get too much meat at the Fishers', but I now try to eat gobs of cheese and an egg every day for breakfast. I did have one excellent meal at the Royal Festival Hall when I attended a Beethoven concert with Marcia Haydée. A melon cocktail, baked chicken with veggies and a green salad. We really paid for it, though. It cost twelve shillings. That is about $1.68. It is a lot for England and a lot for me. But a little splurge makes life at the Fishers' more bearable. The thing is I know Mrs F. does the best she can.

We celebrated the birthday of one of the French girls who turned twenty-one. She still refuses to speak English, so we just do a lot of 'ça-va-ing', which is a tiresome form of conversation. Mr Fisher surprised us with a bottle of champagne. POP! My first glass of champagne. I quite liked it.

Love,
Lynn

November 14

Dearest Mom,

Ever since I got your letter I have been on a tight economy drive. I now itemize every expense. It's a matter of learning how to deal with money. I told Marcia Haydée I could not eat lunch any more at Mrs Honeybun's. Mrs Honeybun has a little café near the school and we went there for roast beef sandwiches. The school lunches are quite OK, only two shillings, about thirty cents. There are always puddings and custards. I try not to eat them because they make me fat. The sight of so many thick puddings and custards turns me quite gooey inside. My face and arms and waist are filling out. But I did have a fine dance class with Miss Edwards, who said, 'Very *nice*, Springbett.' It made the day for me. She was in a rage at some of the girls and snapped at them. I felt sorry for those who are getting it. Her advice is always good. 'Hold your neck and shoulders as if you're wearing diamonds you want everyone to see,' she commands.

After French class I got dressed for point class and I could not find my point shoes anywhere. I hunted high and low. My shoes were missing. I was nearly in hysterics. Marcia found them just as class began. They were in a corner, under a towel. Marcia says one of the girls must have hidden them. It seems so odd! You have no idea what a panicky feeling I had. And of course I was late for class. The dance classes are exhausting, but I've improved my arms – they have more feeling in them, they are not just weights hanging from my shoulders. I am also developing a stronger sense of balance. My tendons may be sore, but they are flexible.

When I reached Orsett Terrace, around six o'clock, pushed along by a torrent of chilly air, I was so tired I couldn't face climbing the four flights to my room. I just sat on the first steps for ten minutes. Jeremy brought me a cup of hot tea and said his Mom had a surprise for me, but I wouldn't know what it was until breakfast. When I awoke and came downstairs I found a tiny muffin sitting on my plate. I had told Mrs F. about your muffins and she made them from the recipe off the Bran box. Then your letter came. Hearing about the mountains and Dad washing the car, and bacon & eggs just made me feel I was looking out our bathroom window and I could hear the bacon sizzle. Sometimes when I wash my face and my eyes are closed I pretend that I'm in our bathroom and just have to go down the hall to my bedroom. I must be an odd little whatnot. Miss Edwards calls me 'little whatnot'.

On Sunday I went to Hampton Court Palace where Henry VIII used to live. The grounds, with the fountains and shrubs and perfect lawns, took me into a historic storybook setting. Saw the old kitchen and wine cellar, the great hall with its massive stained glass windows and vast bedrooms. I also visited the Tower of London where Henry VIII chopped off the heads of two Queens. I was by myself and getting that funny spasm again, but when I thought about prisoners facing death I forgot the spasm. Mrs Fisher says I must concentrate on things other than you, but I don't think she had executions in mind. I'm surprised Henry VIII didn't drown one of his wives in a gigantic vat of custard. That surely would be the worst torture. I also spent some hours at the National Art Gallery. I particularly liked a painting by Rubens of a girl in a felt hat, though the painting is called *The Straw Hat*. The girl has a pure roundish face, big eyes and a full bosom. The portrait, done in opulent colours, is very intense and sensual. The face and eyes sort of reminded me of me.

Last week I went to the Sadler's Wells Theatre (part of the Royal Opera House organization) and saw a new ballet, *Café des Sports*. It was about a bike race in France. Only mildly interesting. I did enjoy watching a lanky dancer in purple tights who played an Existential artist, Kenneth MacMillan – he is also a choreographer. He has great big flashing legs and soft undulating movements. The interval was most dramatic. I spotted Ninette de Valois, Empress of the British Ballet. She is a smallish woman, married to a doctor, whose vivid presence makes her loom very large. I am fearful of the day when she attends a class because she can be quite critical. She started her career in her teens, touring seaside resorts. Of those early days she once said, 'Not only have I danced on every pier, I have also been hissed off every music hall stage in England.' She sounds fiercely irresistible! She is known affectionately as Madam. Some dancers call her the Dame, a title given to her by Queen Elizabeth.

I'm dreading Xmas. Do you know what I'd really like? A Christmas stocking. Would you fill one up and send it to me? In the same package could you also send my rhinestone bracelet, Avon's perfumed deodorant (To a Wild Rose), Kleenex, my camera, bobby pins and sugar cubes. Jeremy Fisher has never seen sugar cubes and I want to show him what they are like. But, most of all for Xmas, I'd like a phone call.

I'm feeling much better but I get awfully tired of having so much responsibility, especially the handling of expenses. (I only spent ten pounds last month.) I don't get so homesick, except in the mornings when I wake up, and need you so badly, Mom. Having someone who cares for you deeply, who always has a shoulder, like yours, is what I miss.

Finally, before my heater goes off and I have to insert another shilling, I must tell you about an extraordinary incident at the Garden. I received a pass to the Paris Opera Ballet and wore my black taffeta skirt and black blouse. The ballet was about a Degas dancer and an Apollo statue that came to life in a museum. WELL – the ballerina threw up on stage. I was not sure what had happened, but she made a jolting gesture and ran off. A man with opera glasses told me during the interval. Imagine, throwing up on the stage at Covent Garden!

Lots of love,
Lynn

December 28

Dearest Mom and Dad,

Xmas is over, I survived. You mustn't take any notice of me. I bought Miss Edwards a little Xmas cake and a box of chocolates for Betty Anderton, a classmate who is very nice. The Fishers were delighted with the tins of salmon you sent them. For some weeks I promised to take Jeremy to the movies. He wanted to see an American gangster film. But I saw *The Red Shoes* was playing at a revival house. You know my missionary zeal. So I took him to that. The dancing is superb, but isn't it absurd for the ballerina to prefer her boyfriend to the ballet? He's such a humourless stick. Not at all dishy (a Brit expression meaning Very Cute) like the impresario. When it was over, Jeremy said, wrinkling his nose, 'You don't look very much like a dancer, do you?' His remark made me feel wretched, because it's true. No long neck. No sunken cheekbones. No dainty will-o'-the-wisp me. I'm all legs and arms. If I succeed, I will have to become someone quite different on stage. We really should have gone to the gangster film.

When the other girls went home for Xmas, the Fisher house was quiet as a tomb. Spooky. The Fishers bought a tree which we decorated. Just a small one, sitting in a pot. Nothing like the dillies *we* had. Knowing how much I dreaded Xmas, Miss Edwards said, 'Lynn' (when she calls me 'Lynn' I just about die), 'I thought I'd try to make your first Xmas in England a little happier so I managed to get some tickets for you to see Margot Fonteyn in *Swan Lake*.' I was ecstatic. Fonteyn is untouchable. It was marvellous how she coped with the worst conducting you've ever heard. Painfully slow. Other dancers would have walked off stage if they had to work to that tempo. But right now I'd be simply thrilled through and through if I could even be the last swan in *Swan Lake*.

I spent Xmas dinner with Arnold Haskell, the school

principal, and his wife. He teaches English literature and History of the Ballet, and knows absolutely everything. He is one of the most intelligent men I have ever met. He saw Pavlova dance many times. Her face was so mobile, he said, although not beautiful, that she could project an illusion of amazing beauty. She also had quite remarkable arms. Did you know that Pavlova died asking for her swan dress? Isadora Duncan resented restrictions of any sort that interfered with her spontaneity. She believed in total freedom. And then he told me a marvellous thing. A French writer, Théophile Gautier, who came up with the scenario for *Giselle*, said that 'ballet is music that one can see'. I wrote the quote down and put it in my diary. Music that one can see – a half-sentence, right on the button, that explains the essence of dance. I could have listened to him for hours.

We had roast lamb, heaps of it! Dinner was by candlelight. Mr Haskell puts sherry in his soup and said I could have a drop. It was delicious. He gave me two lovely books, on Sadler's Wells and Covent Garden. After dinner I sat by the fire with a little rug tucked around my legs, and sipped strong black coffee with a wee slice of lemon in a little china cup decorated with roses. When I came home Mrs Fisher, who had properly hidden away my Xmas stocking, had it out by the tree. The Fishers were going to let me open my presents alone but I asked them to please stay because I wanted someone with me.

The phone call. I wrote down what I was going to say. Then the telephone rang at the agreed hour. I just about fell over myself getting to it, and dropped my note pad in the hall. The operator said a call from Canada and I got goose-bumps all over. I heard clicks and mutterings and then the operator said, 'Hello, Vancouver?' And Bruce roared, 'MOM!' I could just picture him standing in his pants yelling for you. I cried, 'Hello, hello, is that you,

Mom? Can you hear me?' And you said, 'Hello, honey, how are you?' And firecrackers just exploded in my brain. I forgot everything I wanted to say. I realize now we really didn't *say* anything, there was not time, but hearing your voices meant so much to me. Sometimes I feel that life can't still be going on in Vancouver, and then the phone call reminds me that you are truly there. I did not cry. I just sort of danced around and I am sure the Fishers think I am quite nuts. This wonderful happy feeling stayed with me for hours. I miss you so very much. But what an Xmas treat! Oh, someday we will all have Xmas together, won't we? I'll make pots of money and fly you to London. Of course dancers never earn pots of money, so I'll fly to Canada. I am not making much sense.

What Xmas decorations have you put on the mantel and dining room table, the buffet and door? Please remember to tell me. Then I can visualize everything. I am in my room now eating your star- and angel-shaped cookies, Mom. I love you all like mad.

Lynn

If only you knew how urgent I am. If there were only someone here whose shoulder I could lean on – letters, letters.

The reality is that, for many years, these two themes dominated letters home, and my life. Re-reading them I see that I was confused, frightened and a rather grave child, desperately trying to find myself. The ballet *Anastasia* shows how the past haunts our present. I played a terrified woman who claimed to be the only survivor of the Czar's massacred family during the Russian Revolution. *I* believed her story. And what did that grown-up, disoriented child demand? Rising from her bed in the loony bin, arms outstretched, she silently screamed: 'I am me! And I can't go on losing family

– child – husband – *identity*!' Here I am on Woodstock Road, in my blue flannel nightgown, lying in bed, surrounded by letters which remind me, now uncomfortably, that my roles and personal life overlapped, perhaps a bit too often, from Juliet to Janis Joplin, from Manon Lescaut to Mary Vetsera – these were reckless, determined, alienated women who defied society, who said, 'You must pay attention to me, you don't know how urgent I am.'

I turned sixteen in March and did not feel different, except that I was rounder. I shared 'top women of the year' honours, presented by the *Vancouver Sun*, with a seventy-six-year-old grandmother who wrote a book called *I Married the Klondike*. I had an operation, or 'manipulation', on a troubled left foot and woke up in a strange ward to an anvil chorus of feminine snores. For several minutes I did not know where or who I was. 'You mustn't be depressed,' Miss Edwards said. 'If you have the courage, you can make it.' One day Dame Ninette de Valois came to dance class. She sat very regally, glacially on a chair and observed. When she smiled at me, her eyes penetrating every bone in my body, my heart seemed to stop. Every summer teachers from all over the world gathered at the school for a demonstration of the dance syllabus – technical tests required to pass the school's dance examination. I was among two or three girls asked to participate in the demonstration. Miss Edwards was worried about my footwork and didn't want me to demonstrate a certain exercise. 'What do you mean, she's not strong enough?' Madam asked suspiciously. She ordered me on: 'Do them, please.' When I finished she said, 'Splendid. Not strong enough? *You see!*'

I was encouraged by Arnold Haskell, Miss Edwards and Madam, but, at the end of each day, when I took two underground trains to Paddington, to the boarding house on Orsett Terrace, where I existed solely on news from home and continued to disturb my parents with letters of loneliness, the odd spasms consumed me. My parents finally put it to me straightaway: I would have to decide before packing up for the summer whether I wanted to return to the school. I spent an afternoon wandering sightlessly through the green fields of Hyde Park and stumbled back to the greyness of Orsett Terrace at twilight. I skipped dinner and remained in my room, eating raisins and apples sent from Canada, while preparing to pull up the old socks. I even bought a bottle of turquoise ink for the momentous occasion. The letter is in my hand. The ink has not faded, the tissue-thin blue paper is still crisp.

Dear Mom and Dad,

I received your two-page letter and was very much disturbed by the decision you asked. I was hoping that everything was going to be taken for granted. My answer is – I want to return to London and the school. I've thought about it very carefully. I know that when I return from my trip home I shall feel homesick again and I will have quite a time talking myself out of it. But I'm sure I will get over it more quickly. Oh, Mom, it breaks my heart to make this decision, but I want to be a dancer and it's not possible to be one at home in Vancouver. If I said – right, I'll stay at home and be a normal 100 per-cent redblooded Canadian schoolgirl, after a month I'd be weeping and wailing and gnashing my teeth and would never ever forgive myself for giving up this oppor-tunity. Being away from home and people you love is a sacrifice a dancer simply has to make. I would never forgive myself if I gave up this chance. If I stayed at home and was miserable, you would be unhappy too. But if you knew I was doing the thing I love and want to give my life for, you would be happy too.
        Love,
        Lynn

In the fall of 1980, when my life was in psychological tatters, I lay in bed with a fever. I had been rehearsing for the new season at Covent Garden amid darts and arrows of deflating gossip and whispered jabs: 'She's not going to make it.' I did not want to get out of bed, ever. I received a note from Arnold Haskell, who was dying in a hospital. He had seen a clip from *A Month in the Country* on television. 'It is rare to see such depth, such femininity in ballet,' wrote the man with whom I had passed my first Christmas in London. And for a while I wanted to throw off the bedcovers and rush to rehearsals. But I could not.

So I quit.

Months after my defection I longed to ring up Madam, an intensely human woman, but I was afraid to. Just as Mom asked questions that I could not answer, I knew Madam would do the same. An old friend telephoned, however, and was graciously invited to her home one Sunday for lemon tea and cakes. 'The school staff always said Lynn wasn't strong enough,' Madam recalled. 'It was the same with Margot Fonteyn. But it was for me to decide how far she could be pushed. What Lynn constantly had to fight against was her physique. She has a very short torso, but wonderfully long legs and arms that gave her an incredible breadth of movement. She succeeded because of her special virtues – dramatic ability, musicality and a flow of movement, rare among British dancers. Lynn was a rebel. I'm very fond of rebels. They have spark and imagination. But they must be controlled.' Madam quietly laughed, her head thrown back. 'I always have a giggle when I hear the latest Lynn story. She *is* Isadora Duncan, you know.'

Then, quickly, the laugh vanished and her face became sombre, anxious. At eighty-two, Madam sat with great dignity on a small velour chair in a pose of vague uneasiness. 'The Royal Ballet resents losing her. I do wish she'd call me.' Madam had not touched her tea or cake. She moved to a window, her keen clear eyes staring out into the past. 'I don't believe she ever quite got over the isolation of her first year in London. That was a traumatic period. Some people feel she was too young, that she should never have been allowed to come here alone.'

Madam turned away from the window and said hastily, 'But she did become the Royal Ballet's greatest dramatic dancer.'

CHAPTER 4

Growing Pains

The summer at home was not idyllic.

All year I had done nothing but count the months, the weeks and finally the days until I would see my family again. Mom's flow of letters kept me alive, from giving up in despair. On sleepless nights that first winter I thought, 'I can pack my suitcase and trunk, and flee in twenty-four hours. I can go back to my *own* home.' I had no quibble with the school, though I was constantly apprehensive about academic anaemia. The dance classes were the best in the world and became The Reason for getting out of bed each freezing morning in the Fisher house, which seemed even more cheerless when spring made the city gloriously green and breezy. On weekends, the parks were dotted with strolling couples, shouting youths playing cricket and chattering girls lolling in twos and threes, sipping orange drinks. I was a spectator. Alone. Weekends were the hardest, for only at school did I not feel anonymous. When I went to the Garden or Sadler's Wells Theatre I was Cinderella going to a ball. But I always turned into a pumpkin on the tube ride back to Paddington. The Fishers were thoughtful, but Orsett Terrace was not a boarding school of two hundred comradely teenagers who ate, played, studied and danced together, and devised pranks to consternate the headmaster or mistress. It was a solemn, drab house. The Fishers were not paid to be entertaining and loving. They barely eked out an existence themselves.

Mom and Dad, with Bruce, who had just graduated from college, were at the Vancouver airport and I hugged them so long and so tightly, and had such a tear-stained face, that my arrival looked more like a tragic farewell scene. Mom put me on a diet of fish, lean meat, fresh vegetables and heaps of fruit. Gradually, the bready blubber on my waist, arms and cheeks disappeared. Bruce and I swam and raced along beaches. We went clam-digging, with a shovel and a bucket, and toted home large clams which Mom used for chowder. Once we decided to go on an oyster hunt. We rented a boat and sped to a little island in north Vancouver, and climbed over wet rocks, balancing our buckets of salt water. A sharp smack with a shovel knocked the shellfish off the rocks and into our buckets. Then we lazed in the sun and ate the oysters raw. These were gorgeous, heavenly hours. I often thought a bit sadly, as we cracked open oysters looking for seed pearls, that there was no one I truly missed in London. But my bleak memories were burned away by the scorching sun lying happily alongside Bruce, listening to the gentle splashing of water against the rocks. Bruce asked matter-of-factly if I had any boyfriends. He was still dating his highschool sweetheart whom he eventually married. I always envied the closeness of their relationship. Bruce has three children. His one marriage has been steadfast and secure, quite unlike my quixotic partnerships. I confessed that I had no boyfriends. I did not confess that I had *no* friends, really, at all, merely a couple of acquaintances. 'I focus on my dancing,' I said, truthfully. 'Everything else seems minor.' Gazing at his lean, tanned face, his wet hair glistening from a dip in the sea, I asked, 'Do you think I'll ever get a nice thin face? Mine is like a full moon. It's so ugly.' He leaned over and stroked my cheek with his finger. 'I've never seen the moon so bright and clear, it's like a silver dollar.'

After dinner, which I usually helped Mom cook, we all sat at the dining-room table, and talked for hours. I brought out my diaries and read scribbled descriptions of London life: 'Civilized and cold, great unconcern for extreme inconvenience.' And then Bruce would speculate on his upcoming life in San Francisco, where he was entering dental school that fall. I was no longer Big Brother's kid sister. He talked to me like an adult, which I was – a sort of hobbledehoy adult. The sibling rivalry fostered between us by Dad was gone. Bruce and I were in greedy rapport. Mom beamed pridefully. Her two children were establishing careers by themselves in strange cities, in different parts of the world. We were the untamed adventurers. Unfortunately, our puny accomplishments so far and grandiose goals made Dad twitchy. He was a respected dentist, a perfectionist at his work, but instead of forgetting the boy who roamed the snowy Canadian wilderness trapping animals and who crash-landed an airplane in his teens – instead of revelling harmoniously in our homecoming – he turned high-spirited conversations into repetitive alcoholic arguments, which inevitably touched bitterly on his lost adventures. I desperately wanted to put my arms around him reassuringly, but any attempt at reasoning only made him hostile and we would move to other rooms or sit quietly until the punishing mumbling tirade passed, and Mom led him to bed. One night I heard his slurred voice vibrating through the bedroom wall. I was shaking all over and felt nauseous. The first weeks had been peaceful and loving but Dad shattered the secure, affectionate atmosphere as deliberately as smashing a mirror into hundreds of tiny stabbing pieces. I began counting the days until my return to London, and when a day passed without his drinking I heaved a trembling sigh of relief. His outbursts were unexpected and filled the house with tension. Because I had looked forward all year to my summer in Vancouver and had finally reached home at great cost to my parents, I had the numbing feeling that Dad resented me, that he was mocking my holiday. I know today that this was not true. He just never got over the death of his own youthful dreams.

On evenings when the family did not go to the movies, or friends did not stop in, Bruce insisted upon getting me out of the house as soon as dinner was over. We took long meandering drives in Dad's old Buick. Bruce did not want to expose me to any domestic scenes. I resolved that the men I chose to be with, romantically, must allow me to be strong and they must be giving, loving and understanding. Quite a large order, but if I did not find it in marriage, then I would find it in friendship. I further resolved that I would never allow any marriage or relationship to lock me into an untenable situation. Sitting in the Buick, parked alongside a murmuring sea, we talked mostly about Dad's drinking and how it affected Mom. 'I have no patience with people who drink to excess,' Bruce said. 'Shellacked, polluted, tanked – it's all stinko.' Bruce seldom drinks more than a glass or two of wine. The last time we talked Bruce said, 'Dad's drinking left a scar on my psyche,' and then he concluded meaningfully, 'yours too.'

After I returned to London Mom wrote that Dad had stopped drinking. She had been on the verge of leaving him. A friend who belonged to Alcoholics Anonymous persuaded Dad to attend the meetings.

So, the idyllic summer that never was ended in September and, feeling a terrible sense of melancholy, I was again with the Fishers, eating scrambled eggs and raw cabbage sprinkled with pepper and vinegar on my first night there, which promptly made me sick. My three-month visit home gave me a healthy, ruddy glow, and I was astonishingly slim. I vowed to avoid breads, porridge, custards and sausages even if it meant starving. I would stick to tins of salmon, raisins, nuts, and canned fruit and fresh fruit sent from Canada. As the months passed my stomach muscles roped themselves into double knots, decreasing my already limited appetite, for this was my second and last year at the school. The senior teachers and Dame Ninette were sizing us up. In the spring, we would either graduate into one of the companies or be dropped. My absurd diet, coupled with anxiety about the future, produced severe cramps. I did not complain to the Fishers. They had made it quite plain that they wanted to hear no more 'whinings and groanings' from me. 'Unhappiness builds strength of character,' said Mrs Fisher, as she scrubbed the kitchen floor. I began suppressing all emotion. It went into my diaries and dance. Not wishing to make any bid for sympathy – which would be withheld anyway – I went to see a doctor.

I told him about my abdominal pains and that I had not menstruated since settling in London the previous year. He gave me a thorough examination and then peered closely at me over round glasses with thin black frames. 'You appear remarkably calm, but then you *are* an actress, aren't you, or studying to be one?'

I explained that I was a dancer, or studying to be one.

He was silent for a few minutes. 'There's nothing physically wrong with you. It's all nerves. But nerves must be nurtured.' He prescribed endocrine tablets for menstruation and anti-spasmodic tablets for indigestion.

When a senior teacher asked why I missed two classes, I naturally related my visit to the doctor. She was singularly unpleasant because I had not first consulted the school nurse. 'You are stupidly independent,' she said, dismissing me without inquiring how I was or what the doctor prescribed. Her coldness only confirmed that I had no one to rely on but myself. Winifred Edwards, now retired, telephoned me at the Fishers'. Hearing her I wanted to cry but I accepted, in a voice of pure meringue, an invitation to lunch at her house the following Saturday.

Throughout a tenderly prepared meal Miss Edwards indicated that she knew precisely what worried me, and cunningly, carefully drew me out. 'I wish I knew what the school had planned for me,' I said, at last.

Miss Edwards studied me with a knowing smile. 'You must have patience, you must be willing to go forward slowly,' she answered.

My pulse beat furiously. I pushed a salad plate away untasted and began talking about school life. 'I'm sure it's just a façade, but the girls at school never want to discuss ballet. They seem violently irritated when I ask a teacher about a movement or some correction. I asked one if some girls didn't like me and she said, "Yes – but just the silly ones."' Miss Edwards carefully patted her snow-white marcelled hair and glanced at my salad plate. Guiltily, I nibbled at the greens, dabbing my mouth with a linen napkin.

'It's something you'll always have to put up with, little whatnot,' she said. 'Last year, you were pampered, but this year, you are being prepared for a company. You have to show your mettle.' She poured me a glass of cider in a beautifully frosted goblet. We slowly finished the meal in the gathering dusky darkness, except for some lamps in the sitting room and a lamp on the table. Before I slipped on my new gloves and said goodbye, she said very gently, 'You really need to find a good friend at school. Someone your own age. It will help you control your restless emotions and your state of mind.' On the tube ride to Paddington, I knitted away wildly on a scarf. The warm, homey afternoon with Miss Edwards clarified how much I loathed Orsett Terrace and its greasy rigidity, and how I desperately wanted a confidante, wanted to be someone's special mate.

That winter we had two heavy snowstorms, accompanied by gusting gales of wind. I awakened in the morning in an icy room – windows covered with frost – with two hot water bottles on my feet and legs, knowing that cold bones led to injuries and I had spent the fall having my left foot and knee 'manipulated' by a doctor on Wimpole Street. Opera singers cosset their throats, musicians coddle their hands, but anguished dancers can never for a moment forget their *entire* bodies, which are subjected to appalling risks at every rehearsal and every performance. I have extremely loose joints and suffered terribly from nerves. Vigorous warm-ups before a performance, which left me drenched in sweat, exorcized stage fright and kept my muscles sinewy. But I also learned to do warm-ups before class. Protecting my body, I wore three sweaters, wool tights, wool slacks, a jacket, gloves *and* mittens to school. Streets and sidewalks disappeared under packed snow. London turned white. The pipes froze in the Fisher house and we were without heat for almost a week.

I tramped on through the snow and sleet and gale force winds full of enthusiasm because Peter Wright, ballet-master for the Sadler's Wells opera ballet, had chosen several students, including Betty Anderton, Christopher Gable and myself, as 'extras' in the production of *Hansel and Gretel*. We would be paid two pounds five shillings a performance. Betty had dark hair and the pleasing features of a gypsy princess. We were both seventeen, but I was awed by Betty's worldliness. Christopher was sixteen. With his crystal-blue eyes and curly blond hair, he exuded an endearing boyish charm.

We rehearsed at the school and at Sadler's Wells Theatre, which gave me a perfect excuse to miss the evening meal at the Fishers'. I snacked with Christopher and Betty. We were three of fourteen angels who watched over the sleeping Hansel and Gretel. I carried a long gold horn. My costume was made of gold silk. Gold leaves were clipped into my hair and my wings were gold too. This walk-on gave meaning to my existence: I was finally able to express myself in the tiniest way on stage. Our first performance was during the snowy Christmas holiday of 1955. Celebrating my London début Winifred Edwards gave me a red handkerchief and a comb in a red leather case. She came to the opening and assured us that we 'conveyed a lovely feeling as radiant little angels'. I was quite pleased with myself for not tripping down the stairway to heaven.

My knowledge of backstage life became more sophisticated three months later when I was an extra in the last-act wedding party of *Firebird*.

As an extra huddled in the wings I watched many scenes. One dancer, sprinting across the stage during a blackout, let fly an uncommonly noisy fart. 'Sorry, ducks, but that last bit was a killer,' she apologized. One of the corps boys leaped offstage magnificently with his partner, then stood gasping for air, his body shaking. 'She nearly strangled me,' he said to another girl and limped away. I loved it! This was definitely 'home'. I was dazzled by the disciplined beauty of the dancers who concealed physical pain and discomfort until they reached the wings, so that audiences might be swept into an exquisitely enchanted world. The classical ballets – *Firebird, Swan Lake, Sleeping Beauty, La Sylphide* – have similar plots. Prince and princess (who might be a swan or a sylph); manipulative magician and a fairy or bird who brings the lovers together – or pulls them apart. I was once asked to pontificate on the classics at a ballet society. I agreed only if the critic Clement Crisp of the *Financial Times* were moderator. The erudite Clem has a mutinous, lovable sense of humour. Blithely nattering away, I got the Lilac Fairy from *Sleeping Beauty* mixed up with the Firebird and transposed a nest of sylphs into a lake of swans. Clem fed me the most outrageous lines: 'Isn't the Bluebird a remote cousin of the Firebird?' I glared at him, having forgotten that the Bluebird flutters in *Sleeping Beauty*. 'No matter, the birds all gather at the same aviary for cocktails,' I answered reproachfully. Like myself, Clem finds the classic plot thick with whimsical poppycock. 'You sounded just like Anna Russell sending up the Wagnerian operas,' he confided. Between the two of us, we had the crowd in stitches.

Tamara Karsavina, who danced the original Firebird for Diaghilev's company, helped reconstruct the ballet in London and taught the role to Margot Fonteyn. And one freezing wintry day, Karsavina, then in her early seventies, gave a mime lecture at school. I took a notebook and several pencils in case one broke. Karsavina had been Diaghilev's prima ballerina. She was still an arresting, impressive figure, who moved so lightly that you forgot her girlhood had passed forty or fifty years before. I realize today how very fortunate I was to come of age as a dancer when I could absorb dance history directly from what I call the 'historical links'.

Body movement and distinct gesticulation form the creative personality, Karsavina told us, but each movement must have a reality – personal conviction. A dancer's brilliance, she said, resides in the feet, arms, hands and head. The *emotional* content emerges from the neck. After her lecture I concentrated on the placement, the holding, the slow turn of my neck, determined to use it voluptuously, though I did not think of the word then.

The walk-on performances in *Hansel and Gretel* and *Firebird* gave me money for gallery tickets to West End plays and concerts. And I continued to avoid dinners at Orsett Terrace. If Christopher or Betty were available, we'd hustle off to the canteen or a sandwich shop. I tactfully proposed to Mrs Fisher that since I had to be at the theatre several nights a week, perhaps I could separate my dinner bill from the monthly rent. She adjusted her apron – a white cotton smock with sunflowers – and sat me down at the kitchen table, where she peeled potatoes.

'I know you haven't been eating here lately. And I understand you told one of the boarders the food made you fat. Now, I like to think of the girls here as a family.' She put the potato peeler aside. 'I think you would be happier if you moved.' Pause. 'You don't fit in.'

Obviously my absences had been a topic of conversation. At first I blushed with anger at this swift ejection and then I was quite elated. I was now familiar with London. I had no confidante, but I was making 'acquaintances', and I was not being hurled into the street, bag and baggage, with no one to call. Within two weeks I moved to a romantic address: Hamlet Gardens in Ravenscourt Park. My new lodging, found by Miss Edwards, was only a short distance from the school. I packed up everything on a Saturday. Then, on Sunday, I drove away in a taxi without further adieux. That short drive marked the beginning of my nomadic existence. I was the only lodger in the Victorian apartment at Hamlet Gardens. The landlady, Irene Sopwith, a thin, birdlike woman in grey woollies, understood the diets and dilemmas of dancers. Her own daughter, Noreen, who was Ballet Rambert's leading dancer and later displayed her gifts of characterization with the Royal Ballet, was constantly on tour. Mrs Sopwith and I had formal dinners together in the dining room, seated at opposite ends of the table, like Miss Haversham and Estella in *Great Expectations*. Her dinners were quite good. She twittered away endlessly on a variety of subjects, asking all sorts of questions, but never waiting for answers. A typical dinner: 'I'm sorry that someone at the school hasn't taken you under their wing, my dear, if you're cold, put on another sweater, because I mustn't turn on the heat, frightfully expensive, you know. Do you like the chicken? It has no sauce. I don't trust sauces. They're so *devious*. My, you're a poised little thing. Noreen is so reclusive. We're not very close, but I do appreciate the difficulties of a young dancer. Now, if you're chilled, put that shawl around your shoulders. Later we'll have a nice cup of tea. How do you find the divine Beriosova?' She examined a Brussels sprout on the end of her fork and looked at me. My mind, reeling from her chatter, went awry. The Brussels sprout was still on her fork, in mid-air. I quickly ate one or two on my plate and said, 'Delicious!'

'How nicely put,' said Mrs Sopwith. 'The delicious Beriosova. I know we'll get along splendidly.' And we did.

I sat on a pincushion all spring, worrying about summer and fall. In May I ran to Winifred Edwards. We received our dance certificates – or, to put it bluntly, learned our fate. This was the announcement I had been fearing. The anointed dancers joined the godly company at Covent Garden. The most promising were assigned to the touring company. Those still being considered were placed in the opera ballet at Covent Garden. The leftovers humbly accepted seven pounds ten shillings a week in the opera ballet at Sadler's Wells Theatre and did not fuss. Betty Anderton, Christopher Gable and I were lumped together at the bottom. The Sadler's Wells opera ballet was usually a dead end. After one year, you were discreetly asked, 'Had you ever thought of dancing in musical comedy?'

'Madam likes your work very much,' a senior teacher said, watching me turn pale, 'but she wants you to spend this year building up your strength.' I did not believe her. I was certain she sugarcoated the bad news to everyone. Miss Edwards had soothing words. Madam, she asserted, was very much aware of all her students, and a year in a less pressured situation would allow me to gain confidence and maturity.

School was over.

Betty, Christopher and I separated quietly, numbly, until fall. The one thing I now looked forward to was the arrival of Mom. 'I'm pleased your mother is coming,' Miss Edwards said. 'It will make your life in London seem more real.' The day I received her travel plans, I joyously committed my first seditious act. Stuffing my practice bag with shoes that had to be darned, I bought a box of strawberries and went for a stroll in Hyde Park wearing a yellow T-shirt and white pedal pushers – snug pants that stopped below the knee. Mom sent them from Canada. Pedal pushers were not worn in London and the mini-skirt was some years away. I selected a grassy area under a tree, kicked off my sneakers and stretched out, alternately sewing my satin slippers and dropping strawberries into my mouth. No one bothered me. Life can be very pleasant, I decided on that gleeful picnic.

I found a job operating a gurgling espresso machine five nights a week and also rented a bed-sit in Kensington for Mom and me. 'It's always nice to see one's mother – now and then,' Mrs Sopwith said, waving me goodbye as a taxi drove me to new quarters, luxuriously private and over-looking a garden.

Mom cooked hamburgers on a two-burner hot plate and learned how to light the one electric heater with shillings. 'Honey, I'm not homesick, but even *I* long for some of the old comforts,' she said laughing. I planted a whooping kiss on her cheek. Miss Edwards had been right: Mom's visit validated London for me and gave my life a reality that we could share. It was a happy summer, almost carefree, and we went on a Cook's coach tour through France, Belgium and Holland. For three months I had a shoulder – hers – to lean on, and though I dreaded her departure, I sensed that the gloomiest period was over. I even had a chum – a South African girl named Jacqueline Daryl who graduated into the main company. Jackie had been living with her Mom in a bed-sit and since our parents were leaving for South Africa and Canada respectively at the same time, Jackie ended up being my flatmate in Kensington. A tall, fair, beautiful girl, Jackie was very popular with the chaps. I was quite flattered by her friendship. She introduced herself one day after class.

'You have a very curious talent,' she said, 'so free, without angularity. Sorry, but I couldn't stop watching you.' She had the confidence to utter this compliment. There was no awkwardness. She was very matter-of-fact. She invited me to Sunday lunch with her Mom in their bed-sit. We listened to records, talked about the school, our future in the ballet, strange British customs, and for a few hours my own struggle for identity was suspended. I often met Jackie for window shopping expeditions before serving cappuccino at the coffee bar in Kensington. Mom approved of Jackie, found her amusing, intelligent and sensible, and was glad to know that I would be safely settled for the year.

In September Mom had an interview with Dame Ninette. I fussed and fretted unnecessarily over what she would wear and say. Mom is a handsome woman, candid and decisive, like Madam herself. The two women, I am sure, appreciated each other's qualities and Madam spoke in her most forthright manner. 'Quite an impressive gal,' said Mom, after the interview, calmly unpinning a brooch she wore for my sake. 'She certainly doesn't shilly-shally around, does she?' But what did she say? I begged. Mom smiled proudly. 'You mustn't worry, hon, it's unlikely you'll be out in the cold next year.'

The conversation with Madam was relayed to Dad in a letter that I saw for the first time while recently ploughing through boxes of letters: 'Madam believes Lynn has a great future, if all goes well. She says Lynn has a special quality. They want to train her slowly to strengthen her beautiful legs and feet. Naturally she asked me not to tell Lynn any of this. But I thought it was wonderful coming directly from the top.'

Madam gave me the opportunity to succeed. She let the teachers and choreographers know that she liked me. Without her trust I might have wilted away in discouragement. There were times when I must have annoyed her greatly, but she never reproached me for the way I managed or mismanaged my life. Without Ninette de Valois, there would be no Lynn Seymour.

Jesters and fools, favourites who know unspeakable secrets and flatterers of tyrants; lusty men pursued by infatuated women amidst intrigue and treachery – backstage at the ballet? No. I am here referring to the operas in which I danced with Betty Anderton and Christopher Gable. For *The Pearl Fishers*, we smeared our bodies with dark 'Egyptian No. 3', a pancake make-up, very cold to apply. The opera chorus wore long dark brown underwear instead. They looked ridiculous, but felt cosy. We were native dancers in another part of the Ceylon jungle. For *The Bartered Bride* I was a Bohemian peasant whirling to a polka in another part of the village square. In *Rigoletto* and *Eugene Onegin*, we performed a stately minuet and oom-pah-pah waltz in another part of some gleaming ballroom. I seldom attend the opera today. If nostalgia strikes, I just yodel 'The Last Rose of Summer' from *Martha*.

I was happy for the first time in London. Our ballet-master Peter Wright treated the opera corps with respectful affection, and built up a sense of camaraderie. We never once felt like 'rejects', but that shadow stalked us and so we rehearsed with boundless energy and enthusiasm. Appalled by the acting of the opera singers who just leaned against tree trunks or thrones, we studied the period style and effect of each opera. When we were not dancing we sought to make our behaviour and gestures have meaning and purpose. We took great care with hairstyles and make-up. We wanted our acting to be as good as our dancing.

Rigoletto opens in the palace of that rake, the Duke of Mantua, where the cavaliers and their ladies are having courtly fun, contemplating the usual seduction rites. Betty, Christopher and I, with a dancer named Ben Stevenson, now director of the Houston Ballet in America, formed a huddle full of courtly intrigue, whispering naughtily about the Duke's roving eye. Then, seconds before our minuet began, Ben would mutter, 'Now make a flower.' We'd toss our hands out like exotic leaves and lean back elegantly and laugh – a big four-petal flower in bloom. I'm sure no one noticed, but we looked forward to that moment each performance. *Eugene Onegin* left us a bit dizzy. The cruel, world-weary Onegin wilfully flirts with a bewildered alto throughout a second-act ball where the guests accelerate the action by waltzing endlessly faster and faster. Christopher was my partner. While Onegin made a pest of himself with Olga, Lensky and Tatiana in old Russia, we waltzed on and on and on. The room was spinning with us.

'Christopher, how much longer?'

'Hold on, another twelve bars . . .'

'Are you sure?'

'Keep staring at my nose . . .'

'It's spinning *too*.'

'Here we go, five more bars . . .' Then we had to stop, with the lightest of hearts and fairest of smiles, and wander casually to a buffet table of fake food. We could hardly walk in a straight line. We always lurched toward the buffet, holding each other up.

The Sadler's Wells Theatre was giving a gala performance for the Hungarian Relief Fund in December 1956, starring a who's still who of dance, from Margot Fonteyn to Alicia Markova. My flatmate Jackie Daryl heard that the Covent Garden opera ballet had been asked to do the polka from *The Bartered Bride*, which they weren't even performing that season. This gave me the mean reds. The Sadler's Wells opera ballet hadn't been asked to do anything. I complained to Peter Wright, who was properly vexed. He immediately dialled a magic number and we were rewarded with an excerpt from – guess what? – *Eugene Onegin*.

The opera performances and rehearsals were exciting. My heart always did a peculiar pitty-pat each time I passed through the stage door. I once finished a rehearsal so pleasantly exhausted that I decided to get on a double-decker bus and go for a random ride. I fell asleep and woke up in Hampstead. On the day of the performance I always arrived at the theatre about four-thirty – three hours before curtain and sometimes four, depending when the opera ballet did its polka, minuet or tribal dance. As I stood in the wings, the boys in our group, who viewed me as the spinstery Canadian goody-goody, would dart onstage in circus costumes or whatever clucking rude one-liners. 'How's your cherry?' and 'Drop your knickers!' were favourites that sent them into heaps of laughter. Once or twice, Christopher, egged on by peer pressure, joined the teasing game. I hardly noticed – but some titters did filter through.

'*You don't fit in.*' Mrs Fisher's words rang through my ears. But if I did not fit in with the opera ballet, where would I ever *fit*? The ballet was all I had. Christopher accompanied me to the Garden one evening where I was meeting Jackie after a performance. Leaving the Sadler's Wells Theatre on Rosebery Avenue, I took the bull by the horns. 'Sometimes I get the feeling everyone finds me odd,' I said. 'Am I doing something wrong?'

'You take everything so unfashionably seriously,' he said. 'At school you studied English, French, Art Appreciation, History of the Ballet and Dance Notation. You care so bloody much. It's distinctly unstylish, unchic. The English way is to appear not to care about succeeding at all, to be very off-hand, to develop a blasé pose about your work. One is supposed to say, "Oh God, another rehearsal, how boring." You say, "Mr Wright, you mean we aren't going to rehearse any more?" It was super dancing in the Hungarian Relief gala, but some of the kids thought it pushy the way you barged into Peter Wright's office and told him about the opera ballet from the Garden doing *Bartered Bride*. And then you said, "Just because someone's a brain surgeon, that's no reason why you can't talk to him like anyone else."

In England, we're brought up to respect the squire and his relations.'

I couldn't understand.

Christopher looked at me steadily, with close-drawn eyebrows. 'I sound like a dreadful bounder,' he said, lighting a cigarette. 'Anyway, I'm sorry. But I answered your question.' He hadn't completely. I put it to him again six years later on a trans-Atlantic flight after we had knocked off a bottle of champagne. 'The boys wanted to shock you, to be evil, because you lacked colour and flair and glitz. You seemed so bloody sexless.' He laughed, extracting from some hidden recess another memory. 'Do you remember *Orpheus*? I knew differently after that performance.'

The Arts Theatre Club in Cambridge asked Peter Wright to choreograph a student production of Gluck's *Orpheus and Euridice*, with dancers from his opera ballet. The opera deals with the Greek minstrel Orpheus, who is trying to reclaim his wife from death. In one sequence he imagines himself descending into Hades and wresting her from a belligerent horde of demons. The dance between Orpheus and Euridice was full of unfulfilled longing. Christopher and I were chosen for the pas de deux. Rehearsals were amazing. We giggled about our sensual undulations. It was very difficult, however, as Christopher/Orpheus was forbidden to look at Lynn/Euridice: Peter Wright urged us not to be afraid. On the day of the performance Christopher and I were pieced into bits of Grecian drapery. Confronting him in Hades I thought, *well*, he looks awfully sweet to me; don't be afraid, let go, make it real. We started with supreme lightness, hesitant at our reunion, and then gradually moved slowly, ecstatically, into each other's arms. I 'let go' completely and became Euridice, being brought back to life by her beloved Orpheus. Christopher blinked in astonishment and immediately responded with a physical vibrancy that stripped aside my last inhibition.

We finished the dance in a sweat, our costumes clinging to glistening bodies. I did not see Christopher again until we were on the train returning to London. I was sitting in a compartment with my glasses on, knitting. The glasses made my eyes the size of enormous brown lollipops. I wore the Springbett outfit: a pleated skirt, a white blouse, ankle socks and orthopaedic shoes. He looked at me with dazed eyes, as if he had come upon a stranger. 'I'm knackered,' he said in a dry tone, thoughtfully trying to read my face and expecting to find someone else, a young woman, perhaps, who vaguely reminded him of the erotic Euridice. She was nowhere to be seen.

'Me, too,' I said. 'Thank God that's over.'

He nodded uneasily, avoiding my magnified eyes, and took a seat in another compartment. After the Cambridge performance, Christopher never participated in the rude jokes backstage at Sadler's Wells. Gradually, too, there were no further inquiries from the other boys on the state of my cherry. Nobody knew for sure how it was, and I certainly wasn't telling.

CHAPTER 5

Beer and Skittles

The train chugged towards Hull in a torrential downpour.

The seaport town in northern England was the last stop before the touring section of the Royal Ballet returned to London and celebrated the New Year of 1958 with a short season at Covent Garden. After a season in the opera ballet I had been promoted to the company which shuttled up and down the British Isles in cramped, draughty trains, from Bristol and Oxford to Manchester and Edinburgh – all seemingly going via Crewe.

I thought the provincial tours would be a marvellous way to explore the country, but what I glimpsed of massive cliffs, sloping farmlands, medieval castles, baroque cathedrals and swan-studded rivers was from the smudged windows of rattling trains. Once the company debarked we were frequently surrounded by the smoking chimneys and factory gates of industrial towns. There was never time to visit the recommended Botanical Gardens in Birmingham or the ruins of a Cistercian Abbey in Leeds.

Some dancers stretched in the jolting corridor, others played cards or wandered in and out of compartments borrowing magazines and cadging cigarettes. There were those who gossiped and those who slept. I had been dozing, using a bunched-up cardigan as a pillow, but after two hours I put on my glasses and squinted through the window. Betty Anderton and Christopher Gable stood in the corridor, leaning against the compartment door. Christopher was entertaining Betty with an incident that occurred at the beginning of the tour. We were doing *Coppélia* at the Golders Green Hippodrome. Christopher, playing an appealing young peasant lad, leaned against the proscenium arch during a solo and an elderly lady in the first row reached over and tapped his knee. 'Want a sweet, love?' she asked, holding up a chocolate almond. Christopher was so startled that he mumbled, 'No thank you.' His fans later sent presents directly to the stage door at Covent Garden, but this remained his favourite performing story. Christopher and Betty moved on to a most unamusing Number One Topic: a dancer's confidence.

'I read that a dancer is completely confident until the age of twenty-four,' Betty remarked – a bit of information I can now vouch for as accurate.

'And then what happens?' Christopher asked gloomily, passing her a thermos of lukewarm tea.

'I don't want to know,' she answered, taking a swig.

We three were mates and I valued their friendship for I was singularly unpopular with the group, notably the senior girls who resented my eagerness to learn all the roles in the repertory. Betty dismissed them in her breezy, ironic manner. 'Springbett didn't come to England to sit on her butt and eat English food,' she would say.

The girls were peeved that the ballet-master Henry Legerton, a former Shakespearian actor and character dancer, actually liked me, despite my gaffes and naïve outspokenness, which they titteringly labelled 'Canadianisms'. At the first performance of *Les Sylphides* in Golders Green, north London, I was one of the creatures in a long white tulle skirt who danced in a moonlit glade. Amidst a bluish misty light, the sylphs abandoned themselves to the air, then froze and slowly glided into a kneeling position. I was learning the ballet and therefore not certain when to glide. The aerial sprites drifted to the stage floor. I remained standing. When the curtain fell I was ready to be blasted. I had botched the mood; yet, once realizing the mistake, I held the position, hoping to make the grouping appear natural. The audience applauded but as we ran offstage two perspiring sylphs made scornful unsylphlike noises. Henry Legerton awaited me in the wings. My mouth was dry, my palms sweaty.

'Springbett,' Henry said firmly, 'you ruined the performance.' The ballet-master arranges classes, rehearsals and sees that the performances are up to snuff.

I fortified myself with a feigned bravura to keep from caving in. 'Oh, gee, no one could be sorrier than me, boy,' I spurted breathlessly.

Henry, a small man in his early forties, with a merry face and twinkling eyes, stood quite still for a moment, his expression incredulous. 'Don't call me "boy",' he said gruffly. 'Show a little respect for your elders.'

I had not meant to say 'boy'. I was trying to be colloquial and had been groping for the word 'mate', though that was not correct either. I began apologizing nervously. Henry interrupted. 'Best get changed for the next ballet.'

Henry knew I was learning a whole new rep and that I was something of a loner. Henry was a loner himself. He came to England from Australia after the Second World War and worked with the Russian dancer Leonide Massine, who recommended him to the Royal Ballet. He vividly remembered his early years of displacement in a foreign country. We outsiders always sniffed each other out. Immediately I felt a kinship with him. On the train from Glasgow to Aberdeen I saw him absorbed in a book. When he was strolling in the corridor I cornered him.

'Your nose has been between the pages all afternoon,' I said. 'If it's that interesting, maybe I should read it too.' Young dancers never asked Henry what he was reading. He was quite pleased by my schoolgirl curiosity and frankness, when I was not being overly familiar. The book was *To the Lighthouse* by Virginia Woolf. He promised to lend me the novel before we left Hull.

The train was crawling into the station. Betty buttoned her black coat and pulled down her suitcase from the overhead rack. It was just past noon. We now had to locate digs in the pouring rain. With luck, if digs were found quickly, we would have a leisurely afternoon, buying snacks for dinner and writing letters before the chore, night after night, of darning the toes of our ballet shoes and washing tights. By the end of the week and a long train ride, we looked forward to an early sleep. Betty handed me a plaid hound's-tooth coat. Everyone snickered that I looked like John Cranko, a company choreographer, who also wore a Sherlock Holmes coat with billowing sleeves and pockets galore. Christopher had whispered to Betty, 'It's hideous, but I guess it's warm.' I bought the coat in a September sale in London. It was a symbol. The management had given me an advance against my salary because I was penniless, living chiefly on courage, and had to buy clothes for the cold northern tour. The advance confirmed that within the labyrinthine Royal Opera House I existed *as a person* among the powers who gave orders, who could strike down or promote careers.

'Hull,' Betty said loudly, tying a woollen scarf around her neck.

The sprightly company dispersed quickly, like dizzy circus performers hunting for the big tent on the first night in town. Some shared taxis and sped to preferred addresses remembered from previous tours. But most set off doubtfully, in twos and threes, holding umbrellas against the rain, each lugging one large scuffed suitcase with an entire life stuffed inside. We gave eight performances a week and travelled on Sunday. Touring was exhausting, but daily performing removes roughness and rawness from young dancers. On our one free day, the idea was to get settled as fast as possible.

Betty grew up in a hotel that her parents owned in

Bayswater. I decided that she instinctively knew which digs to select and left the decisions to her. Digs were sparsely furnished quarters in drab houses, occupied by even drabber transients. I called digs 'elbow rooms'. They were just a place to sleep. The walls were thin. Doors slammed throughout the night, radios hummed to soppy music, mattresses squeaked to obscene creaks, cars hooted and buses rumbled outside windows. The landladies ranged from garrulous magpies with pink bows in permed hair to tight-lipped biddies who suffered gastric disturbances. Some were like motherly hens.

We took digs in a gargoyled brown brick house within a stone's throw of the theatre. Betty thought it a bit odd that we were the only dancers at Mrs Gorse's boarding house, but a pile of burning logs seemed to bid a warm welcome. We confronted a woman in a wheelchair, swathed in shawls and blankets. Chins bubbled on to her bosom. Fuzzy eyebrows almost reached masses of magenta curls on her forehead. 'Isn't she sweet?' I whispered to Betty, who was trying to make up her mind. The grandmotherly figure was either the very pineapple of goodness or a sharp-tongued termagant who felt she deserved a sedan chair.

Betty explained that we were with the ballet and needed a room with two beds. We received ten pounds ten shillings a week, and had to pay for our own digs. A room on the third floor was available at an acceptable price, breakfast included. We paid for the week. The woman then wheeled herself into the sitting room with the inviting fireplace. 'This is Mrs Gorse's parlour. She does not expect to see you in here. You make your tea in the basement kitchen. She doesn't allow drinking or eating in the rooms. And no gentlemen.' She licked her lips. 'The hot water goes off at nine o'clock.'

Dragging our suitcases up the stairs I moaned, 'Oh, Betty. What a horrible person. And I thought she was sweet.'

'I know, Springbottle. You wanted her to be Ethel Barrymore.'

The room, far worse than the others on the tour, had faded peeling wallpaper. One tiny window peeked on to an alley of dustbins. There was no sink or mirror. 'Oh, gosh,' I said, falling on to the bed. The mattress dipped in the middle like a hammock. Betty's buckled into a series of lumpy hills. 'Terribly sweet, Springbottle,' Betty sighed, 'and it's ours for the week.'

As the tour progressed and the repertory changed from town to town, both Betty and I were getting solos. I had started working on the creation of a ballet to be called *The Burrow*, which would have its première at Covent Garden. After three years of torturous exercise that forced my squishy body into a sculptural shape, I suppressed an excitement that dulled exhaustion. I may have appeared supremely calm, but I secretly trembled as though ice cubes had been dropped down my spine. *The Burrow* was my first role. I would not be recreating something that critics and audiences had seen countless times. No reviewer with a memory of the great ballet names could write, as is customary with the classics, that the dancer, despite a fluency for one so young, lacked the fiery pride, regal majesty, delicate grace, prodigious brilliance, feathery lightness or spellbinding pathos of a dozen favourite predecessors. I took a blue aerogramme note from my suitcase. Lying on the bed, a pillow propping up my head, I began a letter to my parents in Vancouver. 'What can be the matter with me? I'm so involved in all the new happenings, a whirlpool of work and people, that I forgot to write. *The Burrow* is going to be impressive. It's a modern ballet about twenty people hiding in an attic. A claustrophobic prison. There's no good fairy or prince to save them from the inevitable . . .'

I let the ballpoint pen fall to the bed and wriggled my

toes. I could hardly wait until Monday, the 'get-in' day, when rehearsals resumed on the new ballet by Kenneth MacMillan. Kenneth was the company's rising choreographic star. I was in the corps, and understudying the lead of his ballet *Solitaire*, a playful piece about a girl rejected from the games of others. In *The Burrow* he gave me the role of an adolescent who falls in love for the first time. Kenneth was twenty-seven. Not traditionally handsome but extremely dishy, a phrase that I found even more marvellous than the clap or the gout.

A tall, lean, languid chap with soulful brown eyes and dark brown hair – Kenneth was as shy and diffident as a preppie awaiting the results of his first exam. He spoke in a soft tear-drop voice. His melancholy gaze, his delicately furrowed brow gave him the air of a Russian poet. At times he was morbidly sensitive and withdrawn; he had a cool brain and a brooding nature. He carefully selected a few friends with whom he was completely at ease and let go a Rabelaisian wit. His most personal emotion – a feeling of savage alienation in a punishing world filled with contemptible desires – was expressed on stage. He disliked airy-fairy tales. When Kenneth studied the Brothers Grimm we saw the sadism instead of the sentiment. The witch in his ballet *House of Birds*, based on a Grimm fable, was an evil-beaked shrike whose victims were imprisoned in cages. He was very conscious of psychological imprisonments and rejections that impose solitary confinement. Fear was the predominant emotion in his new work, *The Burrow*. The dramatic situation – despairing people hiding from an outside tyranny in a squalid attic – suggested *The Diary of Anne Frank*. But the ballet was also semi-political. The young film critics, directors, and playwrights were striking at genteel British society with a broadsword. The leader of the Angry Young Men was John Osborne who described the royal family as 'the gold filling in a mouthful of decay'.

The post-war rebels detested the courtly bows and duplicities of the rigidly intact class system. They wanted to shake the tip-toeing club rooms of English culture. Their feelings of impotence were intensified, the critic Kenneth Tynan analysed, 'by the knowledge that Britain no longer had a voice strong enough to forbid chaos, if, by some horrific chance, it should impend.' An avid movie and theatregoer, Kenneth MacMillan was mesmerized by Osborne's *Look Back in Anger*, which showed the post-war youth crushed by the barrenness of life. A frowsy, collapsing family of vaudevillians symbolized England's 'nasty little problems' in another Osborne play, *The Entertainer*. He understood Osborne's disillusionment and was so impressed by the play's theatrical brilliance that he cried. And when Kenneth got the rollies so did his theatre-going companion and confidant, Jeffrey Solomons, who became a close friend of mine. Discussing *The Burrow* with Jeffrey, he said, 'It seems as if we're living on an island that has outgrown its use. It's rather like being trapped, isn't it?' He wanted the ballet to make a provocative statement. Jeffrey Solomons, a shrewd and perceptive man who greedily attended all the new plays, movies, and ballets, urged him to be unsparing, to produce a harrowing dance of desperate life, not a mild minuet.

Like Tynan and Osborne, who were fed up with the mythical 'Aunt Edna' of the theatre, for whom Terence Rattigan wrote his mannerly parlour plays upholding middle-class virtues, Kenneth MacMillan regretted that attending the ballet had become similar to visiting an old aunt. Too many ballets were preciously nectared for 'Aunt Edna', the bugaboo of the ballet. Kenneth was a protégé of Dame Ninette. By the late fifties, she was still assembling the finest troupe that England would see for years. Madam had a remarkable eye for finding talent and, as she has said, a particular fondness for rebels. Kenneth was a rebel. He dared to shake out the balletic sop with dramatic story-ballets revealing dark corners of the heart. The touring company was an ideal place for him to experiment with poetic realism.

Kenneth was proud of saying that his dance incentive was picked up at the movies, watching Fred Astaire and Ginger Rogers and Gene Kelly. He saw Hollywood's classic musicals before he saw anyone dance on stage. He seldom discussed his early childhood on a chicken farm in Dunfermline, Scotland, but his confidant, Jeffrey Solomons, knew that his mother's early death left him emotionally wounded at a tender age. Kenneth was then living with his father and two older sisters in Great Yarmouth. His father died when he was in his teens.

He started dancing classes when he was twelve and won a scholarship to the Royal Ballet school (then called Sadler's Wells) after faking a letter from his father. 'My son who is thirteen would like to become a ballet dancer,' he wrote. 'Can you tell me how he gets a scholarship?' He joined the company when he was seventeen. As one of Cinderella's primping stepsisters, he danced opposite the company's princely choreographer, a bewigged and rouged Frederick Ashton. Kenneth was hilarious as a galumphing booby. He effectively mimed the moon in one ballet and a pitiful clown in another. He was good in classical roles. Trying to exorcize a loneliness which Jeffrey chided him for 'carrying around, clutched to his heart', Kenneth began creating dances, mostly about real people with intensive cravings. Along with John Cranko, he was accepted choreographically as one of Madam's Bright Young Men.

Many years later Kenneth related that one day Madam mentioned that a very good dancer had just joined the touring company. (Madam had previously discovered Margaret (Peggy) Hookham who became Margot Fonteyn, England's prima ballerina for over two decades.) 'The new youngster is Canadian,' Madam said. 'She has a preposterous name. Berta Lynn Springbett. It sounds like a special kind of egg. We'll have to do something about that.' Kenneth, who was preparing *The Burrow*, watched the touring section rehearse. I hardly glimpsed him. I vaguely remember a comely man languorously wrapped around a chair. Kenneth was impressed by my fluid movement – 'unlike that of any other member of the company'.

When he chose me for *The Burrow*, after only two weeks in the corps, we both recognized a muscular and psychic empathy between us. I instinctively knew what Kenneth wanted me to do. As a dancer Kenneth's languid frame and soft, supple body did not conform to the formal lyricism of the company's 'style'. Neither did mine. I was more Russian than rigidly English. He saw in me a reflection of his *own* movements and feelings. I did not know it then, but I was to become *his* image of the 'new' ballerina, and, in time, a new image for the Royal Ballet.

The company held daily class and rehearsed in church meeting halls as the provincial theatres had no rehearsal space. The theatres were easy to find; there was usually only one to a town. The rehearsal church required a city map. There was always an abundance of churches. Betty and I showed up on time with the other dancers, many with stories of taking wrong buses in the wrong direction or having to start from scratch back at the railway station, a reasonable place to get one's bearings. The sole advantage to Mrs Gorse's boarding house was its short walk to the theatre. There had been an unpleasant scene in the kitchen that morning. A red-faced man with an inhumanly thick neck sat at the one table dotted with plastic placemats. I took a seat at the far end of the table and waited, nervously.

'You get your own tea here, miss,' he said in a rasping voice, 'and wash up your plates, too. Bread's in that blue tin.'

I filled a scorched teapot with water and turned on the gas. The bread was not day-old. It was weeks old. 'Is there any butter?'

'Butter? You think this is the Ritz?' He laughed bitterly, blowing his bulbous nose. His body shook with a wheezing noise.

Betty came down the kitchen steps and saw me at the stove looking very pale. 'We'll have some lovely tea, Springbottle,' she said smartly, 'and I'm sure there's marmalade here.'

While Betty searched unsuccessfully a waft of lilac perfume drifted into the kitchen and a cadaverously thin woman entered holding a lace handkerchief. She wore a black dress that fitted tightly over a flat bosom. 'Good morning, Colonel,' she said tonelessly without glancing at us. 'I hope you slept well. I did not. There was an odour of cheese in the corridor and Etta told the new guests I do *not* allow eating in my rooms.' She opened the fridge and carried a bowl of pudding to the table. She scooped out a glob and wrapped it in wax paper. 'I made the suet pudding yesterday. Etta's favourite. Give her some for lunch. I'll eat mine at the bank.' Betty and I stared at the pudding – scraps of beef fat whipped together with sugar, flour and eggs, and then steamed. She plopped some raisins into the soggy mess. 'Now, we have a Spotted Dick! Would you like a taste, Colonel?'

The Colonel accepted a spoonful. 'Mighty fine, Mrs Gorse,' he said heartily with the air of a connoisseur.

Betty and I exchanged glances. We both felt queasy and fled from the kitchen instantly, having once mistakenly requested suet pudding in Manchester. Hurrying into the hall, we saw the lady with the magenta curls sitting in her wheelchair beside the parlour door, her hands folded across her chest. 'Leave your room keys on the hook,' she called. We obeyed and dashed into the chilly morning air. At a tea shop, we ordered tea and white bread with a daub of apricot jam. It was going to be a long day but I knew that rehearsing *The Burrow* would make me forget a proper lunch.

The church hall, normally a convivial scene of meat loaf suppers, missionary meetings and singspirations, was a high-ceilinged room with an open hearth. But there was no fire blazing. Four canvas folding screens were arranged like an accordion at one end as a changing area for the girls. The boys changed behind a blackboard used for Bible lessons and the memorizing of holy scriptures. With draughty, windy gusts whirring through multi-paned windows, we quickly sought the warmest niche anywhere, half-hidden from the company staff busily discussing scenery and lighting for the evening performance. Behind the screens and blackboard, the rehearsal piano and chairs clumped together, we tore off street clothes and pulled on practice clothes and leg warmers, making a shivering sexless blur of legs and limbs. Morning class went quickly, though I found myself scratching my leg. I assumed it was a gnarled fibre in my leg warmer until I saw Betty twitch and jab her fingernails into her thigh. I was practising a pas de deux with Donald MacLeary, my partner in *The Burrow*. Donald gave me a sidelong look and said, 'Please go ahead, give yourself a good scratch.'

My face turned beetroot red. 'All right,' I said, 'just watch.'

'Does it feel lots better?'

I shook my head. 'Must be a spider bite. Betty and I are trapped in the most dreadful digs.' I wiped rivulets of sweat from my neck and brow.

'Where're you staying?' Donald's towel was draped around his neck. He always looked marvellously cool, like a model for tennis-anyone? sweaters in the Sunday supplements. He was a young Scotsman, with dark velvety features.

'Mrs Gorse's. Near the theatre. But we're the only dancers there. I think we're the only guests, except for some geezer who wheezes and a dragon with dozens of chins who sits in a wheelchair.'

'Last season a couple of dancers stayed there, but they moved out,' Donald said. 'The fat lady, with the reddish wig . . .' I nodded, urging him to continue. 'Well, she used to go into the rooms . . .'

'How did she get upstairs?'

'She was carried.' Then he added slowly, 'The boys moved out because of bedbugs.' I could not fret over bedbugs when I had to pour all my subconscious fantasies into *The Burrow*. I sat on a folding chair in the emptying hall and ate two apples. He had two hard-boiled eggs. Donald would be my first partner at the Garden. Margot Fonteyn once said that dancers can have bigger and longer careers with partners of complementary authority, emotion and grace. Partnerships create stars – box-office couples – similar to the famous movie teams of Bogart and Bacall, Tracy and Hepburn, Stanwyck and Fonda. Fonteyn's partners were Robert Helpmann, Michael Somes, and later Rudolf Nureyev. Equally the dancer-director relationship is as important in shaping a ballet career as in films, especially if the director has distinct qualities. Garbo was guided by the director Clarence Brown. Dietrich inspired Josef von Sternberg. But the relationships were not exclusive and did not last for ever.

Frederick Ashton's muse at the Royal Ballet was Margot Fonteyn.

Donald was a marvellous natural partner, and everyone longed to dance with him. Partners need the strength to lift you in the air as if you are a feather. My physique is not feathery. He manipulated my body with a light dreaminess and there was enough of him (six feet of taut muscle) to wrap my legs and arms around. Although I was from the corps and Donald had seniority, he was not condescending about rehearsing extra hours with a corps girl. The rehearsal pianist was not there, but we didn't need him. Staring intently at my eyes magnified behind the glasses I wore during moments of fatigue, he said I looked rather like a serious grown-up child. I had no reply. Then he said: 'Let's go. Come on, take your glasses off.'

Our bodies intertwined to non-existent music. When we finally sprawled on the floor massaging our feet, Kenneth MacMillan and Brenda Bolton, a twenty-year-old soloist from Australia, were sitting along the wall in folding chairs, smoking. Brenda, a stunning golden-haired dancer with chiselled cheekbones and a husky voice, was telling Kenneth about her lunchtime walk around Hull. Brenda and Kenneth were quite pally, he liked her effervescent company.

Kenneth, who has the amazing ability to lounge in a metal chair as though it were a chaise for Mme Récamier, let his ash drop on the floor. His grinning brown eyes were on me. 'And what did you find in Hull, Brenda?' he asked.

'Bath salts. I bought rhododendron.'

Kenneth raised his eyebrows towards heaven. He raised his shoulders too. Kenneth enjoyed light-hearted banter with Brenda who could riposte as well as pirouette. Listening to their easy prattle, I doubted that I could ever be as casual with him, or anybody. I was too earnest. My dancing had attracted Kenneth; and Dame Ninette de Valois, a gutsy grande dame, had been kind to me. But I felt hopelessly dull. I must develop, I decided, a public personality, or several, like different roles one played onstage. For the moment it was difficult just being Berta Lynn Springbett.

The cast for *The Burrow* worked through the afternoon as the wind beat against the church windows. In his baggy trousers and sweat shirt, Kenneth went over the movements of the oppressed attic group. He explained that we were living in a murky room, listening tensely at the walls. We could not leave the room, yet staying there was a neurosis. We were imprisoned. But outside was danger, probably death.

During afternoon tea break, I stared moodily at the floor, then twisted nervously to the left and walked with spasmodic steps to a corner behind a dressing screen. Removing my slippers, I rubbed swollen soft corns on my toes. That night was the opening. I was dancing in the *Coppélia* corps. My toes were squashed and raw. Suddenly Brenda was beside me grimly scrutinizing the blisters, the result of eight performances a week for eleven weeks and extra rehearsal time on *The Burrow*.

'Do you have any rubbing alcohol?' Brenda asked. I was silent. 'Wait here. I'll find some for you. It's going to hurt like hell. But it toughens the skin. Otherwise, those corns may get infected.'

I held Brenda's arm. 'Please, don't say anything to Kenneth.'

Brenda smiled. 'He's heard about far worse things in *this* company than blisters.'

Peering through the canvas screen, I saw Brenda borrow a match from Kenneth to light a cigarette, mutter thanks and then fish around in her practice bag. In a quiet, almost yawning voice, Kenneth said he only needed male principals during the last hour. There was a clatter of chatter and chairs. Brenda handed me a bottle of rubbing alcohol. I dressed quickly and left the rehearsal hall.

When I reached Mrs Gorse's boarding house, Etta, the lady with the chins and magenta curls, was coming out of the Colonel's room in her wheelchair. 'You'll find the cheese and crackers in the kitchen,' she said acidly.

I restrained myself from yanking the wig from her head. I feared that the sight of a semi-bald pate would be even more horrific. Also Betty and I would definitely be out of digs — and money. I became aware of a twitchy-itch in my leg forgotten during the afternoon rehearsals. 'I hope there are no bedbugs in this establishment,' I answered with a haughty coldness that shocked her.

Her face became mottled. She remained for an instant paralysed. Then wheeling herself back into the Colonel's room she cackled, 'Life isn't all beer and skittles, you know.'

Half laughing and crying, I flopped on the bed. Stripping myself, I saw three reddish bumps, the size of hives, sprouting on my right leg. I began giggling nuttily until I remembered the swollen corns and blisters on my toes. The laughter stopped as soon as I applied the rubbing alcohol. I had to bite a towel to keep from crying out in pain. By midweek I cut holes in my ballet shoes in order to relieve the pressure on my throbbing toes. But I continued rehearsing with Kenneth and dancing my rep – a peasant maiden, a sylph, a sailor's dimpled lassie, an ethereal fairy, and so on.

Since the company virtually lived in rehearsal halls and theatres – digs were just tatty places to endure the nightly five-hour coma – I made my table in communal dressing rooms, at the top of five flights of winding concrete steps, a sort of picturesque substitute home. This was done by effecting a 'place setting' on the sickly pea-green table facing a mirror framed in bright light bulbs. I bought a red towel, red wash cloth and a red tray for hairpins, jars of creams and make-up tubes, tissues, brushes, cottons and aspirin. Halfway through the tour I dumped the red and splurged on a new 'place setting', switching to a more chic marron. This table – my boudoir – was a refuge from the dreariness of the outside world, and its muddy streets, rain-splashed sidewalks and colourless sandwich shops. After the *Giselle* matinée I peeled off my costume, which was soaked with perspiration, tied a bathrobe around me and again applied rubbing alcohol to the raw pustules. The blisters were tiny oozing volcanoes. The other girls, also in robes, wiped off mascara and greasepaint. Many were smoking and drinking coffee out of thermoses.

'Walter wants to have a little boff with me,' I heard someone say, braggingly.

'Walter boffs everyone. He's a frightful letch.'

'I know. But his teeny-weeny *is* straight.'

My head sank on to the marron 'place setting'. I was burning hot, feverish, and my toes throbbed with the sting of rubbing alcohol. Hearing Brenda Bolton's husky voice on the steps I ran to the landing. In a headlong rush I told Brenda that I didn't think I would be able to dance on pointe that night in *Solitaire*, Kenneth's popular ballet. 'I heard that the best thing for blisters is a piece of meat,' I gasped.

'If you can afford meat, eat it,' Brenda said tartly. 'Don't put it on your bloody toe.'

Then she made a fast decision. She went directly to John Field, the artistic director, and requested that my segment in *Solitaire* be danced on demi-pointe, or tiptoes. John Field had been a premier danseur at the Garden until he was asked to manage the touring company. A skilled administrator, he was enormously sympathetic to the neuroses and physical problems of dancers. Knowing that I was working overtime on *The Burrow* with Kenneth MacMillan, he ordered changes in the evening performance. The senior girls, openly, scornfully referred to me as 'the Canadian upstart' and 'the prairie girl'. Brenda Bolton and Margaret Lee, another Aussie soloist, heard more appalling attacks. I would have crumpled had I known what was being whispered, but Maggie Lee brought the smutty gossip to a halt. Two soloists in Maggie's dressing room, livid that I had a role in *The Burrow*, were nattering over whether I had seduced Kenneth MacMillan or he had seduced me. They had already decided that we were sleeping together.

The vivacious Maggie, aged twenty-two, was the wisest,

maturest member of the young troupe. She had straight black hair, a lovely smile and expressive eyes. Some of the girls mimicked her Australian accent, but her dancing and cool head were respected by the staff and Maggie ignored the petty bitchery of the envious Missy Minivers. However, she had never encountered such meanness, such evil back-biting until *I* joined the company, she told John Field, who asked her to keep a friendly eye on me; he did not want me hurt.

Maggie slammed a lipstick tube on the dressing table. 'Lynn is just a kid,' she said, 'and you two sound like Lady Sneerwell. You're jealous because no one has ever created a role on you, and no one ever will. You don't dance like Lynn, that's why. So leave her alone.' There was an embarrassed silence. The truth is I had only been kissed once – on the cheek – by a Canadian boy and had never even been on a 'date'. The two girls began powdering their faces attentively. When Brenda Bolton heard the story, she warned Maggie, 'I hope they don't trip you on the cement steps.' Someone once tried that on Brenda. But no one bothered Maggie Lee and for the rest of the tour my name was not mentioned in the dressing rooms.

I lived for *The Burrow* and rehearsals with Kenneth. In a letter home, I wrote: 'It's just so marvellous working like this, actually creating a new ballet. My life is cut off from everything else. Tension is high, but for the first time since I've been in England, I feel completely alive. Kenneth MacMillan is very kind to me. I wish you could meet him. Life is a rosy fig. I guess figs aren't rosy, are they, but this fig is.' I was so absorbed in *The Burrow* that, on lunch breaks with Brenda Bolton, I left the church hall without my umbrella or cap or purse.

'It's filthy outside,' Brenda would say patiently. 'Get your brolly.' And I would gaze into the dripping mist as though seeing rain for the first time. We often noticed

Kenneth going into a book store or the tobacconist and conspired to bump into him. I wanted to know what magazines he read, what brand of cigarettes he smoked. 'If we go to the Indian restaurant, maybe Kenneth will be there,' I said. Kenneth liked Indian food. But we never had enough money and usually ended up in sandwich shops.

'Does Kenneth see anyone – in particular?' I finally asked Brenda.

'He had a girlfriend named Margaret Hill, if that's what you mean. He created *Solitaire* on her. She was a wonderful dancer.'

In two days the tour would be over. I would be in London for Christmas and then Covent Garden. That event seemed like a distant dream. But I had to find a flatmate. The English girls lived with their parents. I was afraid to ask Brenda about her plans; a rejection would be too depressing. Then Brenda announced that she, too, needed a flatmate. I told her about a place in Kensington with two small rooms. 'Of course, the bathtub is in the kitchen and the loo is down the hall.'

'Isn't it always,' Brenda said, munching a sugar lump. 'Guys are so lucky. They can just pee in the sink.' We giggled over the possibility of our trying to do the same and strolled back to the church hall, arm in arm, with Brenda urging me to reserve the flat immediately.

The closing party in Hull, on 30 November 1957, put the company in a holiday mood. The tour was over, at last. Rehearsals for the entire repertory would continue in London through the Garden opening, the day after Christmas. We wanted a Christmas theme for the party so everyone, including staff and crew, pitched in, taking turns decorating the church hall. Red and green streamers were suspended from the ceiling and pinned to the walls, making a fluttering crêpe-paper canopy. Bouquets of holly and sprigs of green festooned the mantel over the hearth stacked with logs, and mistletoe was fastened over doorways. Two loudspeakers were connected to a borrowed record player and stacks of Frank Sinatra, Jo Stafford and Peggy Lee records. The church lent an enormous cut glass bowl for a punch, specially invented by Donald MacLeary, that would have made the congregation faint dead away. Donald began with properly Presbyterian grape juice and then poured in non-sacramental vodka, sweet and dry vermouth, angostura bitters and lemon slices – the ingredients purchased from a quickly depleted party fund which only allowed for crisps, French bread and cheddar cheese as munchies. The floor was dusted and polished. Candelabra on four tables, and strings of red and green lights rigged up by the stage crew, transformed the pallid hall into a glowing baronial ballroom. A warm family spirit overspread the group. Rivalries were forgotten. And after two cups of Donald's lethal punch several dancers thought they might as well fall in love, at least for a few hours. Most would be home in another day, under parental scrutiny. 'The only energy I have left is for a romance by mail with a chap in Canada,' said Brenda, concluding that the company blades were either emotionally undeveloped, had the tentacles of an octopus, or were in search of a faultless reflection of themselves. But the jolly party pulled everyone together affectionately. At midnight John Field announced a toast to us and we clinked cups to him. 'Just think, on the spring tour we'll be waking up in Plymouth, Bournemouth and Wolverhampton,' said the sardonic Brenda, attractively Christmassy in a red silk dress found at the flea market in Notting Hill.

Couples began dancing, a bit stiffly at first, unaccustomed to steps without lifts and leaps and jumps. On the record player Jo Stafford saucily admitted, *'I've got the world on a string, sitting on a rainbow . . .'*

'Can I tell you a secret, Maggie?' Christopher Gable said

as he escorted Maggie to the floor. 'It's only an accident that I got into the company.' Maggie often said that he was the most talented of all the new boys.

Maggie laughed. 'You're joking, of course.'

'No. Someday I'll tell you the story.'

'Remember, Christopher, with a few exceptions, successful careers always seem to be accidents.'

> *Sitting on a rainbow . . .*
> *Got the string around my finger . . .*
> *What a world, what a life . . .*

I sat on a stool in front of the fire, watching the golden flames dismember four logs. As the wood took different shapes, crumbling into angular heaps, it resembled a house on fire, or rather a log cabin I had seen as a child in the Canadian Rockies. The cabin was on fire. I sat hypnotized by the flames, unable to take my eyes off the burning cabin. I was not thinking about blisters or bedbugs or the ballet. I sipped Donald's punch, which made me tingle all over, and hoped that the people inside the cabin escaped unharmed. A log toppled over and I sighed sadly. The cabin would soon be ashes, but then Henry Legerton would come along and rebuild the cabin with another log.

The closing-night party is etched deeply because, for the first time, Kenneth and I had a quiet, intimate chat. A soft voice came to me from a few feet away and I heard a chair being pulled up. 'I only asked, why aren't you dancing . . ?' Kenneth repeated again, faintly apologetically. I sipped my punch, thinking I should come up with something terribly witty to hold his attention. Christopher had asked me to dance, but I had refused politely. I could not tell him, or Kenneth, that I had never been social dancing before in my life. 'I just wanted to sit here and stare at the fire and think of nothing,' I said finally.

'But fires always make one think of something,' Kenneth said.

'I know. It's very hard to think of nothing. Actually I was remembering a cabin in the woods. I like staring into roaring fireplaces and sitting on isolated beaches.'

'Fire and water.' He cupped his drink between his hands. 'The elements of mythology . . .'

I finished my drink and tossed the paper cup into the fire. Our eyes met. 'It's delightful here.'

'Hull . . . or England?'

'I mean *here*. Just sitting here.'

He watched the paper cup burn instantly. 'Would you like some more punch?' I did not answer. 'Well, I would,' he said. When he sauntered away, I was certain he would not return, that I would be left alone and have to mingle with the others who had noticed us. Brenda and Maggie were talking with Donald and John Field. They seemed so chic in their knits and silks, so wonderfully dressed and cosmopolitan. I felt extremely plain in a skirt and white sweater with a gold necklace that belonged to my grandmother. I would not be able to buy new clothes until I went home for the summer. But Kenneth ambled back, balancing a plateful of crisps and two cups of punch. He asked when had I decided to become a dancer.

'I'd been going to a dance school, but when I was about eleven, I saw a film. *The Red Shoes*. It was thrilling.' I took a gulp of punch and relaxed. 'It was thrilling in Vancouver, Canada, where I grew up. I'm just a hick, really.'

'I saw the film too. It was glamorous, wasn't it? And we know it isn't.'

'No. But it makes you feel very whole somehow – dancing, I mean. Forcing your body into doing something physically perfect, not once, but again and again.'

Kenneth said that he never told his schoolmates he was studying dancing. It was considered sissy stuff. Then he won a prize and the local paper printed a story. To avoid taunts, he pretended it was another MacMillan.

I nibbled some crisps and sipped a third cup of punch. Kenneth was so *easy* to talk to. His rangy warmth (or was it the punch?) made me feel quietly charming, not as though I were awkwardly hanging in mid-air, somewhere between childhood and sophistication. 'It's always difficult for boys,' I said, 'yet dancers are stronger than footballers. My brother is a terrific athlete. He's seven years older than I am and married now, but his friends were all jocks. They made fun of the boys in my dance class who were very muscular. The jocks were just big slabs of beef. Not my brother. Not Bruce. He was a track star. When his friends teased me about dancing, I'd just sit on the floor and do the splits. That shut them up.'

Kenneth pressed together the tips of his long, slender fingers. 'Were they shocked?'

I hesitated a moment and then said, 'I hope so.' We began laughing like silly children. I was delighted. I had made Kenneth laugh. We were suddenly conscious that we had become subjects of interest to our friends near the punch bowl. As I recall, Kenneth said humorously, 'Miss Springbett, we have to see John Field about something very serious. Now, you must behave.' We threaded our way through the dancers to the punch bowl. John, his wife Anne Heaton, Donald and Maggie and Brenda formed an elegant group, half-leaning on each other, smoking, talking, drinking.

'Are you chatting about us?' I asked.

Anne Heaton answered immediately. 'What's your decision, Lynn?'

'I may sound a little prosy now,' Kenneth said, raising his cup, while Donald refilled it, 'but the time has come to make an appeal to Miss Springbett in the presence of her peers and possibly a few admirers.' He indicated a fresh round of the devil's brew for everyone. 'I want a lemon slice,' Kenneth added. The cups were filled, the group looked towards me. I waited breathlessly. 'You may feel a paroxysm of despair, but here it is. Let us drink first.'

A blue haze of cigarette smoke surrounded us as we took reverential swallows. 'You really shouldn't begin your career in London, at Covent Garden, under the name of Springbett,' Kenneth said. 'The programmes will be printed next week. Now is the time to change your name, if you want to.'

'Madam won't be fit to live with if you don't,' said Brenda, dropping her head in a tragic attitude.

'You took the words right out of my mouth,' Kenneth said.

'Put them back instantly,' Donald insisted, 'or Kenneth won't be fit to live with.'

'I shan't.'

'That was a friendly warning,' John Field sighed.

'Donald, your punch is simply killing.'

'Madam is quite right,' I announced firmly, 'and Kenneth is quite right. I cannot be Berta Lynn Springbett.'

'You don't look like a Berta Lynn.'

'Maggie, do fetch me a crisp. Well . . .' I devoured the crisp, 'now that you have me cornered, give me a name. And give me a chair, please.' John sat me down in a folding chair. The group, pleasantly overcome by Donald's punch, began playing a grand and goofy game: Finding a Name for Springbett. It went something like this: Anne tilted her cup to her lips. 'Do you have monogrammed towels, Lynn, or silver? You see, I'm concentrating on initials and heirlooms.'

'Monograms be damned,' Donald said. 'Lynn, remember your character can change with your name.'

'One thing at a time,' Maggie cautioned, waving a cigarette.

'Frankly, I feel quite thirsty,' Kenneth said, draining his cup.

'Did you all change your names?' I asked.

'I had to fight to keep mine,' Anne said. 'Heaton. Madam thought "Heat-on" sounded like a frightful cat in heat.'

'Madam is seldom wrong,' Kenneth murmured, his back slightly arched, his arm around Brenda's shoulder.

'Well, let me think,' I said gravely. 'Perhaps my name should have a rather French-Canadian sound.'

'Babette. Babette de la Bidet.'

'That's much too refined,' I argued.

'Gladys Powys, how do you like that?'

'It sounds like Glynis Johns,' I complained.

'Let's have another drink,' suggested John.

'If only Madam were here,' said Kenneth.

'Bettina. Bettina Lynn.'

'Yes, couldn't I keep Lynn?'

'Bettina Lynn,' said Kenneth thoughtfully. 'Hmmmm – no, no. It's too Vera Lynn. *Auf wiedersehen*, sweetheart.'

'This may be difficult for you, Lynn. I know how you must feel,' Anne remarked, 'but we'll find something for you. Count on us.' She slipped into a chair beside me. 'Donald, what *did* you put in the punch?'

'Let's all have another drink.'

'Take my cup.'

'Anne, what name did Madam have in mind for you?' asked Kenneth.

'Seymour. And I'd like a lovely steak with *béarnaise* sauce.'

'Bettina Seymour. That's a mouthful.'

'Berta. Berta Seymour.'

'Berta? Oh, you are wicked, darling.'

Kenneth took a pencil from his pocket and wrote something down on a paper napkin. 'Consider how Lynn Seymour looks in print. I like the y's.' He passed the napkin around.

'Bettina Seymour?'

'You aren't listening.'

'Let's have another drink.'

'Take my cup.'

'She might be able to keep the monogrammed towels and silver.'

'I don't have any. You're all being quite dreadful.'

'I think Lynn Seymour is best,' said Kenneth.

'May *I* see the napkin?' I stared at the pencilled scrawl. Seymour. Lynn Seymour sounded very sophisticated, very British, very cool. My parents might be startled, but I would remind them of Seymour Street and Seymour Creek and Seymour Mountain in Canada. Did such places really exist? Well, if I didn't know, they wouldn't either. Canada was very big, with very many small towns. There might be a Seymour City. 'I agree with Kenneth,' I announced, giving him the paper napkin.

'Then it's Seymour. Lynn Seymour at Covent Garden,' Kenneth said. There was another round of drinks. Kenneth huddled with John Field, assuring him that Madam would be pleased with the name and John said a memo would go to the Garden management immediately. Maggie and Brenda and Donald moved into the candlelit room telling friends, such as Henry and Betty and Christopher, that Springbett was now Seymour.

'If someone calls me Lynn Seymour, I'll probably just walk by. I won't know who it is,' I said.

But when Christopher gently put a hand on my head and smoothed my hair saying, 'Your character is going to change, Lynn Seymour, that's what Donald believes,' I was amazingly calm, as if Lynn Seymour had been my name for ever.

'Christopher, we were in ballet school together. I'm not going to change. Except around the edges.'

It was almost four in the morning. The lights blinked.

Our conscientious ballet-master Henry Legerton reminded us that our train departed at eight.

Christopher asked again if I wanted to dance, but I answered that I might even have trouble walking home, so he took Betty in his arms as Frank Sinatra meltingly crooned,

> *Imagination is lazy . . .*
> *Your whole perspective gets hazy . . .*

Our table was already stripped of our cups and napkins. The log cabin was burning out for ever in the hearth. I stood up and swayed to the music by myself, waving goodnight to Brenda and Donald, who had draped a sprig of holly around her neck like a leafy scarf. Two corps boys were doing Gene Kelly steps on a table littered with crisps and blobs of French bread. In the middle of the room, two couples, arms interlocked, formed a sleepy human swing. Simon (Mottie) Mottram, a corps dancer with black curly hair, danced alone, holding a chair above his head with one hand. Kenneth had his coat on. He was leaving with John Field and Anne Heaton.

I continued to sway, my head spinning. Kenneth pressed my hand. I was blushing and knew it, but the dwindling candlelight hid my face. 'Pleasant evening, Miss Seymour,' he said. 'We'll see you on the train.' I nodded silently, letting my body undulate in time with the music, my arms stretching, my fingers caressing the air.

> *Imagination is silly . . .*
> *You go around willy-nilly . . .*
> *I go around wanting you . . .*
> *And yet I can't imagine . . .*
> *That you want me too . . .*

Somehow, after a few hours of strangled sleep or none at all, the last members of the company straggled into Hull station, bleary-eyed and hungover, minutes before the train started the five-hour journey to London. A handful of dietary sticklers remembered to prepare picnics of boiled eggs, tomatoes and apples. But six tubular loaves of French bread, four unopened bags of crisps and two cubes of cheddar had been salvaged from the party. The leftovers were dispersed among the troupe. Hopefully a snack car with sandwiches and soft drinks would be attached as the train moved south. Otherwise there would be pleas to sandwich vendors on platforms. On Sunday, the 'get-out' day, most station snack bars were locked up.

Betty and I ran for the train, with Betty calling, 'Faster, *Seymour!*'

Kenneth and Donald waved from a compartment window. Kenneth comically pantomimed with his long arms that he had seats for us. Donald pointed to a thermos and made drinking gestures. The train was mobbed with Sunday travellers. People were wedged together in corridors, tripping over suitcases and hampers as they hunted for seats, pressing faces against glass compartment doors. A shrill whistle blew, there was a hiccoughing of steam, and, with a loud groan, the long train left Hull. We literally tumbled into the compartment. John and Anne yawned helloes. Kenneth smoked his first cigarette of the day and sipped a cup of coffee from Donald's thermos. Everyone wore coats and mufflers. An icy wind set us shivering and Donald immediately pulled up the open window. Kenneth presented paper cups from the party which Donald filled with coffee. 'If you feel the need of aspirin, we have that too,' Kenneth said. 'We do not have any Bromo-Seltzer, however.' The train creaked along. For a while the compartment dozed, but I was wide awake and positively chuffed that Kenneth had invited Betty and me to join his compartment. The amusing, elusive Scot, with a shock of dark brown hair that fell over his forehead – the man whom

I most admired – was offering friendship, a prized thing in my life. The isolation I felt in England only diminished when I was in the theatre or sweating in a rehearsal room. When I was with Kenneth, the isolation was gone completely. He stimulated my mind and sense of artistry. There was an understanding beyond dance, something unspoken, that was intensely human. And yet the friendship, which I valued as much as the ballet, must not, I knew, be disturbed by restless emotions.

Rain splattering against the train windows turned to sleet and Donald's thermos of coffee was soon replaced by various hip flasks passed among the group. The flasks contained tea and whisky spiced with sugar. The concoction removed the chill that had set us shivering. I thought that I would never, ever, be warm again. Kenneth discussed movie classics he had seen at the National Film Theatre and the new plays of John Osborne, Eugene Ionesco, Samuel Beckett. He asked what book I was reading – or, rather, at the moment, what book I held in my hands. I explained that Henry Legerton had lent me *To the Lighthouse* by Virginia Woolf. Eyes previously sealed in sleep gazed curiously at me. Kenneth asked if I liked her novels. I replied, quite honestly, that I had never read anything by her, that she was a new name for me, like Ionesco and Beckett. All I *did* know was that the lighthouse symbolized the changing light and darkness in relationships. I wondered if the lighthouse was like the room in *The Burrow*, with its outcasts, victims and lovers, trapped between joy and despair, but I kept this thought to myself. The train screeched and lurched on, rocking back and forth on wet tracks, past a bleak countryside of trees bending sorrowfully in the morning wind. Using a scarf as a napkin, Anne Heaton helped Donald break off pieces of bread from the French loaf. She produced a dinner knife and made cheese sandwiches for us. Soon the compartment was cosily aromatic with smells of cheese and bread, and cigarette smoke from everyone except me. Eyes closed again. Kenneth continued to stare out of the window. I sat beside him and tried to read Henry's book, but I was too tired to sleep and too tired to concentrate on the Ramsay family in the novel. Kenneth said, 'I'm glad Henry gave you the book. Too often dancers don't know anything but dance.'

'I don't know very much.'

Giving me a penetrating look, he said, 'But you will, because you want to.'

At a station newsboys hawked the Sunday papers. Windows and doors flew open. People milled on the platform during the brief stop, buying papers and cigarettes and chocolate bars.

When the journey started again, the company shifted seats, found new companions for cards, word games and swapping Sunday papers. I walked through the train searching for Maggie Lee. She had moved to a car with non-dancers, a car with wailing babies, provincial couples clasping hands, grandmotherly ladies in feathered hats and stout businessmen with pinched faces, all going to London. Maggie said that she enjoyed observing their reality, disarmingly human and tenderly undistinguished. She needed moments alone, apart from the company, to keep in touch with the rueful ordinary waywardness of simple people going about their personal affairs. She was leaning against the corridor window, smoking a cigarette.

I had a purpose in seeking out Maggie. I wanted her to teach me how to smoke and knew she would not laugh at my request. I was probably the only member of the company who did not smoke and everyone said it relaxed you. The next two weeks — before the Garden — were going to be very scary. Maggie was reluctant, however. I had to coax and cajole, pointing out that I did not drink, like a lot of dancers, and cigarettes would not catapult me into perdition. So she extended a cigarette, which I brandished theatrically, and explained how to inhale and exhale. I gagged, finding it most curious that people did anything quite so disgusting. Maggie always regretted the smoking lesson. 'There's so much I want to learn,' I insisted, taking a short drag on the cigarette. 'I want to try *everything*.'

The flat I shared with Brenda Bolton in Kensington was on the top floor. There had been a fire in the house, so the flat had been freshly painted. It was anonymously furnished – two beds, two bureaux, and some chairs, lamps, a daybed and table in the sitting room. After my experience in Hull, I luxuriated in the flat's cleanliness and spent the first Sunday submerged in a tub bubbling with Brenda's rhododendron bath salts. I wrote my parents about changing my last name to Seymour, adding, for the sake of politeness, that if they had any other choices, they should wire. 'Please remember, Dame Ninette de Valois, whom we all adore, was born Edris Stannus.' They did not send a telegram.

We rehearsed *The Burrow* through Christmas.

Sitting in the Garden canteen one afternoon, awaiting Kenneth, I waved hello to Maggie and Brenda who were having tea and cigarettes. They were talking about *The Burrow*, and knowing my limited knowledge of life outside the ballet, Maggie said quietly, 'Your dancing reveals things you aren't even aware of.' The dancer to whom Kenneth responded was not a neuter anorexic beauty. He had seen enough of them. The Seymour signature, first seen in *The Burrow*, was feminine, passionate, boldly sexual – but none of it was calculated. The movements resulted from my physicality and a personality that reached its full dimension onstage. 'You have to see Lynsey dance,' my second husband prodded his mates. 'No fey sprite. She's the only ballerina who makes you restless for a woman.' Kenneth appeared, relaxed and smiling, and we also had tea and cigarettes. He advised me about stage make-up, costuming, the effect lighting would have on my face and urged me to change my hair style. 'You don't want to look like all the other dancers, with their tight chignons.' I wrote down everything he said on a note pad.

Leaving the canteen, Brenda stopped at our table. 'Lynn and I are expecting you at our party on Sunday,' Brenda said to Kenneth. 'It's our big fling before the Garden.'

Even with Christmas money from home, we spent a week's pay on the party. We bought a Christmas tree and decked it with tinsel and red and silver balls. We bought red and green candles. I wanted candles everywhere. We nailed a wreath outside the flat. I decided it would be lovely and musical if all the doorknobs had ropes of bells, so we bought bells. 'We have to remember food and drink,' Brenda cautioned. Taking a cue from Donald's devil's brew, we bought grape juice and poured in gin instead of vodka and several bottles of cheap red wine. 'Tastes ghastly,' Brenda burped. Vodka was added. A platter of tuna-fish salad was garnished with tomato wedges, and crackers and crisps surrounded an onion dip. With our last shillings, we bought some glittery costume jewellery and a lipstick called Cranberry. I thought Brenda looked marvellous, but I was hesitant about the lipstick. 'It makes me look tartsy. I want to look mature. Kenneth is coming.'

The party was really an excuse to get Kenneth to the flat. Then I fretted that he might not show up at all. 'He's meeting Nico and Donald for dinner,' Brenda said, 'and Donald promises to bring him.'

I made lots of phone calls to Donald. 'If Nico comes, I'm certain Kenneth will, so you must tell Nico that I want to ask him something about my costume.' Nicholas Georgiadis, a young, abstract painter who infused the stage with striking rather than pretty images, had been discovered by Kenneth and Madam when he was a student at the Slade School of Design. Kenneth respected Nico very much.

His colours for *The Burrow* were mud, ochre and brown. 'And one solitary light bulb, yes? Grim, like Kafka,' Nico said in his Greek-accented English.

On Sunday, I flung myself on the daybed and announced, 'The flat looks lovely. What if Kenneth doesn't come? All our money . . .'

'He'll come. If only out of curiosity.'

I then revealed my plan for midnight. 'When the clock strikes twelve, you say, Merry Christmas and Happy New Year, and kiss Kenneth. You're old chums, it's perfectly natural. Kiss anyone else you like. I'll be right behind you and Kenneth will have to kiss me. By that time everyone will be kissing everyone else.'

'Is that what you really want?' asked Brenda.

'I really do. Now I have to wrap his present.'

'Present? What did you get him?'

'Two packs of Marlboros. That's what he smokes. And that's all I can afford.' I began scissoring a sheet of gold paper.

'How much was that paper?' Brenda demanded.

'I do think presents should be handsomely presented, don't you?' I paused, then added in a very small voice, 'Brenda, you might have to lend me some money next week.'

'We'll rob the piggy bank.'

'Kenneth has *quelque chose*,' I murmured, lighting a cigarette and inhaling deeply. Brenda scattered some ashtrays and excused herself; it was time to put on the Cranberry.

At five o'clock in the morning I was curled up on the daybed, my head buried in the pillow. The party had been a raging success. Brenda knew it was a success because the food and punch vanished quickly and two Australian lads that she invited got violently ill in the bathtub.

Betty Anderton brought a bottle of chilled white wine.

Christopher and Simon (Mottie) Mottram presented us with dates and walnuts. A pretty dancer named Clover Roope brought homemade Christmas cookies. Maggie Lee held two tins of salmon, whispering, 'I thought you might need to eat next week.' Donald MacLeary extended a Brie, also for the cupboard. And Kenneth arrived with him, accompanied by Nico. I was radiantly happy. There were a batch of Australians who had never heard of *Giselle* and several dancers who talked of nothing else. The party was boisterous, with couples doing the rhumba and samba and sitting on the floor yakking in animated clusters. At midnight Brenda followed the scenario and gave Kenneth a playful peck on the lips. Others immediately searched for lips to kiss, not necessarily playfully. But as I moved towards Kenneth someone darted between us and knocked over a candle, spilling wax on the rug and a maddening fuss erupted about the oozing wax. Kenneth drifted away. Brenda pleaded, 'Don't worry about the wax, I'll clean it off in the morning.'

The moment I had been waiting for was lost.

A conga line began dancing around the sitting room and into the kitchen. People were clapping in rhythm. Kenneth reappeared, holding his coat, saying goodnight. I gave him the wrapped Marlboros. He accepted the gift with a gallant bow and said he would see me the next afternoon at rehearsals. I smiled through the rest of the party, swallowing my disappointment with watery eyes and wishing it were over. The party had collapsed for me at midnight. When the last guest leaped wildly down the hall staircase, shouting 'Bah! Humbuggery!' and Brenda surveyed the flat, shuddering at the mess of paper cups and napkins and cigarette butts, I was face down on the daybed, shaking with tears. Brenda had never seen me when I was not poised and thoroughly controlled.

'Lynn, what is it? The party was great. We spent too much money, but what the hell.'

'That fool who tipped over the candle, he spoiled it all for me,' I said between sobs.

'But Lynn, life can't be arranged according to a script. Even if Kenneth had kissed you, so what? A kiss doesn't mean anything. The French do it all the time to perfect strangers.'

'He hardly spoke to me. I don't believe he finds me attractive.'

'Utter rubbish. You're so close with him at rehearsals, you're with him all day.'

I wiped my eyes with a paper napkin. 'That's why the party was important. It was in our flat. Not the theatre, not a company bash. It was ours, and he didn't notice me. I'm just podgy and plain. Why would he be attracted?'

'You have a crush. A schoolgirl crushette on a neat older man who could be your favourite college professor. Kenneth doesn't realize what you feel. Why should he? You are beautiful to him, you are very special to him as a dancer.' Brenda stopped. Obviously there was nothing more to be said. 'I'm going to uncork Betty's wine. Are there any cigarettes?'

'I hid an emergency pack in my top drawer.'

The waxy splotch on the rug represented my Christmas wish for 1957. At least I had not done anything embarrassing. I had confided only in Brenda who would not gossip. If I became a truly beautiful dancer and a beautiful woman, then Kenneth would fancy me. I had confidence in succeeding as a dancer. I would sweat at rehearsals all week because I must be brilliant on the night of *The Burrow* première.

LOVE AND BEST WISHES FOR OPENING NIGHT

THINKING OF YOU   MOTHER DAD

The hired limousines and gleaming Rolls-Royces and coughing taxis converged on the Royal Opera House a half-hour before the curtain. Word filtered through ballet circles that Kenneth MacMillan had created an unusual modern work of terrifying force out of grim non-balletic material. Clive Barnes wrote in the *Daily Express* that *The Burrow* was the first British ballet to express the feelings of the post-war generation. 'Those over thirty may hate its almost hysterical, neurotic pulse,' Barnes warned. 'Controversial and stimulating, this piece seems a landmark destined to do for ballet what *Look Back in Anger* did for the theatre.' *The Burrow*, a twenty-one-minute ballet, with music by Frank Martin, was the second on the programme that opened with the misty blue and soft whiteness of the romantically ethereal *Les Sylphides*. Brenda, Donald and Anne were soloists. I was one of the moonlit sylphs. This was the ballet that I muffed four months earlier at Golders Green. The evening closed with *Veneziana*, a zesty gambol of masked ladies, harlequins and gondoliers. Maggie danced the lead. Christopher was one of six Venetian cavaliers, and I did a tarantella with three other girls.

But the night's event was MacMillan's ballet. Princess Margaret, a great ballet-goer, drew admiring glances and polite greetings from notables of society, public affairs, finance and the arts when she arrived at the opera house, resplendent in a fur jacket, a yellow brocade dress and a single strand of jewels around her neck. It was the second day of the New Year, 1958, and a holiday spirit pervaded the sold-out red and gold house. To Londoners, the ballet is not merely a pleasurable diversion but a prideful ritual, and the opera house is a citadel of culture and civilized sociability. The frescoed theatre, illuminated by pink candelabra along the horseshoe tiers, is not a cold cathedral or an impersonal slab of fresh concrete. The Garden has the period charm and intimacy of a 19th-century drawing room where there are boxes of delicious sweets, leather-bound books, the perfume of roses, and a marmoset on a velvet cushion.

Ten minutes before curtain and the chandeliered crush bar on the second floor, we were told, swarmed with glamorous figures in black tie and satins, drinking champagne and white wine. There was a sense of excitement and gossipy expectation. In the basement of Covent Garden, the dressing rooms for the boys and girls in the corps – two airless cavernous low-ceilinged chambers, already hot with the sweat of bodies at make-up tables – swirled with racks of white sylph costumes, black cloaks and masks, maroon tights and crimson gowns. Amidst the feast of colour were the alien browns and greys – the tattered trousers and skirts for MacMillan's ballet.

In the corridor, costumed in my sylph dress, I went through my movements for *The Burrow*. Christopher, still in practice pants, rehearsed his steps a few feet away. He was one of twenty people also hiding in the attic. He did not have to get into costume for another half-hour. We worked silently, occasionally glancing at each other, but never speaking, oblivious to the flutter of wardrobe, the delivery of telegrams and flowers, the mutterings of the ballet mistress. And then the tension broke. The sylph girls were herded down the corridor towards the stage stairs. Christopher squeezed my hand. Then I disappeared with the detached dispossessed air of a ghost.

'Can you imagine me waiting for my big night?' I wrote home two days later. 'We rehearsed *Les Sylphides* all day, thank God. Got rid of a lot of nerves then. The time came. *Burrow* time. Suddenly I was living in that room, with one naked light bulb, dreading the knock on the door that would shatter our lives. I don't remember going onstage. I changed from my sylph costume into a plain brown (dress) costume during the interval in a kind of trance. This was what I had been waiting for, because nothing has existed for me except this ballet. When the curtain finally fell the audience exploded.'

MacMillan's ballet received eighteen curtain calls. Donald MacLeary and I had a call by ourselves. A bouquet of pink carnations was pressed into my hands. One critic fumed that the morbid subject, which lacked 'lyricism', gave ballet the cramps. But the others described it as powerful, impressive, gripping – a ballet touching a generation that had grown up in a world of panic and the fear of disintegration.

Overnight, Kenneth MacMillan symbolized 'the new school' of ballet in Britain

A beaming Princess Margaret admitted to Kenneth and Madam, 'I had shivers down my back watching. My hands are quite worn out from clapping.' Anne Heaton, Donald MacLeary and Donald Britton also met the Princess. Britton was a prodigious character dancer with an amazing capacity to spin. Many years later he was doing a routine lift and suffered a pinched nerve in his spine which ended his career. He did a lot of Kenneth's early ballets and Madam adored him. Reporters covering the Royal Family observed that I had not been included in the presentation. I was unaware of any particular slight. 'If the bosses at Covent Garden think this is fair, they should think again,' scolded the *Daily Mirror*. When the same story ran in another newspaper, the Garden quickly replied, 'Miss Seymour was dancing for the first time.' One week later the Garden made amends. I was presented to the Queen Mother. 'She was so lovely and wonderfully pink,' I recounted to Brenda over a midnight coffee. 'But nobody gave me any instructions. When it was time to leave the box, I didn't know whether to curtsy or walk out backwards. Finally I just said, "Goodbye now" and *waved*.' Brenda almost spilled her coffee.

I taped the opening-night wire from my parents to the dressing-table mirror, along with other cables from Canadian friends. My parents sent a bouquet of flowers and, by special delivery, a pair of pearl earrings. When the première was over, the corps dressing area was thronged with tearful Moms and Dads hugging their children. I began to wipe off my mascara. 'Where's Seymour?' I heard a man ask gruffly and my hand stopped in mid-air. Who was asking for me? Betty, on her way out, called 'Lynn . . .' and I turned around. A short man with rumpled hair, freckles and stocky build approached. He wore a tan raincoat. A camera was slung around his neck. 'Lynn Seymour?' I nodded mechanically. 'Press,' he said loudly, above the babble of voices.

'Thought we might have a snap, just in case . . .' Flashbulbs popped three times. He patted my shoulder and darted out of the dressing room. The next day a photograph of me appeared in the *Star*. I took a fresh tissue and continued wiping off my make-up. Reflected in the mirror, standing behind me was Donald, his black hair strikingly sleek. He wore dark trousers and a black knit sweater. 'Seymour!' he said, throwing his arms around me. 'Partner,' he murmured affectionately.

'Partner,' I repeated.

'Did you bite your nails?'

'To the quick. I don't think I can do it again.'

'But you will, my love. We both will.'

The performance had been anguish. Now I felt an urge to run away. Everything inside was shaking. I had not been very good. I knew that. My hands trembled as I finished creaming and drying my face. The following morning I had company class at ten o'clock for two hours and *Giselle* rehearsals all afternoon. I put on my blouse and pleated skirt, my cardigan sweater and hound's-tooth coat. I could not run away. There was no place to go. I sat at the dressing table, hands in my lap, waiting, afraid to move, afraid to leave the room. I would never forget the excitement of that night, but I must accept my inevitable failure.

I rose wearily and walked out of the dressing room,

staring straight ahead at the exit sign. Sinuously slumped against the wall, a cigarette dangling from his mouth, was Kenneth MacMillan. There were lines of fatigue around his eyes, but they glistened with an intense light and seemed astonishingly beautiful.

I hesitated.

Kenneth looked at me steadily. 'I was waiting for you,' he said, puffing on his cigarette, 'because I wanted to say,' he paused and a rush of colour streamed into his cheeks, 'I thought you gave a smashing performance.'

CHAPTER 6

The Thirty-two Steps

Life in the Royal Ballet was survival of the fittest and firmest, but even if I was bushed all the time and underpaid and cold and hungry, it was a privilege to be in the company. I was part of an élite family, and my own little family within the Royal Ballet still exists today, twenty-five years later, although we have spun off in diverse directions. Christopher Gable, Betty Anderton and I connected as teenagers, graduated from the school and opera ballet together and went into the touring company and then the main company at Covent Garden. Few schoolmates manage to keep the most solid youthful friendship after they start university but the Royal bonded us. At times closer than blood relatives. So we slog along today with mutual respect, painfully aware of each other's weaknesses and strengths, attainments and failures, remembering ourselves as children with exalted vows, stretching our muscles to the breaking point, in a sweaty nursery lined with mirrors.

'We had no adolescence. One day we were kids, the next day we had adult responsibilities – there was no middle period,' said Donald MacLeary, when he dropped by the other day after a rehearsal at our old school in Barons Court. Donald, one of the youngest dancers to be appointed a *premier danseur*, is now a ballet-master. 'No one really prepared us for life, for paying taxes or finding some emotional balance. We were just kids, tossed into the world, without a proper home.' Donald entered the school when he was thirteen. He came from Inverness. He had only performed Scottish country dancing and the Highland fling but he passed the auditions, and his mum wept when he left

Scotland. He arrived wearing his best kilt. He quickly exchanged the kilt for long pants and tights.

Donald poured himself a glass of Pouilly-Fuissé, which I bought to brighten a light repast of salad and fresh fruit. He held the glass firmly, his eyes fixed on the golden liquid. 'Looking back, it sounds a bit romantic,' he said, 'but making up before a performance I used to get the shakes. I talked myself out of that. "The people out there paid to see you," I'd say.' I admired his rationalism. In his long career with the Royal Ballet, Donald emerged without any serious physical injury. The irony was that today he was wearing a neck brace. He lives in the country, an hour from London, and had taken a tumble horseback riding, his favourite outdoor activity. 'Why don't you come out this weekend?' he asked. 'I'll see if I can find some other old family members.'

'I can't get away. Demian's having a birthday party.'

He drained the contents of his glass, studying me with a curious intentness. 'I don't know how you managed as a dancer with three children. I'm so tired at the end of a day I find it hard to organize my own life, let alone anyone else's.' The truth is I don't know how I managed either, but I loved having children – and seeing them grow up. Just as I spent hours warming-up to exorcize stage fright, the household tensions of raising three babies helped keep life in perspective.

'The legendary Seymour stamina,' Donald said, shaking his head. 'You could have continued dancing, Lynnie.' He removed a peach from a glass bowl in the centre of the table and sliced it. 'One is not supposed to ask questions,' he said ambiguously. 'Of course you always did. On the Australian tour, the perfect little corps girls, putting on their ballerina airs, said, "Yes, sir; no, sir; I'll slit my throat, sir," but you asked questions. You created a sensation – Madam's newest star.' Changing the subject, I told Donald that I definitely wanted to visit him in the country, but I would have to wait until fall when the chaps were back in school. Then I took him by the hand into the garden.

The Australian tour lasted eight months. Most of the time we rehearsed in 100-degree heat. And my partnership continued unexpectedly with Donald. Towards the end of that critical tour, the bedevilling articles and headlines began about Lynn Seymour as 'the logical successor to Dame Margot Fonteyn'. Fonteyn was married to the Panamanian ambassador, Roberto de Arias. Lovingly dubbed Panama Hattie, Fonteyn, who made her début at the age of fourteen in 1934 as a snowflake in *The Nutcracker*, may have hinted that she would be spending less time in London, or the press just assumed it. I do not know. But thinking of the future, Madam watched me with chilling calmness. The tours were used to develop and try-out talent. Madam clearly had something in mind for me. That something was *Swan Lake*.

When the company left for Australia at dawn, after stern warnings from director John Field that anyone who missed the plane would spend the next eight months in London without pay, Madam was already in Sydney. Our repertoire featured the classics on which the Garden prided itself, from the comic *Coppélia* (a village lad develops a pash for a wooden doll but discovers his error before getting any splinters) to the tragic *Giselle* (a village maiden dies of love and is condemned to a supernatural world). It also included Kenneth MacMillan's *The Burrow* and *Solitaire*. Kenneth was supposed to go on tour with us, but, at the last minute, he had to stay in London, presumably to work on new ballets. I was acutely disappointed. That he once patted me paternally on the shoulder required the resuscitating squad of Maggie Lee and Brenda Bolton. Brenda did not come with us either. 'I'm needed to do the gypsy csardas at the Garden or the curtain won't go up,' she wisecracked. 'It hasn't occurred to anyone that Australia is my home and I might like to go.' She expanded her London rep. On a postcard she wrote : 'I'm getting into men and booze and food.' But Maggie Lee was on the plane, still keeping an eye on me at John Field's suggestion. Maggie, Betty and I shared digs in Australia.

The trip took about three flying days, with desperate relief stops in Frankfurt, Rome, Cairo, Karachi, Calcutta, Bangkok and Singapore. For the take-off we had to Look Pretty for publicity shots. Then as soon as we were in the air, everyone changed into jeans, shorts, slacks. I wriggled into pedal pushers. We stretched our legs at each airport, our third stop being Cairo. As we began our descent we were first struck by lightning and then suddenly found ourselves surrounded by an ominous escort of Russian MiG fighters. Submerged in preparations for the long tour, we had failed to take the Suez crisis into account. We got progressively hotter until we finally straggled into monsoon weather. Leaving Calcutta we felt quite wan and could neither sit nor sleep. The two loos became odoriferous. By the time we reached Singapore pale English faces had turned green. We were certain that the plane would be condemned by any board of health. There were jokes about our being the withered survivors of Shangri-La. Donald MacLeary sat mournfully in his seat, grinding his teeth in unspeakable pain. Donald is dying, I thought; his appendix has burst. John Field consulted with the stewardess who nodded briskly and then went to see the pilot. The plane landed in Darwin on the north-east coast of Australia, and Donald was carried off on a stretcher. He looked around the barren airstrip, realizing that we would soon leave him to an unknown fate in a hospital, and he would probably never see us again. He demanded to be returned to the plane. Next stop, Sydney. I took a seat beside him. 'Puss, what's wrong?' He rolled against me and haltingly admitted to an ordinary body dysfunction. I fished out a remedy that Miss Edwards had given me and he disappeared to the rear of the plane. I finally dozed off. When I awoke we were approaching Sydney. Donald was seated three rows ahead of me, looking great and talking animatedly. The company was in fine fettle. *I* had saved Donald's life! His pals gave me a round of applause, and I deplaned feeling quite chuffed.

Madam welcomed her young brood in Sydney. I received a personal message. She planned to coach me in a sequence from *Swan Lake*. Then, one day, at the conclusion of a company rehearsal she fairly knocked me over with the additional news that she wanted me to learn the lead double-role of Odette-Odile in *Swan Lake* and be ready to give the first performance in two months. A four-act classic! I had never danced a lead in a short ballet. I listened to her quite stunned. She was not interested in hearing me stammer concern. Her attitude was, 'The important thing is *I* believe you're ready.' You did not argue with Madam. She was seldom wrong. I fled the rehearsal room clutching my stomach, which churned away like an electric dishwasher. Maggie Lee rushed after me, 'Are you all right, girl?' I collapsed on a staircase, knees hugging my chest, feeling and looking a bit like Donald on the plane. After only fifteen months in the company I was being catapulted into the lead of the most celebrated and difficult ballet in history! It was a genuine make-or-break opportunity. And Madam had chosen me. I had been sending notes to my former teacher Winifred Edwards but decided I mustn't tell her this latest news. Miss Edwards would be quite shocked and say, 'Madam has gone mad again.' I had seen Fonteyn and Beriosova in *Swan Lake*. 'How could I possibly . . . ?' I asked Maggie, who gave me a hug and said that Madam's decision had not surprised her at all.

Once our Sydney opening was under our belts we settled into a routine of eight shows a week and my *Swan Lake* rehearsals began. The company had a full rehearsal schedule which meant that the Odette-Odile studies had to be dovetailed into the early mornings. The day's schedule began with my taking the tram from Bondi to do a solitary warm-up (in preparation for the technical hardships to come), followed by an hour and a half of *Swan Lake*, company class, repertory rehearsals, and then the performance.

This was very deep water for a raw eighteen-year-old. However, Madam and John Field together persevered with the raw lump and the raw lump gave her all. Svetlana Beriosova arrived as guest with David Blair, who was also to be my stoic prince for the first two performances. They both gave me unending support and advice but there were never enough rehearsals.

For the first time I faced the problem of being partnered in lengthy classical adagios. Madam looked bemused when I pleaded that I had never even danced a classical pas de deux on stage or in class. How could I suddenly pull three of the world's most famous adagios out of the bag in one evening?

So Madam decided in her infinite Irish wisdom that I should perform the bravura pas de deux from *Don Quixote*. So saying, she threw a coat around her shoulders, pinned a small hat to her majestic head and returned to London. The following morning I arose at seven o'clock and went for a tramp along Bondi Beach wrapped in my Sherlock Holmes coat. The wind swept against my face and the ocean thundered in my ears. I knew that I was on my own. Madam had put me to the test.

Two figures approached across the sand, hands in pockets. I gradually recognized the drawn faces of Christopher Gable and Simon Mottram. I had seen little of my friends; they now seemed to belong to another world that did not touch me. I was somewhere in outer space. We stood awkwardly and Mottie asked if I had heard about a girl in the company with whom they shared digs. I shook my head. There was a prolonged silence. 'She had a breakdown.' We had been told the tours resulted in one or two breakdowns. The dancer tried to kill herself and was in the hospital. I pulled the hound's-tooth coat closer to me, burying myself in its folds, not wanting any outside realities to interrupt my concentration on Odette-Odile. 'Oh, I'm so sorry,' I mumbled and tramped on, mentally rehearsing entrances, exits, attitudes, gestures, every detail of my life which consisted only of *Swan Lake*.

Robert Helpmann joined us as a guest artist. Madam bolstered the touring company with box-office names from Covent Garden – Beriosova, Anya Linden and, when we reached New Zealand, Margot Fonteyn. An Aussie himself, born in Adelaide, Helpmann studied with Pavlova when she visited Australia. From the early thirties through the early fifties he was the Garden's top male star, an actor-dancer with a vivid sense of theatre. As a performer there was little that Helpmann cannot or has not done. He co-starred on the stage with Vivien Leigh and Katharine Hepburn in plays by Shakespeare and Shaw. He played the choreographer in *The Red Shoes* who notices a promising newcomer in the corps and encourages her in a production of *Swan Lake*. He choreographed for Madam and was one of her earliest 'rebels'. Although more or less retired as a dancer, she lured him into our midst by inviting him to star in a revival of his ballet *Hamlet*. Madam has described him as 'cute as a monkey, quick as a squirrel'. When we met he was still quite a little monkey, a suave, slim, svelte monkey, with big eyes and a devastatingly mobile face. His outrageous wit, companionship and support were just what I needed as I prepared for *Swan Lake*.

One morning before company class I was rehearsing alone on a bare stage. Wiping the sweat from my brow with the inevitably soggy towel, I heard an impish voice say, 'I've been watching you.' He mounted the stage from the darkened stalls, a colourful figure in a yellow shirt and a foulard tied around his throat. 'That variation is already much better.'

Recognizing the eyes, lips, mouth, which are a caricaturist's dream, I fumbled, 'Uh, Mr Helpmann . . .'

'Bobby,' he said, rolling his eyes roguishly. 'Hang something on that lovely body of yours after class. I'm taking you to lunch.' Within seconds he had conquered me; I was his.

Bobby was then in his late forties. He had heaps to teach me about the theatre, ballet, personality and style, and the interpretation of roles. He offered steadfast support like the choreographer in *The Red Shoes*. My aim as a dancer was always to find the realistic 'truth' in a role – even the classics which are ethereal and illusive. This truth was what Kenneth MacMillan also sought with heightened theatricality. But as Kenneth perceived, my work was sometimes misunderstood by critics who found themselves so caught up with my acting that they forgot about the actual dancing and therefore thought it was secondary to the performance.

Bobby Helpmann and I had many long discussions about *Swan Lake* which he first danced with Fonteyn almost twenty-five years earlier. He stressed that the story of bewitchment was more complex than such classics as *Giselle* and *Coppélia*, and that it could be danced dramatically, with complete conviction, once I explored the psychological nuances beneath the airy-fairy froufrou. Stripped of its feathers, *Swan Lake* is about a magician who lures a dashing but rather dim prince away from his true love Odette and seduces him with a startling look-alike Odile. The double-role is technically terrifying. Odette is seen in white, Odile in black. To contrast them effectively, however, requires some concept of their emotional differences, Bobby advised, with his teasing intelligence. Odette is the victim of the magician; Odile, his mirror-image. Having absorbed this interpretation (though, at the time, not fully shaded), I proceeded to work twelve hours a day on the treacherous third act where the vixenish Odile arouses the prince with a series of steps called fouettés – whipping, spinning turns on the point of one foot. A ballerina's reputation rises and falls on whether or not she completes thirty-two dreaded fouettés. These steps not only affect you physically but also mentally. I have heard balletomanes counting, 'She's at twenty-two now, ten more to go,' daring you to tumble into a heap, lungs and legs gone. Cruel blood-thirsty buggers. The countdown simply turns ballet into a gymnastic event.

Practising the fouettés on a raked, or sloping, stage over and over again in the heat was crippling. I once ricocheted into the wings, hit the wall, pushed off non-stop and went careening back onstage, eyes out of focus. An observant Bobby Helpmann saved a limp noodle from spinning into the pit. Donald was learning the role of the prince. The heat was so intense that he fainted at one rehearsal. To cool off I napped in the basement of the theatre, stretched out on empty costume baskets. The scurrying mice, leaping through the basket, did not come near me. Even the mice were sweating.

The rehearsal coach for *Swan Lake*, in any company, has seen hundreds of productions and almost as many ballerinas as Odette-Odile. The coach has a preconceived notion of the role. My body was much too pliant for the traditionally formal elegance of a Fonteyn. My movements are soft and sinuous. 'You're not a swan at all,' our couch cried, interrupting me with a clap of hands. 'Those legs of yours – why, you're like a snake!'

Looking at the floor, breathless with exertion, I answered, 'I've thought a lot about what I'm doing and, for me, it's right.' The only person who fully accepted my style at that time without trying to modify it was Kenneth

MacMillan. Now I had the endorsement of Robert Helpmann. I was never troubled by saying 'No' to a ballet-master or coach. Maggie Lee sat in the stalls with John Field, who worried that I was throwing my arms and arching my back too much. Madam might not approve. 'Let Lynn do it her way and they'll love it,' Maggie protested.

I did ten performances of *Swan Lake* on the tour. My début, coinciding with my nineteenth birthday, was in the sunbaked city of Melbourne. The Canadian flag billowed in a muggy breeze above the theatre. According to the press it signalled a Royal Ballet custom – 'the launching of a new ballerina'. As I got into my white Odette costume I lamented to a dancer in the dressing room, 'Oh, it's going to be a disaster, I shouldn't be doing this.'

Without glancing at me, she replied, 'You're quite right. I don't know why you've been given the role. Madam has always been a bit potty.' She continued painting her eyes.

Stupidly it never occurred to me that the girls who had been in the company three years or so might be jealous. The dancer to whom I wailed was only twenty-two and already very embittered. In show business lore it is considered unlucky to whistle in the dressing room. I quickly learned it is even more gauche to complain. I only completed eight fouettés with David Blair as my partner, but the critics were moved to praise my youth, beauty and strength. One reviewer even commented on my lovely cheekbones!

I wrote my parents: 'The biggest thing ever is now over for a while. First performance of *Lake* was such an experience – the times I nearly crumpled and lost heart. I did some very bad things but when I mentioned them, half had been forgotten. The audience was full of supporters and the company with me all the way. At the end the relief was terrific and the kids gave me a hand!'

The thirty-two fouettés were executed (I use the word advisedly) at the third performance with Donald as my handsome prince. We took nine curtain calls. 'You were travelling, just a bit,' Bobby Helpmann said, giving me a squeeze.

Performing increased my confidence, and so did the excellent partnering of Donald, but offstage I remained a freckled frump. Would I always need a role to project sex and/or beauty, I pouted to Bobby as he shuffled approvingly through the reviews. I sat on the couch in his hotel suite, a mousy little thing in a brown skirt and a blouse with a Peter Pan collar. Bobby pondered a moment, then fixed us both refreshing drinks in tall, tall glasses. Superbly attired himself in a blue blazer and tan slacks, he positively sparkled as he filled the glasses with jagged clumps of ice. Even without his gold cufflinks and gold watchband, Bobby would have sparkled. Bobby had been touring Australia in a Noël Coward comedy and he is like all those Cowardian chaps whose names are Nicky and Toby and Sandy. 'You want to know what I'm really like, do you, underneath all the glittering veneer?' asks the matinée idol in Coward's *Present Laughter*. 'Well, this is it. Fundamentally honest!' That's Bobby Helpmann, fundamentally honest. I had asked a question. He gave me an answer – and a scene – that left an indelible impression.

'I told a reporter that you're a truly great talent, one of the very few ballerinas,' he said, striding towards me. 'The roles you interpret affect you and you affect the roles. That's what being a star is. You have to give a performance offstage, not all of the time but some of the time.' He thumped the reviews with his fist. 'You want to project a bit of magnetism when you leave the theatre? Well, for starters you must stop dressing like the governess of Thrushcross Grange.' He flung the papers on the couch and dramatically sipped his drink. 'You're hiding something. You're hiding *yourself*.' Bobby urged me to start wearing hats – big hats, little hats, floppy hats. 'Hats frame the face. They're sexy. Mysterious. You can be a *femme fatale* or a coquette in a hat.' He told me to wear soft clinging dresses in bright primary colours. And heels. 'With your legs, your arch, high heels are essential.' He sank on the couch beside me and muttered confidentially, 'A child becomes a courtesan in high heels.'

'Now Bobby,' I temporized, 'how would you know so much about heels?'

He glared at me with mock indignation. 'Obviously you never saw me play the Ugly Stepsister in *Cinderella*.'

Bobby Helpmann, Donald MacLeary, John Field and several principals were invited to a yacht party. I decided the hour had come to don my best habiliments. I set out to meet Bobby at the theatre dressed to the nines. Christopher and Mottie were sauntering out the stage door as I approached, wearing my highest heels. The image Christopher saw sent him sprawling. He recalled, 'Mottie and I were going for a milkshake. We noticed this very curvy lady coming towards us. We thought she was some film star giving the boys a thrill. Giant picture hat. Gorgeous legs in the most divine shoes. "Who the hell is that?" Mottie asked. She walked straight up to us. "Is Bobby inside?" "Good Christ, it's Lynn!" The grey thing on Bondi Beach in Sydney was now this extraordinary creature in Melbourne. We were completely dazed. She came out of the theatre with Bobby, got into a taxi and roared off. The transformation was amazing.'

Bobby was very pleased. He thought that I looked madly divine. I feared that I looked divinely mad. When we boarded the yacht I was going to loll in a deck chaise, but Bobby indicated No Lolling and pointed to an upright canvas chair which showed off my 'line'. The guests stared at me with bright, alert eyes. But I did not lose poise or pose. In Adelaide we attended a party arm-in-arm at the Governor's House and I wore the same outfit. A society matron said to Bobby, 'Isn't that little Lynn Seymour wonderful?' Bobby waved her aside impatiently with, 'Oh, don't be so stupid.' Then he dazzled her with a forgiving smile. 'Of course, she's wonderful.' Bobby's mother called me Dame Lynn. Bobby succeeded in converting me into one glamorous presence, up to a point. The ankle socks and pleated skirts disappeared for ever; I became highly conscious of the latest in chic. But the glamorous movie star image offstage was never really me. I always felt most comfortable in a sweat shirt and jeans. I'm like a kid with clothes. I also like to 'dress up'.

Sydney, Melbourne, Brisbane, Adelaide – we hopped around Australia in claptrap planes with grinding motors. I often slept with ice on the bed. The dancers bought insect sprays and trouped in and out of each other's rooms, spraying bed, blankets, shower, and then fell asleep in a steamy vapour of spray. After many performances Betty Anderton and I went for midnight swims. Once we even slept on the beach. In the morning we heard that someone had been 'taken' by a shark. Our ballet-master Henry Legerton, always jovial and full of dance anecdotes that I relished, invited a small group to a hillside farm where a hospitable white-haired lady, whose hearing-aid crackled like a wireless, kept an animal sanctuary for tired creatures. Not members of the touring company, but possums and bandicoots. She had also built an enormous mud dam, in case of fire. We would slide down the wall of the dam, our bodies sleek with mud, and splash in the water, watching bush fires miles and miles away scorch the night sky with orange flames.

On our first weekend in Brisbane Donald and I were invited to view a tropical rain forest. The setting was gorgeous. Thick green foliage enclosed us in an exotic jungle of orchids and fern trees. As we filed gingerly down a muddy path, accompanied by the screeching of birds, I looked down and saw a coiled electric green snake. I let out a piercing shriek, took a gigantic leap, and landed with a splash. To my horror my legs were covered with leeches. Donald, nattily attired as ever in a sort of safari get-up, calmly rescued me. Leeches, he explained, had to be burned off. Spluttering, we chain-lit cigarettes and painstakingly burned off the offenders. I'd had enough of rain forests. It was back to the car.

Meanwhile Donald and I were dancing every night and rehearsing all day. The demands were punishing, but I was loving it. 'No human being could be happier or have such a bursting soul,' I wrote home. 'Perhaps dancing is my best form of transmitting feeling.'

On days off I started reading the life of Isadora Duncan, the first star of modern dance, a true renegade who defied the rules. To me, Isadora Duncan became a romantic figure – a heroine.

'Are you planning to do something Isadora Duncan-ish?' Maggie Lee asked.

'I'd like to. I need the opportunity.'

In Brisbane I found myself one weekend lying on the beach between Donald and my debonair mentor Bobby Helpmann, who had invited us, along with John Field and his wife Anne Heaton, to weekend at his apartment on the Gold Coast. Bobby treated us to heavenly food and drink. At dusk, when the heat abated, we were still relaxing on the sand. I jumped up and dashed into the sea. Donald sped after me. We cavorted like innocent water babies in an Esther Williams musical. For the moment the sea was a surging sanctuary. Cresting on a breaker we saw Bobby waving. We waved back, and continued swimming and singing 'Many a tear has to fall . . . 'cause it's all . . . in the game . . .'

John Field and Anne Heaton also waved. 'Aren't they sweet?' I called to Donald. They soon appeared to be shouting, but we could not hear a word. However, we became alarmingly aware of a forceful undertow. Bobby was beside himself on the beach, leaping and miming. We turned, looked out to sea. About sixty yards away was a black fin. We began thrashing furiously, although the undertow slowed us. The shark seemed to be waiting for a calmer surf before making an attack. A breaker thundered down. Swimming with all our strength, we took great arcing dives and were hurled on to the beach, quaking from head to toe. Bobby practically carried me to the beach towel.

'It would be rather difficult for you to do the thirty-two fouettés with only one leg,' he reprimanded as he dried me off. 'Madam would be *most* displeased.'

When the company reached New Zealand we were a tattered group. Strained and drained. The freezing weather was just like Scotland and the sudden climatic change had us in shock. Margot Fonteyn arrived, bearing tidbits of news from Covent Garden, and perked us with her very presence. Margot and Bobby were dancing a lot together and he suggested that she might coach me in *Swan Lake*. I thought this would be splendid.

At the appointed hour I was so nervous I did not warm up properly. We started with my entrance as Odette, running onstage. She stopped me immediately: 'Why are you looking over your shoulder?' A perfectly reasonable question. Looking fearfully over my shoulder involved my interpretation of Odette and her relationship with the magician – I wondered if he was lurking somewhere. But I was tongue-tied with Margot. I could not open my mouth. She thought Odette should make an entrance facing the audience as a proud Swan Queen. From then on I was in trouble. There wasn't one movement that she did not question. She was trying to help teach me the essence of 'classicism', no holds barred, but I was childishly unprepared for criticism from the goddess herself. The experience unnerved me. Unnerved? I was shattered and feared for my next performance. I thought, well, she has her way of doing it, but this is *mine*; I cannot conform to someone else's style. The session was disastrous. Bobby was worried because rivers of tears flowed from the odd little whatnot. But Margot Fonteyn respected our stylistic differences and we later became very good friends. In New Zealand I was just a kid out of the corps.

I had two more *Swan Lake* performances and I danced them with a deluxe stomach ache. John Field tacitly supported me. He did not ask me to alter one movement. A New Zealand newspaper quoted Field: 'Lynn Seymour certainly has the material Dame Margot Fonteyn's successor must have.' Soon reporters and caption writers referred to me as the girl most likely to succeed Fonteyn, a phrasing which added to my stomach ache. No one has ever 'succeeded' Fonteyn, or will. Then rumours began flying that I was to dance *Swan Lake* at Covent Garden with the main company. Madam had received enthusiastic reports from John Field and Bobby Helpmann. And one memorable afternoon, John Field confirmed the performance. It was set for Wednesday, 6 May 1959, two months after my twentieth birthday.

I accepted the news numbly. The Garden performance, partnered by Donald, had to be viewed as just another performance and played down in my own mind or that swan would never take flight. Repeated dancing in the big roles increases your confidence. The expert method behind Madam's madness was evident: the touring company gave young dancers the same valuable performing experiences that British actors received in the provincial theatres. From this pool of talent emerged names that would draw queues at Covent Garden.

But I would be fibbing if I gave the impression that the Garden date was not brutally thrilling and terrifying. It meant the whole bloody world to me, and I wanted my parents there, I wanted Mom and Dad to see me dance Odette-Odile at Covent Garden. Then I could endure endless stomach contractions. Yet I knew they could not possibly afford the trip; it would be a hardship for Mom to come alone. We had talked about my going home for the summer. Ah. What if we juggled the expense sheet and instead they came to London for *Swan Lake*? I tossed the idea around but did not put it to paper.

My friends thought that as I was the first Canadian to dance a ballerina role with the Royal Ballet, the city of Vancouver or the Ballet Society would celebrate the event by sending Mom. So finally I wrote home and mentioned in an off-hand sentence, 'You should make an appeal to the city to have a Get-the-Springbetts-to-London-fund.' My parents were too proud for that, of course. The Canadian press ran tons of articles on my 'triumph in Australia' but no one approached my parents with the notion of sending them to London.

I have no recollection of the return flight. I remember meeting Kenneth for lunch my third day back at a restaurant in Soho. There was affection in his wistful brown eyes and he gave me a tender hug. I made myself as pretty as possible, without overdoing it, and then fretted that it was all a waste; the lighting in the restaurant was atrocious. Australia, I told him, was terribly wild west; it only lacked hitching posts, and yet I loved the sunburnt countryside. He knew all about *Swan Lake* there and upcoming at the Garden; he filled me in on Garden gossip and vaguely alluded to the ballets he was preparing. We walked down Shaftesbury Avenue towards Piccadilly, a blaze of neon and a babel of noise, and I reflected, yes, I'm home, London is home, and I'm so glad to be here, in this marvellously drippy hazy grey-golden mist. We said goodbye at the tube station and I decided: I'll dance *Swan Lake* for him.

Swan Lake started the first Seymour myth.

To steady nerves, to keep myself distracted, I deliberately left myself small tasks during each interval. Brenda Bolton and Jackie Daryl were swans. Jackie came to my dressing room before the killing third act, with the fouettés, and saw me sewing ribbons on my shoes. She was confounded.

'I expected to find you praying or something,' she gasped.

'Oh, no . . . I have to finish these shoes,' I said in a bored, emotionless voice.

Jackie reported the scene to some of the other swans, shaking her head in amazement, but as the story was passed along, from swan to swan, it came out that Seymour worked slavishly but could not get herself 'together' in time for a performance!

LYNN GAVE BEAUTIFUL PERFORMANCE RECEIVED OVATION
MADAM DELIGHTED LOVE WINIFRED EDWARDS

My dutiful teacher and coach Winifred Edwards informed my parents by cable and letter that *Swan Lake* went down very well.

May 10, 1959

Dear Mrs Springbett:

It was indeed a great occasion for Lynn and it is sad that you and her father were not there. You would have been very proud of Lynn. Her entrance established her as an artist and ballerina in appearance and figure. The thirty-two fouettés were quite good. I earnestly hope all your sacrifices and heartaches will prove to have been worthwhile.

I was rather horrified to learn that she had not written to you on arrival in England. I should keep her up to the mark greatly. Let her feel that you long for her letters.

She is truly humble about herself with deep inner thoughts and aspirations about her work.

Miss Fonteyn's mother sent her the message: 'Tell her it has given me great pleasure to watch her performance.' I don't think Lynn expects to come home this summer. She would think it too expensive I am sure.

Kindest regards and congratulations,
Winifred Edwards

My parents also read a feature in *Time*: 'The brightest new star of England's famed Royal Ballet is Alberta-born Lynn Seymour . . . dancing in the gruelling double-role in *Swan Lake*, she won lavish praise from London's most finicky critics. "My performance was very faulty," she said. "I'm no technical monster, by any means . . ."' The critical endorsements contained such words as power and personality. Alexander Bland in the *Observer* confirmed Madam's decision to teach me the role. 'The grape-vine from Australia had been tingling with the news that an exceptional young dancer had emerged in the touring company . . . Rumour had not outrun the truth. Seymour *is* exceptional – in fact it is safe to say that, barring accidents, a legitimate heir to the dynasty of top British dancers has been born.' Andrew Porter in the *Financial Times* perceptively noted: 'She dared a droop of the hands which strictly speaking should be termed a fault, but in fact was expressive.' Most significantly, I established my own signature, quite distinct from that of Margot Fonteyn.

Great reviews do not mean million-dollar salaries and the pick of the parts. The ballet is not Hollywood or Broadway. And Establishment dance companies across the world operate just like other Establishment organizations: you are kept in line by the unspoken reminder that no employee is indispensable to the system. After the performance my pay went up to twenty pounds a week and I was immediately packed off to the provinces on a six-week tour. A mob of reporters from Canadian papers swamped my dressing room. I sat in a chair beside the make-up table combing my hair while a dozen blurred faces fired questions at me.

'What's your ambition, Miss Seymour?'

'Just do what I'm doing, as best as I can.'

'You seem very calm now. How did you feel during the performance?'

'My heart was in my mouth most of the time.'

'What happens next?'

'Well, immediately next I'm out for a bite to eat, then to bed.'

Kenneth MacMillan took me to Le Petit Club Français, popularly known as the French Club, in St James's Place, to toast my Garden début in swan feathers. The French Club, one of the few restaurants open after eleven, was on the second floor of a wobbly Georgian building. The food and service were sometimes dismal, but it was comfortable and unpretentious, which I liked, and had the ambience of a salon. Lively talk. The smell of Gauloise cigarettes. A musical clatter of dishes, silver and wine glasses. The French Club attracted a medley of people in the arts. For two years or so, Kenneth and I went there for supper about once a month. He would ring me up and announce softly, 'I want to go out. I'm hungry.' Breathless pause. 'Shall we meet at the French Club?' And I would answer quickly, 'Hold on. Let me see if I have enough money.' Going to the French Club meant 'dressing up', so I would slip into a frolicsome dress, high heels and wild hat – something from the flea market to astonish Kenneth.

With a serious face and air of complete detachment, Kenneth guided a battle-weary but keyed-up dancer to a corner table covered in a red-and-white checked cloth. He stopped briefly once, to greet Roy Round, a photographer whom I had met during a posing session for *The Burrow*.

Round was dining with Peter Williams, the editor of *Dance and Dancers*.

'Hello, ducky,' Williams said humorously to Kenneth, 'don't give me any Bolshoi tonight.'

Williams congratulated me on Odette-Odile and said that he was quite unprepared for the feeling of drama I had sustained in a work of such length. Kenneth responded with a slight I-told-you-so inclination of his head, bid the chaps good evening and steered me to our table. We both knew that the dance crowd was eyeing us. We also knew that I had company class at ten o'clock in the morning. But my fatigue had vanished. I did not want to go to bed. There were many times later when I did class and afternoon rehearsal after only four hours of sleep.

Kenneth ordered wine. We lit cigarettes. 'The only eatable thing here is *gigot d'agneau*, I'm told,' said Kenneth, 'but I have yet to see it on the menu.' He studied the card. 'You see, no *gigot*.' He looked at me with hurt, wide-open eyes. We burst into laughter.

Outside there was fog and the sound of rain, but inside the French Club there was only warmth and freedom from anxiety.

CHAPTER 7

Côte d'Azur

Splash!

I have submerged myself in a soapy bath with scented salts. Mid-morning on Woodstock Road. A sensation of supreme content creeps over me as I lean my head against the tub and let the hot water massage the old bones. For twenty-five years, more or less, I was in class at ten o'clock or earlier, six, sometimes seven, days a week. Athletes train for their one big race. Dancers endure the same sort of training every day of the week, and do not retire at twenty-two. The previous night's indulgence in cigarettes and cocktails streams from the pores in rivulets of perspiration while doing turns, jumps, glides, beating and sliding steps, and leg exercises. If you skip one day of class it's like missing four. The most precious commodity – your body – must never fail you. This reality haunts your life, day after day, increasing fears about the span of your career and artistry on stage, for dancers, particularly harrowingly, are only as good as their last performance.

My soapy hands again turned to the morning post stacked on a footstool beside the bath. The Notting Hill Playhouse asked me to choreograph a production of the Kurt Weill musical *Lady in the Dark*. We had some conferences and I was then invited to play the neurotic heroine, a fashion magazine editor who has a nervous breakdown at the pinnacle of her career. Psychoanalysis pulls away the past and reveals that she was rejected by her father. The Playhouse wants an answer, and Lynn Seymour, like *Lady*'s Liza Elliott, must make up her mind. The answer, I decide, is no. I am not keen on the director, I would need singing lessons and half the libretto should be scrapped. A director I admire very much, Lindsay Anderson, has asked if I would be interested in playing Gertrude in a production of *Hamlet*. We met ten years ago at a Christmas party. 'You give some ballets a surprising strength,' he said. 'The truth is you're a very good actress.' I turned down the role of Karsavina in the Herbert Ross film *Nijinsky*. I was too much in awe of this great lady to prance through with a pale imitation. Today, soaping my arms with a sponge, I think that acting has intriguing possibilities. I am not ready for *Hamlet*. But I would adore playing a character named Gertrude in almost anything.

I could have danced another five years but then I would have delayed the transition into another career. The average professional life of a dancer is twenty years, barring physical injuries and breakdowns. The public and youngsters enrolling in dance schools are unaware of the casualties. Names simply disappear from programmes. It takes a lot of courage, and luck, to be a survivor.

The telephone rang in the adjoining bedroom and I wondered if Demian would answer. He was somewhere in the house. I had no intention of interrupting my hot soak. The bedroom door opened and Demian called 'Mum?' I asked him to answer the phone. 'She's in the bathroom,' I heard him mutter. I must remember to tell him not to think of himself as the BBC presenting news bulletins. 'What are you doing, Mum?'

'*Who's* on the phone, my darling?'

'Philip.' Philip is Demian's father. Demian was born about two years after Kenneth MacMillan's daughter, a beautiful child with the creamiest skin and brown hair. But Kenneth and I seldom prattled about our children. There was never time for that. 'Philip wants to talk to you.'

'Tell him I'm having a debauch of luxury.'

'She's in the tub,' Demian reported. 'Are you coming to

my birthday party?' Philip had telephoned about the party and gifts. Demian wanted accessories for his electric train. He has a tank-car and two coaches. I would ask Philip to buy him either a dining-car or wagon-lit. Demian weaves his own fantasies for hours, playing with the train. Sometimes he doesn't even turn on the switch. He pushes the cars up and down narrow-gauge tracks, whispering to imaginary passengers in the coaches. When the twins ask why he doesn't run it electrically, he answers, 'I don't want to,' and they say with exasperation, 'Ohhhhh – Demian – !'

'I'll ring Philip back,' I called out, but he had concluded his chat already. The bedroom door slammed shut. Birthdays are a special pleasure for the children. Demian requested a chocolate cake with pink icing. His instructions were specific. And he definitely wanted a wagon-lit. 'They're quite smart looking, Mum, for the rich passengers.' I idled in the bath, nostalgically recalling my only trip on a wagon-lit. Yes, it was quite smart looking and I was a let's-pretend rich passenger on the most marvellously theatrical summer vacation in my life. For two weeks I did not have to worry about anything. I kept in shape by swimming all day every day. Sheer bliss.

I glanced at the clock. Time to rise from the bath, like Venus from the sea, and organize the day that stretched before me, a day with no worry other than financial. A day without a turbulent stomach, wobbly knees and sweaty pre-performance palms. The first stop is the model train store in Chiswick High Road. I want to price the wagon-lits. Up, Seymour, up.

Splash!

Kenneth MacMillan wanted to go to St Tropez. He proposed the idea to Donald MacLeary and they both urged me to join them. I did not have to be coaxed. I attributed the invitation to my saucy high heels and hats. We decided to leave in late June as soon as the spring provincial tour, following *Swan Lake*, was over. By then I had a principal role in every ballet in the repertory. I had been touring and dancing without a let-up for almost a year. Flopping on a beach with Kenneth and Donald sounded dreamy.

'After the Aussie tour, I could not stand another flight or the publicity that will ensue, and the last thing I want to do now is dance for the Vancouver Ballet Society,' I wrote my parents. 'This must seem terribly mean, but I want to relax with no worries of meeting people. I'll be home any time next year – and ready to perform – if the Ballet Society sponsors a partner and myself.' Odette-Odile at Covent Garden had made Springbett-Seymour a name in Canada, so I spelt out exactly what I wanted from the Ballet Society which wished to see the local girl dance: a round-trip ticket. Two, in fact. For myself and a partner. My parents replied to my vacation plans in the south of France with typical generosity. They sent heaps of love – and a cheque.

During rehearsal breaks Kenneth, Donald and I chatted animatedly about our trip to the lush, decadent sunspot of the Riviera. St Tropez had been a drowsy fishing village until Brigitte Bardot let down her hair and everything else there in the flesh and on-screen in Roger Vadim's charmingly amoral film *And God Created Woman*. Topless movie stars and bottomless millionaires cruised St Tropez in their yachts, cars and espadrilles. The hordes of curious tourists – like ourselves – had not yet invaded the town. We giggled with anticipation over what we might find and carefully planned wardrobes for the beach, café-sitting and night-clubs.

Lorna Mossford, the ballet-mistress for the touring company, approached me one day after a coffee klatch. Mossy, as we called her, was a gritty lady with blondish hair and a bubbly personality. Quite rowdy and wonderful. 'I've been watching the three of you,' she said. 'If you're up to something positively disgusting, *I* want to know about it.' One hand on hip. A cigarette tipped precariously from her lip.

'We're running away together,' I chided.

'Oh, that *is* disgusting,' Mossy averred, flinging her cigarette into an overflowing ashtray and extinguishing it with four quick circular jabs. 'So many butts and I can identify each one.' She rummaged in the bowl. 'This neat one is Donald's. The unfinished atrocity belongs to Seymour. And this, *this* wisp of paper, unspeakably squeezed, reeks of Kenneth.' She sank into a chair opposite me and lit a fresh cigarette. We all smoked like fiends. 'Now tell Mossy more.'

I disclosed the destination of our holiday. Knowing that Kenneth found Mossy a boon companion I suggested that she come along with us, making it a tidy foursome, although, I stressed, we needed Kenneth's formal approval. Mossy stared at me for half an instant, rapping her slender fingers on the table. She closed her eyes as if in a trance and cogitated. Then she leaned forward, gripped my hand conspiratorially and announced in a throaty voice that she was ready for a quadrille. A few days later I bought a bikini and Kenneth made round-trip reservations from Paris to the Côte d'Azur on the Blue Train. We would travel in style and pretend, for two weeks, that we were movie stars and millionaires.

The Blue Train slipped out of the Gare de Lyon in Paris a bit past eight. During its heyday in the twenties it took Isadora Duncan, Scott and Zelda Fitzgerald, and Diaghilev to the Riviera. Diaghilev even commissioned a ballet called *Le Train Bleu*, with a scenario by Jean Cocteau and a front curtain by Picasso. The setting was not the train but *une plage* where a young English dancer whom Diaghilev named Anton Dolin turned cartwheels in a Chanel bathing suit. In the late fifties most celebrities flew to the Riviera, but we wanted a gambol on the train with a glamorous past and Kenneth had a phobia about planes anyway. Today it is just another train. In 1959 the gleaming blue wagon-lits still carried a promise of romantic intrigue locked inside each compartment as the train sped south, stopping at Cannes, Nice and Monte Carlo.

During the following two weeks we took all our meals together, but there was something very special, something magical about our dinner in the Blue Train. We were role-playing to be sure, but we played with a personal gusto. We just opened up spontaneously, indifferent to the pressures – and realities – of London. Kenneth, then a squeak under thirty, was relaxed, witty and, when he chose, provocatively evasive – qualities which attracted me. The crisp, impetuously direct Mossy, a woman in her thirties who was eventually winded by the long tours and 'life', conveyed a raunchy glamour. Donald and I were forever bonded by the endurance contest of *Swan Lake*. He was twenty-two and already receiving fan mail. I was still trying to develop a sophisticated image for myself. Scanning the menu in the pinkly-illuminated restaurant-car, I marvelled that the only worry facing us was a choice of wine. Nothing disturbed our happiness, or hinted that it ever would. The white linen, heaps of crystal and silver and porcelain dishes were stage props for an enchanted *tableau vivant*. Kenneth ordered the wine. 'I want something assertive,' he said, 'but *not* aggressive.'

Glancing around the restaurant-car I noticed people staring at us admiringly. Then I had a petit-thrill. There sat the epitome of chic Rosalind Russell, in a dark blue suit and picture-brim hat. Scrawled in my diary I find: 'Dinner divine. Ros. Rus. Lobster in aspic. Cheese board, fruit.' We lingered at the table over strong coffee and many cigarettes. The train rolled along at seventy-five miles an hour, past darkened countryside and a night sky gleaming with stars.

Kenneth held forth. His head teemed with ballet ideas. He wanted to create a piece for Donald and me; and, someday, he wanted to explore a full-length dramatic 'story ballet'. We listened as if under a potent spell, and would have dawdled longer but the waiters were preparing for the second sitting. Reluctantly, sadly, we pushed back our chairs and slowly returned to our wagon-lits. Kenneth and I leaned against the windows in the corridor and had final cigarettes before turning in. We had to leave the train around seven in the morning and then take a coach to St Tropez. Kenneth finished our dinner conversation. Madam, he reminded me, believed that ballet was very much a part of theatre and so did he. Finding the dramatic 'truth', he went on, with a perfect fusion of music and choreography and décor was the object of the Russian choreographer Michel Fokine, whose ballets, such as *Le Spectre de la Rose* and *Les Sylphides*, were created for Diaghilev's company. Tamara Karsavina had been Fokine's muse. Kenneth said that I was an emotional dancer, 'a Fokine dancer', and he supposed that he was rather a Fokine type himself. 'George Balanchine is a choreographer of pure dance. Both are fine. Nothing is wrong in art. What's important is that it works.' He patted my head and said goodnight. His last words that night on the Blue Train were exhilarating and I stayed in the corridor for some minutes turning them over in my mind while dreamily gazing at a sliver of yellow moon.

Our beds had been made. Mossy, scantily clad in her 'baby dolls', was brushing her teeth. I am familiar with every twitch and nerve and bone in a dancer's body, and oblivious to nudity backstage or onstage, men and women. But outside the theatre I retain a curious modesty, which astonishes many friends, and sleep in flannel nightgowns and layered woollies. I never scamper around the house half-dressed. When Kenneth took snapshots of me on the beach in my bikini, I shyly held a striped beach towel against my front. Away from the footlights I am insecure about my body and feel uncomfortable with the careless, harmless nudity of others. When Mossy bent over the sink I hurriedly undressed and nestled between the sheets in the upper berth.

'Kenneth patted my head,' I said. 'I'm a sucker for anyone who does that.'

She looked up from the sink, a world-weary expression on her face. 'Where men are concerned, one can be too much of a sucker' – she stepped out of her feather mules – 'or not enough of one.' Then she sat down, inspected her feet and began painting her toenails blood red.

The south of France – an ecstasy of sunshine, pine trees and olive trees, pistachio plants, roses and jasmine, and the bluest sea in the world. The air was like champagne and we were blissfully intoxicated from the moment we stepped off the train. One day blended into another of swimming, sunning, biking, eating and sitting in sidewalk cafés. Our hotel was on a narrow winding street lined with boulangeries, pâtisseries and blanchisseries. From behind shuttered windows came muffled music and laughter. Everyone we passed seemed to be a participant in a hedonistic carnival: lusciously lean and golden brown, they had obviously given up their souls to the pursuit of sensual gratification. Bright faces reflected the enjoyment of total abandon. In that atmosphere, even with pallid white skin, it is impossible not to feel sexy too.

'I may lose my self-control here,' quipped Mossy, a peculiar expression in her eyes.

'Give us plenty of warning,' Kenneth answered as, captain of the group, he marched into our hotel, a lopsided mustard-coloured building with a red tiled roof. To economize, Mossy and I had a double, but the chaps booked separately. Kenneth's stay-awake-all-night passion matched mine but did not make him, jested Donald, after one night on the Blue Train, the model room-mate, 'if you like to sleep'.

We plunked our suitcases down in a dark chamber. Then I flung open the shutters and great shafts of sunlight scissored the room, revealing brown tiled floors, tidy beds and an oak armoire. Sparse but clean. The window overlooked other rainbow-coloured shutters, red sloping roofs and a wedge of the blue harbour. I was speechless with wonder. As soon as Kenneth and Donald settled themselves we walked into the centre of town and rented four dilapidated bicycles, our mode of transport for two weeks, bought some bread and cheese, a bottle of Beaujolais, and pedalled off, over hill and dale. Careening cars whizzed past us like entrants in the Grand Prix. We were all headed for the same, *la plage Tahiti*.

Bronzed bodies barely covered by snippets of bathing suits the size of band-aids speckled the sand which sloped into transparent water that rippled from light blue to turquoise to a deep blue as the eye travelled to the horizon. We rented an umbrella and beach mats, and exposed our tender skin to the glare of the sun and the suntanned. I quickly turned bright pink and had to adopt a rôtisserie method by swathing myself in shirts and towels and sticking out one limb at a time. Mossy was also quite careful about her skin, although she tanned readily. 'Too much sun, ducky, and we lose our pure English complexion. Look what happened to Gladys Cooper when she went to live in Hollywood!'

After the tension of the Australian tour, building up to *Swan Lake* at the Garden and then the laborious provincial tour, my body needed the salty sharkless sea and the hot massaging sand of the Med. We lazed on the beach every day all day. A bread company in England called Hovis which produced brown bread then had an advertising campaign that exclaimed, 'Don't say brown, say Hovis!' The second day, when Donald observed that he was turning brown, Kenneth said in his grandest manner, 'Don't say brown, say Hovis!' After that we would ask, 'How's your Hovis coming?' And the replies would be, 'My Hovis is coming along,' or 'I'm worried about my Hovis.'

Hovis was the first word in our coded vocabulary which infuriated many in London. Kenneth turned a nice coppery colour. Donald was the Apollo *anglais* whose presence raised us into the realm of the *beau demi-monde*. As for me, not fretting about fouettés was a curiously pagan experience unto itself, so I didn't worry about my peeling nose and freckling cheeks.

The day started around eight in the morning when I unlatched the shutters and leaned out the window, contemplating the bougainvillaea creeping along the rooftops, and inspected the sky, which descended over a hodge-podge of villas and shops like a rushing blue landslide. Petit-déjeuner was delivered at nine. Seconds later the chaps appeared with their trays of *café au lait* and croissants, and we sat cross-legged on the two beds in pyjamas or bathrobes and organized lunch that we would purchase in the markets before cycling to the beach. There we would divvy up the books. Kenneth introduced us to America's contemporary 'Southern' writers – Truman Capote, Eudora Welty and Carson McCullers. I was reading *The Member of the Wedding*, the story of an anguished adolescent girl searching for companionship. The McCullers novel inspired Kenneth's ballet *Solitaire*. He and I lay under the shade of the umbrella ruminating on the heartbreak of childhood, as depicted in the McCullers portrait. Donald and Mossy meandered in opposite directions on the hot white sand, books tucked under their arms, finding their own place in the sun. There was nothing further to reveal about ourselves when we talked abstractedly. We both understood the cruel insights of McCullers and Capote whose characters were outsiders, traitors to society.

By the middle of the second week, after basking on the beach, sauntering in shops and idling over late-night dinners, my system was thoroughly sautéed. Too much sun. Too much wine. Too much rich food. The mistral had started to blow. I wondered how the others were coping – or if it was just me with the surfeit. I didn't feel like lingering at the dinner table one night but sat quietly, rubbing the stem of my wine glass as Kenneth theorized on the off-beat romanticism in Capote's short stories. Not being British, I wasn't trained to keep a stiff upper lip and smile no matter what. But I was learning, quickly.

We found an outdoor cinema that was showing Louis Malle's disconcertingly erotic exercise in women's liberation, *The Lovers*. Jeanne Moreau, ageless and timeless, the quintessential Frenchwoman, the courtesan-concierge, portrayed a bored society woman. She has a husband who bores her, a child who bores her, a lover who bores her. Moreau of course can even look bored when she's making love but she makes boring interesting. In the film she meets a young man, a stranger, and they spend a night of explicit rapture. When Moreau and her friend proceeded to assume nude Matissian positions to the accompaniment of Brahms's double concerto I sensed calamity and left halfway through. I heard my name called and running footsteps. Donald caught up and put his arm around me. We walked without talking for a while and came upon a deserted café, selecting a darkened corner where we would not be disturbed by midnight strollers or the thriving street trade, single women in open cars and single boys on foot.

Donald ordered 'deux cognacs'. He asked if the movie had upset me. 'Oh, it's so awful,' I blurted out, 'but I think I'm in love with Kenneth.' Donald said nothing. He gently placed his hand over mine. I looked at Donald. 'What am I going to do?'

We finished our cognacs and reordered. Thoughtfully, firmly, Donald counselled that proper emotional timing for an affair was essential on both sides and I must consider Kenneth's feelings too without making a pest of myself. Pest! I shuddered. What an ignominious word. Children and the inexperienced were pests. Kenneth preferred older women.

'How old?' I demanded.

'Not twenty and not virgins,' Donald answered. Kenneth had had a liaison in New York with the dramatic dancer Nora Kaye when he was guest choreographer for the American Ballet Theatre. It had been a frothy adventure, because Kenneth did not want a heavy amorous entanglement. Not yet. I trusted Donald. He had known Kenneth for a couple of years. And when he advised me to suppress my immature outbursts, although his phrasing was more felicitous, I promised, vowed, swore up and down, that such an incident would not happen again. None as far as I can recall ever did, and I decided not to go round baring the secrets of my heart to my dearest mates.

My little drama was mercifully and comically defused the next afternoon. Our holiday was almost at an end. But the scene at least conformed to the time and place: French bedroom farce.

Before apéritifs at six we took siestas in our rooms. Unbeknownst to us, Mossy had a thumping pash for Donald. Drenched in perfume and sashed in her unrestrained satin wrapper she noiselessly surprised the young Scot in his room as he dozed on the bed in his skivvies. Donald was exhausted from his summit conference with me. He smelled perfume. Jasmine. An eye opened and he saw Mossy floating towards him. Donald muttered, 'This is all getting to be *too much*.'

Mossy pounced on the bed.

'What do you want?' he asked idiotically.

'Darling, what do I *want*?' she repeated. 'Must you ask?' They rolled on the bed, back and forth.

'Lynn or Kenneth may come knocking at any moment.' Mossy shook her head and assured him that I was asleep. 'Lynn never sleeps!' he shouted and landed on the floor with a thud.

'Why do you think I gave you all those privates on the Aussie tour?' Mossy said, thoroughly dishevelled from the struggle. She was out of breath. 'Privates' is slang for special coaching between a dancer and a ballet-master/ mistress. Obviously privates can assume a sportive nature that pushes careers.

Donald got up off the floor and sat on the window ledge. It seemed safer than the bed. Mossy gathered herself together. 'I don't mean to be priggish,' Donald said, 'but this is just *not* the right time, if you know what I mean.'

She closed her eyes wearily and asked for a cigarette. He gave her a pack. 'If anyone asks, just say I came to borrow some cigarettes,' she said, and then, with a sensational toss of her blond hair, bleached white by the sun, she opened the door and drifted out. It all happened in about thirty seconds.

Donald recounted the story as we walked to the sidewalk café where we were to meet Mossy and Kenneth. I laughed so hard, with such welcome relief, that he had to hold me up. 'What an amazing holiday! We only have two more days. We really must watch our manners.'

The evening was excessively merry. We all went dancing. I still did not know how to 'social dance' but had practised the cha-cha in London and it was the one step we knew how to perform with high-voltage precision. Our cha-cha elicited more '*magnifiques!*' than the floor show. We concluded the light-hearted night with a bottle of champagne and bought photographs of ourselves from the club photographer. Looking at the picture today I notice that our eyes are a wee bit sad. It had all been too marvellous – the sunshine, the sea, the companionship.

On our final day we dallied on the beach until the last minute, resisting the return to London and our grey life in one-room flats and rehearsal studios. Salty and sandy in beach togs we almost missed the coach to St Raphael. Once there we dallied over drinks in a café and almost missed the train to Paris. We literally scrambled aboard just as it was leaving the station. Kenneth heaved Mossy and me into the vestibule of the wagon-lit, jumped in and then all hands reached out for Donald, running wildly to keep up with the steadily moving train. He landed on top of us, hardly the most composed entrance on The Blue Train.

We did not talk much on the journey home. Our picture postcard vacation was over. The whirligig revelations, all perimeters defined, drew us closer together. Donald and I would continue rehearsing a tepid ballet by Andrée Howard called *La Belle Dame Sans Merci*. We thought the singsong title sounded like a convent in suburban Paris. I played a belle who seduced six gallants.

As usual, in London, I confronted another new address, a vicarage, of all places, in Kensington. Winifred Edwards, ever-considerate, had secured the lodgings with a vicar, his crippled mother and her nurse, an elephantine woman with a stormy red face. The house was dark and dreary. I envied the dancers who lived with their parents or relatives. Our group split up at Victoria Station. Mossy kissed us goodbye, then dashed off to meet Henry Legerton. Kenneth, Donald and I took the underground to our separate abodes, murmuring sad farewells.

I spent the afternoon in my room, suitcase thrown open on the floor, dirty clothes and underwear scattered everywhere, shutting my eyes to the sombre severity of the cubicle and fighting a sense of solitary confinement. I started some letters, pushed them aside and paced restlessly back and forth. No one waited for me in London. No one waited for me anywhere. And after my holiday 'high' I did not want to be alone. I lay down on the bed, trembling and chilled. I longed for the sunshine and music of St Tropez, I longed for the ceaselessly cheerful camaraderie of my chaps, Kenneth and Donald. I made myself a cup of weak tea and was sitting forlornly in the kitchen when the telephone rang. It was Kenneth, and not a moment too soon.

'What are you doing?'

'Nothing.'

'What are you doing for dinner?'

'Nothing.'

'Let's go someplace. I don't want to sit in my room. It's so *grey*. I'll ring up Donald.'

'Yes! Then call me back.'

When I did not hear from Kenneth for half an hour I nervously called him. Had they made plans without me? 'Donald isn't answering,' Kenneth sighed. 'He's probably *washing*.'

Time passed. Then I telephoned Donald. 'Kenneth has been trying to reach you. We're going to dinner.' There followed a series of phone calls about where to meet and when. We decided on a bistro in Soho at seven-thirty. I began sorting out my clothes and then without warning suddenly panicked. I was afraid to leave the vicarage alone. I was afraid to ride the underground alone. How childish, how stupidly childish can one get? I asked myself, bathing my forehead with a damp cloth. I sank on to the bed hugging a pillow. Control yourself, girl, control yourself. I telephoned Kenneth. 'I'm having a bit of trouble, darling,' I said haltingly. 'Could you and Donald fetch me in a taxi?' Kenneth understood. He was feeling rocky too.

An hour later we three were in a taxi, crawling in the

evening traffic towards Soho. I sat between the chaps, secure and tranquil again. Rain pattered against the windows. 'You're still brown,' Kenneth said softly, with a sly smile.

Linking arms we all shouted in a chorus, '*Don't say brown, say Hovis.*'

CHAPTER 8

Bring On the Dancing Girls

'What did you do with that Sherlock Holmes coat? It was so big and you were so small. It made you look like a homeless little waif.'

Chewing on a celery stalk I laughed. 'After the Australian tour, I saved up my money and, one year later, with a cheque from home, I finally had enough to buy a new coat,' I said to my dinner guest Jeffrey Solomons, whom I had not seen in yonks, or at least since my second marriage. Jeffrey, a gangly, cuddly man, sat at the dining-room table, patiently waiting for me to finish brewing a cauldron of soup-and-stew. The children were snug in their beds, and Jeffrey and I were having a late-night supper.

'Do come round,' I had said on the spur of the moment. 'I'm not much in the mood for cooking, but I need to clean out the fridge. I'll throw everything into a pot.' He had planned to go to the cinema with a friend named Nigel. 'Bring him too, darling. I'm longing to hug you. Too much time has gone by.' After my last defection from the Royal Ballet I had time to see old mates, so I was frequently on the telephone scribbling luncheon and dinner dates into the Talmud. I did not call at random. I still lacked the courage to telephone Madam.

Jeffrey Solomons was Kenneth's confidant for many years and when our lives intersected after the St Tropez summer, Jeffrey quickly became someone I adored. He has a marvellous wit, a keen mind and an acute understanding of people. There is not a hypocritical bone in his body. He has a clear sense of identity and has always been completely honest about himself and others, including me. I respect these qualities very much. An authority on ballet and music and art, Jeffrey is an art dealer who first introduced me to abstract expressionism and pop. He took me to a Mark Rothko retrospective in 1961 and forced me to study Rothko's intense bursts of colour, painted on large canvases in rectangular configurations. 'Unabashedly emotional – poetic – even Impressionistic,' Jeffrey explained as we wandered among the paintings at the Whitechapel Gallery.

We listened to recordings of Mahler and Stravinsky, and saw film classics at the National Film Theatre. There was very little he did not know. Kenneth, he mentioned, for example, thought the choreography of Jack Cole was terrific. I hadn't the foggiest as to who Jack Cole was. But I learned that he staged the musical sequences for dozens of Hollywood movies (*Gilda*, *Cover Girl*, *Gentlemen Prefer Blondes*) and Broadway shows. Jack Cole was the only choreographer with his own stable of dancers under studio contract – Gwen Verdon, Buzz Miller, Carol Haney – and although he is a forgotten man of dance his work has inspired and influenced Agnes de Mille, Jerome Robbins and Bob Fosse. Kenneth liked his style – flagellant, opulent and sensuous with an underlying cross-current of conflict.

'You were amazingly intelligent and determined to learn,' Jeffrey said as I poured the stew into a tureen and carried it to the table.

I asked his friend Nigel to light the candles. Nigel's head was completely shorn of hair. He was quite striking. 'Jeffrey, you know the dishiest chaps.'

'But so do you, Lynn. Shall we compare notes?'

'We must. After dinner.' I peered into the stew. 'I'm calling it pot-*luck*.' We were bantering just as we had more than twenty years before when I announced to him, 'I'm a hick. If you step off Vancouver you'll fall off the world.'

Jeffrey turned to Nigel. 'When I first saw her in the foyer at the Sadler's Wells Theatre I thought she was a kooky little girl. Then I heard Kenneth talking about her beautiful arms. Kenneth said, "Her movement is very luscious." He found the general style of the Royal Ballet extremely arch. Lynn was not "arch". She was a very direct dancer.'

Nobody was eating the soup. I had neglected to put soup spoons on the table as well as a fresh loaf of bread. My attention had been focused on Jeffrey, listening to him as I had in the past and learning a bit about myself. Jeffrey and I got the giggles. 'She isn't kooky at all, Nigel, that's the point. It's one of the great Seymour myths.' Nigel fetched the bread and spoons. I leaned over and gave Jeffrey a kiss. 'But she is an odd little thing,' Jeffrey said as Nigel served the stew. 'Odd little thing offstage and then onstage she was someone quite different. Someone we didn't know. That's what stunned and fascinated Kenneth. That's what stunned us all.' Jeffrey sipped the soupy stew. 'Quite good, my dear,' he said. 'Much better than your tuna-fish casserole.'

When I met Jeffrey, Mom's tuna-fish casserole with crisps on top was the only dish I knew how to prepare. But once I was accepted by Kenneth – and Jeffrey – I studied cookbooks because our motley group, which Fred Ashton tabbed the Diners' Club, began meeting weekly for dinners in restaurants or in each other's flats. The Diners' Club membership varied through the early sixties. The initial roster was Kenneth, Jeffrey, Donald MacLeary, designer Nicholas Georgiadis, editor Peter Williams and myself. We were joined from time to time by designer Kenneth Rowell and his then wife Diana. Later Christopher Gable and his wife, an exceptionally intelligent dancer named Carole Needham, were in the club. Ashton said that you had to be a member of the Diners' Club to get into one of Kenneth's ballets, but that was just amusing hyperbole. Kenneth encircled himself with a tightly knit group of people whom he liked and depended upon, and that group doted on him. Ashton had his own clique which we called the Royal

Family. Certainly as Kenneth's reputation increased the management realized that the two choreographers had their own private admiration societies. 'We are *one* organization,' Madam stressed, not wanting to see the company divided into two camps, no pun intended, I think.

'Have you seen Puss lately?' Jeffrey asked.

'Just last week.'

Nigel was bewildered. 'Who's Puss?'

'Donald MacLeary,' answered Jeffrey. We all had nicknames. Donald was called Puss because of a joke he told. The punch-line ended in a meowing-pussy-scratch gesture. Peter Williams was Poffer. Poffer of Poffington. Very upright and grand, with a long cigarette holder. A dancer who came and went briefly was called Vida after nasty Ann Blyth in *Mildred Pierce*. Vida would steal anyone's lover, including his mother's, said Jeffrey, if she had one. 'And I was called Becky,' he explained, 'because it sounded so Jewish.'

I dunked a slice of bread into my soup bowl. 'They called *me* Thinnie Lynnie. The beasts.'

Nigel washed down his stew with a glass of wine and looked at us dazed, as if he had accidentally walked into some secret and ritualistic party. Poffer. Puss. Becky. Vida. Heavens, what must the poor lad have thought? But our nicknames and code language helped relieve myriad tensions.

'Thinnie Lynnie?' murmured Jeffrey. 'That must have been later, when I wasn't around. I remember Kenneth always called you *La* Lynnie.'

Nigel set down his spoon with a resigned sigh. 'What was Kenneth called?'

Conversation stopped. Jeffrey and I stared at each other. A smile broke across Jeffrey's lips, but his voice seemed to have faded away. When he spoke it was raised scarcely above a whisper. 'Kenneth?' he asked, gently squeezing my fingers. 'Kenneth was always,' he said, with a jack-o'-lantern grin, 'just Kenneth.'

The summer preceding my *Swan Lake* début in Australia I visited my parents in Vancouver. Mom and Dad had moved from our old house with a rose trellis, which I once used as a barre, to an apartment. 'You won't be living with us again, honey,' Mom said. 'We've lost you to London.' They bought me new clothes at a department store where Mom worked part-time and then we drove to San Francisco. Bruce was married and finishing dental school there. He bartended at night in a saloon called the Red Garter in the raffish North Beach area. His wife Patricia was expecting their first child. The 'Beat Generation' poets and writers of the fifties, such as Jack Kerouac, put North Beach on the tourist map. Bruce and I went to scruffy coffee-house clubs where 'Beat' poetry was read and jazz was played. Bruce also walked me up creaky staircases to obscure Chinese dens. Waiters with long braided pigtails, doped to the gills on opium, perhaps, sat us down on bamboo mats and served cups of thick sweet tea. We even ventured into a famous transvestite cabaret. A painted and powdered entertainer in a jewelled costume who called himself Lola Montes flung rubber spiders on the stage and danced around them, swatting the spiders with a riding crop. 'I am Lola, mistress of King Ludwig,' he lisped. 'Ludie's last gift to me,' and he-she spun the whip, 'was the clap.' That was the cue for the crowd to applaud. Lola Montes then engaged in some primordial kicks. I absorbed everything, calmly smoking a cigarette. Bruce was impressed by my sophistication. It was only skin deep.

On nights when Bruce mixed drinks I sat at the bar waiting for him to finish work. The Red Garter was one of those joints with sawdust on the floor. The waiters wore boaters, striped shirts and red braces. The women who frequented the saloon, and quite a few of the men too, could not take their eyes off Bruce. I was very proud of him. 'I wish I could show you off in London,' I said, but he never crossed the Atlantic, alone or with his family.

Remembering my early letters, Bruce asked about my friends – who they were and how many did I have. I explained that since I was always on tour it was difficult to make solid, lasting friendships, but there was one chap I liked very much, a bashful type who spent Saturday afternoons with his mates at a restaurant in Soho. I did not know how to crash the party. The Red Garter served its drinks on cork coasters. Imprinted on the coasters was a nude woman of ample proportions, perched on a bar stool with a straw boater set at an inviting angle. The coasters carried the exclamatory demand: 'Bring On the Dancing Girls!' Bruce put six coasters in a paper bag. 'Pass them out to your pals. Don't be a bashful type yourself.'

Jeffrey Solomons, I had discovered, often waited for Kenneth in a pub opposite the stage door at Covent Garden. I had had a lager one noonday and sat down next to him, a muffet on a tuffet. 'Do you like walking?' I asked. Yes, Jeffrey answered, gazing intently at me. 'Would you like to go for a walk with me?' Yes, he answered again, and we strolled around the market and flower stalls of Covent Garden. It was very pleasant being with him. We talked about *The Burrow* and Madam and Kenneth. Then glancing at his wristwatch he said that he had to run; it was Saturday and he always lunched with Kenneth and Nico at Madame Maurer's in Soho. They were probably looking for him at the pub. Madame Maurer, a plump Bavarian Frau from Munich, served heaped portions of heavy German food. If she liked you the bill was low. If you were not her 'sort of person' the price was so high you never went back again. There were only eight tables in the cubby-hole restaurant usually occupied by actors and dancers with little money –

her 'sort of people'. Longing to be accepted socially by Kenneth and his intimates, Jeffrey and Nico, I decided, quite literally, to crash their luncheon the Saturday before flying to Australia. Party-crashing is a risky way of winning approval, but, I thought, it was now or never. I missed masculine companionship. The three chaps, several years my senior, were sensitive and sweet and chock-full of knowledge that I wanted. Burying the coasters in one of the half-dozen pockets of my Sherlock Holmes coat, I set off for Greek Street in Soho on a drizzly afternoon. Their lunches started around one o'clock, went on until six and concluded at a cinema. If my bolt from the blue entrance met with disaster, I would be in Australia for eight months, time enough for the intrusion to be forgiven.

They were flabbergasted to see me.

I barged right up to their table, fished out the coasters and said in a small voice, 'Here's a memento from San Francisco.'

I gave them two each. There was an uncomfortable silence. Biting my lip I turned to walk away. Nico spoke up. 'Lynn, come back. Please, you must join us.' I dashed to the table, and sat down beside Nico. When they politely asked about San Francisco, puzzling over the cork coasters, I let forth a giddy account of Lola Montes. They howled. '*You* were in that club?' Yes, yes, yes. They howled louder. Acceptance! I ordered a baked potato, surely the best I ever tasted. Did I want to go to the cinema with them? Oh, yes. Unofficially that was the first meeting of the Diners' Club.

Regular 'club' meetings did not resume until one year later, with *Swan Lake* and St Tropez in the recent past. It was autumn and a foot injury knocked me out of the first weeks of the provincial tour. I had been learning three ballets – *La Belle Dame Sans Merci*, *The Sleeping Beauty* and *Solitaire*. Rehearsals had been tense and fatiguing. Dancing is as precarious as tightrope walking. One mental or physical slip and there's a plummeting fall. The strain sapped me and I sprained my ankle. I was not even allowed to take class. I thought: That's it, I'll never dance again, I won't be able to catch up with the others. In a letter home I lamented, 'It's extraordinary how, once one has the self-discipline of class, one's life falls into a more disciplinary pattern. I am nearly a case for the nut house.' Eventually I was allowed to take class for half an hour and have private coaching lessons with Winifred Edwards. But I did not dance for most of that autumn.

The Diners' Club – long convivial Saturday lunches, followed by a film – saved me from complete despondency. At last I had a 'family' in London: Kenneth, Jeffrey and Nico. We went to museums and art galleries and saw the new plays by Harold Pinter and John Osborne. On Sundays when London shut down we had tea parties, usually in Belgravia at the flat of Peter (Poffer) Williams. '*You don't fit in here.*' The words had haunted me for years. But now I did fit in, now I belonged.

'You can't stay at the vicarage,' Jeffrey groaned. 'It sounds frightful.'

'The atmosphere cannot be good for you,' Nico agreed.

The pious tiptoeing solemnity was not improving my perverse soul or spiritually depressed mind, so I rented a top-floor room in the home of a dancer named Clover Roope. Clover had been at school with me and had graduated into the main company. She was the first person we knew who owned a tape recorder and on many rainy Sundays the Club gathered in her sitting room for 'electronic' concerts which we taped. Our antic musical group was called the Lesbos Ensemble.

The American composer John Cage was then the rage of the avant-garde. Cage created his own form of music with new sounds from non-harmonic instruments fashioned out of Dadaesque junk – electric buzzers, aspirin bottles, whistles, and screws and bolts installed between the strings of a 'prepared piano'. Accordingly the Lesbos Ensemble composed and taped a twelve-minute composition, *Fanny or the Demon Barber of Fleet Street*, a sonorous send-up of Cage. Jeffrey dropped shillings into milk bottles full of water. Nico uttered muffled noises in Greek. Clover sang into a dustbin with a paper bag inside. I hammered on a leather suitcase with a wooden spoon. Kenneth of course conducted.

'Is Puss coming?'

'Not until later. He has a date.'

'*Really?* With whom?'

'He didn't say.'

'In that case we shan't wait. Is the Lesbos Ensemble ready?' We ran to our places and seized our instruments. Kenneth pointed to the Vibrowumphff, Clover's instrument which opened the concert, and pressed the tape recorder.

Wumphff! Plink-plink-thud!

Bang-plunk-apopoulus-plunk-ping-wumphff!

The sitting-room door opened. Donald stopped on the threshold in a raincoat, a cashmere scarf tied around his neck. 'What a lot of farting.'

Kenneth glared at Donald and waved a chop-stick baton. 'That was a *wumphff*. You've interrupted us. We must start again.' The Lesbos Ensemble was sprawled on the floor, laughing until the tears rolled.

'Isn't it wonderful to have Kenneth here to amuse us,' I said to Jeffrey.

'No, no, you have it all wrong,' he corrected. 'Kenneth thinks we're here to amuse *him*.'

Kenneth wandered over bearing a tray of cakes. 'Sweets?' he asked innocently. Jeffrey took two coconut cookies with a red cherry in the middle. We called them Nipples. I reached for one. Kenneth withdrew the tray in dismay.

'Isn't he dreadful?' Jeffrey said. 'You can nibble on my nipple.'

'*Becky*, that would be most improper. La Lynnie would be eating for two. Herself and Giselle. She may have four raisins.'

Madam had decreed that I should learn the classics. With my foot fully mended by Christmas – 'Slaving over a hot stove all day,' moaned Kenneth, who cooked a sumptuous roast beef Christmas dinner for Donald and me – I bid a temporary adieu to the Diners' Club and rejoined the touring company in Brighton where I began rehearsing *Giselle*. A Garden performance was scheduled for early March.

I spent mornings on *Giselle* and afternoons with Sergei Grigoriev who was coaching me in *Les Sylphides*. It was a privilege to be working with Grigoriev, then seventy-three years old. He had been régisseur for Diaghilev's company and had seen Fokine's ballet mounted for the Paris season of 1909. He had perfect recall and subsequently restaged many of these masterpieces for the Royal Ballet. The principal dancers were Karsavina, Nijinsky and Pavlova. Madam wanted him and his wife Liubov Tchernicheva to enrich us with their first-hand knowledge of dance history, which keeps the classics historically accurate and a company historically alive. Ballets are 'preserved' today on videotape. But this is a comparatively new memory-bank for choreographers. The subtleties and nuances of a performance can only be gleaned from a living performer or coach who participated in the original production. I learned both the Karsavina and Pavlova roles. Karsavina, he recalled, had the slowly floating-to-earth quality of autumn leaves. Pavlova leaped through the forest like a mountain stag. His wife adored Christopher Gable who was dancing the Nijinsky role. She showed Christopher how Nijinsky delicately fondled the ringlets on his wig and then touched his shoulder with his hand – an absent-minded gesture, in reverie. In a ballet these details are like the shading light of a lamp in a brightly lit room.

Giselle was far more problematic than a sylphide. That little peasant girl haunted me, as a theatrical riddle, for years.

One of the most popular ballets, *Giselle* balances romanticism and mysticism in a story of the unattainable perfect love. Balletomanes, critics and dance historians flock to *Giselle* to compare and contrast Fonteyn and Alicia Alonso, Beriosova and Antoinette Sibley, Natalia Makarova and Gelsey Kirkland. There are a few people around who may recall performances by Pavlova, Karsavina and Spessivtseva.

Giselle's plight: she falls in love with a man she can never have, a playboy prince betrothed to a noblewoman. Discovering that he deceived her into believing he was just another ruddy peasant, she goes mad, dies of a broken heart, and becomes a spirit in the supernatural world – or is it just the imagination of the remorseful prince? A ballet of emotional and stylistic complexity, it moves from a rustic village on the Rhine into a fantasy forest glade. 'It is a thoroughly deceptive role,' Peter Williams cautioned at a meeting of the Diners' Club. 'Technique alone won't make Giselle work. She has to be completely convincing, first as an innocent passionate human and then as a tragically lost spiritual being.' I called myself the Great Sponge because I absorbed all the dance information possible in Poffer's smoky salon where we drank gin and Dubonnet. Like journalists, actors, professors or artists anywhere, the Club not only gossiped and giggled but also talked a lot of serious shop.

The key to Giselle's character is her death – the mad scene. I could not understand the motivation of her collapse unless it was mental. Giselle had been romantically deceived, but then who hasn't? There seemed to be very little logic behind her lunatic disintegration. And when I danced Giselle, it was an absurdity to portray her as a fragile flower who died of a broken heart. I don't look flowery or fragile. Nonetheless I sweated on the role in the provinces and in London. At the age of twenty I had danced *Swan Lake*. Now, one year later, Madam was presenting me in *Giselle*. There were churlish remarks that the path to ballerina-status was being laid out 'like a red carpet', but Madam had placed utter confidence in me. Instead of floating high on a cloud of elation I was unable to sleep nights. A migraine stomach had me hobbling around the bathroom in pain. I envisioned myself onstage, unable to finish a movement and ending up on my bum. The ultimate terror. The Diners' Club was a supportive rooting team. When the riotous laughter stopped, laughter which steadied jangled nerves, my 'family' was there, loyal to the last beat.

I danced Giselle at the Garden as an impulsive girl consumed by love who goes mad without warning. And that vexed me. I was bouncy and exuberant, radiant and confident and healthy – 'a Giselle by Rubens', remarked one critic who found it unlikely my Giselle would die of love, true or false. But I was also described as 'a true original' and the *Observer*'s Alexander Bland stated that I was as different from the run of home-trained dancers as butter from margarine. 'It is now practically certain she will be the British ballet star of the future.'

I had not let Madam down. I had not disappointed her.

Dancing Giselle over the years I was never quite satisfied with the concluding first-act mad scene, even when I removed all 'bounce'. It still seemed like silly nonsense. The difficult second act of pure dancing in the supernatural world never presented a problem of 'logic' – or caused me too much technical anxiety. When I solved the riddle, her death was acceptable and the ballet, as a whole, became dramatically valid. Giselle, I decided, did not look like the rest of the peasant girls. She was a wee bit different. She never cavorted with the peasants; she was never out gathering grapes, or whatever peasants do along the Rhine. Her mother probably brushed her hair for hours. She did not have much fun at all, poor sensitive thing, until she fell manically in love with the disguised prince. She depended on that stalwart youth and when she learned of his deception, of his nobility, she simply snapped. Her dreams for her future dashed, she did not wish to live any more. And so she killed herself. The story, as danced in the first act, became plausible. She was not frail but rather a highly-strung individual who suddenly committed a savage act against herself. However, it was quite a while before I was allowed to dance that interpretation at Covent Garden.

Giselle was no sooner performed and in my rep than I started rehearsing Kenneth MacMillan's new ballet, *Le Baiser de la Fée* (*The Fairy's Kiss*). Kenneth mulled his ballets for months, poring over the scenario once it was ready, listening and listening to every note of the score, imagining steps and combinations thereof, and jotting down concepts for the sets and costumes. He created ballets as a cohesive unit, contemplating the artistic ingredients as an artist considers his canvas, brushes, and paint in relation to his images. His eye encompasses the ballet virtually down to the last detail. For this reason Kenneth likes his collaborators, designers and dancers around him as part of his daily life. They are necessary 'tools' in the MacMillan atelier. On our St Tropez holiday Kenneth had said that he wanted to choreograph a ballet for Donald and me. What emerged was his extremely personal version of a Stravinsky work first produced in the late twenties.

Kenneth was enthralled by the brilliant composer and had choreographed other ballets to his music. He also wanted to demonstrate that he could effectively stage a romantic ballet in the 'classic' idiom. Stravinsky's scenario was drawn from *The Ice Maiden*, a Hans Christian Andersen story about a young bride who loses her fiancé to a fairy who kissed him at birth. It was dedicated to Tchaikovsky and is an arrangement of Tchaikovsky melodies. Stravinsky wrote that Tchaikovsky had been marked with a fatal kiss, a mysterious mark of genius that set him apart from other artists. The fairy represented Tchaikovsky's artistic muse. Freudian specialists believe that the 'fatal kiss' is a reference to Tchaikovsky's homosexuality that further set him apart in torment from society. This material of magic kisses in never-never-land, of fairies and gypsies and villagers, does not seem particularly MacMillanesque. But Kenneth saw the ballet as a study of alienation, a recurring theme in his work. He did not identify with the young man or the ravishing Ice Queen who both achieve some kind of satisfaction in the beyond; he identified with the betrayed bride who is left in the lurch.

'She's the one who is lost,' he said, fingering a glass of wine as Stravinsky's music came to an end on the record player in Poffer's flat, an uncommonly cosy room lined with books, dance photographs, leather chairs and cushions, where the Diners' Club spent many Sundays discussing *Baiser*. Some people, Kenneth ruminated, would always be alone. I knew exactly what he meant. Donald would dance the graceful fiancé snatched away from me, the pathetic bride, by the imperious, enigmatic Svetlana Beriosova. 'At the conclusion, you'll be alone,' murmured Kenneth, 'hopelessly searching for your lost love in the fresh snow.' Sitting on the floor I shivered involuntarily, staring at the flickering flames in the fireplace.

Kenneth specifically did not want a cutesy-wootsy rendition of fairyland. 'Oh, no, no, not *that*!' we all exclaimed heartily. Our esteemed host Poffer, refilling glasses and offering light snacks, allowed that fairyland, as traditionally depicted onstage, was, 'Let's be frank, duckies, a crashing bore.' So designer Ken Rowell extended himself, conjuring up a threatening landscape of abstract icebergs and rock formations. To those with a knowledge of art, such as Poffer himself, the ambitious sets evoked the ominous alien world of Max Ernst and Tchelitchev, a world inhabited by dark, deranged dream-monsters. The meetings of the Diners' Club expanded my education, from modern music to surreal art. Even when our behaviour was ribald, as with the Lesbos Ensemble, I acquired bits and bobs of erudition.

Sexuality, in all its unpoetic aspects, was also discussed and we tittered over juicy morsels, passed along like hors d'oeuvres on a dish of indiscretion, as to the latest supposedly secret seduction at the Garden. Madam deplored hanky-panky within the ranks, but deceits of the flesh went on aplenty. One simply turned the other cheek. The only club member who openly admitted to having a private life was Jeffrey Solomons. He always wanted to bring a current favourite to dinner. 'But will your guest amuse me?' Kenneth drawled, daring Jeffrey to lumber us with a Potential Bore. Donald frequently missed meetings. Svetlana Beriosova was acquainting him with *la jeunesse dorée* of London. 'Now, Puss, where did you find that silver cigarette lighter?' Kenneth would ask, lounging on a stack of pillows at Poffer's, and moodily exhaling a stream of cigarette smoke. 'No one gives *me* expensive presents.'

I had turned my mind off sex. I was too preoccupied with the cycle of roles I was performing and the rapture of creating a new ballet with Kenneth. My emotions were put in storage, so to speak. But Kenneth and I, alone together, timorously wondered aloud about the romantic nature of love and what it would be like finding some kind of satisfaction with that very special person. At night I fell asleep dreaming only of *Baiser*. I would envision the ballet, step by step. Tossing in bed after an arduous rehearsal, I suddenly 'saw' a movement I wanted to do. The next morning I rang up Kenneth and excitedly related the pattern. Then I hurried to Barons Court. He was already there, smoking and sipping coffee. I did it for him: spin-spin-spin, *melt*. 'It's the Violet Crumble,' he said ecstatically. Thereafter when he wanted my signature movement he would say, 'Violet Crumble'. Our code vocabulary increased.

Weekday rehearsals. Saturday at Madame Maurer's and then a film, usually a Hollywood classic or the French *nouvelle vague*. And Sunday the Diners' Club. In between constant telephone calls with Kenneth on *Baiser* and Jeffrey Solomons on the state of the world. Our deceptively cloudless world of fierce cravings, wistful obsessions and forbidden dreams. I had stopped eating anything except cheese and boiled eggs. With *Baiser*'s April opening only days away nothing else went down. 'Lynnie, the club meets at my flat tomorrow,' Jeffrey would say. 'What would you like? A ripe Brie?' Jeffrey had lived in Paris for a while after the war. He was a cheese and wine expert. But none of us had any money. 'Becky, you know I still adore plain old English cheddar,' I would reply.

If we all went to the French Club Peter Williams quietly picked up the bill. He was extremely generous. One night we sat around a big table – Kenneth, Peter, Ken Rowell and his wife Diana, a fashion model with a flowing mane of red hair. I was persuaded to order a chicken leg and eat what I could. Half-heartedly I forked the chicken, enviously staring at Diana Rowell's cheekbones. When I danced *Giselle* a critic hinted that my round cheeks needed shading. 'Bones!' I spluttered, flinging down the chicken leg, my appetite gone. Baffled eyes looked at my plate. 'Not that one,' I said, squeezing my cheeks. 'I want them here.' Diana Rowell came to my dressing room two days later with a box of paints and feathery brushes, and daubed my cheeks with light brown hues. I was, after all, dancing with the heavenly, womanly Beriosova, second at the Garden to Fonteyn. I did not want to come off looking frumpy. When I inspected myself in the mirror, yes, I had bones. I ran to the wardrobe department where Kenneth was fretting over the completion of the costumes. He held up one of mine – a pink cape with white embroidery – but I didn't see it. 'Kenneth, bones, bones!' I cried delightedly.

He giggled, 'Oh, you *are* dotty.'

The press interviewed me just before the opening. I smothered the tension within by issuing some outrageous quotes. Outrageous, that is, for a 'rising star' at Covent Garden. Asked about the dietary problems of a dancer I chirped, 'A little whisky's good for you – just like tea,' and went on to say, 'I'm mad about ice-cream, too.' I detest ice-cream and I only occasionally drank whisky. As for the ballet? 'Sometimes I ask myself why I go on with this dreary old drudge,' I continued, 'and then I get caught up in it all over again.' Fleet Street discovered that I made good copy. I was not Miss Dainty Little Two-Shoes, ever so prim, ever so perfect. When the feature appeared, however, I worried that Madam would be non-plussed by such uninhibited disclosures. She wasn't but I suspect others flinched. 'You're not British,' consoled Diana Rowell, 'so you're not expected to sound like some nice little dancer from Ipswich.' Chrisopher Gable said pridefully, 'No one in the Royal Ballet *ever* made such public statements, "A little whisky's good for you!" Oh, Lynnie, how smashing.'

Baiser was Kenneth's homage to Frederick Ashton, who had mounted his version in the late thirties with Margot Fonteyn as the bride. The parallels of Ashton-Fonteyn and MacMillan-Seymour did not go unnoticed in print or backstage at the Garden. I trod gingerly on the 'red carpet', not wanting to trip. The allusions to Fonteyn and the possibility that future dance historians would find the casting significant left me, after the première, lying nervously awake until four in the morning, dreading the second performance, which frightened me more than the first. The ballet received curious reviews. One critic recalled that neither the original nor productions by Ashton or George Balanchine had survived and was dubious about Kenneth's version. Richard Buckle in the *Sunday Times* hailed it as a tremendous success, and was captivated by the 'shimmering insect splendour' of the choreography. The hard-edged sets troubled traditionalists but Dicky Buckle endorsed this new kind of fairyland, saying we had seen enough gothic, baroque and rococo. The performances were found charming and spontaneous. It was observed that after the drama of *Swan Lake* and *Giselle* I had an opportunity to exhibit 'an enchanting piquancy and irresistible pathos'.

All in all, the rave personal reviews describing me as triumphant in a ballet of icy beauty froze my heart. The wise-cracking Lynn Seymour who prattled to the press about her extravagances, shoes and scent, was a miserable bunch of humanity suffering from bottled-up fears. Performing fears. I spent Sunday in bed. The Diners' Club sent fruit juices, cheese and mineral water to my room. I needed someone to assure me that I could do the second performance. I simply needed an uncritical confidant to whom I could spill out my heart. Another dancer was useless. My career was moving upwards so fast that the slightest suggestion of weakness would result in scornful glances. And since I did not want the Diners' Club to think me childish I could not go weeping to them. I was fifteen years old again, in the Fisher house on Orsett Terrace, desperately crying for assurances from Mom. But I had lost my parents years ago the day my plane first took off from Vancouver. My heart began skipping beats. I rang up Kenneth and asked him to send round his doctor, 'but don't tell anyone,' I said. In a letter home I whimpered: 'The doctor came, he was terribly sweet and explained that all I had to do was relax and stop the anxiety, but how can I?' He prescribed some tranquillizers. I slept peacefully for several hours and then went for a promenade on the King's Road with Kenneth and Jeffrey. 'How about a hot fudge sundae piled high with nuts and whipped cream?' Jeffrey said, giving me a sidelong look. 'You *are* mad about ice-cream, aren't you?' I leaned against his shoulder and felt much better instantly.

When the monthly magazine 'crits' appeared, one reviewer expressed his disgruntlement over Beriosova's 'pink cheeks'. Svetlana Beriosova has exceptional bone structure. But criticism is personal or it is nothing. Diana Rowell and I had some thumping laughs. 'You gave me cheeks, Diana,' I said, hugging her. 'You see, I *know* what they look for.' A dancer learns that any imperfection, even 'pink cheeks', is fair game for criticism and my own camouflaged blemishes added to my fears. When I tussled later with weight problems – two or three pounds are enough to put ripples in your 'line' – Kenneth would say, 'You're not dancing tonight, it's for your own protection', and I would physically puff up in despair. Film stars go on strict diets before the start of a six-week shoot – and two months later the physical worry is over. A few extra pounds on a stage actor are seldom noticeable, not with clever costuming. But a dancer can never let go. Your body is exposed for two thousand people at a performance. Getting down to the nitty-gritty – and why not? – the public pays to see beautiful bodies in flight, to realize fantasies of grace and perfection. The American dance critic-essayist Carl Van Vechten said, 'Sex is both concealed and awakened.' This fosters a detestable narcissism among many dancers who are having love affairs with their form. To me it's onanistic.

Six months after the Garden première I was touring the provinces when the main company went to America. Madam had some news for me: I was to fly immediately to New York and dance three *Baiser* performances at the Metropolitan Opera House with Donald and Svetlana. I turned helplessly to Kenneth. 'There's nothing to be afraid of,' he counselled. 'It's a role you created. The critics can't compare you to predecessors.' Madam of course knew precisely what she was doing. For my first exposure to the tough New York critics and impresario Sol Hurok who arranged the American tours – and had input into the American rep, so I was told – the circumstances were perfect. Madam was not introducing me in a familiar classic but a new work by another protégé, Kenneth MacMillan. Naturally I caught a cold from the air-conditioning on the plane. I straggled through customs with a temperature and runny nose, and took a bleary-eyed taxi ride to a midtown hotel. Approaching the city for the first time in my life I gazed in awe at the monumental skyline, heart skipping beats again. The taxi was swallowed into the darkness of a tunnel and we surfaced in canyons of steel and glass and concrete. The immensity of New York left me breathless. I fell into bed with a raging fever. Svetlana came to my room, which overlooked a dismal air shaft, with flu-and-cold pills, ointments to rub on aching joints, throat lozenges and fruit juice. She also gave me a copy of the *New York Times* which carried an item headlined: BALLET STAR FLYING HERE FOR A ONE-ROLE STAND.

'That's you, Lynnie.' Svetlana forced two aspirin down my throat. 'You can't be sick. Madam would never forgive you,' she said sternly, 'and neither would Kenneth.'

Madam. Kenneth. 'Oh God,' I wailed.

I telephoned my parents in Vancouver who pepped me up. 'You'll be fine in the morning, honey,' Mom said. 'You'll give a great performance.' I begged Mom to tell me that again, more emphatically. She did. In the morning I felt absolutely rotten. Must I go through this torture before *every* performance? I asked myself. When Fred Ashton's *A Month in the Country* had its London premièrc in 1976 I lay abed with a 102-degree fever. The doctors did not know until two hours before curtain-time if I would be able to dance. Sir Fred was biting his fingernails at home, awaiting their decision. But I went on.

I bought some postcards in the hotel lobby and attempted to pay for them with a $100 bill, thinking it was one dollar or not thinking at all. Donald, who fetched me for the afternoon stage-call, settled the financial matter and trundled me into a taxi. We bumped down Broadway over sizzling pot-holes to the old Met on Thirty-ninth Street. *I'm not going to make it*, I thought, frantically holding on to Donald.

Backstage I glimpsed Madam's unmistakable shadow behind a costume rack. The hour had come to pull up the old socks or pull them off completely. I attempted napping in a dressing room after the rehearsal but two senior dancers, the most prim and proper *poseuses*, seemed intent on irritating me. They had bought a sex manual in a Times Square bookshop and were whooping hilariously over the drawings and text '. . . "put an ice pack on his balls" . . .' Screams of wicked laughter. Svetlana let me nap in her dressing room. Four aspirin later it was time to make up and warm up.

The gold curtain parted.

Madam sat in a box with Martha Graham. She had invited that consummate artist-actress and leader of modern dance in America to see me. Martha Graham's verdict was positive. 'She's got it,' she declared. 'I'd also like to see her in comedy.' It took Jerome Robbins to do that. The New York critics were rather cool towards *Baiser*, carping about an excess of décor and costumes and a not very danceable score. I was 'a darling' to one critic, 'scintillating' to a second and 'a brilliant seductress with a pair of supple steel pins for legs' to a third. The *Herald-Tribune* said that Kenneth MacMillan 'truly invented a new kind of movement for Lynn Seymour in which she seems fairly to melt from one step to another.'

Svetlana meanwhile had snaffled Donald for her partner in the main company. Madam saw that he was a fine physical match for the statuesque Svetlana. 'Lynn is average height,' Madam said. 'She can dance with anyone.' During Madam's reign you were assigned a partner and that was it; you tried to make it work as best as possible, without complaints. But times change. In the late seventies a technician with delusions of misplaced grandeur announced that she wouldn't dance with one young dynamo. Years earlier that same little vixen had lied about the hour of casting call to Brenda Bolton and several girls hanging around the Garden canteen. She was the only one to show up and she got the part.

I was livid when she pulled rank on a chap of terrific talent, for I remembered the male soloists who nursed and partnered me tenderly, without affectation – during my first shaky performances in *Swan Lake* and *Giselle*. I had a heated encounter with the artistic director Norman Morrice. 'There's constant talk about fairness at the Royal Ballet. Is it fair that he lose a performance because of this, this *person*? Madam would never permit such a thing. *Give him to me.*' He did and we danced a whiz-bang performance.

When the three *Baiser* performances were over I rejoined the touring company in Liverpool. The last days in New York I clung to Donald and Svetlana as I shuttled from my hotel and the Met to suppers at Sardi's and penthouse parties. I had a taste of society, like Cole Porter's oyster, and society had a taste of me, but I much preferred lunches at Madame Maurer's in Soho – pea-green walls with a faded mural and oil-cloths on the table. Despite all my efforts at glam, it is an 'act' which I can perform effectively, but an 'act' it is. If I try to name drop, you can be sure I'll get the names wrong. Essentially I'm still the girl in the Sherlock Holmes coat.

The kitchen clock on Woodstock Road struck twelve.

My stew of fridge left-overs was not bad at all. Nigel

kindly emptied the last drop into our soup bowls and I replaced the candles burnt down to the nub with fresh ones. It was so nice seeing Jeffrey. I wanted him to stay for hours and hours. 'You know I nearly choked on my Wiener Schnitzel when I saw you in the doorway that Saturday at Madame Maurer's, wearing your Sherlock Holmes coat, and dripping wet. Kenneth said to me, "My God, she has a nerve." We were quite hostile at first. Where did you get the nerve?'

I lit a cigarette and leaned my head against the back of the rocker which is placed at the head of the table. 'I honestly don't know. I liked you all and I just knew that I had to make some friends.'

'Kenneth was so reclusive, it was amazing how quickly he let you into his life,' said Jeffrey. 'I thought you might be inhibiting. I wanted to say, "No room! No room at the table!" But Nico was the mediator, and you sat down in that horrendous coat and handed out those dreadful little coasters.'

'Bring On the Dancing Girls!' I smiled at Jeffrey, not wanting to tell him that I still had a coaster tucked away in a box.

'We felt comfortable with you. It was instinctive.' Jeffrey pursed his lips and looked at me with a brooding, penetrating glitter in his eyes. 'And you smiled so beguilingly, it was almost sad.'

CHAPTER 9

Bouquets and Bows

Life hinges on chance and coincidence. A friend persuades you to attend a party and you meet your future lover. One day you're casually walking down the street when a car veers out of control and flattens you, breaking several bones. I am not religious. I do not believe in a Master Plan for our life. Neither do I believe 'Talent Will Out', a dumb cliché disproved by the mediocre talent often found at the powerful top. The role Fate plays in transforming lives can be either wonderful or frightening. My partnership with Christopher Gable was sheer happenstance. Fate brought us together and for four years we blazed brightly, two glorious shooting stars, scorching the moon in a glowing make-believe sky. And later Fate hurled us to earth, the bottom fell out of my world, and the lights went out. But, for a brief period, life onstage and off was one of total enchantment, and this is when it began.

During the *Baiser* production my friendship with Kenneth MacMillan deepened. We were chemically attuned to each other. We had a communion of spirit. I confided to a Canadian friend, 'My joy in being with him is really due to his way of transmitting *his* world to me and greatly appreciating what I have to offer him. You can imagine how my heart soared with that realization.' Kenneth was creating a new work, far removed from Hans Christian Andersen. He had merged Colette's novel *The Ripening Seed* with *House of the Angel* by a South American writer named Beatriz Guido. These novels about the loss of virginity were moulded by Kenneth into a dramatic scenario of innocence plundered. I was to portray a sensitive girl who has a fluttery flirtation with her handsome young cousin during a party at her home. The two are hothouse plants trembling with mutual longing but too awkward, too shy for anything more physical than passionate playing on the edge of a dangerously sexual garden. The fresh, dewy-eyed youngsters are enviously observed by a cynical married couple. The wife seduces the lad, who is grateful for his initiation with an older woman. But the girl's experience is brutalizing. Attracted to the husband, she coquettishly provokes him into an encounter which starts affectionately enough, and then becomes violent. The husband loses control and rapes her. Left alone in the garden, the girl is trapped in the silent agony of her despair, shunning the cousin whom she loves.

The sheltered girl, taunted by cruel children and forced to examine the nudity of male and female statues, is at the churning centre of this maelstrom which Kenneth called *The Invitation*. Her hidden desires, savagely released, have made her an alienated outsider for ever. It would not be a ballet, Kenneth mused, for those who attended tea-dances with Palm Court orchestras. 'When you lose your innocence, physically or psychologically, it can be a shattering experience. I'm interested in the way people behave. I'm sick of fairy tales.' With this balletically shocking material, reminiscent of Antony Tudor's *Pillar of Fire*, in which a rejected girl gives herself to a stranger, a theme further explored by Tennessee Williams in his play *Summer and Smoke*, Kenneth was determined to show the psychological damage of prudery and hypocrisy. His corrupted characters in the tragedy of manners, set in the Edwardian period, were not young adults, but self-conscious adolescents, starved of parental love and pleading for attention, as they try to reconcile physical hunger with suppressed emotions.

The ballet was a turbulent dance-drama of poetic imagery with tremendous acting requirements. 'Particular artists especially appeal to me,' Kenneth told an interviewer. 'Among dancers, for example, there is Lynn Seymour. She has a wonderfully expressive body, great musicality and independence. I try to cast dancers with something in their own personalities that might be in my story or theme.' He cast Anne Heaton (with whom I had danced in *The Burrow*) and Desmond Doyle as the jaded married couple. On the spring provincial tour I was dancing the lead in *Sleeping Beauty* and Desmond Doyle was my patient prince. He kissed me once after a performance and I fairly swooned. I informed the Diners' Club about the insignificant kiss; it seemed necessary to reveal some sexual trivia. Desmond Doyle was married and our involvement was confined to the stage. Christopher Gable was also on the tour. He played one of the suitors eager to win Aurora's royal hand.

Kenneth might have cast Donald MacLeary as the cousin, a part he danced much later, but he had already transferred to the main company. The chap that Kenneth wanted suffered a knee injury and quit the ballet to find a new career before it was too late. Dancers hate to hear about such injuries; the possibility of a crippling accident shadows every morning class, every rehearsal, every performance. It is another constant fear that fragments minds: '*Will I be next?*' Various replacements had been suggested but Kenneth was not enthused about any of them. He wanted an extremely youthful, virile dancer who could act with his face and hands and feet.

We were just beginning to rehearse *The Invitation* in Belfast when the tour ended. Rehearsals would resume again after our summer vacation. The ballet would have its première on the fall tour and then open at the Garden. In the interim I was flying to Canada for a month, but this time my trip was sponsored by the Vancouver Ballet Society which also agreed to finance a partner. I guessed, and correctly so, that Donald was lost to Svetlana. Remembering how Christopher and I had sparked in *Orpheus*, my eyes fell upon him. Christopher has an ebullient personality. He is funny and smart and sexy. He would make a super partner, I thought. A natural. Not just in Vancouver but in London. But you did not tell the management – at least in those days – whom you chose to dance with. Madam would have a conniption. I put the Vancouver offer to Christopher straightaway. Would he like an all expenses-paid trip to Canada in exchange for two evenings of duets from *Les Patineurs*, *Solitaire*,and *Don Quixote*. He said yes. I was delighted. (The Ballet Society had requested excerpts from *Swan Lake* and *Giselle* but I adamantly refused, explaining to Mom, 'They must be willing to see something new.' I drew up the programme and organized the music myself.) Christopher was just another boy in the company. He was getting bigger roles but, as he admits, nobody paid serious attention to him. One wet noonday in Belfast when an unexpected downpour splattered against the windows of a sandwich shop where Kenneth and I were having our ritualistic coffee, cigarettes and snacks, I said tentatively, 'What about Christopher for the cousin in *The Invitation*?' Kenneth puffed on his cigarette thoughtfully. 'He knows how to make a story come alive, he is an incredibly swift dancer and very musical. He dances the way the music sounds.' Kenneth listened in silence. 'You know I'm dragging him off to Canada with me for two dance concerts. We do *move* so well together.'

'It's an idea, Lynnie,' Kenneth said. 'I can have him learn the part,' he knocked the ash from his cigarette, 'and we'll see.'

That afternoon Christopher's name went up on the rehearsal sheet for *The Invitation*. He was speechless. 'Just wait until Kenneth sees us rehearse a pas de deux,' I said excitedly. We were a gorgeous complementary match and Kenneth watched us, two young innocents, expressing bewilderment and joy, with liquid arms and legs. He inclined his head with a veiled smile. The three of us were in sublime rapport.

In London I said goodbye to Kenneth, Jeffrey and Nico at Madame Maurer's. The sole luncheon conversation was Kenneth's new ballet. We all sensed that it was going to be an important controversial work. Nico was designing the scenery and Edwardian costumes evoking luxury and decadence with splashes of sun-kissed colours. He showed me the preliminary sketches for my entrance – a summer dress and a picture hat with gauzy flowers. The realistic drama would be framed impressionistically. Nico said that he wanted me to look as if I had stepped out of a painting by Renoir. I jotted down pages of notes from our conversation, slipped them into my tote bag with a copy of the Colette novel, which I would share with Christopher across the Atlantic, and then excused myself from the weekly cinema outing, for I still had to pack. Christopher and I were leaving for Canada in the morning. Thus began an escapade with Christopher Gable that consolidated our partnership, though, for a couple of moments in Amsterdam, I feared I had taxed his good nature.

'Amsterdam?' Jeffrey asked, when I dutifully recounted the epic excursion to the Diners' Club on my return. He turned in pseudo dismay to Kenneth and Nico. 'How peculiar. I always thought Canada was in the *opposite* direction.'

The Canadian flight, a no-frills venture, indeed started in the opposite direction. The cheapest fare was on a charter leaving from Amsterdam. But we were in high spirits and did not mind flying backwards, as it were, to reach Vancouver where the mayor himself would preside over a hometown-girl-makes-good ceremony at city hall. Mom warned that a mob of reporters and photographers would be awaiting 'Vancouver's own ballerina'. My carefully selected arrival clothes for 'the dentist's daughter', citizen of merit, would have warmed the cockles of Bobby Helpmann's heart. I wore a pearl-grey suit, black patent leather shoes and a floppy white Greta Garbo hat. As soon as the No Smoking sign blinked off and we ascended from Amsterdam into the sky above Holland, I doffed my finery and slipped into slacks and a knit jersey. Christopher changed from his smart brown suit into jeans and striped shirt. We hugged in excitement and ordered champagne, chattering as we sipped about the relationships of the cousins in *The Invitation* – their adolescent isolation and how it would be translated into Kenneth's balletic language.

'Kenneth's ballet is going to shake the roof off the Garden,' I said dreamily. 'Working with him is amazing, you'll see.'

'But – suppose he finds another dancer to replace me?'

'Oh, he won't. Kenneth thinks cinematically. He repeatedly says it's important for partners to have an emotional and physical mix. And Christopher, *we fit*.' That fit resulted in a mercurial excitement that inspired Kenneth and us. 'The three of you, what a team!' exclaimed Jeffrey Solomons years later after watching a rehearsal of *Romeo and Juliet*. Christopher and I expected to go on dancing together forever. Or until we were carried offstage.

Dad had sent me a sleeping pill so I could nap on the long flight and meet the mayor as fresh as a daisy. I swallowed the Seconal, instructing Christopher to wake me up one hour before we landed in Vancouver. Without a qualm in the world I sank peacefully into the arms of Morpheus, unaware, even while Christopher read the Colette novel, that the pilot was announcing engine trouble and a speedy return to Amsterdam. The passengers were shooed off the plane with their carry-ons. Assuming we would only be on the ground for an hour or two Christopher decided to let me sleep. The sepulchral silence must have discomforted my subconscious. I opened a heavy-lidded eye, looked around and saw vast rows of empty seats. The little buggers, I thought groggily, they've left me behind *somewhere*.

My small head, bobbing around at the rear of the plane, was seen by a stewardess who charged down the aisle. What was I doing there? she demanded. I had to get off instantly. We would not be leaving until morning. In my dopey condition I had very little ability to move. I muttered something about a sleeping pill. The stewardess, now assisted by a steward, regarded me dubiously. They hauled me up and began tugging me to the exit. My legs were made of rubber. I could not walk properly. At the open door, with a gusty breeze whipping my face, I stared dizzily, dazedly at the two thousand stairs (so it seemed) leading to the ground. Propped between the two attendants like a Raggedy Anne doll I swayed on to the stairs in a state of limp confusion. Somehow we reached the terminal. I was met by Christopher who assured the crew that I had not been rendered unconscious by two glasses of champagne.

'When she's feeling herself again, tell Miss Seymour that she should never take a sleeping pill until a plane has been in the air for over half an hour,' the steward sniffed.

We were loaded on to coaches and transported to a hotel. Christopher plunked me down on a chair in the lobby with our carry-ons while he secured room assignments. The lobby was going round me in circles. I heard a hubbub of voices and languages. And then I tumbled to the floor, scattering our baggage and books. I lay in a heap, unmindful of disapproving stares from the other passengers who thought I was squiffed. Christopher gathered me up, saying, 'We're in a double. Will your mum be upset?' If I could have replied I would have asked, 'What about Carole?' He married Carole Needham shortly after this drugged scuffle. He scooped up our belongings, threw me over his shoulder and swept me off to the unknown.

I awoke the next morning bright as a button. I did not understand why I was curled on a bed, fully dressed, with Christopher – or *where* we were.

The telephone rang. 'This is your seven o'clock wake-up,' said the operator in a vague accent. Well. How very odd. Christopher stirred.

'Welcome to Amsterdam,' he yawned.

'Don't be silly.'

'We haven't left yet.'

'You mean we *still* have a fifteen-hour flight?' I gasped, pulling open the drapes, and squinting in disbelief at the windy Dutch countryside. He explained the delay, jolting my memory. I leaped off the bed. 'Let's shower and eat. I'm absolutely ravenous.'

'Are you always this lively in the morning?' he groaned. 'It's positively morbid.'

I'm usually disgustingly bright in the morning and had just had the soundest of Seconal sleeps. Christopher lay crumpled and pale. He needed perking up. A bottle of champagne was what we needed.

We hastened to the hotel restaurant, oblivious to the passengers queuing at the coffee bar, and ordered champagne and poached eggs. We had finished a glass each and were anticipating our eggs when our dour travelling companions began filing on to the coach. 'Not to worry,' I insisted, pouring more champagne. 'Isn't this fun? Let's ring up Kenneth.' Christopher doubted that Kenneth would be convulsed by a Sunday wake-up at six forty-five London time.

The eggs were served and I attacked them greedily, recalling that I had not eaten since the previous afternoon at Madame Maurer's. The coach tooted its horn. Christopher put down his fork. I assured him that the horn was meant to deceive and torment. The poached eggs were divine. So was the champagne. We saw the stewardess climb aboard the coach. The door slammed shut. 'Quick, we must fly!' I cried. Christopher grabbed the bags and settled the bill. I ran to the coach with the champagne bottle hidden in my tote and pounded on the door. The passengers and stewardess glared at me with glacial, unfriendly eyes. I burped.

'I simply don't understand it,' I said to Christopher as we bumped along in the last two seats, polishing off the champagne. 'I always seem to be running for trains and planes no matter who I'm with.'

He looked at me speculatively, throwing an arm around my shoulder. 'Life with you, Lynnie, *is* a bit wilder than normal,' said Christopher, his blue eyes flashing brightly. I snuggled against him. That was the sweetest thing a mate had ever said to me and he became 'My darling Christopher'. By the time we reached Vancouver, bedraggled and wrinkled and worn out, the mayor had gone to bed but we received tons of publicity the following day. Our two concerts were sold out. Christopher's vitality and passion affected me like an elixir of love. With Christopher as partner I was confident, beautiful, irresistible. There was no fantasy onstage. For a few hours I lost myself in a rhapsodic reality that made my ordinary existence extraordinary. I never wanted the curtain to fall.

Likewise, the doleful pessimism which often enveloped Kenneth during the creation of a ballet vanished in a puff of cigarette smoke when we three rehearsed. On the fall tour Christopher and I danced *Solitaire* together and he was my prince in *Swan Lake*. Christopher was reading the books of Stanislavsky, in which the famous director of the Moscow Art Theatre theorized on naturalistic acting – that is, the identification of an actor with a part, for the taut 'technical performance' lacks emotional colour. We spent hours discussing the internals and externals of the characters we portrayed – all of them. Rehearsing *Swan Lake* Christopher said, 'Stanislavsky defines love as being the most total attention to somebody. Now, when all is lost for the lovers, I think they should never stop looking at each other.'

I bounced off another idea. 'Their lives are finished, so they should never let go of each other, it's too unbearable.'

We danced many *Swan Lakes* on tour and gave both interpretations, depending on our mood. Nothing was prearranged. We intuitively *knew* what was right for us when the moment came. This lightning intuition extended beyond characterization into the nuts and bolts of a performance which is why our partnership was unique. During *Romeo and Juliet* some seasons later in Rome, the Italian conductor began the balcony pas de deux at a frenzied steeplechase speed. It was undanceable (the only theatre people I have ever screamed at are conductors, who can unbalance a performance, unbeknownst to audiences). Without so much as a conferred whisper, we instinctively cut half the steps, the same steps, and stayed with the mad conductor's beat. Now, that's partnership!

The fall tour was thrilling. Kenneth saw that Christopher and I were a matchless combination and *The Invitation* role was definitely his. Kenneth choreographed two yearning duets for us, presented me with a *tour de force* role in which I dominated the stage as a gauche child, a blossoming adolescent awakening to love and finally a disillusioned and deflowered woman. The excitement of creating a new ballet is – for me – the very essence of dance. This creation stimulated every nerve in my body. I was not tired or depressed or lonely or unwanted. I was liberated from such mundane earthbound emotions. The classics are very demanding and not that rewarding – so many dancers have done them before and reached a point of acknowledged excellence. But a new ballet, created for my body and my personality, gave me the power and energy of unlimited expression.

The company worked at tense high-fever pitch while nightly performing the touring rep. The only absent creator from *The Invitation* was the composer Matyas Seiber who had been killed in a tragic car accident. I did not want the critics merely to 'accept' *The Invitation*. I wanted them to be astounded. And yet I was worried, we were all worried. 'We have given our life blood,' I wrote home after rehearsing the last scene in which the raped girl, with revulsion in her heart, staggers alone towards the footlights, mentally and physically broken. 'Kenneth has undoubtedly produced a masterpiece. We all know it, but we also have a feeling that it will be ill-treated by the critics. It's amazing how we live by praise and recognition.' Anyone who tells you otherwise is a liar.

The provincial opening was in Oxford. The London dance crowd, hearing that Kenneth had staged an X-rated ballet to shock the fairy tale fans, descended on the university town. Both Martha Graham and Antony Tudor had created ballets that might be called unsuitable for children but they were not choreographers for the staid Royal Ballet, a hallowed British institution, which normally did not explore what Freud calls 'the repression in the emotional life of humanity'. Dame Ninette, who crammed thirty hours of work into an average day, also appeared in Oxford, and her presence became an inexhaustible topic of conversation. Madam could wither us with a word: what would she think of a ballet in which a depraved Edwardian gentleman abuses a teenage girl?

The afternoon run-through left Madam stunned. She is disarmingly honest and expects the same from others. A commanding eyebrow twitched ever so slightly. She seemed to be coolly musing, 'No elves or happy peasants in this one, eh, Kenneth?' We waited, half frozen with fear.

'It's a beautiful ballet,' she said, her eloquent eyes piercing the cast, 'but don't you think the seduction' – she refused to say 'rape', we duly noted – 'could take place off-stage?'

Mumble, mumble. Murmur, murmur.

Our ballet-master Henry Legerton volunteered to play a dirty old gardener who observed and reacted to the offstage 'seduction'. Henry's mischievous suggestion had us tittering. His expert miming would earn the ballet a triple-X rating. Kenneth explained that the 'seduction' was essential to the dramatic continuity of the piece. It was as obligatory as the scene in *A Streetcar Named Desire* when the brutish Stanley disarms his sister-in-law Blanche with the deadly line, now a classic, 'We've had this date with each other from the beginning.' Madam realized there were plenty of prigs on the board of directors – and among the press – who might be offended. But her faith in Kenneth's integrity was unshakable. That valiant Dame of the British Empire made a farewell gesture. 'It's your ballet, Kenneth,' she said without further ado and drove back to London.

Kenneth and I were staying in the same hotel. On my new stipend of twenty-five pounds a week I had treated myself to decent lodgings for the Oxford première. I simply had no endurance for crabby landladies, bedbugs, wheezing neighbours and a communal loo. After the opening I sat with Kenneth in the lobby, a handsomely appointed room with a fireplace, wing chairs and fling-thyself-upon-me sofas, sipping coffee, brandy and smoking cigarettes. Kenneth slumped against a cushion in the far corner of the sofa. He looked utterly dejected. I was certain he would have a serious depression if his ballet was not a huge success, so I prattled on, as second brandies were served, about my pleasure in dancing with Christopher and how delighted I was that Nico had promised me two costume sketches as a gift – they hang in my sitting room on Woodstock Road.

Kenneth's wintry face turned crimson. His eyes narrowed. Oh, Kenneth, I thought, please don't be sick *now*. If you get sick, who'll look after me if I run a temperature before the London opening?

'Lynnie,' Kenneth said softly. 'Turn your head slowly to the left and tell me if you see what I think *I* see.'

I turned my head and noticed several tweedy chaps reading newspapers and a bosomy woman in a horrendous black-and-white checked suit grasping a glass of sherry. 'Not *right*,' Kenneth said exasperatedly. 'Left! Sharp left.'

I stifled a yelp. Crossing the lobby, rosary in hand, swished a pixy with an exceedingly mean face. The odd creature was a midget nun. I wondered aloud if it might be a London critic in drag. We both started laughing uncontrollably. When we looked around she was gone. 'It's a good sign,' I cried, 'it has to be. But why do you suppose she looked so mean?'

Kenneth buried his face in a cushion. Coming up for air he fairly choked. 'If you were a midget . . .' We fell upon each other, two naughty, noisy children, '. . . and a nun,' he said in a mirthful crescendo, 'would you look *happy*?'

Divine Kenneth.

Marvellous madness. This joyous spirit must never end, never, I reflected, and many years later I wished that we had seen a midget nun again.

The Invitation was a smash. It was called brilliant, powerful, a work of major importance and Kenneth's best ballet to date. With such headline reviews in London as 'Rape at the Ballet' and 'A Massacre of Innocence', it quickly became the shock-of-the-town. When some critics coughed that it was too melodramatic and sexually cynical and said they were nauseated by the distressingly loveless copulation, the Garden sold out. *The Invitation* was a 'hot ticket'.

Kenneth, who had been so worried, accepted the acclaim with his customary shyness and Little Boy Lost, Little Boy Found grin. We were all too dazed, too super-charged to make much post-performance sense. In his first created role, Christopher's sensitive dancing caught the fancy of critics and audiences – and the management. He sent me a bouquet of yellow roses with a note, 'Thank you, Lynnie. I don't believe any of it!'

Lying abed with the sniffles I read that my performance catapulted me straight into the ballerina class, that it ranked as one of the outstanding interpretations of the decade. It was quite a heady experience when I further read that I could give movement shades of meaning almost as precise as the intonation of speech. *The Invitation* was an artistic breakthrough – firmly establishing me as a 'remarkable' dramatic dancer.

Many Aunt Ednas pursed their scabby lips in 1961 and stomped out of the theatre when we toured the provinces. They preferred warmed-over myths and gussied-up fairy tales. Out of ugly material Kenneth fashioned an expressive sexual battle, although the real war resided within the tragic girl herself who would never resolve her conflicts, who would never be cleansed of guilt or fear.

'I'm puzzled, your performance is so realistic, so frightening,' Christopher said when things calmed down. 'What you're dancing and acting is miles away from your personal knowledge. What are you drawing on, where does your performance come from?' Some cast members wondered if I had long suppressed a hideous trauma. My conception of the role was purely imaginative. At a meeting of the Diners' Club Kenneth had shown me a critique of Ionesco who was trying to discover true theatre, to push everything to the 'climax where the sources of the tragic lie'. Without dialogue I knew that I had to transmit feelings within me to the audience – or the performance would fracture the ballet. *The Invitation* was a form of liberation. It allowed me to abandon the outward poise I presented to my friends and convey with utmost 'truth' the desolation and isolation that haunted me, and convincingly 'act' out the sorrow of a girl who would never discover a fulfilling love. The ballet was a kind of psycho-drama and at the end of each performance I felt gloriously purged. But could I do it next time?

An actor in a hit play, with sensational personal reviews, can bask in the publicity for a few weeks and then settle down for a long run in a role that becomes as familiar as an old shoe. Dancers seldom have a second to bask in anything. There is always morning class and another role to learn while still keeping your rep fresh – at this time I was also dancing *Swan Lake, Solitaire, Les Sylphides* and *Don Quixote*. When *The Invitation* opened at Covent Garden I began receiving Society party invites but seldom had the inclination to accept. I still bought my clothes in thrift shops and at flea markets – it was all my budget could afford. I had two smart outfits which I saved for special occasions. I could not join Café Society even if I wanted to, and I did not want to. It was jollier being with Poffer and Becky and Nico and Puss (if he was in town), and going to the theatre with them, or having a late-night snack with Kenneth at the French Club. I was photographed for various glossies by Zoë Dominic and Roy Round. I had known Roy casually for a while. He was a mate of Peter (Poffer) Williams and would soon marry a striking dancer named Georgina Parkinson. I did not feel self-conscious posing for Roy. Relaxed and amiable, he quietly chattered away as he carefully lighted me so that I looked enigmatic, elusive, provocative – all the things I was not.

'Saw you last night at the French Club,' he said, gently tilting my chin over a naked shoulder.

'Why didn't you say hello?'

'It was very much Do Not Disturb. You and Kenneth seemed to be having a private conversation.'

'Oh, we probably were,' I said, playing the enigmatic role. When Kenneth and I dined *à deux* he discouraged table-hoppers. We had been discussing my latest crushette. The Danish dancer Flemming Flindt was appearing in London with the Festival Ballet and I had fantasies about him. 'He's so healthy and hunky, a lovely Danish delight,' I confessed to Kenneth. 'Why don't you invite him to a performance?'

Some days later Kenneth announced that we had a celebrity house that night. He rattled off the list: 'Liz Taylor, Gene Kelly, Nora Kaye and Herbert Ross. And your Danish delight, Flemming Flindt.' I attacked the role with such force that I almost bruised Christopher and upended Desmond Doyle during the 'rape' sequence. Nora and Herbert lured a bunch of us, including Flindt, back to their flat where we ate and drank and gabbed until three in the morning. Herbert, a choreographer who wanted to direct films, was in London on a movie project. Herbert and his wife Nora Kaye were a warm-hearted couple. I had just opened in *The Invitation*. Twenty years earlier Nora Kaye had created a similar stir in New York dancing a similar role in Antony Tudor's *Pillar of Fire*. I never saw Nora Kaye perform but I was very much aware of her reputation as a dramatic dancer and I respected her friendship. I was sitting with Kenneth and Donald MacLeary when she came over and said to Kenneth, 'I think this child is marvellous.' She clasped my hand and sighed in her low, gravelly voice, 'I'm battered from your performance.' (The following day I received a bouquet of peonies with a pink box. Inside were pearl earrings and a brooch. The card was signed: 'Nora Kaye'.) Before guests began leaving the Ross flat, Flemming Flindt complimented me on my performance. He was 'knocked out', he said. I squirmed with delight.

'I'm going to be dancing at the Paris Opera,' he said, running his eyes up and down my body. 'You must come and see me when I'm there. I'd like to show you Paris.' I was completely enamoured and said breathlessly, 'But of course . . .'

Sharing a taxi with Donald, who had just leased a two-room flat in Kensington Park Gardens, I confided, 'Puss, I think he fancies me. Shall I succumb?'

'Ta-ra-ra-boom-de-ay,' Donald sang.

'But it means a trip to Paris.'

'Well, that's the best place for it.'

Paris had to wait. Frederick Ashton wanted to see me.

Since that November day when I auditioned for Frederick Ashton in Vancouver, I had only glimpsed him fleetingly around the school or at the Garden. On the fall tour, while rehearsing *The Invitation*, he visited the company and asked me to dinner. My head throbbed with apprehension. Ashton represented the essence of sophistication and I was a hoydenish oddity. He had met Gertrude Stein who declared that he was a genius. He knew the Royal Family – the one that lived at Buckingham Palace. He was intimate friends with Margot Fonteyn and Bobby Helpmann and Cecil Beaton. Ashton's world was that of the silken drawing room, mine a spartan bed-sit, at best. When he dined with Fonteyn she was dressed by Dior. What was I to wear?

I donned a black skirt and sweater, topped with my Sherlock Holmes coat. I was so nervous about the dinner that I scrupulously refrained from ordering anything that might drip, squirt, leak, run or be dicey to cut. I did not want to spray his white breast-pocket handkerchief with a gooey sauce. Honeycombed with the charm of a rare engraving, Ashton put me at ease immediately.

He was taking an old ballet called *The Two Pigeons*, first produced at the Paris Opera in the 19th century, and restoring it to life with his own choreography. The Ashton version of another French oldie, *La Fille Mal Gardée*, had just been hailed as a 'pure classic' and is considered the brightest gem in Ashton's choreographic crown. *The Two Pigeons* would be especially created for the touring company and he wanted me to play the heroine – an adoring artist's model whose lover strays from their nest with a flashy gypsy girl but who contritely flies home again. The story of the wayward 'pigeon' is based on a fable by La Fontaine.

Two new ballets in one season? I was struck dumb. Here was the chance of a lifetime. I had danced two big ballerina roles in London, Giselle and Odette-Odile, and was creating my third for Kenneth. Now, Frederick Ashton, whose ballets were usually created for Margot Fonteyn, warned that he expected me to start rehearsing his 'little love-bird' as soon as *The Invitation* bowed in London. He had been highly impressed, he said, by the warm lyricism of my movements which were precisely what he wanted to develop in his romantic St Valentine's Day ballet.

'Once we begin rehearsals, I'm going to bully you, so be prepared,' he said with a great dollop of humour. Then he glanced at my untouched plate and murmured in a fatherly manner, 'Do you really like scrambled eggs for dinner?'

Ashton's *Cinderella* was added to my rep, as a sort of preparation for *The Two Pigeons*, and I made my Garden début during the Christmas holidays as the chimney-sweep child who is transformed into a princess. Fonteyn and Beriosova each did two performances. I was given five. 'You're carrying the whole company,' said Christopher, who was also in the three-act production with Betty Anderton.

Hearing that I was to work with Ashton on a new ballet, Winifred Edwards positively cooed. I had never seen her quite so happy. 'It's so *very good* for you to be working with Mr Ashton,' she said, her delicate hands patting her snow-white hair. 'His style is so adult, so mature, so *formidable*. You'll have to exert everything you have to please him.'

Ashton did not bully me at all. I have worked with

choreographers outside the Royal Ballet who bully and shout and stomp and enjoy grinding dancers into dust. It is their favourite form of self-expression. Ashton was always sensitive and sweet. Kenneth MacMillan likes to work with dancers he knows and trusts because he gives them room to experiment spontaneously with their own body movements. Ashton does the same to a lesser degree. But I have also worked with choreographers outside the Royal Ballet who fiercely reject any artistic input from dancers. Kenneth is intrigued by idiosyncratic movement. Ashton prefers a cool purity. An Ashton ballet seems breathtaking in its lightness, but is killing to dance. The linking foot movements must fluently flow from one to another like unseen threads in yards and yards of the frilliest lace.

Ashton takes the personal qualities of his dancers and embroiders them with the sharpest needle on to lace. 'He allows you to do your own characterization,' Bobby Helpmann has accurately said, 'he doesn't attempt to impose anything. Choreographically, he insists quite naturally on his line and his method of doing things.' And his line is classical. Every Ashton ballet, Bobby observed, would have been ideal for Pavlova, and Fred, who saw Pavlova dance, admitted that he thought of her when creating a ballet. Fred loved my arched feet and choreographed some intricate Pavlova steps.

The Two Pigeons, which had a gala première at the Garden two months after *The Invitation*, gave me an opportunity to display my versatility as a dancer and an actress. Kenneth's ballet of corruption was contrasted with true love rewarded. As the wistful model with a Degas smile in the Ashton confection, I was, by turn, insouciante, coltish, humorous and womanly. If I was uncertain of a gesture or Ashton uncertain of a 'fussy' movement, he would say, 'Useless embroidery. Lovely, yes. But let's cut it.' Unlike Kenneth, a Chaplinesque figure, who wore baggy sweat-pants to rehearsals and had a cigarette clamped between his teeth, Fred, with a cigarette in hand, one finger crooked, was serenely grand and as British as a furled umbrella and the bowler hat.

One night Kenneth and I attended Harold Pinter's *The Caretaker* and concluded our outing at the French Club. Throughout supper I kept thinking of Pinter's spare sardonic comedy-drama of two brothers who befriend a scabrous tramp. The three characters in the modern parable of emotional isolation, fraught with unspoken doubts and tensions, made *The Two Pigeons* seem terribly old-fashioned: Bohemian Paris. Swirling gypsies. Fluttering doves. Squabbling lovers. Not fully appreciating Ashton's distinct vision and worried that the ballet was too sugary, I asked Kenneth to sneak into the balcony on the day of our stage-call and give me a critique. 'The girl is much too cute,' I said. 'I'm going to remove some of the sugar and make her more irreverent.'

'Get on with it your way,' Kenneth said. '*You always do.*'

Kenneth hid in the balcony as his presence, unless invited by Ashton, was against protocol. Besides, Ashton knew that Kenneth was president of the Diners' Club and I was under-secretary. I removed the girl's pouts and moues, substituting some impish mischief and wilful sexuality. Kenneth muttered later, 'Mmmm, I like it.' Fred, who misses nothing, caught the minuscule changes and expressed his hesitation, but everything fell into place at the première and I was rewarded with some laughs. The critics applauded the ballet's strong choreography, heartfelt emotion and feeling of youth. Ashton, it was agreed, had given me a marvellous role and, wrote Clive Barnes, 'Seymour has succeeded in drawing something new out of Ashton, something typically Ashton yet individual to herself.' The ballet was not popular in America. Sol Hurok, who prided himself on divining American taste, blamed the title. The small, sturdy showman expounded in his Brooklyn accent, '*Two Pigeons* – I can't sell it. You know what pigeons do to our park benches?'

Fate interrupted the Ashton production just as it had MacMillan's *The Invitation*.

My assigned partner Donald Britton came down with the flu a few days before the première. If a stage star becomes ill the opening is postponed. If a film actor is bedded down with flu, the director shoots around him. But dancers are instantly replaced. Ballets are allotted a specific number of performances and the Royal Ballet shares Covent Garden with the opera company. There are no postponements. Who could step in for ailing Donald Britton? 'Well, there's Christopher Gable . . .' said I. Ashton made some minor alterations and, for the second time that season, Christopher created a new role opposite me, learning an intricate part in record time. Betty Anderton was dancing the gypsy girl. The three of us, who had cavorted at the Duke of Mantua's palace in the opera corps of *Rigoletto*, were unexpectedly reunited as the leads in *The Two Pigeons*. We were still disgracefully young. Christopher was only twenty. It was a tender occasion. Christopher, nobody's darling but my own, won plaudits for his stylish, masculine dancing. Ballet buffs and critics began to say that our partnership might one day be historic.

My life away from the theatre, away from the Diners' Club was not a rollicking party. I lived on the top floor of Clover Roope's house and saved my money for suppers with Kenneth. My wardrobe was only decently replenished when I received a cheque from home. I was woefully restless once I stepped outside the stage door and drifted anonymously with the passing throngs towards the tube station, feeling very much like a tired waitress with aching feet.

The idea of having a boyfriend, just a chap to hold hands

with and kiss, filled me with a curious eager anticipation. The applause from a packed house was no substitute. I seldom heard the applause, even when there were eighteen curtain calls. The bows were a courtesy to an audience which I never sought to please. My goal during a performance was finding a perfection that satisfied me. Would Fate step in? The little-girl crushettes were as palatable as suet pudding. The Danish dancer Flemming Flindt wanted to show me Paris. Would I return to London a true Woman of the World? With *The Two Pigeons* happily launched, I wrote Flindt that I would pop over to Paris the first weekend in March. He responded enthusiastically. I could already smell the fresh croissants and *confiture* we would have in a big brass bed the morning after.

I wrote home that I really needed a short holiday in Paris and my parents sent the money for a plane ticket. I then selected my hats, shoes, lingerie and clothes with the care of someone going on a honeymoon.

Donald sweetly provided moral support for the Parisian jaunt. We flew to Paris on a Friday afternoon and booked a double room on the Left Bank. One room was cheaper than two. Paris was a delicate wash of pinks and blues and glorious golden greys, not the depressing greys of London. Donald and I meandered through shops and art galleries and then sat on the *terrasse* of the Café aux Deux Magots, staring at the sleek young men and women and drinking glasses of Pernod. It evoked memories of St Tropez and we wished Kenneth were with us, but he had declined our bid.

Flemming Flindt telephoned the hotel at seven and invited us both to dinner. 'I wanted to make the trip sound casual,' I explained hastily to Donald, 'so I told him you were here, too.' The hearty and rugged Flindt whisked us off to a Russian restaurant called Le Coq d'Or and we stuffed ourselves on caviar, iced vodka and meat from flaming swords. 'Now I want to take you to a cabaret where you'll hear beautiful Basque folk songs,' Flindt said. Donald asked *sotto voce* if I wanted him to disappear. I clutched his hand under the table and whispered, 'Not yet.' The night ended for the three of us at dawn in Les Halles, festively noisy and lively, sipping piping hot onion soup and *blanc de blanc*. Flindt suggested that I rendezvous at his apartment later that afternoon, around four and, nodding coyly, a soubrette smile from *The Two Pigeons*, scene one, I said goodnight. The sun was coming up.

'You look super,' Donald said after an awkward sleep as I stepped into spiky heels. I wore a full Oxford grey skirt and a new silk shirt. Flindt was dancing that night in *Swan Lake* at the Paris Opera and had given us tickets. I arranged to meet Donald in the lobby and sallied forth to my assignation.

Flindt awaited me in a small apartment, obviously on loan. Thick rugs. Low divans. Vases of flowers. Expensive knick-knacks. Satie on the record player. He took my hand and led me to a divan. I floated like one in a dream. 'You know I have a performance tonight,' he said, and I inclined my head, calculating that we had one hour. 'I will just drink tea, but you might want some wine.'

'Don't open any wine for me. I *adore* tea.'

He said that was lovely and produced a silver tea service with biscuits. He glided on to the divan. He poured. I lit a cigarette. He passed me a cup. I exhaled smoke. He poured himself a cup. He leaned against the cushions and said how pleased he was that I had flown to Paris, and so on. And so on. I smoked a pack of cigarettes. We finished the pot of tea. It was twilight and Flemming left to prepare for the performance. We were to meet at the Café de la Paix after the show.

I fidgeted through *Swan Lake*.

Afterwards Donald and I sat on the *terrasse* of the Café de la Paix, waiting for Flindt and his next move. 'Why don't I leave you?' Donald said. I insisted that he stay. If plans went awry I needed him. Looking over Donald's head I saw Flindt approaching our table, and, yes, I really needed him. Flindt joined us with a young woman of extreme loveliness. She could not keep her hands off him. He introduced his 'girlfriend'. I felt like a complete idiot. Donald was an angel. He rescued me with smart talk and clever jokes, then quickly pulled me out of the café, saying we had to dash off to meet some other friends. We jumped into a taxi. I was a deplorable figure of sorrow. 'We're going to a club,' Donald said. Not just any club, I countered, we must go someplace larger than life. We ended up at a club where a line of Junoesque chorus girls wore monocles, tuxedos and top hats, and did the most surprising things with gold-headed canes. Blinded by tears, I laughed anyway, and when the show was over we did the cha-cha. Again and again.

'Shall we leave *now*?' Donald asked.

'No. Let's keep dancing.' We danced until dawn, and Donald finally chaperoned me back to the Left Bank.

That summer, following my success in *Cinderella*, *The Invitation* and *The Two Pigeons* at Covent Garden, and more articles about me in the Sunday supplements and *Newsweek* ('Lynn Seymour: In the Fonteyn Sweepstakes'), Kenneth was going to Venice with Diana and Kenneth Rowell. 'You need to get away,' he said, 'why don't you come?' I did not know what to do with myself or where to go. I didn't want to lumber anybody. Kenneth was very persuasive. Venice is an opera set, he said, with religious processions and music and delectable platters of prosciutto, and we would drink Bellinis at Harry's Bar – champagne and peach juice.

Naturally I went.

We stayed in a quiet pension near the Grand Canal. One morning I arose very early and wandered down to the port and went for a boat ride with a grizzled fisherman. When I strolled back to the pension Kenneth was pacing on the marble floors in the frescoed lobby. 'I've been looking for you,' he said almost angrily. 'I woke up and you weren't there.' He smiled and breathed a sigh of relief. 'I was so worried, Lynnie.'

194   *Lynn: An Autobiography*

strolled back to the pension Kenneth was pacing on the marble floors in the frescoed lobby. 'I've been looking for you,' he said almost angrily. 'I woke up and you weren't there.' He smiled and breathed a sigh of relief. 'I was so worried, Lynnie.'

CHAPTER 10

Cupid's Dart

Last week I telephoned Colin Jones but he was away on an assignment. When he rang up an hour ago, he caught me by surprise. I had not seen him in years and he had never been to Woodstock Road. Colin is an expert photojournalist. Backstage at the ballet, peasants in Russia, merchant seamen on a trawler in the North Sea, the Dickensian shopkeepers and servants of Olde London, racial riots in America – Colin's camera snapped them all from fresh, unorthodox angles for the *Observer*, the *Sunday Times* and other publications. On a tour of the Middle East in 1961, Colin Jones took a picture of me exploring the Great Mosque in Damascus with Margot Fonteyn. We were not dressed properly for entrance into the ancient temple and had to don huge cloaks and remove our shoes. Colin's camera captured us, cloaked and barefoot, looking preposterously medieval.

Margot persuaded me, with very little effort, to accompany her on lively sight seeing expeditions in her chauffeur-driven car with Fred Ashton. She recalled how she kept losing her balance when learning one of his ballets in the early forties. 'Fred's steps are frightfully speedy,' I agreed, and Fred was highly amused by my nonchalant admission as we sped down a narrow road towards a ruin, another temple or a palace. I was quite chuffed by their companionship and conversation, a refreshingly sedate change from the tumultuous revelry of the Diners' Club, but as Madam had remarked to Kenneth, 'Lynn is amazingly adaptable.'

Fred bought me a tangerine-coloured caftan in Damascus. I posed for Colin against a backdrop of heavily veiled

women, men wearing fezzes and baggy pants, and homeless
children in the crowded bazaar, jumping around like stray
puppies whimpering for a morsel of food. I tossed them my
small change. Fred's caftan went with me to Ibiza, Fire
Island and Key West. The garment is shredded now, but I
am still fond of it. I last wore the caftan as a turban to the
New York première of *The Wild Boy*, Kenneth's new piece
for American Ballet Theatre. I said hello to the company's
co-founder Lucia Chase, a resplendent and courageous
benefactor of American dance, and knelt at her feet. 'Lynn,
I didn't realize it was *you*,' Lucia said graciously, her eyes
floating to Fred Ashton's caftan wrapped around my cropped brown hair. The evening was a homage to Kenneth,
with Fred's caftan.

The big boys, Jers and Addie, are at Scouts. Demian has
been assembling his electric train, very pleased with his
various birthday accessories – a station, a tunnel, trees and
a wagon-lit 'for the rich people'. I rushed upstairs, feeling a
trifle reckless, and slipped into a beige body stocking. Then
I shimmied into Fred's caftan, this time as a dress. The
tears and slits give it the air of a funky high-fashion frock.
Colin Jones likes clothes and admires the way they are
worn. He was the first man who ever told me I was
attractive, and my heart nearly stopped. I was always so
physically insecure and never quite sure what the men I
knew wanted or expected of me. But I could not live
without their companionship. When Desmond Doyle, my
prince in *Sleeping Beauty* and heartless violator in *The
Invitation*, kissed me, I shivered with pleasure. When Kenneth held my hand as we moved to our table at the French
Club, I was dazed by his sweetness. Sexually I was still
stumbling in the dark. But Colin Jones was very much his
own man. He had imagination. He really liked me.

I pinned mirrored bits of jewellery to the tangerine
caftan. Costume jewellery – gold bracelets and rubies –

adorned my arms and neck. A shiny belt with a dangling chain circled my waist. I stared into the mirror. Not bad, not *too* bad, though I did sparkle like a Christmas tree. For a final dash of colour, I clipped two hydrangeas from the vase of flowers on my glass dressing table and pinned them in my hair. Some powder, some eye make-up – dark and dramatic. Eyes reflect the soul. Kenneth once said they are, perhaps, the most expressive, the most revealing feature of the human body.

I needed a drink, a slug of something before Colin arrived, but there was no booze in the house.

Colin Jones, a youth with curly sandy-brown hair, slight and sensitive, my romantic image of a Venetian lad in a velvet doublet from another century, was my first love. It had been so perfect. For a while.

Contrary to what readers of the popular press might believe, the dramas in my house seldom happen in the bedroom but around the dining-room table, a permanent set-piece for farewells and reunions. Colin unwrapped two bottles of red wine. 'Can you open them, Lynnie? I'm thirsty.' The good humour and bonhomie are still with Colin, but his face is graver and his eyes have a solemn introspection. Some years ago on assignment in Africa he contracted a non-specific virus that has never been fully cured. We sat alongside each other at the table, both nervous, indeed possibly frightened.

'My wife gave me your message, Lynnie. I had to get a bit drunk before I could make the call, before I could see you. Said you wanted a snap of you and Margot. Sorry. I forgot it. Do you mind? Well, here's to you, Lynnie.' We clinked glasses. His hand touched my shoulder ever so slightly. 'You're beautiful, Lynnie, you really are, and I should not be here. No, I definitely should not be here. I came because I was curious. I heard you want to muck around in the past. Photographs and stuff. I wish you'd leave it alone. We had good times, great times, didn't we, the two of us? We were quite a little couple. *Lynnie*. That's what Kenneth called you. La Lynnie.' His words carried an air of suspense. My self-control amazed me. I sat quite still. 'Kenneth and Lynnie – yes, you two were quite a couple, weren't you? Pour me another, love, and I thank you.' I refilled our glasses. 'So, how is Kenneth?' I paused for a moment before speaking, fiddling with a cigarette to pass the time.

'Kenneth? Fine, I suppose. I really don't know. I haven't seen him in yonks.'

Colin's eyes had become little points of light. A frown darkened his forehead. He appeared to be mulling a matter of vital importance. 'Well, well, well,' he muttered. 'And you've quit the Royal Ballet?'

'Yes.' My tone was emotionless, too obvious to be ignored.

An odd flush burnished Colin's cheek. He drank a full glass of wine. Turning in his chair, he regarded the photograph on the wall of Christopher Gable as Romeo. 'I really should not be here,' he repeated, tapping his fingers on the table. 'Hullo, who's this now?'

Demian had toddled into the kitchen. He opened the fridge and poked around. I made perfunctory introductions. Demian stuck his head back in the fridge. 'Mum, there's a cup of blood here.'

'Demian, don't be absurd. That's tomato juice. Run along and play with your train.'

Colin was laughing. 'A cup of blood in the fridge. *Lovely*. Would you say, Lynnie, that he has your sense of theatre?'

'His father's a bit of a character, too.'

The front door opened and Alex, or the chap I call Australian Alex, entered the dimly lit hallway. Alex was the house guest of the week, sleeping on a stack of pillows in the sitting room.

'Is that your latest whatever you happen to like?' Colin asked caustically. 'Sorry, love, I'm a bit drunk. But you always said making love was the best way to cement a friendship. I mean, after you got *into* it. That's what I heard. You announced it one night at a party when you were wearing a pink wig. Anyway, that's what I heard.'

I considered his remark for a moment and answered humorously, 'If you look out the kitchen window, you'll find a cement-mixer at the bottom of my garden.'

Colin scowled. 'Mate, we've finished this.' He held up the empty bottle. 'Let's have a go at the second. Now, what I want to know, between friends,' he thumped the table, 'is that your lover?'

If Madam had any romantic notions for me, she may have hoped that I would marry a young lord or a country squire or a moneyed mittel-European. Karsavina and Fonteyn both married diplomats. But I never had enough ego to believe that I could land a grandee. To the astonishment of friends I never acquired a Swiss bank account, diamond chokers, sables and chinchillas, a bungalow in the Cotswolds or a villa in Provence. I haven't even paid off the mortgage on my Chiswick house. 'Lynn is such a bloody romantic,' my chums despair, 'she's downright old-fashioned.'

Colin's intense curiosity about Australian Alex amused me. I'm always amused when people jump to the wrong conclusions and frequently cannot resist leaving them in error. But I did not wish to tease Colin. 'My boyfriend is upstairs in bed.'

'I want to see him.'

'You can't. He's sick. He made an Indian curry the other night and got violently ill. Fortunately after one bite, neither I nor the boys touched it.' I leaned towards him conspiratorially. 'We were smart.' Suddenly we were both laughing through a fog of cigarette smoke, laughing about the cup of blood in the fridge and the cement-mixer at the bottom of the garden and a Christmas, so very long ago, when I put the turkey stuffing in a milk bottle and rammed the bottle into the turkey. It exploded – showering turkey, glass, chestnuts, and bread crumbs on to the floor and ceiling. We laughed until our sides ached, and we finished the second bottle of wine.

The front door opened again. Ads and Jers, home from their Scout meeting. They strode into the kitchen, curious about the laughter and the stranger at the table. Colin sat back in his chair and sized them up with a vacant expression. He took the last sip of wine from his glass. The lads removed their jackets, waiting. The laughter had faded away. The final set of introductions had to be made. My head began spinning. It was going to explode like the Christmas turkey.

'Lads, I'd like you to meet Colin Jones,' I said quietly, playing with a match-box. 'I haven't seen him in years. Colin was my first husband.'

Extremely athletic and physical, Colin Jones, a dancer in the corps, played one of the acrobats who entertained the guests at the party in *The Invitation*. I hardly noticed him. My partners were Christopher Gable and Desmond Doyle. I was with them and Kenneth throughout rehearsals and my concentration was solely on the role that Kenneth had created for me. I was not radiating any sexual come-and-get-me. It all went into the ballet. After *la bombe* in Paris with Flemming Flindt, I prepared for a two-month overseas tour which took my mind off that sticky-wicket of a weekend. The company was going to Tokyo, Osaka, Hong Kong and Manila. My rep included *Giselle*, *Solitaire* and *Les Sylphides*. On the long flight the 'family' swapped seats. Henry Legerton, Lorna Mossford, Christopher Gable, Betty Anderton – we were all together. As the plane dipped through fleecy clouds over the Pacific, I found myself sitting next to Colin Jones. He was extremely nice; funny without being strident, sensitive without being precious. Colin was two years older than me and lived with his parents in suburban London. Colin knew that he was no great shakes as a dancer and was already planning a new career as a photographer, with sincere encouragement from Margot Fonteyn, who thought his portraits of ballet life, taken in the wings when dancers were gasping for breath and faces were contorted in pain, caught the unseen dance world with devastating accuracy and affection. We had an occasional meal in Manila, but I had a heart murmur for a Philippine dancer named Pineda with whom I indulged in some heavy breathing one morning at five o'clock after a swim. 'Pineda?' mused Jeffrey Solomons when I presented my Asian report to the Diners' Club in London. 'It sounds like one of those fruity American cocktails. How do you make it?'

'I never did,' was my reply.

A lasting friendship was also developing with Anya Linden, a rather shy, serene young soloist with a Grecian profile and a fresh newly-minted loveliness. Anya was dancing leads in *Swan Lake* and *Les Patineurs*. She was a 'guest' from the main company. A season later we were in *The Invitation* at Covent Garden. Anya played the wife, softening her brittleness with Gallic chic. This tour was not like the horrific endless Australian booking in which some dancers stepped off the plane in London looking quite ghastly. I did not have the pressure of learning a full-length role. And by now there was a convivial closeness among the surviving mates of my 'family'. We knew each other's fears and flaws, vices and virtues, and our attitude was nothing less than compassionate, accepting, admiring.

Like Australia, the Asian tour was hideously hot and humid, but when we went swimming after a performance we did not have to worry about sharks. On some nights I drove to the beach with Colin and his friends, or Desmond Doyle and Anya Linden. Aching from the tension of class-rehearsal-performance, we flung ourselves into the starry gently murmuring sea, naked as the fish, floating and kicking in the starry blue night. Playful porpoises. After two hours of straining muscles and nerves onstage, you have to unwind. I longed to emulate Anya's aristocratic freshness and coolness, though my own headstrong impulsiveness saved us – possibly – from confinement in a house of bamboo in Hong Kong, bowing and kow-towing, and opening up gentlemen's fortune cookies.

Advising Colin and Henry Legerton, my rosy confidant on all tours, that we'd meet them at our hotel for a nightcap, Anya and I slipped away from the theatre for a swim and a private little chat about life – that is, the relevance of the male-female relationship and a woman's independence in a world dominated by the passions and loyalties, sentiments and aggressions of men. Our driver, a burly fellow who smoked American cigars, sat in the taxi while Anya and I raced to the beach in the pale moonlight, dropped our clothes in a heap, and plunged into the sea. In the splashy darkness, we tittle-tattled about the men we liked, their weaknesses and strengths, and Anya astounded me by saying, 'You have an understanding of men far beyond your years – or experience,' attributing to me a psychological aplomb of which I was unaware. Some basic instincts about men were put to the test minutes later. We dried ourselves off, dressed and ran back to the taxi. It was almost midnight and the chaps would be in the hotel bar. The highway to downtown Hong Kong seemed darker, wilder and more deserted than I remembered. I peered out the window, searching for a familiar landmark.

We were on another road, driving at an accelerated speed.

'Stop! We want to go into Hong Kong,' I demanded.

The driver paid no attention. He chewed on his cigar.

Again I ordered him to stop the car. He pretended not to speak English. He seemed unconscious of our presence. The delicate beauty of Anya's face tightened into a grim mask. We were out in the middle of nowhere, but the driver clearly had a destination in mind. In the distance we saw small flickers of light. 'Englees girls,' I could hear as he drove us towards a bawdy-house.

I reached into my practice bag, bulging with such items as shoes, pins, needles, ribbons, tissues, make-up – and a pair of steel scissors with sharp pointed blades. I jabbed the open scissors against his neck and, once again, demanded that he take us immediately to our hotel. He mumbled, 'Faster woote.' I scraped the back of his neck with the blade. He slowed down, made a swift U-turn and drove back into town on the highway I remembered. The scissors remained against his neck until we arrived at the hotel and Anya opened the taxi door. We did not speak of the incident again. It had been too frightening and there was no need to alarm the chaps who made jokes about our tardiness, our being swept out to sea. The company, they had heard, was being trailed very closely by a typhoon.

Colin and I sat in the bar until closing, smoking and drinking – the things I usually did with Kenneth, but Kenneth was in London. I told Colin about the Diners' Club and a nutsy letter I was dispatching to Kenneth. The bartender said we had to leave. Colin sighed. I said goodnight and went to my room. I got in bed writing Kenneth how Anya and I almost ended up in a brothel operated by Mother Goddamn – my own literary licence. Kenneth would howl.

The Asian tour was followed by dates in Baalbek, Damascus and Athens.

One sultry afternoon in Athens I strolled with Colin

through the Plaka – the old town. He was taking photographs, looking quite saucy in white slacks and a pale blue shirt. I stood out of camera range, in the shade of the market stall, and watched admiringly. On Sunday nights in London when Kenneth and I had sandwiches at a tea shop in Kensington, he would say, 'I'm doing a new ballet. It's what I want to do. Why can't I find someone I love . . .' Since I felt exactly the same, we propped up each other. Kenneth revealed his lonely boyhood in Scotland, I recounted my adolescence in London. There was personal supportiveness. Anya Linden once said, 'You and Kenneth held each other together.' As I watched Colin eagerly, happily dashing around with his camera, I despaired of always being the person left behind like the girl in Kenneth's ballets, seeking a connection, seeking a meaningful attachment. Seeking *love*.

That afternoon Colin and I climbed around the Acropolis. 'Are you all right, Lynn?' he asked. 'You look feverish.' I toppled into his arms and he held me close. It was not the way I had ever been held by a dance partner, or anyone else. I did not want him to let go.

I snivelled. 'I wish there wasn't a performance tonight, Colin. I really do.'

He threw back his head and laughed boisterously, kissing me on the mouth. 'You are a silly thing. And sexy and gorgeous. I love seeing you dance. I love being with you.' Sexy and gorgeous? No one had ever said *that* to me.

I danced *Solitaire* that night in the Roman theatre near the Acropolis with light, breezy childlike jumps. I had not been so transported since Kenneth first told me, 'I want you to do my ballet.'

Trains, planes, coaches. Packing, unpacking. Hotels, digs, lodgings. I was dancing constantly but I needed London now – and the main company – as a base to perfect my technique. I wanted to resume private lessons with

Winifred Edwards. I wanted to stop the jarring sense of disorientation, the terrifying rootlessness that drained me after four seasons of touring. A provincial tour loomed ahead – Bournemouth, Torquay, Oxford, Manchester, Glasgow, and *on and on and on*. I would definitely talk to Madam about transferring to the main company. Another year on tour would corrode my spirit. Madam promised to have me moved after the tour. I was even more excited to learn that I would dance *Sleeping Beauty* at the Garden.

Time, once again, to find new 'temporary' living quarters in London.

Donald MacLeary, who had acquired a two-room flat in Kensington, had an ingenious proposal. 'Why don't you share with me? When you're on tour, I'm in London. When I'm on tour, you'll be in London. And if we're both here at the same time, it doesn't really matter.' When I informed Jeffrey about Donald's offer, he said, 'Well, even your friends are the same – the dreadnoughts of the Diners' Club.' Donald knew I would respect his private life. I had no private life to respect or conceal, though, in later years, when all that changed, I vexed the Garden because I never attempted to conceal anything. I am too open a person for secrets and clandestine affairs.

Donald's flat was a walk-up on the fifth floor. I moved in, pushed two suitcases, which contained all my worldly possessions, under the bed, and immediately repacked for Bournemouth, the first booking on the provincial tour. When Kenneth or Jeffrey or Nico visited we threw down the key in a rolled-up sock. During my last weekend in Bournemouth, Donald went to see his family in Scotland. I hurled down the sock. The visitor was Colin Jones. He bounded up the stairs with a bouquet of chrysanthemums and a bottle of Scotch. We were extremely timid at first, but Colin was fairly experienced with women. He knew what to do.

Ballet life is so overtly physical and tactile that you

quickly become immune to the thrill of a well-sculpted chest. A man's attractiveness for me involves his brains and energy and inner spirit, his career and belief in it. Colin had all these qualities. His expression of love moved me deeply.

Donald and Colin had attended ballet school together. When Donald reappeared from his family visit, I shyly confessed everything as I sorted out clothes for the provincial tour.

'Colin Jones. Oh, yes, a nice quiet boy,' Donald said. His mild reaction disappointed me.

'Is that all you have to say?' I asked, clamping shut a suitcase.

Donald kissed my cheek. 'Lynnie, I'm thrilled for you.' He mustered up the required élan. 'Let me take you out to dinner. We'll celebrate. Does anyone else know?'

'Kenneth. And *he's* taking me to dinner.'

I danced *Sleeping Beauty* on the tour, with the Garden performance scheduled for November. But my partner had not danced the role before and he did not give me confidence. I missed Christopher Gable, my darling Christopher. Why can't I have Christopher? I asked out of sheer curiosity. We were a natural partnership. The critics had heaped us with verbal bouquets in *The Invitation* and *The Two Pigeons*. Christopher instilled me with confidence, confidence, confidence – but I dared not say that or I'd be told to pull up the old socks. 'You can't have Christopher all the time,' was the terse word from management. In the middle of one provincial performance my legs went completely numb. Leaping offstage into the cramped wings of a dingy theatre I bashed my right arm against a wall. It turned black-and-blue by the last act. Colin Jones, who was in the corps, consoled me with a skittish hug. 'Stop weeping, milady,' he joked, 'and move that arse for Aurora's wedding.' The tour would have been utterly dismal without Colin. We began to live in each other's pockets. As Donald said, Colin was a nice quiet boy, sweetly congenial and even-tempered. The affair did not arouse much notice. Our behaviour was low-key, but I was smitten.

After Saturday-night performances in southern England, we charged into his car and drove to historic unspoilt fishing villages on the Cornish coast, stumbling into old Georgian inns or ivy-covered guest cottages in the early morning. Sundays were spent roaming the countryside. Colin loved *his* England; he spoke of it possessively, as his very own England. He wanted to show me everything: the remains of an old castle, traces of a Roman causeway, churches built in the 16th century, pirate coves and cobbled streets with greystone houses. We tramped across grassy hills bountifully clustered with shrubs and wild flowers and went rowing in sleepy inlets and dined on fresh mackerel at sunset in quaint sea-salty restaurants facing little harbours dotted with all kinds of boats. 'Lynnie, look at that coast-line!' Colin would exclaim, grasping my hand. 'Isn't it beautiful? It's a *proud* coastline.' I saw England through his eyes and it was truly beautiful. Even the smelly bait and tackle which the grizzled fishermen carried were beautiful. We pushed off Mondays at dawn, before the sun came up, so we always drove with the last evening star.

'I'm leaving the company after this season,' Colin said. 'I'm getting a job as a photographer.' I knew he would succeed. I believed in his work. I believed in him. I dozed with my head against his shoulder, thinking, oh, this *is* happiness, nothing can go wrong. And he held me close.

My Garden début as Aurora was only two weeks away when I strained my Achilles tendon – that vital sinewy tissue running from the heel bone to the calf muscle. This is an injury that gives dancers nightmares – it disables and ends careers.

Sleeping Beauty went on without me.

The provincial tour went on without me – Newcastle, Liverpool, Sheffield and Monte Carlo for Christmas. Fighting tears I kissed Colin farewell and took the train back to London. I was 'without legs' – unable to dance – a blobby little thing, until spring.

I was of course in black despair about missing *Sleeping Beauty* at the Garden. And my promotion to the main company was now delayed one year while I took class daily with Winifred Edwards, the Florence Nightingale of lame dancers, who used the lengthy offstage siege to refine my technique until I was as perfectly buffed and polished as a silver figurine. Appreciating the turmoil, clearly visible by the piteous sorrow indelibly marked on my face, Madam invited me to her home for the weekend. Madam did not, to my knowledge, extend such invitations at random; her home was not a ward for weepy injured dancers, but she was always concerned about her 'family' and remarkably unselfish. Kenneth reminded me that during the Second World War she worried that two young lads were not eating enough vegetables. A crate of greens arrived at their lodgings. No one knew where she found the crate, but her Irish charm and iron determination, coupled with a bit of blarney, worked miracles, despite the bombs and blackouts.

I stuttered an apology about intruding on her time. '*Nonsense*! If this was an intrusion, I wouldn't ask you, would I?' she asserted. 'It's settled then. I'll let my husband know we're having a guest.' She described that evening the Christmas pantomimes she danced as a youngster throughout the First World War and her years in the twenties with Diaghilev in Paris, Barcelona, Munich, Berlin and Monte Carlo. A hectic life, but she loved every minute of it and I loved hearing every minute of it.

I slept peacefully between crisp white sheets in a big soft bed with a satin comforter. Early the following morning, not wanting to seem like a lazy bones, I quickly dressed and hurried to the kitchen. Madam was preparing a tray of bacon and eggs and a pot of tea. Fortunately she did not see me. I dashed upstairs, undressed, and sank into bed. Moments later she tiptoed into the bedroom with the breakfast tray. Her kindness constricted my nervous system. I wanted to throw my arms around her but that would have been against protocol. Madam abhorred sloppy sentiment.

I returned to Donald's flat in Kensington with a lighter step and a much lighter heart.

Donald was lumbered with a convalescent flatmate – one who was not dancing but who was now a fixture in London, which upset the apple-cart of his proposal. 'I'll sleep on the couch,' I said. 'I promise not to be in your way and I won't interrupt your life. Just close the bedroom door.' Donald chucked me under the chin and said that as long as I did not snore, I would never interrupt anything. And he announced that he was giving me a Welcome Home/Get Well party.

The Diners' Club – Kenneth, Nico and Jeffrey – hollered for the sock and we tossed it out the window. Svetlana Beriosova ventured into the icy November night and climbed the five flights. A Spanish boy who said his name was Jésus Ximinez de Vega arrived with a blue and red parrot on his shoulder. He got frightfully tipsy on Donald's punch and landed in the bathtub with his parrot. Nobody knew exactly whom he belonged to or how he got to the party. Kenneth mumbled that a party never really took off until somebody fell in the tub.

'I think we just throw the key to anyone in the street who looks dishy,' said Svetlana, as the sock went hurtling again out of the window.

The last venturesome souls were a bunch of kids from an American musical comedy on the West End. It had begun snowing and they shivered up the stairs covered in clumps of snow. There was dancing and drinking and shrieks of laughter to ribald jokes and scenarios we invented about two or three toffs at the Garden. Kenneth took over, presiding like a sit-down comedian. Kenneth did not stand up very much, not even when he was choreographing. 'Kenneth can do *anything* from a chair,' Jeffrey declared, and spirits soared higher and higher as the temperature dropped lower and lower.

'We are freezing to death in here,' Kenneth said, scowling at the dying embers in the fireplace. '*We* bring bottles of wine. Is it too much to ask for some warmth from our hosts?' Shivering himself, Donald confessed that there were no more logs. 'Then let's burn the piano,' Kenneth said craftily. 'It's *so* ugly.' Donald had acquired the flat furnished. It came with tons of misfit furniture – some tables, a chest of drawers, and a piano which neither of us played. Kenneth emerged from the kitchen with a hammer. He gave the piano several hearty whacks. It collapsed on the floor like a house of wooden cards.

'Oh, dear Jesus,' gasped Nico.

'My name is pronounced *Eaysu*,' said the Spanish boy.

'Go away,' said Jeffrey. 'He's not talking to you.'

Kenneth allotted everyone tasks. 'Svetlana, bring the keyboard!' he commanded. 'Lynnie, isn't there another leg?' The piano was ripped apart and flung into the fireplace. Kenneth, we cried, it's a work of art, an environment, a Happening, and clustered closer to the roaring upright, which burned brilliantly in the open hearth. The piano burning was accompanied by jazz records, and we ate apples and cheese. The snow continued to fall heavily. We ran out of punch and bottles of wine, but no one wanted to leave. It was too cold outside. When the flames consumed the last particle of piano, it was almost too cold to remain inside. Kenneth sighed grumpily, dramatically, as if

Donald and I simply did not know how to keep house. 'This cold is bad for your limbs,' he reminded the dancers. 'And Lynnie's already injured.' He sauntered into the bedroom and stared pensively at Donald's chest of drawers. 'Now that piece is ugly too,' he pronounced, tossing Donald's cashmere sweaters and French shirts on the bed. 'Wood! Wood!' he chanted, carrying an empty drawer into the sitting room. 'We will not freeze to death tonight.' He kicked the drawer into the fireplace. Soon the entire chest of drawers was flickering with an eerie intensity. Kenneth received a huge round of applause. Donald's clothes and some of mine were strewn across the bed and on the bedroom floor.

'Kenneth, you absolutely cannot burn anything else,' Donald said.

'I won't,' he said obediently, and sank on to the sofa. 'I'm warm now. We're all warm now.' He looked outside the frosted window. 'You see, it's still snowing.' He purred contentedly.

Around midnight I received a phone call.

'Who's calling Lynnie at this hour?'

'La Lynnie has a friend.'

'You mean – a friend-*friend*?'

I smiled enigmatically. Colin Jones was ringing me from his provincial digs in Liverpool. He said that he missed me and wondered how I was feeling. 'What's all that noise?' he asked as Kenneth sprang to life again.

'Donald, we will need more wood. Can't we burn the chairs? Oh, please.' There was a hue and outcry for 'Chairs! Chairs!'

'I called at a bad time,' Colin said awkwardly.

'It's just a *little* party,' I said lamely. 'You know, the Diners' Club.' I told Colin that I missed him too, and he rang off as several chairs, smuggled into the flat from the ballet school, were pitched into the fireplace. The guests reluctantly departed around two-thirty, braving the snow-storm, leaving Donald and Kenneth and me, curled on cushions and pillows in front of the fireplace.

The chairs from the ballet school warmed us until the wee hours.

'Did you have a good time, Lynnie?' Kenneth asked, yawning.

It was in fact the most colossal party I had ever attended and Kenneth's performance was the grandest of all from those early pleasure-filled days and nights when we giggled until dawn. I gazed sleepily at the glowing embers, saying nothing. I was so very happy, but I wanted to be with Colin Jones.

The weather stayed bitterly cold for the next two months. I took class with Winifred Edwards, went to the cinema and art galleries with Kenneth and Nico and Jeffrey, and caught up on piles of reading. Colin passed through London before going to Monte Carlo for Christmas with the touring company. It would have been wildly romantic to spend Christmas with my lover, *my lover Colin* – the words thrilled me! – dancing in Monte Carlo, an indolent setting of villas, gambling casinos and luxurious hotels. Instead I was stuck in dark, wet London with aching joints. I did not flaunt our relationship because I sensed that the Diners' Club would send me up. I did not babble about my emotions. But I did tell Donald that I would start looking for a flat. I would soon be twenty-three years old. I was now a *femme du monde*. I wanted a place of my own.

The week before Christmas Donald received a message from a young American actress named Jane Fonda whom he had met on his last American tour. She had appeared on Broadway and made a film or two but had not yet married the French director Roger Vadim who turned her into a sumptuous star. Jane Fonda was quite enamoured of Donald's dark sleek looks and social finesse. She was in

Paris and wanted to spend Christmas with him in London. He tactfully explained that his flatmate was very much in residence. Jane Fonda said she would stay in a hotel. She called back an hour later. The hotels were all booked. In the early sixties her name meant nothing to the reservation clerks. But Donald knew the house doctor at the Connaught who immediately arranged for a suite. 'Puss, you're so bloody glamorous,' I said, 'you have contacts *everywhere*.' Even Jane Fonda was impressed.

We were an odd little Christmas group. Jane Fonda, sparkling like an expensive Burgundy, listened with astonishment while Donald re-enacted our furniture burning party. We had plenty of logs on Christmas Day. I doubt if she believed that the instigator was Kenneth MacMillan who reclined on the sofa, a quiet, lanky lamb, who occasionally bleated for a drink, and he purposely did nothing to verify the tale by word or deed. He just smoked and smiled and ate bits of cheese, and smiled and smoked and ate more bits of cheese. Jane was accompanied by two French youths who periodically murmured, '*Ce n'est pas vrai*,' and stared uncertainly at Kenneth. He ignored them. I was handsomely turned out, Donald assured me, but rather cowed by Jane's smart leather boots, her ribbed pullover and brown chamois skirt fitted to an hour-glass waist.

With great subtlety she inspected me closely – 'the kooky dancer' who shared Donald's flat. Kenneth whispered that I withstood the inspection admirably. 'You are a star,' he said persuasively. 'Now go talk to her. She might think you're peculiar.'

'Why don't you?' I asked.

Kenneth slouched deeper in the sofa. 'I don't want to,' he replied, stretching his long legs.

Jane Fonda had studied with Lee Strasberg, director of the Actor's Studio in New York. Strasberg's school came out of the Stanislavsky Method – that an actor identify completely with the role he plays, drawing on every emotional and physical experience, quite often past events. We exchanged civilities and briefly discussed the business of acting-dancing. Did I not find the naturalistic method essential to understanding a part? she asked sweetly.

'I always try to find that kernel of truth,' I answered feebly, 'but then I just do it, it's instinctive. Dancing is my expression of feeling because sometimes I feel rather empty as a person. You know, almost backward, lacking in experience, why . . .'

Donald quickly handed me a glass of champagne. Suddenly I had two glasses. 'Lynn has her *own* method,' he said deliberately. Then he quickly asked Jane if she had seen the new Truffaut film.

I retreated to the sofa where Kenneth was examining the ceiling as if it had just been painted by Michelangelo. He pretended not to have overheard our chit-chat. 'I am peculiar,' I said, sinking on the cushions beside him. Kenneth nodded his head and exhaled a long stream of smoke from a stubby cigarette, continuing to examine the ceiling with big, wide innocent eyes. 'Do *you* think I'm peculiar?' I asked, cadging a cigarette from him.

He ignored the question and went right on smoking.

Two months later I rented my own flat in Pimlico. The house belonged to Johnny Cranko, who had left the Royal Ballet to become artistic director of the Stuttgart Ballet. Colin painted the one large room and built some shelves. My parents sent sheets and towels. I bought a bed. Decorating the flat took my mind off the anxiety of Not Dancing. 'I feel like a deaf mute,' I cried out in frustration to Kenneth who stopped over for afternoon tea. 'Here I am, in my first London flat, *mine*, and I have my first boyfriend, *mine*, and my life is out of synch because I can't perform. Grey days. Grey skies. *Grey me*.' I was not concentrating on the tea. Kenneth took a sip and then implored me to make another pot of tea, fresh tea, that didn't have 'blobby little black things floating around it'.

As the wintry weeks slowly dragged into spring, Kenneth and Colin – both seemed to possess an inexhaustible fund of patience – kept me from leaping out the window, although I would not have injured myself. The flat was in the basement. By summer I was allowed to do an occasional pas de deux and some dancing in the corps. The grey skies lifted when I was cast in a revival of Leonide Massine's stylized ballet *The Good-Humoured Ladies*, first produced by Diaghilev, to music by Scarlatti, in 1917. Massine had replaced Nijinsky as Diaghilev's personal favourite, a position he held until he dared exert some independence of his own. Eager to keep the old ballets alive, even the most obscure ones, Madam, who had danced in the Diaghilev production, invited Massine, then in his late seventies, to restage his work. Lydia Sokolova, a former Diaghilev star, was also in the revival. The short ballet was considerably less engaging than rehearsal chats and tea-breaks with Sokolova, one of the first British girls to join the Ballet Russe. Her real name was Hilda Munnings. 'My audition was here, in Covent Garden,' she said as we folded our limbs on some packing crates in the wings. 'I wore new ballet shoes. Very silly thing to do. I slipped onstage. Three times.' I promised never to appear on any stage in new ballet shoes. She clapped her hands delightedly, and squinted out at the semi-darkened stage and the tiers of empty seats. An endearing woman who knew every unspeakable folly and unmentionable foible of the ballet world, Sokolova, at sixty-six, convinced me that endurance, to a great degree, depends on a sense of humour. 'I see it in your eyes,' she said, 'yes, there is humour.' During a particularly black hour, after I left the Royal Ballet, the critic Dicky Buckle passed along a note that he had received from Lydia Sokolova written at this time. 'What of the divine Seymour

– quite lovely,' she said. 'With unspoilt charm and wit. I feel there is a real English ballerina in the bud at long last. Feet like Pavlova (but they work better). That is dancing as it should be, for the joy alone.'

Kenneth completed a new 'abstract' ballet, to music by Shostakovich, that he called *Symphony*. He was forking my tuna-fish casserole with chips on top in the Pimlico flat when he announced that the leading role was mine. The other guest of course was Colin Jones, who was sleeping over most of the time. Colin had left dancing and was working very hard as a photojournalist. Once I began seeing Colin steadily I dropped out of the meetings of the Diners' Club because Colin whisked me off to crumbling castles and museums in the Cotswolds. But the two most important chaps in my life were fond of each other, which relieved me, and Kenneth was the first to hear that I intended to marry Colin. We giggled privately over my becoming plain old 'Lynn Jones', after burying 'Berta Lynn Springbett', but I assured him that I would always be 'Lynn Seymour' to him.

Two days before the première of *Symphony* at Covent Garden I lay in a feverish pool of sweat, racked in pain. I was dead sick with a temperature that had me hallucinating. I saw myself running along a windy beach towards a strange distant figure who awaited me, whose face was hidden by the sun, a huge ball of fire. I took a short cut through a forest of pine and rock and then crashed violently against a sharp rock, unable to get up because I was bleeding profusely. The stranger disappeared, with the rocks and the pine trees and the sea. I looked around: I was lying on a stage, the curtain was ready to go up, and I was bleeding.

I awoke with a scream that would have normally aroused my neighbours, but it was midday, and the house, except for myself, was empty. I looked in the mirror. My complexion had a corpse-like pallor – waxen and bluish-white. My pulse beat furiously. Trembling fiercely from the nightmare, I poured myself a shot of whisky and crawled back into bed. Colin was out of town on assignment. Kenneth was with my replacement, a dancer of fragile beauty named Antoinette Sibley. Malicious popinjays tried to pit us against each other as rivals, but we were physically and emotionally opposites, and I always had a respectful affection for her. We had gone through ballet school together and she had graduated into the main company while I languished in the opera ballet with Betty Anderton and Christopher Gable.

I had to talk to someone, anyone. I had to hear myself speak. So I picked up the phone and dialled an international airline, inquiring about round-trip fares from London to Rome, with a Rome to New York return. The airlines are so polite; the voices are so confident and mellifluous. And would you like to make a reservation? I heard. Possibly next week, I answered, it depends on my husband. When the doctor came to the flat my temperature had gone down. I rang Kenneth. He had created a new ballet and I was stricken with fever. *Oh God, what is wrong with me?* I wept.

'The doctor says it's all right – I can do the second performance. Will you let me?' There was a pause, an intake of breath. My heart pounded with fear.

'Obviously,' Kenneth answered.

The following day my temperature fell, but the première had been and gone.

Colin and I decided to be married in Vancouver in the summer of 1963. The nuptials would take place after an American tour with the main company. Christopher Gable and I were in the main company – at last. Colin hoped to arrange magazine assignments that would keep him busy in the States while I danced *Symphony* with Donald MacLeary and *The Invitation* and a couple of *Swan Lakes* with Christopher. The tour started in New York. It was only my second visit. Nora Kaye and Herbert Ross said that I must stay with them in their house on Jane Street in Greenwich Village. I accepted, gratefully. Years of touring had given me a phobia about hotels, even the poshest ones, and Nora and Herbert are the sort of people you can be completely natural with, shoes kicked off. Herbert was having quite a bit of success on Broadway. He had just choreographed and directed the musical version of *Tovarich*, co-starring Vivien Leigh and Jean-Pierre Aumont, and was basking in a winner from the previous year – *I Can Get It for You Wholesale*, the musical that introduced a funny-looking little Brooklyn girl with the untheatrical name of Barbra Streisand.

The Jane Street house was disarmingly homey – casually furnished with plump chairs and couches, clusters of roses and violets in glass bowls, stacks of books on every subject, heaps of newspapers, magazines and theatre-dance memorabilia. Humming away, her face wreathed in smiles, Nora cooked breakfast in the morning before shooing me off to class. If Herbert had not appeared by our second cup of coffee, Nora would call upstairs, '*Her-BIT!* I want to hear those two feet on the floor!'

Then she wriggled an eyebrow, implying that one had to prod the dears or they did get into mischief. I spent more hours browsing around the antique shops, bookstores and boutiques in the Village where I always houseguest on New York visits, though the Rosses have moved uptown to a skyscraper on Central Park West. I am very comfortable amidst the easy sophistication of Greenwich Village. The zigzaggy streets, outdoor flower stalls, and mews houses remind me of London. I even found a pub where I could read the morning paper undisturbed.

'What pub?' Nora asked with motherly solicitude.

'Julius, on Waverly Place.'

Nora and Herbert howled with laughter. 'It's not just a pub,' Nora said. 'It's a gay bar.'

I shrugged away the news. 'Well, it looks like any pub in London to me,' I said. 'It's just a matter of how one sees other people.'

After performances at the new Met in Lincoln Center, Nora's mother had a light supper on the table for me. This was usually borsch – a beetroot soup with a dollop of sour cream. The Rosses, so winsomely hospitable, brought out bowls of borsch, prepared by Nora's mum, for Donald MacLeary and Georgina Parkinson. A stately dancer with jet-black hair, blue eyes framed by silky lashes and a flawless complexion, Georgina, who was nicknamed George or 'the-beautiful-Georgina' or simply 'the BGP', danced with us in *Symphony*.

One Sunday evening we were gossiping around the kitchen table when the phone rang. Nora answered. 'What time is it over there?' She winked at me extravagantly and mouthed in a stage-whisper that could be heard to Battery Park, 'It's Kenneth!' We replied in a loud volley, *'WHO?'* Nora handed me the phone.

'How are the *Pigeons*?' Kenneth asked in his unmistakably languid voice. I replied that the reviews were all good but Sol Hurok was either dropping *The Pigeons* from the rep or just keeping the second act at the gypsy encampment in which I did not appear. But Kenneth had not telephoned from London to inquire about the reviews of Ashton's ballet. He had a specific and surprising message: he was sailing from Southampton in two days on the SS *France*. Colin was coming with him. I had not expected to see Colin until Vancouver, three months hence, but he had cleverly wangled two photo assignments in America. Kenneth, who refused to fly at that time, and hated travelling alone, had speedily booked a stateroom on the French line. 'My two chaps will be here in a week,' I announced breathlessly to the kitchen klatch, which was desperate to see Kenneth. I was particularly desperate to see Colin. I missed being with him. I missed seeing the world through his sage photographer's eyes. And I missed crossing the Atlantic with him and Kenneth on the *France*, and playing shuffleboard with them. Since Nora and Herbert, coincidentally, were themselves sailing for London, they generously insisted that we all stay in the Jane Street house with Nora's mother, who worshipped Kenneth. She was constantly fluffing his pillows.

Kenneth, Colin and I only had a short time together. Kenneth was departing for London after our New York engagement and Colin had a photo assignment in Alabama and Mississippi. There was another departure that had Kenneth and me in the doldrums. Dame Ninette was making her last visit to New York as director of the Royal Ballet. The woman who had created the company and brought it to an apogee of artistic achievement never surpassed, was retiring. Her successor was Frederick Ashton. We were going to miss her terribly. In a mood of muted sadness, like children being separated from a beloved parent, the chaps and I went to hear Mabel Mercer in a dilapidated midtown club called The Upstairs at the Downstairs. 'I can't sing for toffee anymore,' said the incomparable Mabel, an adorable *café-au-lait* dumpling who had sung at Bricktop's club in Paris during the thirties, 'so what I'm going to do is tell you a story, to music.' Her clarity and subtle use of inflection, her elegant phrasing of a lyric, brought tears to our eyes when she sang 'Down in the Depths (on the 90th Floor)'. The song expressed our own emotions. Kenneth slumped in the rickety chair, an elbow propped on our table, not much bigger than a saucer, and tightly closed his eyes. I slipped my hand into Colin's, unsettled, unnerved and convulsed with a throbbing heart.

'What's up, Lynnie?' Colin whispered tenderly.

'Nothing.' I blubbed. 'Everything.'

The Wedding.

'How excited and half-pleased, half-apprehensive you must be over Lynn's forthcoming marriage,' Winifred Edwards exclaimed in a letter to my mom. 'I think my main feeling is one of great gladness for her. I believe the loving companionship and security of marriage will give her what she has lacked so much through all these years. Colin Jones is a likeable, manly young man. He was a tough, rather naughty boy in the ballet school. Then went into the opera ballet, army and touring company. Realizing he would not go to the top as a dancer, he wisely decided to leave the ballet and return to "real life". I think they will start life together as comrades, on a level with each other, give and take. Lynn will no longer have to wear the armour these children build who are proud, reserved and lonely. She is tired after the long season and cruel winter, and needs this time *with you* and rest!'

I danced again for the Vancouver Ballet Society and three days later Colin and I were married at the Vancouver yacht club. Colin had been brought up as a Roman Catholic, a faith which he had cast aside but not too far. He thought we should be married by a priest. So we found a cleric who espoused a reasonable faith.

A nifty young English graphic designer named Johnny Hogarth, who entertained us for hours at the Diners' Club with obscene tales of the fashion world, made my wedding outfit – a dainty snow-white suit with a vested jacket that fitted snugly over a diaphanous blouse. My hat was what Kenneth called 'a slightly Bea Lillie beanie'. Colin presented me with an exquisite French antique ring of two golden hands holding a diamond heart-shaped solitaire. Bruce was best man and gave a stag party for Colin the day before the wedding. He also made certain that Colin had a haircut. The mini-skirt and the shaggy Beatle-style hair – the two most visible trademarks of soon to be 'Swinging London' – had not yet reached Vancouver. Colin's hair was just thick and curly. But, in 1963, any man in North America whose hair wasn't closely clipped was very iffy. 'You're being stuffy and provincial,' I argued with Bruce, to no avail. Colin wanted to please the Springbetts and then I accused *him* of being provincial. A few years later the world was inundated with lads whose hair was long, short, curled, twirled, bunched and pinioned. So much for conventions. Our honeymoon was spent in the Canadian woods, swimming and fishing.

Another new address awaited me in London. 'Colin, this is it. I am not moving again for years.' Anya Linden had recently married and we inherited her flat in Charleyville Mansions for eight pounds a week. The neighbourhood was shabby – grand old houses peeling, chipped and tilting ominously like dominoes ready to fall. But we had four rooms, including a cold comfort cubicle for overnight guests – usually Kenneth – and a narrow space that Colin quickly fixed up as his own darkroom where he pridefully showed me the wonder of developing and printing photographs. The flat was a short walk from the ballet school in Barons Court where I took daily classes and rehearsed whatever management decided I would be performing. Best of all, Christopher Gable and Carole Needham lived across the road. The original Diners' Club sadly disbanded – or regrouped. Like most young marrieds, Colin and I entertained other young marrieds: Christopher and Carole, Kenneth and Diana Rowell, Georgina Parkinson and Roy Round.

But Kenneth MacMillan was always with us. He looked upon the lot at Charleyville Mansions as *his* special little brood and we looked upon him as *our* precocious little boy. I saw him daily and talked with him on the phone every night, even after we just had drinks or dinner together.

That winter Colin and I were both struck down simultaneously with severe colds. We lay in our new brass bed, swathed in sweaters, under a mountain of blankets. Kenneth volunteered to play doctor. He came over with aspirin and juices and a bottle of whisky. 'I don't know why you're always sick,' he muttered, un-ravelling himself at the foot of the bed after pouring us cups of hot tea with whisky. Colin said that Kenneth maintained his health by keeping his body temperature the same all year long.

The concept appealed to Kenneth. 'You might be right,' he agreed.

'You're both potty. Give me the phone, I'm going to call Christopher.' Kenneth shook his head and made tut-tut-nurse noises; if I phoned anyone he would not make dinner. '*Dinner?* Oh, Kenneth, you lovely old thing!' My char lady had already done the shopping. Kenneth broiled chops, tossed a salad and replenished our cups of tea-and-whisky. We all ate on the bed, picnic-style, finishing off the Scotch which produced a state of euphoric and inoperable bliss. When Colin and I began to nod off, Kenneth asked timidly, 'Do I have to go home now?'

Kenneth was the first guest in the Box & Bumpf Room, so named because the cubicle was a repository of unpacked books and bric-à-brac which would be attended to someday in the future.

It was a happy, loving period. Colin wanted his parents to meet our friends, so we threw a buffet party. Colin invited reporters and photographers from the *Observer*. I invited members of the Diners' Club, past and present. We were nervous at first, but as people arrived with bottles of wine and I mixed American cocktails, forgetting the ratio of gin to dry vermouth, we unconcernedly prepared to blend the pagan and parental worlds. Minutes before Colin's parents were due, we lost our self-possession.

The lights fused.

The entire flat was plunged into blackness, a situation dramatized a short time later by Peter Shaffer in his play *Black Comedy*. I gave everyone candles which produced the bawdiest remarks, as the Diners' Club membership asked the press to perform unseemly services with the candles. Amidst this rambunctious pandemonium, my in-laws arrived. 'It's like the blitz, isn't it?' I said cheerfully, leading them by the hand into the darkened sitting room. I was bereft of further words and sank on to a chair only to discover that Nico was already sitting there. Kenneth had withdrawn to the Box & Bumpf room and locked the door. 'He said to tell you he was wanda,' said Nico. 'Wanda' was a code word for depleted, prostrate, spaced-out. We were all a bit wanda that evening. I am afraid Colin's parents assumed that wanda was our way of life.

Not quite.

I was dancing a full rep at Covent Garden. Some critics who had previously reacted mildly to *The Invitation* reversed themselves and were unanimous in their praise. Critics seldom reverse opinions in any of the arts, so I have the deepest respect for the rare few who have the supreme confidence to confess, 'I've changed my mind.' Reporters consistently asked to interview me and my outspoken quotes always amused. 'Dancers are assumed to be stupid or tiresome,' I informed one journalist. 'I'm painfully aware of all the things I don't *know*.'

'Your mates at the Garden will love that comment,' said Colin.

'But it's true. I certainly couldn't tell the writer about Schnubia. How do you think that would go down with Sir Fred?'

Schnubia was also part of our private vocabulary. The

word evolved one night at dinner when Kenneth joined Christopher and Carole at our table. After a hard day, whatever your business, you are just tuckered out. And if you relax, you want to really let go with friends. We were all tense. Christopher and Carole were suffering rehearsal fatigue. Kenneth was fretting over a new ballet. Colin was anxiously waiting for his negatives to dissolve into prints; and I had been working on that lugubrious peasant Giselle. We had a date again at the Garden. I was so tired that I mixed the salad with detergent instead of vinegar. That set us off. Dinner came to a halt and, chortling like maniacs on leave from an asylum, we opened a bottle of this and a bottle of that, and began expanding our private vocabulary. Code words drew us even closer together and permitted flights of wild Rabelaisian fancy, which Kenneth loved. The saga of Schnubia, concocted mostly by Christopher and Kenneth, illustrates the lunatic camaraderie.

Kenneth's sweat pants, which he wore to rehearsal, were always stretched out of shape because, as Christopher jested, 'You spend so much time on your bum, sitting down.' Expressing mock horror, Kenneth retorted that his bum was his own territory, and not our business.

'It's a free country,' said Colin.

'It's Schnubia!' announced Christopher, who had been reading Evelyn Waugh's *Scoop*, a comic novel about a diffident nature columnist dispatched by mistake to cover a crisis in the fictional country of Ishmaelia. Waugh had Ishmaelia, we had Schnubia. Kenneth, we decided, was an émigré from Schnubia. Before the Great Revolution he had been the High Priest of Schnubia because of his famous bum, the Schnubian Bum, a mark of great beauty and excellence. In Schnubia the men were known as the Hemorroids and the women were the Dammoroids. They lived near a mountain range called the Mighty Piles. Each year, until the Great Revolution, seven beautiful maidens brought gifts of fruit and vegetables to the temple where Kenneth presided. At the culmination of the ceremony in which the Dammoroids submitted to the desires of the High Priest, their pears and apples and potatoes and cauliflowers were stuffed up his arse, which accounted for the distinctive shape of the Schnubian Bum. The Hemorroids looked upon these rites with disfavour, for they were envious of the High Priest, and made him flee through the Mighty Piles to – where else? – *England*.

I never finished making dinner that evening. Carole took over. She opened the fridge. 'Oh. Here are three artichokes.' She turned to Kenneth, who squirmed in his chair. Tugging at his sweat pants, he fled to the Box & Bumpf room.

We had many evenings like that, riotously pissed, gloriously ribald.

Our first wedding anniversary was celebrated on the island of Ibiza with Christopher and Carole. Two other younger company dancers, also married – David Wall and Alfreda Thorogood – happened to be there. The holiday was languorous and sun-drenched. One blistering day we explored the inlets and beaches around the town of Santa Eulalia, where we had booked rooms. Carrying picnic baskets of cheeses, lusciously ripe tomatoes, bread and bottles of wine we hiked over craggy cliffs and steep rocks until we found an isolated cove of pink sand and a warm blue sea. We idled for an hour or more, playing in the water, nipping the wine, sunning ourselves, nipping more wine, taking huge bites of tomatoes, and then rinsing off in the sea, and nipping some more wine. Christopher noticed a white villa, set far back among palm trees swaying gently in the afternoon breeze. A rotund gentleman was watching us through binoculars. We were in bikinis, more or less, and there was quite a lot of flesh to see.

'Tell him to come and join us,' I said, waving to the chap.

Christopher relayed the message in English. The binoculars did not budge. 'Try Spanish, my darling,' I sighed, dropping my head on Colin's golden-brown shoulder. Christopher answered that he did not know that much Spanish, so he gestured towards the sand and the sea. Nothing happened. Christopher pointed to us. 'Don't overdo it, my darling, he might misunderstand,' I said.

The man was just a peeping Tom. Irritated at his lack of sociability, we agreed, after guzzling another bottle of wine, to 'fix him'.

Facing the sea, with our backs to him, we formed a tipsy chorus line.

'Uno. Dos. Tres,' Christopher called out. Down came our bikini bottoms and up went six sets of white curvy behinds. The man exploded in Spanish, shouting, '*Guardia civil*'. He hurried down the steps of the white villa, jumped into a jeep and roared off, whipping up a cloud of dust. 'We don't have to worry about him,' I protested. 'It's a long way to Seville from here.'

The chaps thought we had better push off anyway. 'I have a sense of foreboding,' Colin said, as the last empty bottle floated out to sea. Stumbling against each other, our bikinis once again in place, we hustled over rocks, through bushes and fresh water ponds, and a forest of prickly trees, finally reaching the public beach. Quite a sight we were – sweaty, out of breath, and plastered. We went directly to a cabaña-bar run by an Englishman who called himself Bunty. Bunty had lived in Santa Eulalia so long that he spoke 'Catalonian English'. His hands gyrated like airplane propellers and he used a rinse that made his grey hair saffron or amber, depending on the day's wash. He was a dear. Over Cuba Libres, his treat, we related our peccadillo on the pink beach. He thought we might be in for a tthfpot of trouble. We had trespassed on to the private beach of a wealthy landowner and he had gone to fetch,

Bunty suspected, *la guardia civil* – the police. Bunty urged us to scatter. Christopher and Colin dashed into the sea. The others stretched out on separate clumps of sand. I was in no condition to endure the blinding sun. I stayed in the bar with Bunty, who gave me another Cuba Libre.

'Don't you have anything to read? I need to focus my eyes on something.' Bunty gave me a tattered old muscle magazine. I pulled a face.

'What tew you want? Proufftt?'

At that moment *la guardia civil*, as Bunty predicted, swaggered into the bar. Two of them – Dos and Dishy were my names for them. They interrupted Bunty. He answered in perfect Spanish, without any impediment. They proceeded to the public beach where four other guardsmen trudged in boots through the sand, accompanied by the landowner, his eyes scanning every face. 'It's not the faces he'd recognize,' I muttered to Bunty, who refilled my drink. Our humourless pursuer came into the bar and sat down next to me, jabbering away in Spanish. Expressing shock and dismay, Bunty served him a Cuba Libre. The jowly-cheeked señor, whose shirt was damp with perspiration, turned to me. Bunty said casually, *'française'*. I flipped the pages of Bunty's magazine, issuing a series of *'mon dieu*'s and *'Oooo-la-la*'s! The señor finished his drink and stomped out, reconnoitring with the guardsmen who slapped their thighs angrily and sauntered off in disgust. The señor, Bunty said, owned a hotel in town, a Mercedes and a yacht. I thanked Bunty for saving us from arrest and sensational tabloid headlines in London.

'What a shame,' I sighed. 'We could have shown him *tthuch* a good time.'

Some months after the Ibiza holiday Johnny Cranko invited me to Stuttgart to dance in his production of *Romeo and Juliet*. Cranko was building a prestigious company, a miniature Royal Ballet, in the provincial German town. Marcia Haydée, one of my first friends at ballet school in London, was Cranko's muse. Johnny, who died tragically of a heart attack in 1973 at the age of forty-five, had a remarkable gift of language. He articulated what he wanted from his dancers with a vibrant Oscar Wildean wit. Words flowed easily, his thoughts were communicated briskly, precisely, with a razor-sharp clarity. No mutters, stutters, murmurs or mumbles. Dancers loved working with Cranko, a man with large blue childlike eyes and shaggy hair, and he had collected a marvellous group of ballet zanies who sparked the dreary town of Stuttgart. Cranko's dancers came from top companies all over the world; both they and guest choreographers knew there was no existing dance establishment to compare with the Stuttgart Ballet. I was in Stuttgart for Juliet while Kenneth MacMillan was directing a ballet there. 'I'm so nervous, Kenneth, what's wrong with me? I adore Johnny, the dancers and even *you're* here.'

'It's the first time you're dancing away from the Royal Ballet,' he reminded me, laughing softly, 'and you want to make a good impression on Marcia.' Of course I had told him about my teenage forays to Covent Garden with Marcia Haydée and our lunches at Mrs Honeybun's. I still envied Marcia's lovely long neck and back. She envied my feet and legs. A superbly talented and unaffected woman, Marcia now directs the Stuttgart company. She taught me the role of Juliet and was a loyal friend. Cranko's dancers had their own code vocabulary, so Kenneth and I returned to London with a whole new batch of words. Marcia christened a step in which the legs open in a balletic spreadiness as the Wide-On. In Stuttgart the word Ninny was a euphemism for private parts and their satisfaction.

'How's Ninny this morning? Did Ninny have a good time last night?' The most commonly heard combination of words, singly, doubly, or all together, was Hilda Monica Riva.

'What did you think of the performance?'

'Oh, my dear. *Hilda*. Absolutely Hilda.' Hilda was Stuttgartese for horrible.

'Hilda *Monica*, do you s'pose?' Monica referred to the menstrual cycle. Riva was revolting. And if a dancer's performance was described as Hilda Monica *Riva*, well, that was the worst. You could not sink much lower.

My Romeo partner was Ray Barra, a personable, funny chap who had danced with American Ballet Theatre. Ray's parents were Spanish and he had romantic Andalusian eyes. His nickname was Theda Bara. The atmosphere was comfortable, bitchy, easy – and entirely professional. Kenneth and I were naturally delighted by the comradeship of Johnny Cranko, Marcia Haydée and the whole Stuttgart crew. I danced one performance and half-expected to hear mutters of 'Hilda Monica Riva', or just 'Hilda', but when Cranko and Kenneth both complimented me, I breathed a sigh of relief: it had gone down well. If choreographers have doubts, they don't waste words. They say nothing. Then you go home and spend the night with your head over a toilet bowl. Cranko's production, to Prokofiev's music, stirred Kenneth's intensely imaginative mind. He wanted to choreograph a full-length ballet. He wanted to create a spectacular ballet in which I would be acclaimed as an international star. The obvious ballet was *Romeo and Juliet* and the obvious partner was Christopher Gable. Our three-way collaboration would be electric. Covent Garden would have a new 'star team' – Seymour and Gable. But such a project was extremely costly and required – obviously – the agreement of the Garden. Kenneth was ready, indeed itching, to extend himself on a full-length romantic classic, and Christopher and I were willing to slave with him night and day and dawn.

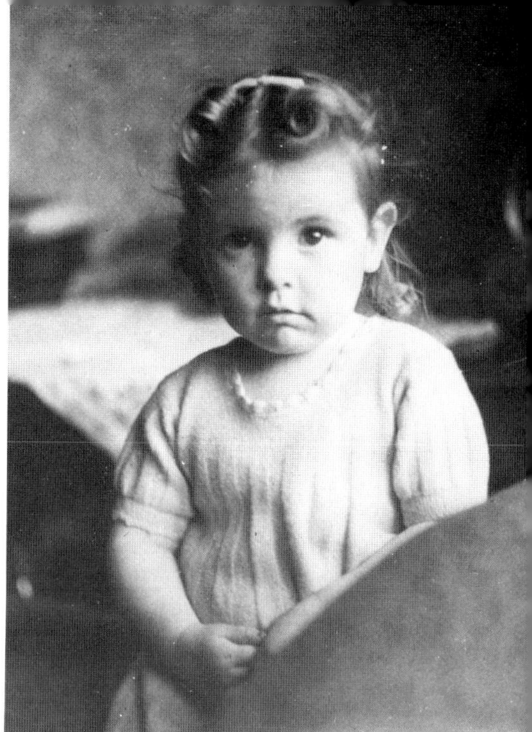

Memories of Canada: myself looking apprehensive aged 2 (in 1941); with my brother Bruce; at Kitsilano beach, Vancouver, in the pose I was to use many years later in *Anastasia*

ABOVE 'Among Jean Jepson's tulips' (front row, centre) in the Sun-Ray Revue

LEFT The rooftops of Paddington: I was 15 when I came to London in 1954

BELOW Fledgling in the garden – from cygnet to Isadorable

The Invitation: the role in which I acquired
actress status

The Invitation: two innocents in the garden – first encounter with Christopher Gable, who played the role of my cousin, and the last moments of horrified disillusionment

ABOVE Corpsing at a rehearsal of
Images of Love – Christopher Gable,
'Kabuki Lil' and Rudi Nureyev

RIGHT With Marcia Haydée, learning
Cranko's *Romeo and Juliet,* during her
early days at Stuttgart. She is now the
Stuttgart's director

BELOW The can-can from *La Boutique
Fantasque* with Alexander Grant. I
was taught the role by Moira Shearer

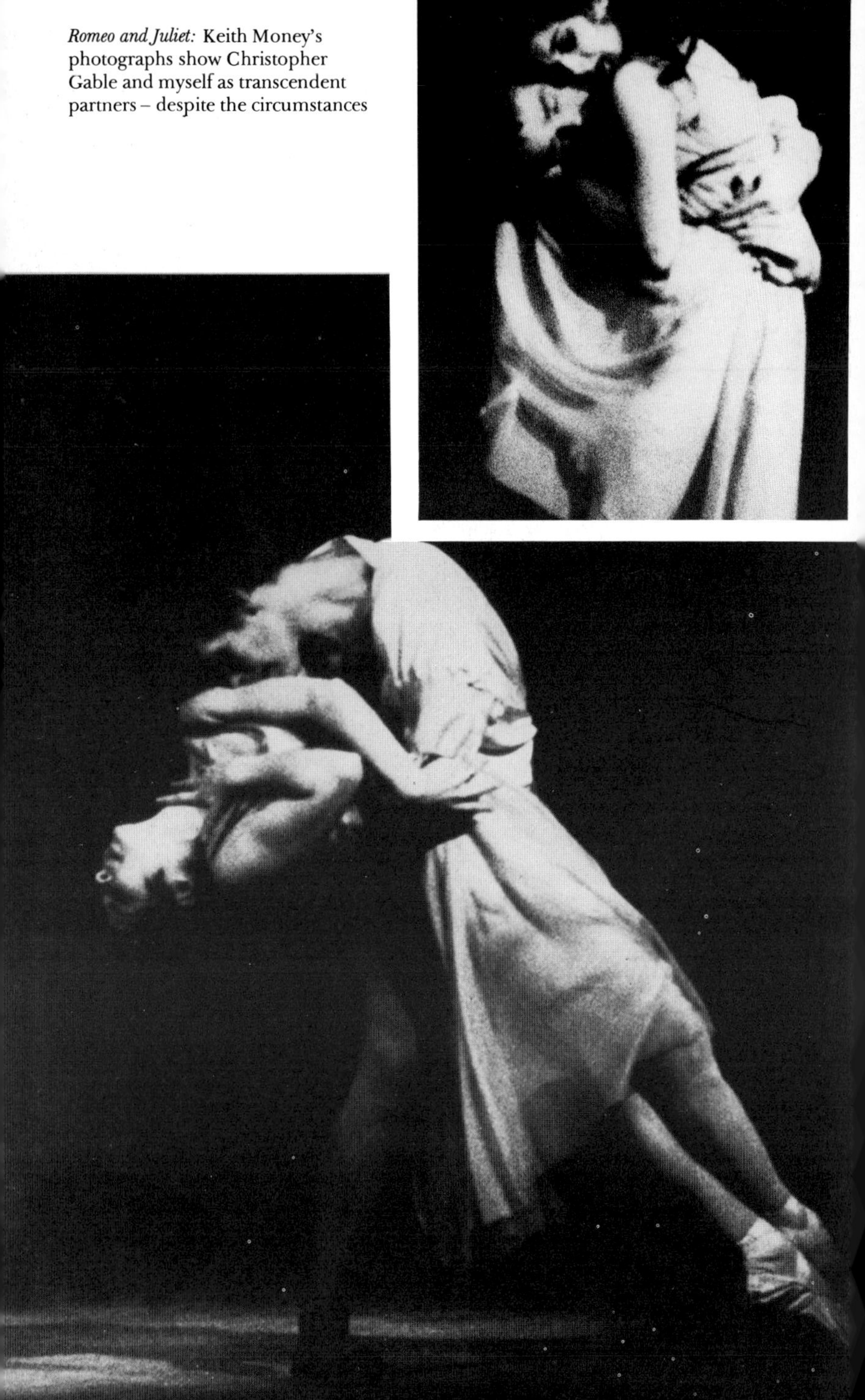

Romeo and Juliet: Keith Money's photographs show Christopher Gable and myself as transcendent partners – despite the circumstances

With Christopher – somewhere in Verona

Conscripted *Voluntaries* with David
Wall, Tetley's tribute to John Cranko;
a Russian jeté in *Symphony;*
'kamiquasi' *Rituals;* and Alvin Ailey's
Flowers – the created Janis Joplin role

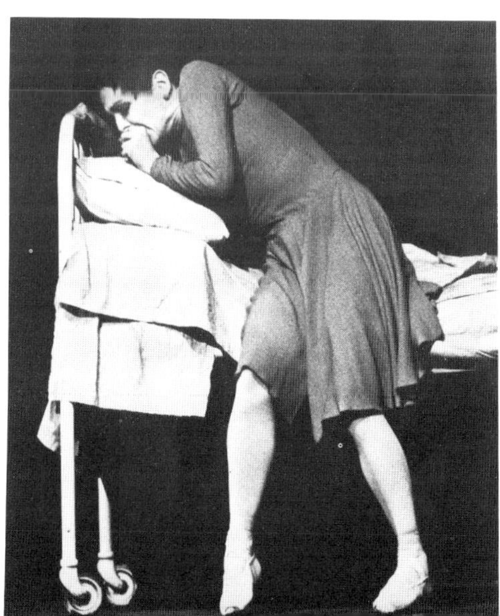

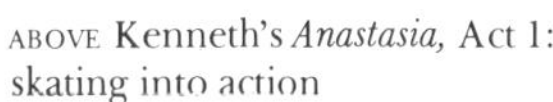

ABOVE Kenneth's *Anastasia,* Act 1:
skating into action

RIGHT *Anastasia,* Act III: alienation –
the harrying aftermath of the
Revolution and the massacre at
Ekaterinburg

Crickmay's photographs show my 'Vidal Sassoon crop' in close-up. Further scenes from *Anastasia*

Rehearsing *Laborintus* with Glen Tetley (David Ashmol looks suitably perplexed) . . and 'bemused' by Kenneth Macmillan (1980)

RIGHT Jerome Robbin's
Dances at a Gathering

BELOW Mayerling with David
Wall. The closest I ever
came to social climbing!

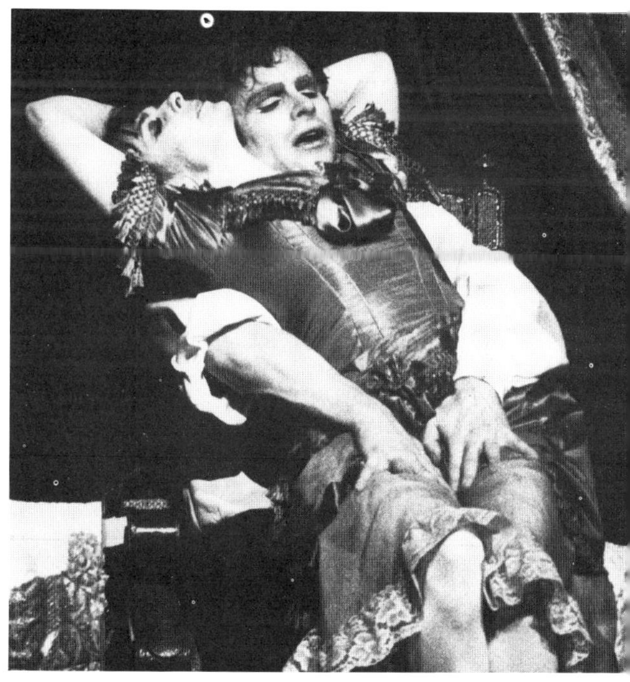

OPPOSITE The Divine Fred: with Sir
Frederick Ashton rehearsing *A Month in the
Country*

BELOW Ashton's *Isadora*

ABOVE On hols with Rudi in Corfu: Demian navigating

LEFT One-parent family at Sainsbury's, Palladium gala 1980 . . .

BELOW Vanya and Lynn Hackel, 1983. I feel more like I do now!

In September, I was asked to dance on Canadian television and said to Christopher, 'Partner, you're coming with me. We'll fly direct from London. No more junkets to Amsterdam!' Kenneth, who had been mulling his *Romeo* project and had even proposed it to the management, said he would create a pas de deux for us from his envisioned production, though he had not been given a firm go-ahead. In rehearsal Kenneth first conceived a pas de deux, which serves as the fulcrum for his work. Christopher and I – both in fine fettle – responded to what Kenneth wanted as if we three were under a potent spell. Like a man possessed, Kenneth completed the balcony pas de deux in three rehearsals.

'Lynnie, do you think they'll let Kenneth do *Romeo*?' Christopher asked as we flew to Toronto.

'Why not, my darling? And it's going to change our lives.'

We danced the *Romeo* pas de deux, and returned to London via New York, stopping to see Nora Kaye and Herbert Ross, who predicted that MacMillan's *Romeo*, co-starring us, would be a major event in the dance world. We talked of nothing but the *Romeo* possibility. It was thrilling and, for me, one day, utterly nauseous.

Christopher and I shared a borrowed flat in the Village. I was in the kitchen opening a bottle of club soda. I suddenly felt sick to my stomach. I thought I was going to faint. I leaned against the dishwasher, accidentally pressing various buttons. Disgorging water, the machine thumped and groaned. I cried out for Christopher. Holding me in one arm he finally managed to turn off the machine. We were, after all, quite unfamiliar with American gadgetry. I slid to the floor. 'I'll be all right, Christopher. I just went dizzy . . .' He carried me to the couch.

'Lynn's flaking out, she seems awfully tired,' Christopher confided to Nora. But this was no normal 'flake-out'. I suspected what was wrong and the knowledge struck me like a merciless karate chop. Panic-stricken, I told Nora, 'I think I'm pregnant.' I said nothing to Christopher – or anyone else. First I wanted to consult my doctor in London.

'Well, Miss Seymour – I mean, Mrs Jones – you're going to have a baby,' he confirmed with a smile.

I walked aimlessly for hours, from Marble Arch to Hyde Park, from Piccadilly Circus to Covent Garden, trying not to cry or scream or fling myself in front of a lorry. Dancers do *not* have babies in their mid-twenties; it changes, said everyone, the stomach muscles. Most dancers do not have children until their early thirties. Some do not have any children at all. I was then twenty-four. The timing was off. A child would remove me from the ballet for too long. The struggle, the misery, the poverty – no, it wasn't worth it, I repeated over and over, staring blankly ahead. The years of loneliness, of provincial tours and blistered bleeding feet – but, at last, I was married, my husband loved me, and I had friends, and a very special friend, Kenneth, whose dream of *Romeo and Juliet* was coming true, not just for him, but for me, too.

Colin was in his darkroom when I entered the flat. I sat in a bentwood rocking-chair I had bought in New York, and rocked idly, overwhelmed by a despairing trance. Pouring a shot of whisky, I telephoned Kenneth. 'Hullo, Lynnie,' he said. 'Colin didn't know where you were. But you know about *Romeo*. What shall we do tonight? Christopher has two bottles of champagne.'

I was on the verge of hysteria. My voice was breaking when I explained my visit to the doctor and his findings. There followed a long silence and I thought I heard a stifled sob at the other end of the line.

'I have the Garden dates,' Kenneth said. His voice was a mere whisper. '*Romeo* opens in February.' Another long silence. I could not speak. 'Have you told Colin?' When I answered, no, he said, 'It seems to me you should.'

I made a pot of tea and was slicing a lemon with trembling fingers when Colin came into the kitchen, exuberant and boyishly handsome. He kissed me. 'Kenneth's been phoning, and Christopher – Oh, Romeo, Romeo.' He poured himself a cup of tea. 'Do come and see my new pictures.' I sank clumsily into a kitchen chair. 'Lynnie, you look dreadful. Maybe you should see a doctor.' In a dead voice I reported in detail that I already had.

Minutes ticked by. I said nothing. My heart beat furiously. Colin waited, tense and silent.

'You're thinking of *Romeo*, aren't you?' He stubbed out his cigarette and retreated to the darkroom.

The telephone was ringing again. It was Christopher. 'Lynnie, you were right. *Romeo* is going to change our lives.'

Change? I was wrong. It did more than that.

Romeo broke hearts and shattered my life.

CHAPTER 11

Star-Cross'd Lovers

'You didn't fit neatly into any box. You didn't come wrapped in a nice safe package. The Royal Ballet didn't know what they had.'

'But what about you, Christopher? They should never have let *you* get away.'

Christopher Gable and I are lying on a pile of cushions in the garden, facing each other in the full glare of August sunshine. He is now the father of two children and, at forty-one, more handsome than ever. He wears an outfit we associate with Kenneth – a sweat shirt and pants. 'Kenneth called it a track suit,' Christopher frequently corrected me. I have on sweat pants, too, and a Mickey Mouse T-shirt. I bought it for one of my boys and then requisitioned it for myself. For Christopher's visit to Woodstock Road I stuck purple dahlias hither and thither in my hair. A bit of around-the-house glam. Christopher is closer than an old mate. He is the one partner with whom I took death-defying risks – without fear. I love Christopher, the brother I always wanted in London, and finally had.

Lying on his back, gazing into the summer day, a hot colour burning his cheeks, Christopher recounted for the first time how his being in the Royal Ballet was a lucky 'accident'. He had mentioned this to Maggie Lee at our closing night party in Hull years ago, on our first provincial tour. Maggie thought he was joking. But his story is important to me, because Christopher is important to me. And it demonstrates, as Maggie Lee said, how the most astonishing careers can be accidental. It was pure chance that brought us together in *The Invitation* and *The Two Pigeons*.

Christopher grew up in the East End of London, a cockney kid. His weekly treat, like mine in Vancouver, was to see a movie at a big glittering picture palace. The great old Hollywood movies gave us all surreal fantasies. He conceived a lust for Carmen Miranda, the Brazilian bombshell in the tutti-frutti hat who danced in tropical production numbers surrounded by strawberries and bananas. He wanted to dance on polished floors with cauliflowers and avocados on his head. But boys who danced were something nameless. His mum said he could have dancing lessons if he also had piano lessons. The piano was respectable. At the age of eleven he was accepted at the ballet school and valiantly withstood the taunts of neighbourhood toughs. He graduated in the Sadler's Wells opera ballet and we created a heatwave in the pas de deux for *Orpheus*. When I was promoted into the touring company, Christopher, unbeknownst to me, had been unofficially discarded. He was moved into the Covent Garden opera ballet, an official – and cruel – snub. He had a month's vacation before getting into his slave costume and bronze paint for *Aida*. Feeling desperate, he rang up John Field, director of the touring company, and told an outrageous fib. 'I've sprained my ankle and would like to take company class so I can get into shape for *Aida*.' He hoped John Field would appreciate his talent – as others clearly had not. When the company opened its tour in Golders Green, Christopher was, of course, left behind. But a dancer injured his back and John Field remembered Christopher. 'That blond lad, is he free – where can I reach him?' Field asked. And so Christopher found himself with Betty Anderton and me in the touring company as a replacement, hoping that he would become a permanent member. *The Burrow* had its première at Covent Garden, we prepared for the spring provincial tour and Christopher received word that he had to return to the opera ballet: our injured corps boy was in fine fettle and

Christopher was not needed. Morally demolished, he dragged himself home and sat in an armchair, staring into space. He did not even go to opera rehearsals. Then Fate intervened. One of the corps girls discovered she was pregnant and dropped out of the tour. Her husband, a corps dancer, departed with her, accepting a chorus role in the West End production of *My Fair Lady*. Christopher received another phone call. He returned to the company and stayed, without ever revealing his weeks of worry.

When Christopher left the Royal Ballet for the theatre and films, the press said he stopped dancing because of injuries. He had already struggled back once from a terrifying operation removing a joint from both big toes because of the presence of osteo-arthritis. After months of patient exercise he had regained the flexibility of those joints and learnt to dance again. When, a few years later, the condition began to reappear and the pain returned, he lost heart and decided to turn his mind to an acting career.

In later years I danced *Romeo* with Rudolf Nureyev, Mikhail Baryshnikov and David Wall. But my partnership with Christopher ended with Kenneth's first production of *Romeo* at Covent Garden in 1965.

My maturest performances as a dancer in the Royal Ballet rep were in the mid-seventies, when, for almost four years, I seemed unable to make a wrong move. Nora Kaye remarked that I was the phoenix risen from the ashes, and there were plenty of ashes scattered across England and Europe. But I never recovered from the loss of Christopher Gable. Great partnerships are based on personality, temperament, physicality, musicality and the magnetic coupling you find in a love affair. Great partnerships are as rare as the Koh-i-noor diamond. Kenneth MacMillan was cutting that diamond, and it was lost.

I was never a good partner for Baryshnikov, incidentally. When we danced *Romeo* we hardly knew each other. There had been no time to build up the partner rapport *I* need. The ballet has two exacting duets and unless the dancers are familiar with each other's bodies – the hollows and curves and quirky corners – a tempestuous Juliet can easily overbalance her Romeo. Mischa and I rehearsed before the evening performance. At one point I over-balanced, bringing with me the robust Mischa, who was unaccustomed to my difficult body. That evening I danced very carefully. I knew Kenneth's choreography inside and out. Mischa did not. And since every performance is *dangerous*, I wanted Mischa to feel utterly confident.

'*Romeo* was far more traumatic for you,' Christopher was saying. 'Do you think much about . . .' he stopped, cautiously, moistened his lips, and said, 'it.' *It*. I shook my head, but there was something unsatisfactory about the movement. Christopher knew I was fibbing. My headshake was entirely false. 'You needed to be protected, Lynnie. There was no one to do that.' He shifted his position so that he sat cross-legged on the cushions, gazing down at me. 'Rather like a mystery, a whodunit,' he sighed wistfully.

'There cannot be many suspects,' I replied, pulling a flower from my hair and stripping off the petals, one by one. 'I was just good old Seymour. *Reliable* Seymour. I am certain no one really considered that I had been smacked in the face.' For years I blocked out the memory of the première of *Romeo*. I pulled up the old socks, soiling with age, and focused on my three boys who awaited me at home, snuggled in bed, after Garden performances. 'How'd it go, Mum?' the twins would ask at breakfast, with grave concern. 'All right,' I would answer, spooning cornflakes into cereal bowls. 'And how many curtain calls?' they always wanted to know. 'I don't count them any more,' I responded truthfully.

Christopher took my hand and rubbed it against his cheek. '"In fair Verona, where we lay our scene . . ."' We had gone over every line in the play with Kenneth, word by word. Peter (Poffer) Williams has said, 'The game of love and death is the theatre's trump card.' *Romeo and Juliet* was a memorable ballet. Kenneth knew what made great theatre and great dance.

But the Seymour-Gable partnership never became historic.

With the ballet announcement of *Romeo and Juliet*, MacMillan's first full-length ballet, Kenneth, Christopher and I became an inseparable threesome. Kenneth was choreographically weaving a monumental tapestry, a multi-coloured tragic dream of passion. We were his tools – and inspiration. We immersed ourselves in each scene and character, analysing the feud between the Montagues and Capulets, the unnecessary deaths of Tybalt and Mercutio, which sealed the lovers' doom, and the bumbling of Friar Laurence who never got to tell Romeo that Juliet was merely in a deathlike sleep, a bit of trickery, so that the two could flee to safety. 'If only they'd had a telephone, their lives would have been saved,' I said facetiously to Christopher during one of our midnight telephone chats, for when we were not at Barons Court or at Christopher's flat or mine, Kenneth, Christopher and I constantly rang each other up with ideas. We were living every moment of the ballet – 'our ballet'.

Kenneth instructed Nico, the set and costume designer, who was often with us, that he was not choreographing a Renaissance fairyland; he wanted a 'realistic' Verona where young horny aristocrats roamed the town full of romantic, adventurous spirits. The virile Romeo and his randy chums would do anything for a lark – or a favour – and think nothing of crashing a party given by a competitive noble family. The fourteen-year-old Juliet did not miss her dolls or seriously ponder her betrothal to Paris once she saw Romeo. Their meeting was one of instant attraction – an exciting shock to them.

The rehearsals, starting with the various pas de deux, were exclamations of wonder at every step – a joyous exchange of insights and motivations. We had seen Franco Zeffirelli's stage production co-starring Judi Dench and John Stride, and Kenneth was determined that his ballet, full of slashing vigour, should overflow with the same vital accent on youth.

Christopher and I, he said, were the very anatomy of young love – earthy and emotional. He choreographed lilting and dipping and spinning movements that emphasized the mutual cravings of the teenage Romeo and his fair Juliet. Kenneth intended to reveal for balletgoers at Covent Garden what Zeffirelli had done for the theatregoers at the Old Vic – a surging romance performed by ardent youngsters whose gusto matched the naturalistic fury of the sword play.

The stimulating artistic atmosphere between Kenneth and myself vexed some people. I heard spiteful rumours that we *were* lovers, or participants in a curiously sophisticated arrangement that, depending on whom you talked with, involved either Colin or Christopher. The gossip did not trouble me. It never has. Some people feed on gossip to make themselves sound interesting.

There was, however, one chilling problem – my pregnancy.

My life was dedicated to the ballet. We could have other children, I reasoned. Juliet was mine. Juliet was the bonding of my partnership with Christopher Gable. Juliet was a priceless gift from Kenneth, glazed especially for me. Juliet, the classic heroine of the theatre, was the culmination of all my fantasy roles as a dancer.

Colin was going to Leningrad on a posh assignment with Nigel Gosling. A man of impeccable taste and enormous knowledge, Nigel was art critic for the *Observer*. Under the *nom de plume* of Alexander Bland he was also a distinguished dance critic, with the collaboration of his wife Maude Lloyd, a former dancer with the Ballet Rambert. Their intelligence and integrity, their kindness and compassion for others, made them a remarkable couple. I did not know them well, but Colin worked with Nigel Gosling on the *Observer* and Nigel was a beloved father-figure. An author of art and ballet books, Nigel was preparing a pictorial book on Leningrad and had asked Colin to take photographs. He specifically chose a young collaborator with a vigorous youthful eye.

Before Colin departed I said in a quivering voice, 'Colin, a dancer's life is very short. You know the politics at the Garden. It might be years before another full-length ballet will be created on me.'

Dressed in a stylish Edwardian jacket, the latest fashion from the King's Road, Colin picked up his camera, suitcase and a copy of *Crime and Punishment* (which the Russians confiscated). He could not bear to look at me as he left. If only he could have communicated his feelings or helped me to decide . . .

I stalked doctors' surgeries across London. Hilda Monica Riva. The same scene, the same dialogue, was replayed six or seven times with unctuous gentlemen in tailcoats.

'I must have an abortion immediately.'

'You're married?'

'Yes.'

'Why do you want an abortion?'

'It's impossible for us to have a child now.'

'We'll take some tests. You may not be pregnant.'

'I don't need any . . . I know . . .'

'This is highly irregular. Where is your husband?'

'*Please* – will you help me?'

'An abortion is against the law, unless there are health or mental problems.'

'This is *mental*, that's why I'm here.'

'Let me recommend a therapist.'

After each gruelling inquisition, concluding with a pontifical lecture on Moral Responsibility, I ended up in a pub slugging down glasses of whisky and returning to Charleyville Mansions damp with sweat. Panic-stricken, I confessed my plight to a Garden administrator who gave me the address of a 'clinic' in north London. The abortion would cost five hundred pounds. I saw the administrator again. Most of the money was advanced to me against my weekly salary of forty pounds a week.

At eight o'clock on a Friday morning, while passers-by hurried to offices, I stepped off a bus in north London and crawled towards a Victorian house, redbrick and almost hidden by masses of ivy. The interior was depressingly functional – bare walls, linoleum floors and the smell of disinfectant. It had seen better days.

I was led into the 'operating theatre' . . .

Hours later, a mini-cab deposited me at Charleyville Mansions. Feeling bruised and swollen, I darted into the flat seconds before the heavens opened in a late afternoon summer lightning storm. Kenneth was at my bedside within ten minutes, coming directly from Barons Court where he had been waiting to hear from me. His face was grey and seemed unusually gaunt. He fixed two stiff drinks for us.

'Here lies the great train wreck,' I said weakly, clearing away the thickness in my throat. 'But I'll be running again at Barons Court on Monday.' I finished my drink in three gulps and leaned against the pillows on the brass bed. 'Please don't leave me alone.' Kenneth slept that night in the Box & Bumpf room.

The following day a hamper with cold chicken, boiled eggs and wine arrived unexpectedly from Winifred Edwards. She had heard I was 'ill'. On Sunday, after a long struggle, I finally reached Colin in Leningrad. He had been trying unsuccessfully to ring London.

'I'm sorry,' I said. 'It seemed the only way.'

Colin had his book, I had the ballet. But we no longer had each other.

An iron curtain was drawn across the episode in north London. On Colin's return from Leningrad, the subject was never mentioned. We were a silent couple, moving about the flat with measured footsteps. I wanted some reassurance from him which he was too heartsick to give. He spent more and more evenings at the paper or in his darkroom, particularly when Kenneth dropped over.

Romeo and Juliet was the talk of the Garden, the unquestioned dazzler-to-come of London's winter season. And I resumed rehearsals three days after the abortion, eager to forget the weekend in the buoyancy of the headstrong Juliet. Because Kenneth was creating the ballet on Christopher and me – dancers he knew and trusted – he allowed us tremendous freedom. He was familiar with every muscle in our bodies as well as our temperaments. He did not always 'order' a specific step; he would suggest a shape, or visual image. 'You're two smouldering creatures. You've just made love. It's Juliet's first experience. The image – the movement – is breathless, *smouldering*,' he drawled, lounging in his Schnubian sweat pants, and opening a second pack of cigarettes. Kenneth challenged us to *interpret* his thoughts, which is intellectually more bracing for a dancer than just concentrating on your feet. He seldom wanted straight pretty-pretty lines. Working with Kenneth, who is not a shrill, rigid taskmaster and who never makes a dancer feel *dumb*, I realized that I could move my body in oddly extended shapes that might otherwise have seemed impossible or improbable.

Kenneth centred the ballet on Juliet. He saw her as a

dominant, self-willed girl – the catalyst of the tragedy – who fell head over heels in love with a rather poetic youth. Romeo first sees Juliet at the Capulets' ball. The eye contact is a split-second look-away, look-again flash, that recognition, that knowledge of like souls so rarely experienced in daily life. We were not ethereal lovers, miming impassioned vows, but two sexually alive teenagers whose passions were unbuttoned. 'Romeo is a nice, normal fellow,' said Kenneth, 'but it is Juliet's decisive personality and rebellious temperament that provokes the affair.' Kenneth did not believe that, given all the obstacles, Romeo would have pursued the relationship if Juliet were a delicate little rosebud or a self-possessed young lady indulging in a forbidden adventure. The Juliet I developed was part child, part woman; impulsive and impractical, but always loving – a modern free spirit who knew exactly what she wanted and would risk all to get it.

Over countless cigarettes and cups of tepid coffee, we listened again and again to the music and then Christopher and I demonstrated for Kenneth how we reacted emotionally to a scene. Kenneth's choreography flowed organically from the yearning of the lovers which he integrated, without traditional show-stopping leaps, into the 'reality', or neo reality, of old Verona. We surrendered ourselves to Kenneth's sensuous lifts, tender rocking motions and smouldering glides of whirlwind love.

'When I climb out of the window after our one night together – and it's incredible,' said Christopher, 'what are *you* thinking?'

I replied that I could not dream of living without him forever. 'I would never be forced by family or convention to give you up or do something against my will.' The words, somewhat altered, sounded frightfully familiar. That was Lynn Seymour talking, not Juliet Capulet.

We pondered Juliet's emotional state after Romeo had

left her bed and she is agonizing over her future. 'She *is* going to find a way out,' said Kenneth, 'but she's despairing.' He inhaled wistfully on a cigarette. 'I don't want her prancing around the bedroom.'

'Could she just sit on the bed?' he asked provocatively.

My eyes lit up. 'Shall we dare?'

It was an audacious idea that could be either theatrically suspenseful – or disastrous. It required the careful building of a character whose desolation stirred the audience – without words, without movement. A scene of silent acting is not easy to sustain by a dramatic actress in a play. Would it work in a ballet? Dancers are not expected to sit alone onstage, hands in lap, during long passages of music. 'We must do it, Lynnie,' said Kenneth.

'Hold on. What if the audience gets restless? That musical sequence goes on for an eternity. I already hear programmes rustling.'

Kenneth crossed his legs and rubbed his chin. He stared at the floor. A shock of unkempt brown hair half-covered his forehead. He flushed with colour. 'Let's try it. *I know you can do it.*' If Kenneth believed I could hold two thousand spectators on sheer stage presence alone – doing nothing – I would meet the dare.

Our creation of *Romeo* was filled with such outlandish invention. Ideas for gesture, movement and nuance spilled freely, hypnotically among the three of us. 'When you've taken the sleeping potion, which you think just might be poison,' continued Kenneth, as we considered the climax, 'would you slowly fall asleep or, perhaps, expect to be ill?'

'I'd be frightened. I'd probably want to keep from throwing up.'

Kenneth urged me to mime a violent upchucking cough and clap a hand over my mouth. He then devised a necrophiliac pas de deux in the tomb when Romeo discovers the drugged Juliet, whom he assumes is dead. 'You want your object of love to wake up, to dance with you,' he told Christopher. 'She can't be dead, that's too awful.' He rehearsed Christopher dragging me around the stage advising me, 'Don't be afraid to look ugly. *You're just a lump of dead meat.*' And the last duet was ugly and unromantic, with my legs rubbery, exposed, open. When I killed myself, after Romeo's death, I died with my legs askew. Watching a rehearsal, a Garden executive sniffed, 'That's vulgar. Juliet should die with her legs crossed. Nobody wants to see what she had for breakfast.'

But the death scene was crucial to Kenneth. His lovers were not united in death. They did not die in each other's arms. 'Two beautiful young people are dead,' he said. 'Two beautiful lives have been totally wasted.'

In his studio our fourth partner Nico was busily designing glowing red and gold candlelit chambers, palazzo façades of pink and green marble, and silk and velvet costumes. He proudly showed me his costume sketch for my first scene: a dark velvet dress with a high waist, 'a Renaissance line – you'll look like a child.' I gasped with astonishment.

Putting an arm around my shoulders, he said, 'Lynn, this is the première we've been waiting for.' He produced the other costume sketches.

'Oh, Nico . . .' I whispered, kissing him, 'they're gorgeous.' He blushed with embarrassment. Removing goblets from a cupboard, he poured us each a glass of sherry.

'Remember the day you interrupted our luncheon at Madame Maurer's?' he asked. The humour in his voice was irresistible.

'I was rather naughty.'

'No. You were wonderful.' He lifted the sherry glass. 'So. To you, Lynn. To Juliet.'

* * *

Early one autumn evening Christopher rang me up. 'Have you talked to Kenneth?' he asked, nervously.

'Not since rehearsal.'

'I know he must be home. He's not answering his phone. I've even tried the code.' To avoid pestiferous calls, Kenneth gave his intimates a code signal which he varied from time to time. Two rings, hang up, call back; three rings, hang up, call back.

'What's the trouble, my darling?'

'Oh God – then you haven't seen the paper?' He paused. 'We've got to reach Kenneth.' Christopher's voice sounded unusually jittery, on edge. When I asked again the cause of his discomfort, Christopher read: '"Nureyev and Fonteyn, as Romeo and Juliet. That is the Royal Ballet's top attraction for the new season announced by Sir Frederick Ashton today."' He sighed, breathing heavily. 'Shall I go on?'

My lower lip quivered. 'Does it mention . . . us?'

'No,' he said very quietly.

I was overwhelmed with a weariness that I could not articulate. But not fear.

'Christopher, this is a costly production. There will be several casts. Rudi and Margot are the big stars. They're "news". But it *is* Kenneth's ballet. Everyone knows he created it on us. Of course Rudi and Margot will be dancing it as well.'

Rudolf Nureyev, who had defected from the Kirov Ballet in 1961, was known as the Russian comet. He was – and still is – the most exciting dance personality in the world. Madam had invited him to join the Royal Ballet as a guest artist. His partnership with Margot Fonteyn, to quote Margot herself, brought her 'a second career, like an Indian summer'. She was the undisputed queen of the opera house. Together they thrilled audiences in *Giselle, Swan Lake* and *Marguerite and Armand*. They could skip rope on stage and

Covent Garden would sell out. But *Romeo and Juliet* was Kenneth's ballet – I repeated – just as *Marguerite and Armand* was Sir Fred's. In fact, no one but Rudi and Margot ever danced the lovers in Ashton's work. It was their vehicle. I assured Christopher that the management would not impose itself on Kenneth in any way. It wouldn't be fair play, and the Royal Ballet was very concerned about 'fair play'.

Later I tried reaching Kenneth myself, using a variety of coded rings. I just wanted to hear Kenneth tell me that Christopher and I would *naturally* dance the première of *Romeo*. Kenneth was not answering. And then I understood. He was hiding out because something dreadful was going on and he could not bear to talk about it.

When we finally cornered Kenneth at our next rehearsal, he looked positively sickly. His sad brown eyes were embedded in deep dark hollows. The Garden had already hurt him by refusing to let him mount a ballet to Mahler's *Song of the Earth*, which he staged for Cranko's company in Stuttgart. Jeffrey Solomons, whose information is generally accurate, said that one fusty board member objected to Mahler's musical genius being 'sullied by choreography'. *Song of the Earth* was added to the Garden rep only after tremendous acclaim in Germany. We knew of his grievous disappointment about first performing the Mahler at the Garden. Now, with *Romeo*, he was once again up against the Establishment. Nothing was decided, yet, about the première, he said, but it was impossible not to assume that decisions had already been made.

In December the Garden announced the gala première of *Romeo* would be danced on 9 February 1965, by Margot and Rudi. Other dancers, stated the press release, including Lynn Seymour and Christopher Gable, would portray the star-cross'd lovers.

Childishly I stuffed the morning newspaper in my

practice bag. I could not face Colin with the news. But he knew it already. 'Margot and Rudi are the glam names,' I said disinterestedly, 'it's still *our* ballet.' And I merrily romped out of the flat, with a carefree goodbye. We had not touched each other since his trip to Leningrad and my 'trip' to north London. Life was tumbling to pieces around me, but I could still smile because I could still act. The smile became increasingly difficult to maintain. At Barons Court I had been assigned the most humbling of all tasks: I had to teach the role to Margot Fonteyn – and three other Juliets.

'Can't someone else do it?'

'You're the only one who knows the role.'

'But that's the point. My body is entirely *different* from theirs. The movements – the interpretation won't be the same. The ballet-mistress knows the choreography . . .'

Kenneth had gone into a depression. I could not reach him. And I could not explain why teaching my role to four Juliets was a bitter pill to swallow. So, with the good-natured sportiveness of a Girl Guide leader, I called in the troupes and began demonstrating Kenneth's steps. Margot wisely, understandably, wanted to create her own Juliet. Her position was vulnerable. She was expected to learn the highly individual movements specifically shaped for another dancer. I gave her the gist and she instinctively made adjustments. She did not choose to die with her legs askew or sit quietly on the bed during a long musical passage. These decisions were absolutely right for Margot. Her Juliet, she decided, must have more moonlit enchantment. To Margot's consternation and Kenneth's aggravation, the other Juliets immediately emulated her every move. Ravaged from lack of sleep, Kenneth moaned, 'They are completely ruining my vision of the ballet.' Romeo also underwent changes, along with some of Nico's costume designs. 'If they ask me to repaint the sets, I quit,' said Nico.

There were many gloomy evenings at Charleyville Mansions. Christopher and Carole came for uneaten pot-luck suppers. Kenneth and Nico, both haggard, turned up around midnight. We tried to console each other. Nico said that Kenneth had taken the case for our doing the première straight to the top, above Ashton, but his efforts had been futile.

'It's bloody unfair,' said Colin.

'Oh, it is not,' I countered argumentatively. 'It would be an insult to Margot and Rudi if they *didn't* have the première.' I extended my glass. 'Give me another drink, please.' We were all drinking a lot.

Colin made no reply. He was considering how to deal with me. 'All right, love, I hear you. The Garden doesn't want another famous partnership.'

I ignored the remark. 'Christopher and I will do just fine as the second pair of lovers, won't we, my darling?' I held my glass in trembling hands.

Kenneth said he would explain the situation. A big American tour was coming up in the spring. The American impresario Sol Hurok had stressed the box-office necessity of a starring vehicle for Margot and Rudi. American audiences had seen them in *Giselle* and *Swan Lake*. Rumours floated that Margot and Rudi might not even go on the four-month tour unless they had the incentive of a new work.

'Ohhh! So, it's Sol Hurok's fault.'

'You might say that.'

'It still doesn't explain why Christopher and Lynnie can't dance the première.'

More wine and whisky were poured. More cigarette smoke engulfed the kitchen. The American choreographer Glen Tetley was in London then. He attended one of these midnight sessions and recalled that the mood was very tense. There was the unspoken hope, he felt, that Kenneth would withdraw the ballet. Kenneth worried that he had let us down. 'It doesn't matter, Kenneth, it's a beautiful ballet. You haven't let us down. Just wait till the second partners go on,' I said.

The days passed.

I continued teaching the role to the Juliets, who requested the same costume alterations as Margot, and when my eyes became glassy, and spasms shook my stomach, I stealthily excused myself 'for some air'. Christopher and I span wild, absurd fantasies. In one, Sol Hurok miraculously descended on London hours before the première, like a cigar-chomping producer in a Busby Berkeley musical, and announced that we had to give the first performance.

Miracles were happening for many hitherto unknown names in the 'Swinging London' of the mid-sixties. This was the era of fashions by Michael Fish, Biba and Mary Quant; of music by the Beatles and the Rolling Stones. The international cover girl was Jean Shrimpton. The artist David Hockney exhibited his paintings of youths splashing in swimming pools. And Julie Christie, with her streaming blond hair and not-quite-censorable mini-skirts, symbolized on screen the socially and sexually liberated scene as the amoral heroine of *Darling*, an incisive comedy of modern manners, directed with an artistic conscience by John Schlesinger. For a few fleeting moments it seemed that life could reach an exalted level. The unattainable was being attained. Dreams were becoming realities. Defeatism was non-existent in the new optimistic temperature zone – 'Swinging London'.

The *Romeo* cast list and sequence of performance were posted about the same time that over a thousand people began sleeping outside the Garden box office, waiting for the first tickets to go on sale. I glanced casually at the list, to verify the date of my pairing with Christopher. 'Christopher

Gable – Feb. 17' I read, and then looked again. A mutilating pain, as horrible as anything I experienced at the ivy-covered house in north London, ripped through me. What I saw had to be a mistake. A secretarial error. There was no other explanation. I brushed past Christopher and other dancers huddled around the board.

'*Lynnie – why? – what does it mean?*' Christopher cried out, chasing after me.

Christopher was indeed the second Romeo on the list. But he had been given *another* partner.

I was at the bottom of the cast list.

The fifth and last Juliet.

I ran the four blocks to Charleyville Mansions and telephoned Kenneth. There was no answer. I telephoned Nico in the Garden workshop. 'It cannot be true, Lynn,' Nico said. 'You must reach Kenneth. He left here an hour ago. He should be home by now.' I sat on the bed holding a cigarette until it burned my fingers. There was no mistake. There is never a mistake on a cast list. I knew that. Why pretend otherwise? I could not weep or shout. I had been rendered speechless. I could not even move. My thoughts became incoherent, endless, tangled, unendurable thoughts.

The cast list for *Romeo* was the ultimate betrayal.

Colin opened the front door. I heard him drop his camera and briefcase and some packages in the sitting room. He walked slowly into the bedroom, removing his raincoat. Alone together, we seldom talked. I still loved Colin. But that love, or what was left of it – those pitiful remains – were utterly trivial, because my life, my worth as a dancer, had been trivialized by the management, so I was trivial, a worthless, stupid dancing doll who had spent ten years taking orders from teachers, ballet-masters, company managers, choreographers and artistic directors. I had believed in them and the sacrifices I had made. And now my ego had been surgically removed, leaving me lobotomized and impotent.

I had lost the première. I had taught the role to four Juliets. My reward, or perhaps more accurately my *punishment*, for falling in love and getting married and then being careless enough to get pregnant – a greater offence for a young dancer than an abortion – had been primitively and publicly printed on a sheet of paper and pinned to a bulletin board.

'I just saw Christopher,' faltered Colin. He knelt beside the bed. I turned away and buried my head in a pillow. 'Christopher said you were the last, the very last mug on. *Fifth cast.*' He gently stroked my leg. 'Lynnie, who did this to you?' The last mug on at a matinée with Christopher, whom the critics would have already seen, thereby diffusing the glory of our partnership. Someone at the Garden wanted to teach me a lesson, wanted to play God, wanted to strike me into submission. But whom had I offended so gravely? The première had gone to Margot and Rudi. Fine. I accepted that. But since *Romeo* had been made for Christopher and me, with Christopher and me planning every attitude and gesture with Kenneth, why were we deliberately split? Why was I the last Juliet?

I did not attend Garden performances in black satin and pearls. I wore mini-skirts from Biba's, the in-shop on Kensington Church Street. My practice clothes were not chic. Most of the dancers did their barre work in thin pastels. Always chilled, I showed up in woollen tights and a striped T-shirt. But this managerial decision had nothing to do with fashion. It seemed a consciously political act to put me in 'my place'. But I had never stepped out of 'my place'. I was respectful to everyone at the Garden. It was my one true solid home.

There were no dreams any more, just a sense of weariness and hopelessness. The brief spell of living, which started with my début in *Swan Lake* and continued with the Diners' Club, through *The Invitation*, my wedding to Colin and the first pas de deux for *Romeo*, had passed away.

'Lynnie . . .' Colin began, 'I am – so sorry . . .' Instinct told him that further words were unnecessary. He looked absolutely miserable.

I stood up and groped for a sweater. 'Sir Fred says Juliet is a snap. Anyone can do it. Christopher and I, we'll flatten 'em anyway . . .' I took my coat from the closet.

The red carpet, which one critic said was being laid out for me, had just been pulled out – for ever. On that red carpet, which had justified a five-hundred-pound misunderstanding, went Colin and my marriage – my decisive deed would always be there to ridicule me.

One day I passed Dame Ninette at Barons Court, or, rather, she passed me. Madam was devoting most of her energy at the time to supervising the ballet school. My limbs were lifeless, my eyes unseeing.

She later ran into Kenneth. 'What's wrong with Lynn? She looks frightful. She didn't seem to recognize me.'

'She's been made fifth cast in *Romeo*,' Kenneth said.

According to Kenneth, Madam arched her eyebrows. She was bewildered. 'Oh, I see.' She hurried down the corridor.

Romeo and Juliet was a prodigious success. Margot and Rudi danced superbly, and who would have expected anything less?

The second Juliet whom Christopher was scheduled to partner strained a tendon in her right foot and had to cancel performances for one month. Her slot, on 17 February 1965, was given to me so, quite accidentally, Christopher and I followed Margot and Rudi as the star-cross'd lovers. After I was made up and had my wig pinned on, I went to Christopher's dressing room.

'Lynnie!' he gasped. 'My God – you are ravishing.'

Nico's high-waisted costume gave me the slim shape of a child. My long eyelashes were black and silky, my face was painted in deep peach-pink hues. Luxuriously wavy hair tumbled down my back. I shrugged my shoulders. Christopher gathered me into his arms.

'Frightened?'

'Not with you, mate.'

A spot of colour burned on his cheeks. I nuzzled against him. He held me silently for some seconds. Then I broke away. The overture was beginning.

The critics turned somersaults.

Seymour-Gable – 'an impeccable dramatic partnership', they cheered, in reviews which overshadowed the première. Seymour-Gable – 'they simply break hearts'. We danced with the infectious gaiety of first love, it was noted, blending a perfect balance of physical youth and artistic maturity. There was no moderation in the praise: MacMillan's ballet became a new drama of life and beauty, of passions tinged with foreboding and despair. 'These two bodies are special instruments for MacMillan choreography,' said *The Times*. 'They can stand on a stage, without flickering a muscle, and yet empires tremble. For a dancer this is one of the supreme gifts.' We were lauded for attributing deep emotions to conventional lovers, for breathing ferocious vitality into the Shakespearian tragedy. One headline blared: IN LYNN SEYMOUR WE HAVE THE JULIET OF OUR DREAMS. The critic Eric Johns continued, 'There are even moments when Seymour's acting seems audible. I swear I heard a piercing scream of pain as she stabbed herself in the tomb scene. Her little face haunted me for days.'

I had some acting surprises up my sleeve. I decided that Juliet would not stab herself in the heart. Her lover was dead.

My Juliet stabbed herself in the womb.

Immediately I was lavished with attention from the media, reading once again, distressingly, about Lynn Seymour as 'the new Fonteyn'. The sequence of my sitting alone on the bed, fearful of the future, had a singularly terrifying effect on the scalps of balletgoers, and every journalist asked, 'What do you think about during that passage?' I answered, 'I can never lose myself in a ballet. I have to be completely conscious of everything – the conductor, the music, the scene, the next movement. I am concentrating only on the ballet.' I fibbed to a degree. I thought of more than my departed Romeo. I thought of my departed life – the secure happiness of the last three years.

Juliet became associated with me. At a party in London, a titled gentleman said, 'I still remember the première of Kenneth's *Romeo*. Your performance was a spirit of flame.'

'But I never danced the première.'

He was quite perturbed. 'Well, I saw *you*, and it seemed like the première.'

When we packed for the American tour, photographer Roy Round (whose wife Georgina Parkinson would dance Rosaline) said, 'After the sensational London reviews I'm sure the Garden will give you and Christopher the New York première. The Royal Ballet will then have two star partnerships.' I smiled sweetly and said nothing. We were known in America as 'The Fonteyn-Nureyev troupe' – that's what Sol Hurok was selling, said Kenneth.

'Tell Hurok to go screw himself,' answered Roy.

Roy even proposed a publicity stunt in New York to focus attention on Christopher and me. What if we disappeared for a night or two, he said to Kenneth, and word leaked to the gossip columnists that the Royal Ballet's Romeo and Juliet were shacked up in a Manhattan love nest? Roy desperately wanted us to stagger New York and flummox Hurok. He wanted to see us snag some press coverage from the couple American journalists always pursued – Margot and Rudi. But his suggestion, Kenneth answered, would only create animosity. The choreographer Glen Tetley alerted the New York dance crowd that our performance 'should not be missed'. Christopher and I were the second pair of lovers to face New York audiences and, although I had stopped counting curtain calls, the *New York Times* recorded that we received twenty-two, 'an unprecedented number for a second cast in the Royal Ballet's New York history'.

Christopher was always mobbed at the stage door by youngsters wanting his autograph. Out of costume I was not recognized. One Saturday afternoon we went in our glamour clothes to Edward Albee's play *Tiny Alice*. We spent the intermission clacking over the presumed identity of the immensely rich Miss Alice, not to be confused with the unseen Tiny Alice, who resided in an altar-like model of Miss Alice's baronial mansion. 'Is she God – or only Temptation? And do we care?' A teenage girl tapped my arm. She wanted *my* autograph. I flashed Christopher a so-there look and scrawled my name, with a grand flourish. The girl studied the signature and then grumbled, 'Huhh? I thought you were Elizabeth Taylor.'

Christopher hooted. 'It's still a compliment.'

My physical insecurities surfaced. 'No. It's because I'm fat,' I replied glumly.

Dance *aficionados* in New York invited us to fabulous midnight suppers. Champagne. Goose liver pâté. Salmon mousse. We were treated like 'stars'. But there was no doubt about our status in America when we reached the Mid-west. For some now-forgotten reason we were given the opening night in Chicago. Allowing plenty of time for warm-ups, we reached the theatre at five-thirty. The stage door was locked, so we had to enter through the lobby. The atmosphere was funereal. Dozens of tearful women were standing in line trying to exchange their tickets. They had expected to see Margot and Rudi; they wanted their money back. We froze when we heard, 'I'm not paying these prices to see *understudies*.' Christopher bristled. 'Imagine people crying because they have to see us – and the ballet was created on us.' The house was hostile throughout most of the long first act – Romeo quarrelling with Tybalt in the market place, Juliet playing with a doll in her bedroom, the two making eye contact at the ball. But we won them with our duet in the garden. Suddenly we could feel the house rhythmically with us. We collided, intoxicated with Veronese desire, aware of the tremors beyond the footlights. Christopher looked at me with his lovely blue eyes which asked, 'All the way, Lynnie?' My silent response was, 'Darling, let 'er rip. I'm ready for anything.'

It was all bravado.

When the tour ended on the West Coast, where my parents and Bruce saw me dance Juliet, I drove with my brother to the beach and confided that I was mentally knocked out. I leant on his shoulder.

After a four-month separation, Colin was joining me for a holiday in California. We hoped to restore our marriage on a second honeymoon. It seemed to me as if I were preparing for a blind date. We were both tense and tired. We pretended to enjoy ourselves, gambling at Lake Tahoe with Bruce and his wife, and exhausting ourselves swimming and boating and hiking.

We returned to London still strangers. I was distressed and depressed. The future looked grim and unresolved.

The Royal Ballet had performances in Italy. I wondered if I could dance Juliet again. I trembled in class and trembled when I reached the flat. Knowing that my marriage was coming undone Kenneth stayed away from Charleyville Mansions. Knowing that I was coming undone Georgina Parkinson took me to a Freudian analyst. We discussed my fractured self-esteem and the fact that I was putting on weight – always a sign of tension. I admitted that I could not venture down the road that morning to buy a quart of milk. I was halfway to the store, then turned around and ran home. I was incapable of communicating anything to my husband. I did not feel as if *anyone* liked me. I was prescribed new tranquillizers, the latest on the market. The tranquillizers made me cry and the crying turned my face into a swollen reddish blob.

On the morning the company was gathering to fly to Milan I lay in bed, terrified to move. I had awakened in the night with an agonizing cry. The dream about struggling through a forest to reach a man who awaited me and then finding myself on the Garden stage bleeding profusely had recurred, piercing my consciousness again, leaving me insensible.

I telephoned Kenneth. 'I'm not going to Milan. I can't leave the flat.'

Georgina Parkinson, exuding efficiency and good cheer, arrived at Charleyville Mansions within half an hour. She packed my clothes and cosmetics. 'Lynnie, hurry up. Get dressed. We have to catch that plane.'

My hands fell to my sides and I sat inert on the bed. In a heavy voice I said, 'I'm afraid, Georgina. I've seen something – horrendous. Once you've gone over that awful edge, you don't want to go there again, ever.' Georgina put her arms around me comfortingly. She was fighting back tears. She begged me not to be afraid. She assured me that she would be with me in Italy, she would not let me go near 'that awful edge', and Christopher would be there too, so I must not be afraid.

'Please, Lynnie,' she coaxed, 'just get through the Italian tour – four weeks. It'll be warm and sunny in Italy and much better than sitting here. Don't let's alarm management.'

Pull up the old socks, again.

I managed to climb into a hideous black mini-skirt with a zebra-striped blouse and zebra-striped stockings which I had bought at Bloomingdale's in New York. Georgina personally escorted me on to the plane. When we landed in Milan I declined to be in the company photograph. I didn't feel like a suitable advertisement for the Royal Ballet.

To my amazement I danced two good Juliets in Italy. But I could not have wriggled a toe without my steadfast partner Christopher. His smile, an expression of faith and love, calmed my nerves. We were given the opening of the London season in *Romeo*.

Christmas at Charleyville Mansions. The candles flickered very low and gradually went out. Colin and I refused to confront the past. It was too recent, too raw. I did not send a Christmas card or a present, not even to my parents. I did not want to hear any humbug carols or decorate a humbug tree. One night when Colin was at the newspaper I stuck my head in the oven, thinking, let's end it *now*, and I found a half roasted chicken inside. This is utterly ridiculous, I muttered: you're unhappy. You must go. Tonight. The decision was instantaneous. But where would I go? Our situation was too entangled for me to park temporarily with Christopher or Kenneth. I needed neutral ground, preferably with friends of Colin. I rang up Nigel and Maude Gosling. Colin had mentioned that they had a studio in their house with a private entrance.

'Every day I stay here, it's more and more painful for Colin,' I told Nigel Gosling.

'This is an awkward position for us,' Nigel said after hearing my request. 'If it was for anyone else, Lynn, I'd say no. But I won't turn you down.'

I stayed in the Gosling studio for six months.

My bolt from Charleyville Mansions was cowardly. I fled without saying goodbye to Colin. But I simply *had* to leave, at once, and I tore into the bedroom, hands pressed to my ears as if shutting out the noise of some distant roar – and flung clothes and shoes into two suitcases. I feared Colin might return at any moment and I lacked the courage to say: 'I am leaving.' Darting from room to room like a frenzied animal about to be cornered, I picked up a memento or two – a straw hat from Ibiza, Art Deco salt shakes from Bleecker Street in Greenwich Village. I scribbled a note and placed it beside my wedding ring on the kitchen table. I had worn Colin's beautiful ring with pride. Taking it from him would be a contemptible gesture. 'Forgive me. I must go away and think,' my note said, giving the Gosling address.

Nigel and Maude Gosling received the runaway wife without one question or cryptic glance. Theirs was a quiet, sympathetic reception on a December night which I have never forgotten. Colin had been with Nigel in Leningrad when I was tramping through London searching for a doctor. 'Colin was beside himself, a man quite lost for several days,' Nigel Gosling reminisced years later. 'He wanted to be with you, but it was too late.'

Maude Gosling, a small, fair woman with beauty and brains, as graceful and tactful as her husband, had a pot of tea and a plate of sandwiches waiting for me in the studio. I had not eaten since morning and ravenously finished the snack in two or three bites. The bed was turned down.

I wrote my parents:

An explanation for the long silence. I don't want to upset you. I just want you to write back with words of encouragement – nothing to give me more doubt about myself. I feel very alone. It's horrible to burden people with this sort of crap, and I know I'm the only person that can really help, thus the turmoil. Some day I will try to tell you everything, the events of the past year, but for now I can only say that the happiness I thought was mine – is not.

I have left Colin. I had to leave because we have both suffered a great deal and there was no point in continued months of this suffering. I 'collapsed' after the American tour and if it had not been for Christopher's support as a partner, I might not have been able to perform. Colin and I had been living separate lives. The situation was intolerable. Oh, Mom, I have been in a black aching hell for such a long time, but now a feeling of tremendous relief is coming over. I am very sad tonight, but this sadness is a joy compared to what went before. Please write very soon and tell me that you love me.

Some time later Colin invited me to lunch at a small, fashionable restaurant near the Brompton Road. All wood and deep brown. Sparkling glass. Choice wines. And secluded tables where couples could meet unnoticed by the rest of the clientèle. He wanted it to be a perfect lunch. He did not want it to be our last, though it was. His pale, sensitive face was hopeful, smiling. I do not recall if we ever got around to ordering. Colin said the caviar omelette was smashing. We drank two bottles of expensive Médoc and smoked dozens of cigarettes.

Colin apologized for things he had not done. He accepted blame that was not his. He said everything that should have brought us together, closer than ever, but I said it would be dishonest if I pretended that we could be newlyweds again. I had to recover my confidence, my ego, my belief in myself and it would be further selfishness on my part to involve him in the pursuit of my freedom and self-determination. I would only continue to disappoint him.

We had to find the answers to our woefully confused lives elsewhere, with other people. I did not see Colin again after our lunch for over seven years. And then we had a curious encounter – lasting only silent seconds, just two staring faces, detached and impersonal – at a traffic light near

Wimbledon. I was being driven by my second husband in a
hired white Rolls-Royce to the hospital where I was due to
give birth to Demian. The twins, Jers and Ads, were
cavorting noisily in the back seat. Five bottles of champagne, to celebrate the occasion, were locked in the trunk.
We halted at a red light. I looked idly out the window of the
Rolls. A gleaming sports car pulled up in the adjoining lane.
My gaze wandered to the chap behind the wheel in a natty
tweed jacket and cap. His eyes, in that instant, caught
mine. It was Colin. I waved. He tipped his cap. The light
changed. We drove off in opposite directions. That was the
last time I saw Colin Jones until he visited Woodstock Road
for the first time the other night and met my family, Jers
and Ads and Demian.

Throughout my residency at the Goslings, I saw an analyst,
and Bobby Helpmann, who had been to-ing and fro-ing
between England and Australia, noticing that I was acquir-
ing a ripple of flesh here and there, sent me off to a weight
specialist. Inactivity and anxiety affect me like three chocolate bars. 'Oh, Bobby, when I get upset I just wrap my flesh
around me,' I wailed. The doctor diagnosed a thyroid
deficiency, but a strict diet of zero calories transformed me
into a mere sylph in four weeks.

Reports of new productions and new ballets at the
Garden did not include my name. Nureyev had discovered
a compelling lad in the corps named Anthony Dowell, who
had been dancing with Antoinette Sibley, and Sir Fred was
highly enthusiastic about their partnership. Kenneth and I
had long dinners in Indian restaurants and sat up until the
small hours ruminating about Garden politics and a curious
feeling that we were being shunted aside by the powers. My
private life had come to a peculiar stand-still at the same
time as my career. Ideally circumstances force decisions,
removing the responsibility of choice from us. Like Mr

Micawber we all want something – or someone – to turn up. Don't we? *I do*. He came along one day, dressed as Kenneth MacMillan, and asked me to meet him at a pub in Covent Garden, a theatrical hang-out with playbills and theatre photographs and posters on the panelled walls. 'Lynnie, I've been offered the directorship of the German Opera Ballet in Berlin,' Kenneth said softly, lolling in a velour banquette, as he poked uninterestedly at a steak-and-kidney pie. We were surrounded by a midday crowd of theatre managers, designers, actors and journalists. My fingers were trembling. 'I have to tell Ashton about it,' he went on.

'The Royal Ballet can't let you go, Kenneth.' I sipped a Perrier slowly, concentrating on the bubbles in the glass. He laughed, half-amused, half-sadly, a frazzled laugh that recalled his tensions during the imbroglio over *Romeo* and *Song of the Earth*. Fumbling for a cigarette, amid loud calls for 'two lagers, and Scotch', while the barmaid was entertaining her customers with a ribald joke, I stammered, 'They won't let you go, Kenneth.' Voices around us became louder and louder, drowning out everything else. Kenneth smiled distantly and signalled the barmaid, ordering another drink. He was not with me any more. He was mulling the scene with Sir Frederick Ashton.

'Bad news for the Royal Ballet. Kenneth MacMillan is leaving them,' reported the *Sunday Times*. 'MacMillan is thirty-six and probably the most brilliant young choreographer anywhere in the world.' Kenneth had relayed the Berlin offer to Sir Fred, hoping he would say, 'Stay here, we need you.' Kenneth did not want to leave the Royal Ballet. But Ashton had replied, 'I think it'll be a marvellous experience for you.' With Kenneth gone, I naturally assumed that I would be permanently put in 'my place' – third, fourth and fifth casts of all ballets. The uncertainty of my position at the Royal Ballet filled me with alarm. Kenneth repeatedly said, 'I can't play political games.' Neither can I.

'I'll be the management in Berlin,' Kenneth said, his eyes shining. 'This is *our chance*. You'll be the prima ballerina.' In Berlin Kenneth could do whatever he wanted. The heavily subsidized opera house would open its coffers for new productions of the classics and experimental works. MacMillan's Berlin company would surpass Cranko's in Stuttgart. Rome, London, Caracas, Vienna, Rio, New York – the international clamour for MacMillan's company, with Seymour as ballerina, stretched my mind.

Berlin would be the start of a rich new dancing life.

I wrote Bruce: 'The worst is over, I can escape the memories of the last year. If I stay in London I risk being smothered by the system at the Royal Ballet. The truth is, I do not think I am wanted there. I need to feel appreciated. So I'm off to Berlin. I have accepted Kenneth's offer.' The night I gave Kenneth my decision, he took me to a Russian restaurant. I ate lightly. I only ordered borsch, but it wasn't as good as the borsch I had with the Rosses on Jane Street. And I sipped one glass of champagne, pleased that I was incredibly slim and bony. Kenneth came to the Gosling studio for a nightcap. I lit candles and put a Stravinsky record on the record player. I carefully laid an ashtray at his elbow. Kenneth smiled very shyly. Bathed in the golden glow of candlelight, we talked animatedly of Berlin and the ballets we would create there.

I nestled against him for a moment. He stroked my hair. His touch, which I already knew from rehearsals, seemed wonderfully natural. He kissed me. His lips were very soft. 'This is impossible, Lynnie,' he said, 'if we're going to work together.' He put his hand on mine. 'I'll always love you,' he went on, kindly, fatherly. 'You know that.'

I clasped his hand tightly. 'Yes. I know that.' I fetched

his overcoat and scarf from the window, hidden by a spray of fluttering white blossoms. I watched him open the iron gate and saunter down the road in the starry night.

We would never be so intimate again.

Part Two

. . . and Boundaries

CHAPTER 12

The Divided City

In the 1920s Berlin rivalled Paris as the centre of international modernist culture, becoming a crossroads for artists and bohemians as well as political émigrés from Russia and central Europe. If you conquered Berlin, so went the saying, you had conquered the world. There were exhibitions by such artists as George Grosz, Max Beckmann and Otto Dix, who endowed German Expressionism with a new hard-hitting realism and sharp social criticism. Berlin's theatre marquees announced productions by Max Reinhardt and Erwin Piscator. There were works by Bertolt Brecht and Kurt Weill, culminating in their masterpiece, *The Threepenny Opera*. Maria Magdelena Deitrich shortened her name to Marlene Deitrich and became a timeless sex symbol in *The Blue Angel*. Under Walter Gropius and Mies van der Rohe, the Bauhaus group of architects and designers formulated principles that transformed the skyline of the modern world. An aggressively cosmopolitan and cynical city, Berlin survived the turmoil of the Second World War and the Cold War. With its gaudy Las Vegas neon in the western sector and its rubble and barbed wire in the eastern zone, Berlin is rather like a tarted-up courtesan of an uncertain age, suffering from schizophrenia. But Berlin endures, seeming to thrive on a pervasive sense of upheaval, welcoming the daring and the different. Recalling Berlin of yesteryear, the violinist Yehudi Menuhin once said, 'Berlin had a most advanced and neurotic society. Everything became Experience, with a capital E − and with a capital X.' In some respects, Berlin has not changed at all.

Enter Kenneth MacMillan and Lynn Seymour in 1966.

I was a woman reborn. 'You look gorgeous,' friends exclaimed before I departed from London. Colin Jones was the only person who had ever used the word 'gorgeous' in reference to me *offstage*. The traumas of the past year were washed away by a high-tide of optimism. The Seymour complexion was milky white and unlined. My eyes shone and my dark hair had a natural lustre. I was very slender – a seductive figure in clinging crêpe de Chine dresses. Cool as a breeze, with great energy, I could hardly wait to abandon myself to a new city and a new ballet company. A dancer's growth depends on the chief choreographer or the artistic director. Without challenges in an expanding repertory you stagnate. Then you lose performing confidence and live in a state of anxiety about your talent, stamina and the possibility of physical injury. Kenneth MacMillan and I – as his ballerina – would spur each other to glorious new heights. In Berlin Kenneth would call the tune and I would be there, at his side, ready and eager to dance. We had no worries about the reigning ballet Establishment. There was none. We were the tastemakers.

Kenneth asked Christopher Gable, disillusioned by the *Romeo* episode, to join the Berlin ensemble, but he pursued an acting career and showed his dexterity in Ken Russell's film *The Boy Friend*, with Twiggy and Tommy Tune. But Kenneth snagged a dancer named Vergie Derman. A soloist with the Royal Ballet, Vergie was a tall, leggy blonde whose quietly droll manner and sensibility reminded me of Brenda Bolton, another blonde Kenneth preferred, during *The Burrow* days. Kenneth put the offer to Vergie one evening at dinner.

'Vergie, why don't you come to Berlin with Lynn and me?'

Vergie thought he was joking. 'Yes, that would be nice,' she answered, playing along.

Kenneth liked surprising his friends with provocative –

usually ribald – statements and he was peeved if you were lumpish about a bit of fun. Vergie assumed this was his 'Let's-all-go-to-Berlin' game and did not want to spoil the charade with practical questions. That would be too utterly-utterly lumpish. Early the next morning Kenneth rang her up while she was in bed. 'You'll need a visa,' said Kenneth. 'I'll meet you at the German Embassy in two hours.' Vergie was nonplussed. Kenneth had *not* been making amusing chatter. Berlin was a serious offer. She asked questions concerning roles and salary. Zestfully he outlined the best with such persuasive urgency that she was looking for her passport before she hung up.

Kenneth awaited her outside the German Embassy. Vergie filled out scads of forms, with Kenneth supplying the needed information. After standing in a long line, Vergie was told she had to secure a signature from a commissioner in another building verifying that she was Vergie Derman. Kenneth tugged her into the foyer. 'This will take *hours*,' he moaned. '*I* have appointments. Typical bureaucratic red tape.' Vergie sighed in resignation and calmly lit a cigarette, saying there was nothing else to do. 'Nothing else to do? Oh, yes, there is.' He extracted a pen from his pocket and signed a fictitious name for the commissioner. Vergie protested. She saw herself in a dank Berlin prison hauling slop cans. 'Now, we can't go back immediately, so let's have a drink,' Kenneth said imperturbably, leading her down the street to a pub. Vergie Derman got her visa two lagers later. The other member of our Berlin group was Ray Barra, my *Romeo* partner in Stuttgart. Ray had snapped his Achilles tendon, ending his dancing career. Kenneth hired him as ballet-master.

Just before the Berlin exodus Maggie Lee visited London. I had not seen her since the Australian tour when she left the company to marry an American physicist. We passed a long afternoon catching up on the intervening years.

Maggie had been my first confidante. Unashamedly I revealed bottled-up emotions I had not discussed with my analyst. 'I thought I was going mad for a while. The final blow was being made fifth cast in *Romeo*. I can't unravel that. But in Berlin there won't be any reminders of *Romeo* or my marriage or – anything else. I probably shan't marry again. It makes life so complicated. I just want to have beautiful, intelligent children.' We laughed heartily.

'And, Maggie, I won't be lonely either. I'll have a little family. Kenneth has rented a vast apartment. I'll be living with Kenneth and Ray Barra.' Maggie questioned the wisdom of that round-the-clock proximity. Kenneth, she responded, tended to get very attached to two or three people and then only wanted to see them exclusively, and no one else. 'It's just until we settle down, so we won't feel like exiles,' I said. We were foreigners – outsiders invading the opera house. We had to stick together.

The communal arrangement seemed to make perfect sense.

The apartment was a duplex on the sixth and top floor of an opulent Art Deco building occupied by Berlin film and stage actors during the thirties. The rooms were painted white and flooded with light from double windows. A large sitting room, which we seldom used, was sparsely furnished with bits and bobs of communal furniture – a couch, an armchair, some lamps. Kenneth installed an oil painting by Nico and floated a multi-coloured carpet from Mexico in the middle of the floor. A small staircase led to Kenneth's quarters from the foyer. Ray Barra had a suite of two rooms directly off the foyer. Mine was at the far end, next to the white-tiled kitchen Ipnd guest room, which Vergie Derman eventually took over. My Japanese prints and Nico's framed costume designs for *The Invitation* leaned against a bedroom wall. I intended to hang them, but never got round to that. My suite was furnished with a Victorian desk, a three-cornered Victorian chair and a bed piled with heaps of pillows. Two sets of double windows were curtained in white lace – a farewell present from Nigel and Maude Gosling.

All in all, the space was luxurious and ideal for sharing. We respected each other's privacy and never went knocking on bedroom doors for cups of sugar. The sugar was in the kitchen and the kitchen was Kenneth's sanctuary – his Most Holy of Holy Places. In bathrobe or Schnubian attire, Kenneth held court in the kitchen. He cooked and read there and contemplated the world, our world, from the kitchen. Late-night talkfests concerned his plans for the company, new ballets, opera house protocol and Berlin customs. As in London, Kenneth entertained us with his Rabelaisian badinage. A prime subject for humour was the bewilderment of our stolid cleaning woman, Frau Schneider, who silently surveyed our threesome, trying to guess who was doing what to whom. No one was doing anything to anyone in the apartment. 'Mustn't tell her *that*,' cautioned Kenneth. 'She'd be devastated.' During the day the opera house was Kenneth's domain. No matter what hour he got to bed, he was in his office, conscientiously, every morning at ten. The opera house was a new building with ample backstage facilities, rehearsal space and dressing rooms. Kenneth presided over the company, *his* company, like a superior host at a distinctive party. The dancers carefully scrutinized his hand-picked star – me – described in the Berlin press as 'the Royal Ballet's best dramatic dancer'. So there we were – the artistic director and his ballerina. A tight twosome to be contended with. But our achievements in London would be topped in Berlin, giving the opera house international popularity and recognition.

I secured the Seymour persona immediately.

Audiences at the opera house dressed very formally – the old bib and tucker for the men and long out-of-fashion dresses for the women. Attending a performance, I sashayed into a sixth-row stall in a purple velvet suit from Biba's, the mini-skirt stopping inches above the knee. I heard disapproving whispers about my outfit which blazed with silver bracelets and a silver satin blouse. 'They don't understand *style*,' I groused to Kenneth and Vergie. 'I'll have to shorten the skirt another inch.'

Rehearsals for the first season began in a rhapsody of work, English-to-German dictionaries in hand. We were learning German. The most used word was '*Zigarette*'. The Berlin schedule split our day in half: we rehearsed mornings and evenings. This disrupted our social calendar but allowed afternoons for shopping and wandering through museums and parks. Vergie lived in a *pension* but she joined our 'family' at the end of the day or, rather, evening, for dinner which Kenneth prepared – a relaxing exercise for him. The MacMillan speciality was not ready until midnight, hence the kitchen klatches: chatter and laughter over endless *Zigaretten* while Kenneth mixed an esoteric sauce and speculated on romances in the company, another favourite topic.

My first partner in Berlin was a dancer named Falco. He had dark curly hair, a taut physique, and a girlfriend in the company. Falco only spoke pidgin English, but he took direction easily and Kenneth was pleased to find a boyishly virile successor to Christopher Gable. To my delight Falco acted as if I were a Hollywood movie star. Alluring. Mysterious. During the long afternoon breaks – we were rehearsing *Giselle* and *The Invitation* – he drove me around Berlin and gave me a tour of Charlottenburg Palace, with its sumptuous suites of Prussian royalty. We attended a performance of the Bolshoi in East Berlin. The border guards, humourless boors, delayed our return, hassling us over papers. When I reached the apartment at two-thirty in the morning Kenneth was sitting pensively at the kitchen table, smoking. He feared that I had vanished behind The Wall.

I did vanish most afternoons for trysts with Falco. 'I'm off to the zoo,' I would announce brightly. 'Frau Schneider says the elephants shouldn't be missed.'

The liberating affair with Falco made life in Berlin fun. Did anyone else notice a change? Kenneth, who reads me like a book, said nothing. But instinctively I thought it unwise to flaunt our relationship. One day I tipped over a coffee-pot in my dressing room. Scalding water cascaded down my leg. Falco hustled me to an emergency hospital. The accident started rumours that we had been doing imprudent exercises in the dressing room. Utter bilge. My dressing room is where I have final calming moments, without ruining make-up, costumes or hair. I never even did warm-ups in the dressing room. To my knowledge the only dancer who may have used her dressing room for warm-ups, real warm-ups, was Alicia Markova, an early Diaghilev discovery who went on to become England's first ballerina. We met towards the end of her career when I was in the touring company. A classical dancer of sweeping purity, Markova was guesting in *Les Sylphides*. Her elevation was gone but she still moved swiftly, with the delicacy of a butterfly. We were appearing in Oxford and Madam attended a performance. I was passing Markova's dressing room and came upon Dame Ninette listening intently outside Markova's door. 'I hear scratching sounds,' Madam said. 'I think Markova's warming up. No one ever sees her in class. She has to do it somewhere, *it's not possible otherwise!*'

Throwing caution to the wind Falco wooed me openly with the presentation of a gigantic fish tank which I placed on a Victorian armoire in my suite. The tank contained dozens of tropical fish. Scattered on the bottom of the tank were white pebbles and rocks. Falco added two miniature castles and coils of floating greenery. Kenneth and Ray Barra disapproved of my lithe and lusty swain. They believed he was using me to upgrade his status – in sum, to get starring roles. Vergie Derman refused to be drawn into the tittle-tattle. The chaps may have been right, to a degree, but their suspicions cut deeply. Was the notion of my capturing an impressive stud who was also an impressive dancer so patently absurd? Was it not possible that he genuinely responded to me, just a little bit? Bloody hell. I had nothing to do with casting. That was up to Kenneth.

After dinner one night Kenneth made a caustic remark about ballerinas whose hearts rule their heads. Angrily, I poured myself a glass of whisky from Kenneth's bottle and marched off to my suite where I nursed the drink until dawn, sitting in front of the fish tank. I had lived my entire life for the ballet. For years only dance had ruled my head and, ultimately, that commitment had me seeing a Freudian analyst. If other ballerinas chose to be neuter thingies, that was their business. Following my collapse in London, I decided that I could – and would – be a total woman and a total dancer. The two need not be separate. Yes, dancing requires rigorous daily discipline, I reasoned, watching one greedy fish swallow up a smaller one, but that discipline need not overwhelm your life. You cannot disconnect the brain from the body, *and live*. Happiness, I believe, like Isadora Duncan, is only attained through a freedom of spirit that ennobles your dancing.

And yet . . .

I did not wish to displease Kenneth. Nagging fears that I might kept me awake and I began drinking to lull myself to sleep, though Vergie said I never drank that much and I trust her memory. Kenneth discussed the affair with Vergie. His mood was distracted.

'This Falco thing, it's so silly, isn't it, Vergie?'

'I don't know, Kenneth.'

'Do you think she's in love with him?'
'I don't know, Kenneth.'
'Do you suppose he really *wants* her?'
'I must go home, it's late.'
'She's *so* emotional. I don't like him using her.'
'I really must go now, Kenneth.'
'One more drink, then I'll put you in a cab.'

The Berlin première. I danced *The Invitation* with Falco as the young cousin. Kenneth choreographed two new pieces for an imposing inaugural evening. For the first time Kenneth created under administrative pressures – dealing with unions, budgets, casts and the entire directorial apparatus. Malicious melodrama added to the opening pressures. An Austrian dancer, married to a wealthy Berliner, was jealous that I had the lead in *The Invitation*. She tried to drum up a court case on the grounds that the ballet was overtly sexual and should not be performed. She got nowhere. But the incident reminded us that we were Outsiders.

For his new *Valses Nobles et Sentimentales*, which Balanchine and Ashton had previously arranged to Ravel, Kenneth conceived a work to Ravel's charmingly simple *Ma Mère l'Oie (Mother Goose Suite)*. Shortly before the première the music publishers turned feisty with financial demands. Kenneth had to change all his choreography to fit a totally different score at the very last minute. The third ballet was *Concerto*, a plotless piece set to Shostakovich's second piano concerto. I danced the middle movement, a romantic impressionistic sequence which resulted from Kenneth slyly observing me working alone, an hour on pointe before evening rehearsals. He transported curving movements of concentrated simplicity – an arm slowly dropping, a leg stretching sensuously – into a joyous pas de deux. The Berlin season was launched with a rep that included *Giselle* and *Firebird*.

I continued seeing Falco, but our affair was short-lived. It was impossible for me to come and go from my suite without passing the kitchen where Kenneth lounged until the wee hours, smoking and sipping tea splashed with whisky. At first it was comforting to know that *Mein Herr Direktor* was there, next door, if uppity Russians proceeded to sack the city. Kenneth would lower his eyes, I fancied, and haughtily wave them off. 'You chaps really are deeply boring and grossly overweight.' When I succumbed to Falco, however, the kitchen became an inescapable Checkpoint Charlie. When I tiptoed in at a tardy hour, Kenneth would call out, 'Well, what have you been up to?' Our eyes would meet and he would glare at his wristwatch.

'Falco is not good enough for Lynn,' he told Vergie. 'And those late nights are going to affect her dancing . . .'

He lost interest in Falco as a dancer and upbraided him, at rehearsal, for sloppy work. Falco read the clear message: Hands off the director's moll. He dropped me like a hot brick. I was furious and helpless. Dinners at the apartment became indigestible. I gained weight alarmingly fast. I thought I was pregnant, but a doctor dispelled that anxiety. My nervous system was acting up and, predictably, producing blubber.

By Christmas I lay abed with the flu, which developed into glandular fever – a debilitating illness in which you run a slight fever all the time and your glands are swollen. I wanted to leave the flat – with my fever it seemed hideously claustrophobic – but I was too weak. Finally I mustered enough strength to see my own doctor in London. Two good Samaritans, Georgina Parkinson and Roy Round, opened their home to me in Battersea. Georgina carried on her full schedule with the Royal Ballet and still managed to rush up and down the stairs, bringing me food, juices, magazines and bright chat. I stayed in London six weeks, transferring myself to a hospital and then recuperating with Winifred Edwards, who got my wobbly legs stirring again.

Kenneth thought I was malingering. Why did I have to be ill in London? he asked. Why couldn't I be ill in Berlin?

Christopher Gable came to the hospital one day and we had an old-shoe talk. 'Do you think I'm sick because of general naughtiness?' I murmured after he expressed astonishment at my sallow complexion.

'How general? How naughty?'

'Well, I did have a lover.'

'People usually get sick from *not* having one,' he answered laughing.

'It must be mental. I'm so faint – so confused, dear Christopher,' I replied, sending him away. My head was drooping. I could not keep my eyes open any longer. My parents were worried about my health and the decisions that led me to leave the Royal Ballet which had been a solid base. In a letter I relieved them on a troublesome subject: 'Please do not dwell on my early departure from home. I wanted to come to England to be a dancer. If we went back in time I would still fly off to the ballet school. My heart and soul are free – I believe – of the blackest moments, although they carry a shadowy memory. My main problem is finding a way to be a ballerina and a woman, because I'm just not the type to live a one-sided life.'

Vergie Derman moved into the Berlin apartment while I was in London. Her humour and unflappability were just what our oddball household needed. Kenneth, coping with Teutonic tempers at the opera house and formulating a new ballet, concealed any vexation on my return. 'We missed you,' he said.

Kenneth's potent personality is only appreciated by a handful of intimates who have known him over the years. He does not go out of his way to ingratiate himself with the press or the public. Outside his circle of friends, people find him vague, diffident, monosyllabic, unwilling to talk. He does not spread around his affection. He confines it to a few and withdraws from the masses. When he succeeded Fred Ashton as artistic director of the Royal Ballet, his private nature was alienating to American ballet buffs who missed Ashton's outgoing Savile Row sophistication and ability to charm anybody. Nigel Gosling said, 'Kenneth is one of those large men who look as though they would like to be small.'

Although he is not readily receptive to newcomers, Kenneth's intelligence, raffish wit and acute sensitivity to theatre, with all its bravura and bitchery, intrigue insiders who concede that his languor, fugitive smile, silences and hesitations are part and parcel of his curious character. The effect is quietly calculated. When Kenneth sits on a sofa, he doesn't have to say a word: you know the rumpled rajah is *there*. We had been the closest of mates for almost seven years but, until Berlin, we had never been around each other constantly. Now that we were living and working together I was vividly reminded of his dominating presence. And to be quite blunt, I like to do a little dominating myself. We all do.

Kenneth had known me since my teens. He influenced and moulded my taste and gave me, with his ballets, his expression of love. We were tied by a mystical devotion. We did not act like lovers, but rather like father and daughter. Wanting to see me healthy and strong, he shooed away any interloper who might distract from home and homework. But I was equally determined to have my own life. If he resented my illness, I resented the manner in which Falco had been dispatched. On my return from London we started bickering, as parents do with children, over eating, sleeping and social habits. I did not want to be scolded or told by anyone how to conduct myself outside the opera house.

I went to a dancer's birthday party and came home past midnight. Kenneth and Vergie were finishing dinner with

Ray Barra. There was no way I could sneak past the kitchen without being seen. Kenneth sat facing the door.

'Do you know what time it is?' he asked, slumping dejectedly in his chair. His voice was flat, almost a whisper. He stared at me through a formidable bonfire of cigarette smoke.

'I've been sick – on my back – for weeks, which you don't seem to believe,' I retorted, childishly fighting tears. 'Why don't you ring up Georgina? She'll tell you.' He called Georgina quite often. 'I was having a little fun with some of the dancers. If I don't see *other people* I'll go bonkers.'

Kenneth brushed aside a lock of hair and looked sadly at Vergie and Ray, who excused themselves and withdrew to their rooms. I have seen Kenneth smoke thousands of cigarettes and he has certainly watched film actors smoke thousands of cigarettes in movies. He knows every theatrical flick, twist, turn and jab, and handled cigarettes with greater timing of a meaningful inhale-exhale than any hero of the screen. He pursed his lips, and inhaled deeply. He simply did not want me to get sick again or put on weight, he explained with a sigh, exhaling dramatically.

I stomped off to my suite: the cell of the condemned. Unable to sleep I sat, again, in front of the fish tank, drinking Campari which we bought in small bottles, along with wine and cigarettes, at a dispensing machine in the building. I was weepy and angry with myself for making Kenneth unhappy. I needed to talk to someone, so waited until eight-fifteen when I might rouse Vergie. I fixed a Campari for her, with lemons and ice.

'Vergie, are you asleep?' I asked, rapping on the door.

'I was asleep,' she answered drowsily.

Throwing some cushions on the floor by her bed, I sat cross-legged on them. 'Oh, Vergie. I wasn't very nice last night. Do you think Kenneth is all right?'

She looked at me with foggy eyes and adjusted her

pillows. 'It's only past eight. So I haven't talked to him. But I'm sure Kenneth is fine.'

'I couldn't sleep all night. I behaved badly.' My eyes lit up. 'Now, you must try this heavenly drink. The Italians gulp it like water.' I handed her the glass which she reluctantly accepted. Awfully bitter she complained. I urged her to drink it down swiftly. She glanced at the clock. '*Oh God*. It's not even nine and I'm pissed out of my mind!' I said I'd fetch more ice.

Kenneth was shuffling around the kitchen in his bath-robe, bleary-eyed and unshaven. He had not slept that night either. We did not speak. He poured himself a slug of whisky and I refilled the Campari glass with ice. Ray Barra wandered into the kitchen, wrapped in a diminutive bath towel, smelling pleasantly of shaving lotion and soapsuds. Ray rummaged for the coffee. When Kenneth spied the Campari glass, he set his whisky down on the table and berated me for drinking before breakfast.

'The two of you – you're off again,' said Ray Barra. 'Lynn and Kenneth, Kenneth and Lynn. It's a goddamn scene from a Pinter play. I'm having breakfast out.' His tone was fanciful but there was an edge to the banter.

Vergie lurched into the kitchen with a splitting headache and asked huskily, 'What's going on? Where's Ray? Is there any coffee?' Vergie and I had less than an hour before company class. A tense moment had passed. Flashing his most attractive smile, Kenneth announced that he would brew the morning coffee. He would not send us off to class without coffee. This operation, between sips of whisky and many cigarettes, took half an hour but the herbal blend was deliciously aromatic.

'Oh, Kenneth, the blend is brill,' I said.

'Absolutely marvellous,' agreed Vergie.

He clutched at his bathrobe, bereft of words, so very pleased that we were pleased.

Then we quickly dressed for our morning class at the opera house.

Our *ménage* – or *ménagerie* – was a strange quartet indeed, interrupted only by Frau Schneider with her vacuum cleaner. Occasionally an innocuous beau picked me up at the apartment for a movie or dinner, but the rigid screening process discouraged the faint-hearted. Away from the opera house we lived in an incestuous one-dimensional world. Kenneth cooked the evening meal. Shopping chores were rotated amongst Vergie, Ray and myself. 'Don't forget my stamps!' Kenneth always ordered. The shops gave stamps with food and liquor purchases. After three weeks we could do a weekend of free shopping in exchange for our stamp-books. Kenneth delighted in the green-blue stamps. He stayed at the kitchen table late at night like a precocious little boy, licking the rolls of stamps and sticking them in the books. Vergie estimated that he must have already licked four hundred stamps. 'Keep that up, you're going to get trench mouth,' I said. He coolly ignored the remark.

One night we patiently waited while Kenneth prepared a recipe for pork chops. Midnight came and went. Kenneth chatted merrily, sketching crackling observations about the alliances and misalliances within the company. Two hours later we were a captive yawning audience. Shrivelled burnt chops were finally put on the table. My head reeled from the smell of grease, cigarette smoke and general tiredness. 'I'm not having any,' I said abruptly. 'Those chops look horrible and fattening. I'm going to bed.' Kenneth's face flushed scarlet. We had words and I ran to my room in tears.

What was wrong with me? What was wrong with *us*? I was sobbing when Vergie, hair pinned up and face creamed for the night, knocked on my door. Vergie, the angelic go-between. 'Kenneth asked me to see if there was anything you needed. He felt he was unkind.'

I downed two sleeping pills. 'No, it was my fault, Vergie. You better go see how Kenneth is. It's quiet in the kitchen.'

Vergie said that we teased each other like an old married couple. 'It's because we're living together,' I answered. Then she announced that Ray Barra was moving out because he wanted a place of his own. Kenneth was depressed, she said, about Ray's exit. He was troubled by company pressures and did not want his Berlin family to break up.

Vergie moved to the door, ready to turn out the light. I asked her not to touch the light. I wanted to fall asleep with the bedroom lights blazing. They made waking up in the morning seem ever so much brighter.

Despite growing domestic tensions at the apartment, we performed with spectacular control at the opera house. Dancing was a release for all emotions. And Kenneth escaped his own *Angst* through the fulfilling unrestricted art of choreography. A voracious reader, he was fascinated by Anna Anderson's *I, Anastasia*, the story of a woman who claimed to be the daughter of the last Russian tsar. He chose to use this material as the basis of his new ballet. I too began reading all the available information on Anna Anderson. Was this individual disconnected from reality? Was her life a tragic dream, a way of handling secret frustrations? Kenneth and I believed her story. The one-act ballet centred on the theory that she was telling the truth. The viewpoint was not hazy. Anna-Anastasia was not an ephemeral character.

The Berlin opera house, which had lured Kenneth from London with promises of money for new productions, tightened its purse. So the ballet *Anastasia* had to be done on a simple Expressionistic set, essentially a revolving platform on a bare stage which represented a Berlin hospital or mental ward in 1920 where Anna-Anastasia relives the past and tries to find her identity. My partner was a muscular dancer whose diverting manoeuvre at parties was tearing up telephone books in his hands. If the telephone books were hidden, he could do the same trick with an encyclopedia.

Kenneth's choreography was extremely physical and involved a dramatic lift – under my right arm. Recalling her flight from Russia, Anna remembers being saved from pursuing soldiers by the man who becomes her lover and literally scoops her up, for a running-twisting pas de deux. We rehearsed the lift over and over again. It was a powerful moment in the ballet. I was not lifted from the waist. My partner's hands went under my armpits, thrusting me high into the air. At mid-point, he balanced me with only one brawny hand under my right armpit.

During rehearsals my upper right arm became extremely stiff and tender but I attributed it to the usual ballet aches. Dancers often have to rehearse and perform disregarding painful limbs, joints and extremities.

When I was in London recovering from glandular fever my hair had been daringly shorn by Vidal Sassoon on a rehabilitating visit to his salon. This style was to become a sort of trademark with me. Kenneth liked it so much that it was decided I should not wear a wig for *Anastasia*.

Kenneth created some harrowing moments for Anna Anderson, who was forced to confront her spiritual death in an uninterested world. She was betrayed by people who would not give her comfort. The truth, as she knew it, was horrifying: the theme was the loss of identity. I found the role physically and mentally depleting, but we collaborated with a complex creative tension which illuminated a work, even when our own illusions about each other were stripped away.

Certainly by the time *Anastasia* had its Berlin première in late June 1967, the disorder and distress in our friendship was fully exposed. Wanting to avoid further rows, I stayed away from the apartment as much as possible. During rehearsals Kenneth seldom spoke to me. Instructions were passed on through my partner. But I was so absorbed in the ballet that I dismissed the slights – and steady pain in my right arm.

A corps dancer named Eike Waltz invited me to tea and cakes at his flat. Half-German, half-Polish, Eike was an attractive loner. We had secretly named him 'Maddy' because of his idiosyncratic behaviour and exuberant dance style.

We had a couple of outings and slowly he opened up and recounted his past.

Eike was born in Frankfurt in 1939. His father, a scholar who spoke several languages, was in his twenties when Hitler came to power. Hitler drew crowds, said Eike, like a royal wedding. Eike's father became a highly placed member of the new government. After the war, occupying soldiers captured relatives of surviving officials who had gone underground. The Russians conducted midnight raids, and the Americans were on the lookout for Nazis. Eike's mother fled with her three children from village to village. Eventually the Russians caught up with them on a railway platform. They seized Eike as a hostage for his father. He was not quite seven years old. The next nine years of his life were spent near Kassel on a farm, originally built as a camp for the Hitler Youth Movement, with two other children and fifty adults. He was not released until 1954.

Reunited with his family as a teenager, Eike was too alienated to remain peacefully with them. One day his mother introduced him to an 'uncle'. He instantly disliked the man – his posturing and attitudinizing. When he learned that the man was his father, and when he discovered his past relationship with the SS, Eike ran away from home and was adopted by a woman who lived near

Munich. Her husband, a stage actor, had been drafted into the German Army and was killed in Russia. Eike took engineering courses but could not find work. He restored baroque churches and published a book of poems. The local opera needed youths in the corps de ballet for *Countess Maritza* and *Die Fledermaus*. His adopted mother taught him how to dance. At twenty he waltzed with the girls at Maxim's in *The Merry Widow* and other operettas. Eventually he danced in Hamburg and was hired by the Berlin opera three months before I arrived.

'I think Eike has taken quite a fancy to you,' Ray Barra said, grinning. A chap in the corps could not be viewed as a serious distraction for La Lynnie. What nobody realized was that I find celebrity collecting a frightful bore. I like people who interest me, whatever their status or background, and I found Eike rather curious.

Eike danced in the *Anastasia* corps. He noticed that I was ashen at rehearsals. I looked, he said later, as though I were gradually fading away with a mysterious illness. Kenneth was not looking well himself. He had to battle over budgets and bargain with unions. And he was choreographing a new ballet. A change of scene, with Johnny Cranko and his irreverent troupe in Stuttgart, would take his mind off the machinery and machinations at the opera house. Accordingly, he planned a weekend respite in Stuttgart and invited Vergie. Ray Barra and I said goodbye to them, anticipating an uneventful spring weekend. It wasn't quiet for them or me.

Their excursion was a Cold War mêlée. Kenneth, who organized the train tickets, neglected to secure visas for the ride through East Germany. They were both hauled off the train at gun-point by the border bogeymen and surrounded by yapping dogs. The helmeted guards in leather boots grilled Kenneth. Name. Address. Nationality. Occupation. That was a problem. Kenneth replied, 'I'm a choreographer.' The guards were stumped. 'Choreographer,' Kenneth repeated. The guards hadn't a clue. Kenneth and Vergie were marched across a bridge and seated on a wooden bench. Sweating from the tremors of interrogation Kenneth whispered to Vergie that he was going to bolt. The dogs growled. Without batting an eye Vergie counselled, 'Sit *still*. You can't run very far here or very fast. And don't reach for your flask. Don't reach for anything.' Hours later visas were issued and they boarded the train to Stuttgart, arriving one day late. The incident was reported in the London press.

'I panicked and when you panic your first reaction is to run,' Kenneth told a journalist. 'But if I'd done that I would have got a bullet in my back.'

In Berlin, meanwhile, another drama was ready to unfold.

It was a brilliantly sunny weekend and just nippy enough for a rambling walk in a thick knitted sweater. I planned to spend it alone, browsing in antique shops. I was padding about the apartment when the telephone rang. The caller was Eike Waltz. With unassuming delicacy of tone and manner, he asked if I would like to go sailing. Charmed by the proposal, I accepted. The glimmering sun and crisp air were blissful. Eike's friends – a Eurasian girl and a French man – were dashingly international. There was no ballet talk, no dance chatter. How marvellous to be out of that apartment, I thought – a release from house arrest. The outing brought colour to my cheeks and light into very tired eyes. I did not even notice the throbbing in my upper right arm.

The following morning, Sunday, I climbed into the big white tub next to my suite and filled it with fragrant bath salts. At the far end of the apartment Ray Barra was in the final throes of moving his books, bedding and boxes of clothes to his new flat. I settled into the tub, sponging my legs and tummy, eyes half closed in reverie. Then I ran the sponge along my arms. My right hand was curiously dirty, as though covered with newsprint. I scrubbed my hand. The filth would not wash off. I raised my arm. It was blue-grey and bulging near my shoulder like a balloon. Purple veins, the width of heavy rope, were rigidly knotted. I screamed and leaped out of the tub. Grabbing a towel, I tore down the hall.

'Ray – my arm – *what is it?*'

He dropped a load of books. His face went white. He telephoned a doctor who examined me in the apartment. I heard him tell me, half in German, half in English, that I might have a travelling thrombosis. Ray consulted the opera house which advised that I be admitted to a hospital immediately. The *Anastasia* première was weeks away. I could not be ill again. I could not disappoint Kenneth. A second doctor said that if I were not hospitalized instantly, I might die.

Kenneth and Vergie returned to an empty apartment. Ray had moved out. I was lying in a hospital bed ten miles away, with my arm straight up, in a sling.

Wondering why I was absent from rehearsals, Eike asked Kenneth about me.

'She has a blood clot,' Kenneth answered in a subdued voice. 'Go see her. She needs visitors.'

His eyes fixed on the floor, Eike experienced a moment of panic. The director's ballerina had accepted an invitation for an innocent sail with a member of the corps and one day later was gravely ill. Eike had heard the rumours that flew months earlier when I scalded myself in the dressing room with Falco. He was worried. I had not tripped or fallen on the boat; there had been no 'accident'. What had happened? He drove to the hospital. 'I saw a grey, shrivelled woman, someone I did not recognize,' he told Vergie. 'She was cold and lifeless. I asked the doctor if she was dying.'

During the next weeks the hospital was my new home. When medication effectively reduced the blood clot I was allowed to attend class and rehearse, but I was commuting between the hospital and the opera house. A vein specialist said the thrombosis was caused by the strenuous partnering – particularly the running-struggling lift – in *Anastasia*. Eike visited me regularly, bearing reading materials and news of the corps. Ravaged by wretched health and my second misfortune in Berlin, I was plagued with anxiety over Kenneth's reaction. *I will dance the première, I will do Kenneth's ballet*, I swore. Lying in the hospital bed, I reflected that it would be much healthier, for Kenneth's sake and mine, if I had my own apartment. I did not want Kenneth to feel abandoned, but I also knew that the pressures of the opera house, combined with our living together, threatened the essence of our rapport. I rented a three-roomed flat in Grunewald, a parklike suburb a few miles from the centre of Berlin.

At my request Eike started transferring my clothes to Grunewald while I was still in the hospital. Meditatively smoking in the kitchen, Kenneth observed Eike packing boxes and suitcases. For some days I lacked the courage to articulate an explanation to Kenneth directly. One morning when he was at the opera house, I telephoned him, and muttered something about our kindred souls working without hypersensitivity or unconscious hostilities, if I had a place of my own. He agreed that the separate living quarters would simplify various matters and, besides, he would not be alone in the apartment. Vergie occupied the guest room.

I was finally released from the antiseptic hospital with its whining patients, unsmiling nurses and the odours of medicine bottles and bedpans. My arm still gives me trouble. It is not an alabaster arm any more, so I never wear sleeveless dresses. In the early seventies, when I was rehearsing with Nureyev at Covent Garden, Rudi – a most considerate partner – experimented with a lightning lift, his hand suddenly pressing against the old wound. I fell screaming to the stage in pain, certain that this time I had suffered another thrombosis, that I would surely die. But I survived.

Pale, tight-lipped and withdrawn, Kenneth said little to me as we concluded rehearsals.

I asked Vergie if Kenneth liked my Anna-Anastasia. She said he was thrilled. 'Why doesn't he tell *me*?' I asked weakly.

The première was a whooping success. I danced despite considerable discomfort, hurling the blood and bone of Anna Anderson across the stage, lashing the audience with that poor woman's fury. My costume was a plain bluish-grey dress, a hospital patient's uniform with a flared skirt. Anna's past was conveyed through newsreels and photographs projected on enormous white sheets. The only prop onstage was the hospital bed. The bed slowly revolved on a platform and we danced on the same revolve. The ballet ended with Anna poised on the bed, floating triumphantly around the stage, ready to accept the recognition of the world.

Vergie told me that my Anna-Anastasia was the most frightening and pitiful characterization she had ever seen in the theatre. I was exhilarated, exultant, flushed with the driving energy of a locomotive that could not slow down. My dressing room was filled with carnations from the management. Flowers of illness and disease. I jammed two bouquets into Vergie's arms. 'Give them away, I don't want to see any more carnations!' Kenneth poked his head into the dressing room. He too was exultant and exhausted. He congratulated me on the performance. And then, scratching his chin thoughtfully, he added that my cropped St-Joan-at-the-stake hair style was marvellous.

*   *   *

Towards the end of the season Eike and I had drifted into living together. This arrangement was somewhat disturbed by an unusual telephone call in the middle of one rehearsal. 'Must be Hollywood,' I quipped. It was! Herbert Ross was on the line from the States. He had directed the musical numbers for the film version of *Funny Girl*, which would make him a very popular film director. Herbert and *Funny Girl*'s producer Ray Stark were developing a Broadway musical, with a dance setting, that could be transferred to the screen. Americans were swooning over 'Swinging London', and Ray Stark, said Herbert, sought a 'real London kook' as the heroine. Herbert preferred a new face – an actress-dancer who would bowl over New York theatre critics. He wanted me. 'I told Ray you were perfect,' said Herbert. Could I fly to New York to hear details first-hand from Stark and Terence Rattigan, who was writing the script? The Berlin season was over. Fantasizing a new life, I packed a suitcase full of 'kooky clothes' – mini-skirts, beaded vests, glitzy costume jewellery and hats galore.

Seymour on Broadway? Seymour in Hollywood? It sounded good. It even sounded quite possible.

Within a week I was surrounded by Empire furniture in a suite at the Drake Hotel on a suffocating July day when the humidity billows over Manhattan like an airtight canopy. A secretary in Ray Stark's office at Columbia Pictures advised me to relax and do whatever I wanted. *They* would be in touch with me. *They* were waiting for Terence Rattigan. Rattigan was in Bermuda. I telephoned New York chums, but maids and houseboys informed me that everyone was out of town, on other islands: Minorca, Capri, Martha's Vineyard, Fire Island.

Since I didn't know when *they* might telephone, I did not leave my hotel. The humidity would frizz my hair. My 'kooky clothes' would be stained by perspiration and as-saulted by dusty grit. Not daring to put on a wrinkle of weight, I sat in the air-conditioned suite consuming gallons of iced tea and eating watercress salads.

Finally *they* called.

Ray Stark was giving a party that evening and his limousine would pick me up at eight o'clock. I bathed and perfumed and powdered myself. I painted my cheekbones in a three-way mirror: were they too high or too low? I asked the same about my eyebrows. And the heels of my shoes. I needed Bobby Helpmann to command, 'Lower the brow. Unbutton your blouse. Wear slinky shoes. You mustn't strut like a majorette.' The chauffeur waited while I changed the colour of my lips from pale pomegranate to rosebud pink. We drove three or four blocks and he opened the door. O Hollywood! O Broadway! I would never even have to walk to the loo again. As soon as I entered the midtown apartment, smiling at a mass of faces, Ray Stark, a small amiable man who fitted my image of a movie magnate, rushed to greet me. 'Lynn Seymour?' I nodded. He stood back, looking me up and down. 'Herbie's right. You're perfect!'

Ray Stark led me into a room as vast as a museum gallery and solicitously made a little speech about me to various lean blonde-haired women who seemed to have stepped from the pages of *Vogue* and sunburnt chaps in aviator shades, loafers and shirts open to the navels that I did not particularly want to see. The chaps were discussing 'deals' and 'grosses'. I heard two muttering, 'But is she bankable ...? *Ray* says she is ...' The chaps were agents who packaged multi-million-dollar film projects. I began to feel slightly self-conscious. Herbert Ross arrived. Hugging me, he repeated that Ray Stark thought *I was perfect* and we would all meet for dinner with Terence Rattigan in a day or two. Rattigan would outline the scenario. 'But Herbert, I can't sing,' I said, pondering my bankability. The musical was about a dancer, he answered. All I had to do was act and dance and talk-sing a couple of songs. Could Vivien Leigh sing? Hell, no. But she did warble in *Tovarich.* I mustn't worry, Herbert went on. He and Stark wanted a dancy show.

Again the chauffeur picked me up at eight and we drove a couple of blocks. I was deposited in front of some town-houses with black wrought-iron grillework and cast-iron jockey statues, world-famous symbols of the '21' club. You can have hamburgers with a $200 bottle of wine at '21' or Chicken Hash Pompadour with a $2,500 bottle of wine. A varied menu. We gathered in the club's main dining room on the second floor. The downstairs bar is less formal, but Rudi was the first man to be served there without a tie. Some rather heavy mouths dropped into their cherrystone clams when I crossed the dining room. The maître d' was undecided as to whether I was wearing a skirt or a sash. Ray Stark beamed. Herbert winked. Terence Rattigan – well, he looked as if he had just taken a laxative.

Rattigan was not my type. And not because he had the mouth of a crocodile and petulant reddish eyes. In the early days of the Diners' Club Jeffrey Solomons had a flat in Chelsea where we converged for Sunday teas. One Sunday Jeffrey appeared at the door highly agitated. 'The boy across the hall tried to kill himself for the second time. First it was sleeping pills. Last night it was the gas. Dear Aunt Edna – he's Terence Rattigan's lover. Poor boy. I wonder *what goes on.*' Jeffrey had opened all his windows. 'I'm airing out the room. It's not very amusing to live in a flat where your neighbour always wants to do himself in.' I remember pitying the boy and wondering *what goes on?*

The master of the well-made play, as critics describe Rattigan, was horribly elegant in a grey suit and silk maroon tie. He gestured with a cigarette holder. Smoked with it, too. Beneath the tailored, exquisitely groomed surface lurked a cruel individual, I suspected. His face was rather set. Rattigan expressed his enthusiasm for the eloquence and beauty of dance – the spirituality of the body in motion. 'Yes, that's all quite true,' I said sweetly. 'But the reality is sweat. Sweat that won't wash out of your practice clothes. And farting in rehearsal is not uncommon either.' Terence Rattigan shuddered. Ray Stark hid his mirth behind a linen napkin. Herbert had warned that I was a 'kook'. He quickly manoeuvred our waiter into asking if we desired another cocktail before dinner.

We settled down to a serious conference. Rattigan outlined the story, entitled *Pas de Deux*. Wretched title, thought I, but . . . who knows? I was to play a kooky young dancer who lived in Chelsea. My boyfriend, whom I had known since childhood, was also a dancer. We both developed a pash for a mesmerizing Diaghilev figure. The lad, far more ambitious than the kooky girl, woos and wins the choreographer-impresario for himself. Quite crushed, the girl stops dancing, presumably to open a needlepoint shop on Clapham Common.

I listened without comment but two days later told Herbert that the story was utterly phony, fake, untrue, naïve, a pansy rewrite of *Design for Living*, which is pretty gay itself, but astutely modern and funny, with the two chaps and their worldly girlfriend all having sex, at the final curtain, we assume, with each other. And that sexual triangle was written in 1932. Noël Coward was ahead of his time. Rattigan was not. The project died a natural death but Herbert did make his ballet movie. It was called *The Turning Point*. Anne Bancroft portrayed the lonely, loveless – childless – ballerina. Shirley MacLaine played a married dancer who gave up a promising career. She wanted to have children. The two, it seems, were not compatible.

The waiting-around period for further conferences on *Pas de Deux* seemed destined to drag on for weeks. Rudi had offered Eike and me his villa in La Turbie. I was eager to escape muggy New York and bask in the sunshine and fresh air of the Riviera. So I told Herbert that I was returning to Europe. If I stayed in New York another month, I would have to send for winter clothes. We agreed to continue the discussions 'later'. My plane ticket, he said, would be with Ray Stark's secretary at Columbia Pictures.

I had been treated handsomely. Limousines. '21'. The St Regis. But when I telephoned Columbia Pictures about my plane ticket, nobody had heard of Lynn Seymour. Suddenly I did not exist! Was I hallucinating the New York trip? Would I wake up . . . in Berlin? There were several phone calls from Herbert and Ray Stark, both profusely apologetic. The plane tickets arrived by messenger and I was sent to the airport in an air-conditioned Cadillac. Goodbye to Broadway. Goodbye to Hollywood.

I had been handled like a new superstar for two weeks. But in the end, she never existed.

Goodbye to all that.

Eike and I tried to have a restful holiday in La Turbie. The beauty of Monaco before high-rise condominiums disrupted the landscape helped me forget the frustrations of the New York trip, the periodic pain from my thrombosis and glandular fever, and the coming season in Berlin. I had not talked to Kenneth in weeks. I wanted to give our relationship breathing space. Vergie was worried sick about Kenneth. 'He's drinking too much. He's very unhappy. His nerves are frayed. Somehow he can still choreograph marvels like *Anastasia*.' That fall Kenneth mounted a new production of *Sleeping Beauty* using a wintry Russian motif, with giant sleighs and furs. Kenneth's stylishly snowy approach to the ballet froze the sentiment and emphasized the sensuality. The production was popular with the public but not with the critics. I had danced appallingly at the previews, still suffering from the insidious effects of glandular fever. My stamina was not up to the rigours of that most testing of ballets. It was another blow for Kenneth, and I felt that he blamed my weak performance for the lack of critical fervour.

In *The Member of the Wedding*, Frankie, the lonely adolescent, has a tender soliloquy on 'belongingness': we all want to belong to someone, but Frankie feels left out; she is an 'I' person. Her friends can all say 'we'. Vergie Derman and Ray Barra could say 'we'. Ray lived with his friend from Stuttgart. Vergie's London boyfriend visited her in Berlin. I had Eike. Kenneth, however, was an 'I' person like Frankie and very lonely. He came to the flat in Grunewald almost every night. And I understand his loneliness because for so many years I too had been an 'I' person. Kenneth missed that 'belongingness' and he missed London. His solace came from creating new ballets and recreating the old, such as *Sleeping Beauty*. But he was becoming a shrunken shadow of his former self. His skin had lost its colour, his face was creased with anxiety. Somehow, as Vergie said, he still managed to choreograph marvellous ballets. His creative imagination towered above all pressures and problems.

He was baffled by my relationship with Eike. To the melody of the hit song 'Alfie', he would fling himself on our sofa and harmonize, 'What's it all about . . . *Eik-eeeee . . . ?*' Eike was not amused. He maintained silence; Kenneth was his boss. Sometimes Kenneth showed up long past midnight. Once, when it was snowing, he rang the bell at two in the morning. 'Please, Kenneth – you must not come after midnight,' Eike said. 'Lynn's arm still hurts and it takes her hours to fall asleep.' I stood in my bathrobe and slippers, caught between the two men in my life. Kenneth wiped the snow from his face. I held my breath, afraid to speak, to utter a sound. He smiled politely and was gone. We saw him less and less in Grunewald after that snowy night. Two months later he was completely alone in the once populated

Berlin apartment. Vergie Derman, who'd been on leave from the Royal Ballet, had returned to London.

Snow and ice mantled Berlin through February. I was dancing *Sleeping Beauty* and *Anastasia* at the opera house and Kenneth added *Las Hermanas*, his ballet based on Garcia Lorca's play *The House of Bernarda Alba*, originally for Cranko's company. I played the eldest of five sisters who lusted after the one eligible man in a Spanish village. The sisters are kept from the world of men by a tyrannical mother. The play is a study in frustration but Kenneth rejected a mood of lyric tragedy and choreographed a swirling duet between the repressed elder sister and the man she expects to marry. I had some difficulty finding a way of portraying this anxious, fussy, pathetic – yet somehow expectant – woman. I remembered how my beloved teacher, Winifred Edwards, would – in an unconscious gesture – pat back a stray hair on her always immaculate head. My wig was tightly marcelled, so I adopted this gesture during moments of tension. I thought it gave the spinster's character more depth because of this endearing, unexpected vanity. The marcelled wig did as much for establishing her personality as my own shorn locks added to the illusion of Anastasia's displacement. *Las Hermanas* is one of Kenneth's most poignant ballets, in which the virile outside world clashes with the sterile inside world of the Alba household.

The challenge of *Las Hermanas* was, however, not enough to make me look forward to the future. I was still physically depleted from my illness and depressed about Kenneth's attitude towards me. There was really nowhere to go. I decided to do something joyous and positive – I would have a baby. After three months of trying, it worked.

I dreaded the impact of my news on Kenneth. His ballerina in Berlin had been sick with glandular fever and a thrombosis in her arm. Now she would be out of the company for several months. Kenneth's emotional and physical state was very fragile. I did not want to let him down. But I would not give up my baby again for unfulfilled promises and ephemeral reviews.

I asked Kenneth if I could see him privately after the company class in my dressing room. I had changed into street clothes and was applying eye shadow when he sauntered into the airless chamber, a confusion of costumes, tights, dance shoes, make-up brushes and bottles, and a fair amount of cigarette smoke. I hesitated. Then it was done in a rush. In one sentence. His appearance of languid calm was unshaken. His eyelids dropped a little, he smiled the faintest of smiles and said in a tight voice, 'That's wonderful, Lynnie.'

News of my condition quickly reached Covent Garden. The gossips prattled: 'Pregnant? . . . But she's still married to Colin Jones, isn't she? . . . Who's the father? . . . Someone in the corps? . . . What does Kenneth say? . . .' Eike took quite a bit of chaff. The scandalmongers said that Eike was manipulating me for his dance career, particularly after he was given a leading part in *Carmina Catulli* by Carl Orff.

In late August 1968, nearly two months before our baby was due, I began having contractions. The doctor informed me, 'You're going to give birth six weeks early.' I managed a feeble joke: 'I've never been this early for *anything*.'

My parents were flabbergasted beyond words when they received our telegram: WE HAVE TWO BOYS. Twins!

Eike and I were quite dazed ourselves. Mother Nature, I secretly thought, was making up for the loss during *Romeo*. 'How very Lynn,' said Nigel Gosling. 'She never does things in halves.' Now we had to double up on cribs, nappies, blankets and baby clothes.

The two little sparrows were put in an incubator for six

weeks to nurse them through that critical period. We named them Jerszy and Adrian. Adrian was as British a choice as Jerszy was Polish.

When I emerged from hospital I started lessons in baby care and driving a car. The twins were strong enough to leave hospital in October. Eike and I agreed that the lads should have Canadian citizenship. This presented a farcical situation which took four years to untangle. Since I was still married to Colin Jones, the last name on their birth certificate (under German law) read Jones. Not the biggest giggle for Colin. After much to-ing and fro-ing with official-dom, I received permission to have the birth certificates in my name. Even this raised a problem: My name remained – legally – Springbett. So first I had to get a divorce from Colin and then have my name legally changed to Seymour. When it was all straightened out years later, a foxy Canadian official wrote to the British consul, 'If only Miss Seymour had consulted us before she had conceived the children, we should have found a solution to her peculiar riddle much quicker.'

Some months after I reluctantly returned to the stage Juliet entered my life again. The Royal Swedish Ballet, under the directorship of Erik Bruhn, asked Kenneth to stage his *Romeo and Juliet* and Kenneth invited me to star in the Stockholm production. I had been back in class several months and found, to my pleasure, that my technique was more assured. Everyone said I looked younger. What rubbish that dancers shouldn't have babies! I advised Kenneth's office that my only special request for Stockholm was an extra hotel room for the twins and their nanny. A week later Kenneth announced glumly that my guest artist fee was too high for Stockholm. He was engaging Georgina Parkinson.

I was dumbfounded. Too high? My fee was about £250,

hardly a huge sum for a guest in a famous opera house. It did not make sense. Glen Tetley was a personal friend of Erik Bruhn's. He would get to the bottom of the matter. Glen was staging one of his ballets in Stockholm at the same time as *Romeo*. I telephoned Glen in Amsterdam where he was co-director of the Netherlands Dance Theatre. Hearing his solid voice, I lost control and burst into tears. 'I've been told Stockholm won't have me – my price is too high – please ring up Erik for me.' I was quivering from head to toe.

An hour passed, then Glen was on the line. 'Erik says they wanted you. In fact the opera house was preparing its publicity . . .' He muttered something about Kenneth not looking forward to staging *Romeo* with the disruptive Seymour circus under foot.

When Eike walked into the flat after a rehearsal, I said accusingly, 'Juliet is off. I've been cancelled.'

Eike methodically removed his coat and scarf without saying a word. He sat down opposite me. 'Cancelled?' he asked slowly. 'Why?'

'Because of you. And the twins. And the nanny. It's too much confusion for Kenneth.'

'I'll talk to Kenneth tomorrow,' Eike said.

Eike is a man who thinks a lot and says what he thinks. The following day he had a conclusive interview in Kenneth's office. Ray Barra was also present.

The page and the prince, the corps boy and the director. 'I'm not trying to undermine Lynn,' said Eike. 'I'm not ruining her chance of being your star. Why are you punishing her? Stop behaving like a child.' Ray Barra squirmed in acute discomfort. Before Kenneth could reply, Eike went on, 'As for me, I'd like to work with you, but I lose performances. Do you want me or not?' A heavy silence smothered the office.

Leaning across the desk Kenneth rumbled a loud NO.

He said that Eike was never going to be a very good dancer; he should look for another profession. 'I'm doing you a favour, though it may not seem like that.' Eike accepted the decision and left the office with dignity. The dance union urged Eike to appeal his case, which they said he would win, but he declined, refusing to be a stooge for union gripes. A few days later the management fired me, stating that I had missed too many performances because of illness and pregnancy. Kenneth's own three-year contract was not renewed.

We were all given six months' notice.

Kenneth's swan song was a new production of *Swan Lake*. I danced Odette-Odile. Kenneth reconstructed the fairy tale as a troubled dream in which the prince awakens to find the creature of his imagination, divested of swan wings, coming to him as a real woman. The production of this classic was an uneven but rather pure rendition. My feelings toward Kenneth were ambivalent. I was angry about Eike's brusque dismissal and my being cancelled from *Romeo* in Stockholm. Yet Kenneth's health was deteriorating rapidly. He was a shrinking figure, pale and nervous. He seldom laughed any more. He seldom smiled. We had a drink together, just the two of us, and I realized with a despairing wrench that the old Kenneth, the Rabelaisian hero of the Diners' Club, was nowhere in sight. He reminded me of someone who had just recovered consciousness after suffering a bad fall, or worse. He was quite ill, and I longed to comfort him, but I had no idea what was wrong. I wrote my parents: 'Kenneth and I are friendly but he is in pretty rough shape and I have very little hope that he can help himself, let alone me.'

In the spring of 1969 I learned that Kenneth, en route to resuming life in London, had suffered a heart attack while visiting friends in Munich. I was feeding the twins when I heard the news. I could not finish the task. A world without

Kenneth? We may have provoked each other, at times, but it was unthinkable that I might never see him again. I stumbled on to the balcony. Sunlight cast uneven patches of brightness on the dark budding trees and grassy meadowland. Two shrieking children ran with kites, chased by a nanny. But instead of the children I saw two teenage dancers with suitcases, running for a train. I closed my eyes. Oh, how swiftly it had all vanished!

I sent Kenneth a telegram, saying, 'I'm always here if you need me.'

Kenneth recuperated in London for some months at the home of Georgina Parkinson and Roy Round. When I saw him again his hair had turned grey. But he is a Scotsman made of iron. He managed to stop drinking and smoking. He married a handsome Australian and fathered a daughter. And he continues to produce ballets. The critics who lean towards candy box ballets quibble over MacMillan, but, like him or not, his contribution as a choreographer has been both prolific and important.

Clement Crisp is a critic who frequently tweaks the noses of smug balletomanes. The other day, over lunch at his home in Islington, Clem said, 'So many people want to keep ballet nice and cosy. Whatever regrets you may have, remember – you and Kenneth kicked and pushed the Royal Ballet into a new era.'

When I left Clem, bound for the tube station, I was utterly turned around. 'Oh, Clem, I hope I'm going in the right direction.'

Watching from the door he called out with a tickling laugh, 'My dear Lynn, you're *always* going in the right direction.'

CHAPTER 13

Fly Away Home

The Studio Club, just off Turnham Green, is for me a hide-out – a convivial retreat, a shelter amid a pelting rainstorm and, all-around, a very pleasant place to while away a beautiful hour. When the house is too chaotic, with jangling telephones, reporters rapping on the door, promoters for benefits gathered at the dining-room table and the neighbourhood Boy Scouts inflating rubber rafts in the sitting room, I sometimes go to the Studio Club to have business meetings. A television producer showed up the other night. Demian's electric train was chugging through the sitting room and the twins were engaged in a game of darts, so we adjourned to the Club with script in hand.

The producer brought drinks to the table. He outlined the script. A fiction writer, a woman in her early forties, is confronted with the chance of a reunion with her former husband. She has two children and lives in an unpretentious cluttered house not unlike mine. The house symbolizes her independence – her one secure niche in an insecure world. Did I think the story required a so-called happy ending? 'What *is* a happy ending?' The producer said he liked my spontaneity and lack of self-consciousness on camera.

The camera picks up every wart and wrinkle, but never caused me the anxiety which increased at every performance on stage. The panic had always been there, but it deepened noticeably after Christopher Gable's departure from dance. 'Your script sounds interesting,' I said to the producer. He still had to raise the money and find a co-star. 'What about Christopher Gable? He's a marvellous actor and we've always worked well together.' He thought Christopher was too handsome. 'But the novelist wouldn't be renewing an *affaire de coeur* with a booby. Her former husband has to have had *quelque chose* for her even to consider taking him back.' We concluded drinks at the Studio Club, agreeing to meet soon.

And now today, Eike Waltz, father of the twins, has telephoned from his home in Essex. I am leaving for New York and he wants to talk about visiting dates while I am gone. Eike has prospered. He is the technical manager of an international electronics company and the father of a daughter by his girlfriend. He still considers the legality of marriage a degrading money-making scheme.

Today is Saturday and he is taking the boys to his cottage for the weekend. We walk to the local. The tables and benches are wooden, the kind families use for picnics in public parks. Eike fetched sandwiches and lagers topped with foam. I explained again that I would be in the States for three weeks, arranging a dance project for Canadian television and the American première of my ballet *Rashomon*. Our topic: his visiting availability. A friend will live in for the first week; then, when the twins go to Scout camp, Demian will stay with his father. For a single mum who must periodically be in New York and Toronto, these manoeuvres, involving three lads, are veritable troop movements, requiring the strategy of Generals Montgomery and Patton together.

An east wind sweeps across the terrace, blowing ash from my cigarette on to my jeans, leaving a black smudge, and I hear Eike worrying about my lifestyle and my ability to cope. 'Cope!' I raged inwardly. 'That suggests scraping through.' Eike describes himself as someone who 'likes to hold his finger on the trigger'. 'But why keep the gun pointed at my head?' Was he saying 'hopeless woman'? Rudi, on the other hand, always gave me hope – dear friend. 'Oh God, let's go,' I said, slamming down my lager.

We returned uneasily down Woodstock Road, Eike very sporty-looking in corduroy slacks and a tweed jacket. The twins, Ads and Jers, were loading their sleeping bags into his car. They had raked the leaves from the front of the house, their last chore of the day, and were eager to be off.

'Where's Demian?'

The twins rolled their eyes and shrugged.

'Demian?' I called into the house.

A small voice answered, 'I'm coming, Mum.' Demian swayed unsteadily out the front door and down the stone path. He was wearing roller-skates.

'Demian, why are you wearing those skates?'

'Oh, please, Mum.' He whisked abruptly past me to the sidewalk. His older, more serious brothers, Eike's sons, sternly advised him to remove the skates. Eike, with an 'I-can-cope-with-it-all' laugh, packed him into the back seat. Demi tossed me a so-there face. The little villain. As Eike locked the doors and climbed into the driver's seat, I sighed, 'Well, chaps, don't let him skate in the car.'

My three lads – smart, handsome, rugged individualists with very strong personalities. Just what I always wanted. I closed the front door and ambled listlessly through the silent house, thinking, yes, I am an odd whatnot, for I would like to have more children . . . a houseful. Too late for *that*. I miss the giggles and chatter and pranks of my lads. I miss their company. And what do they think of their mum? I wonder. Amongst ourselves we shy away from a display of sentiment. It embarrasses them. It is difficult for a mum to tell her growing chaps that she loves them, but that is understood even if not articulated. The lads are protective of their mum and their home. They seldom invite schoolmates over for a visit. 'Our friends would find the way we live a bit peculiar – do you know what I mean, Mum?' Jers said. Addie elaborated diplomatically, 'I sus they have dinner at six o'clock. Sounds quite *boring*.'

The house is mine alone for several hours. Some musicians and dancers are turning up later and, round about midnight, I will scramble eggs and mix a salad. One gossip writer said that I did not know how to boil an egg.

Tosh! Time for a little music? Time for another load of washing. The basket is full every day and I can do pliés to the melody of the spin-dryer. Meantime I am recalling the alienating conversation – the snide asides – in the pub. Oh for a friendly face! I wish Rudi was here.

Rudolf Nureyev saved my life.

I was a mother of two children. A dancer without a dance company. A dancer with no fixed income hovering at the age of thirty. Rudi extended a rescuing hand. I cannot forget that.

Nureyev is the most courageous and intelligent and magnetic man I have ever known. His courage and intelligence, wrapped in a lithe, muscly body, contribute to his exotic, erotic persona. Rudi is also the most creative and energetic person I have ever encountered. After a day of class and rehearsal he will rush off to see the newest film or play or avant-garde musical event. He reads constantly. His ability to absorb information is astounding. Rudi has a machine in his head that sorts out everything immediately and gives him the right answer. If he gives anyone flak, you can be sure it is for a good reason. Rudi is a completely 'honest' dancer – he won't cheat or take a cheap way out. He will fall on his bum trying to do something right and he has a defined sense of what that is. Rudi taught me a great respect for the classics. He urged me to study the classic roles with a scholarly eye, to feel the excitement of making my body fit into a rigid form. During rehearsals, when movements became messy, we would both get angry with our bodies. Covered in sweat I lamented to Rudi about my 'technique'. He mopped rivulets of perspiration from his neck and stared at me with his deep-set, piercing eyes. 'We have funny bodies, Lil. One could say we have excellent technique. We both use an extra force of energy onstage to make our bodies *do* what they naturally don't want to.' Making your body do what it naturally won't is part of Rudi's definition of technique. Like Nijinsky, Rudi seems to defy the law of gravity, but he will be remembered as someone far greater than Nijinsky. The boyish tousle-haired Rudi, with a dangerously wayward smile, is responsible for turning ballet into a mass entertainment. He, most of all, changed the image of the male dancer. His virile, electric personality, which has the vivid colouring of a flamingo, removed such words as 'effete, bland, dumb, asexual' from the public's impression of dancers in general.

Rudi dominates the stage with a mixture of tenderness, brutality and sensuality. He once said, 'I am a Tartar. Our blood runs faster, is always ready to boil. We are more languid than the Russians, more sensuous.' He teased me, asking if I were a Tartar, because of the sensuality of my dancing. 'I may have some gypsy blood,' I answered, 'but, remember, I was taught by a Russian émigré in Canada.' Nureyev and I believe that dance movement is first expressed in the body – and finished in the face. Many dancers do not appreciate that the audience looks at *your eyes*. Eyes reflect either a Being or Nothingness. A born rebel, Rudi flouts convention, but, unlike myself, he never allows his heart to rule his head. 'You should never have gone to Berlin, Lil,' Rudi said. 'You were the only dancer at the Royal Ballet who could have pushed Margot offstage.' He hummed a Russian folk ditty and then added very deliberately, 'But you always followed your heart, Lil.'

Rudi and I do not float in the same social stream.

I am basically a homebody who finds the silvery tinkle of protocol, whether it be the rules of Beverly Hills or Mayfair, extremely discomforting. But our relationship is very special. We have shared secrets strolling arm-in-arm down Las Ramblas in Barcelona and swimming in the Mediterranean at Tel Aviv – nocturnal confessionals before the sky is streaked with the light of a new day. Touring with the Royal Ballet or guesting with other companies in *Giselle, Swan Lake, Romeo* and *Sleeping Beauty*, Rudi and I always managed to find ourselves with adjoining rooms and adjoining balconies, watching the sun come up with a bottle of champagne beside us. And slowly, as the sun overwhelmed the sky, we would polish off the champagne.

Rudi and I danced on the same programme at a London gala in 1961 shortly after he defected from the Kirov Ballet in Paris. With pantherlike grace, the rebellious Rudi leaped away from Russian agents at Le Bourget airport and made sensational international news. He was the first Russian dancer to pull off that spectacular stunt. For the gala, Fred Ashton created a solo for Rudi. Robert Helpmann and I dipped and tipped tempestuously to the tango from *Façade*. Madam brought Rudi into the company, paired him with Margot Fonteyn, who was mulling a retirement, and their partnership throughout the sixties is now dance history. Rudi came to dinner at Charleyville Mansions. He recognized in me a soulmate impetuous but passionate about dance. And he further recognized that the shaping and phrasing of my movements – arms, legs and head flowing in one liquid line – were similar to his. Rudi has no inflated ego. He is not bespotted with such emotions as jealousy and envy. He is generous with praise. He told a television interviewer, 'Lynn possesses a genius. When she goes onstage, Heaven descends on your lap.' I would never ascribe the word 'genius' to myself. But I let the quote stand for the record.

When the Royal Ballet celebrated a Shakespeare centenary in 1964, I was Ophelia to Rudi's brooding Hamlet in a revival of Robert Helpmann's ballet, structured as a flash-back fantasy in the mind of the dying prince. Delighted to find that I shaded the role inwardly like a dramatic actress and imposed the choreography on the grief-stricken Ophelia, Rudi said admiringly, 'You go mad – but so *sweetly*!'

Our affection deepened in Kenneth's ballet *Images of Love*, also part of the Shakespeare salute. Rudi joined Christopher Gable and me in a pas de trois, inspired by the quotation, 'Two loves I have of comfort and despair.' Kenneth interspersed the ballet with prerecorded lines from plays and sonnets. Christopher was the comforting angel (sacred love) and I was the despairingly Dark Lady (profane love). We struggled for possession of the 'poetic' Rudi. Our threesome was a lightning flash of arms and legs, reaching ravenously towards some ceaseless pleasure. An agitated critic said that our costumes for expressing 'the very naked name of love' were in questionable taste, but they showed our line to maximum advantage, complementing Kenneth's choreography, which explored the oriental plasticism of Japan's Kabuki Theatre. Rudi nicknamed me Kabuki Lil, which he shortened to Lil. The name stuck and is Rudi's sole property.

Amid the tense *Romeo* rehearsals, Rudi's close friend Erik Bruhn was mounting *La Sylphide* for the National Ballet of Canada. The ballet is another retelling of a mortal youth who falls under the fatal spell of an enchanted creature. Erik needed a partner. Rudi recommended me at a time when I needed to take my mind off everything and everyone relating to *Romeo*. I needed to get out of London. The invitation from the extraordinary *danseur noble* was extremely prestigious. I arrived in my home country for the December engagement feeling as enchanted as a sylphide. Rudi had sprained his ankle in London and was sitting around growing bored. London was wet and gloomy. Toronto glistened with snowflakes. He hopped across the

Atlantic and surprised us at rehearsals, bursting in one afternoon in sleek boots and a black fur speckled with snow. It was heaven to see him. Erik had been wildly busy with other aspects of the production; I had had to work alone and was desperate for a stern eye and some moral support.

Rudi insisted on taking Erik and me to dinner that night. We trudged through the snow, braving knee-high drifts. Rudi was quite magnificent in his fur coat and cap, but the maître d' of a posh restaurant refused to seat him because he wore a turtleneck, not a tie. Never mind that his cashmere sweater was more elegant than any tie you could buy. The maître d' asked us to leave. Rudi whipped around, grabbed his shirt and jabbed the man's nose into the fur collar. 'Feel this!' he ordered. 'If the coat isn't worthy of your restaurant,' he pushed the man's hands away, 'then nothing is.' He stalked out and began throwing snowballs at the restaurant window. I applauded, inwardly approving of Rudi's attitude. I also needed to keep warm.

Erik was less than pleased by Rudi's behaviour. They had a row. Erik walked off – exit snowy street left. Rudi walked off – exit snowy street right. I was alone in front of the restaurant, with only room service to look forward to. After a moment Rudi dashed back and greeted me with a shivering hug. We passed an empty parking lot white with fresh snow. 'Do you know how to make snow angels?' he asked, his dark eyes glittering. He leaped into the snow and lay down, fanning his arms back and forth like wings. I jumped into the snow and began making angels. We played in the snow as children play on the beach, tumbling over each other, singing, laughing and throwing snowballs into the sky. Our wintry tussle was halted by a policeman who gazed at us with baleful eyes. 'Hey, you two, get moving, or you can spend the night in the clink.' Breathlessly, we ambled sombrely down the icy street and had dinner at our hotel.

One of many times in my career when I was resoundly smacked for not living up to a critic's image of a ballerina occurred on this trip. The *Toronto Star*'s Nathan Cohen was in a snit because I had 'an oval face, short neck, squarish body, plump and shaky arms and heavy legs'. The one defect he did not spot was a loose right molar. 'Don't worry about such rubbish,' said Rudi. 'He could say the same about me: short neck, squarish body, heavy legs and low-slung backside.' He flipped the paper into a waste paper basket. Erik Bruhn injured his knee. On two days notice Rudi learned the role and we danced *La Sylphide*. Rudi strapped up his ankle. 'I don't care if it's broken. I've wanted to do this ballet for a long time. And here's a chance to do it with you, Lil.' Before the curtain went up, the house manager informed the audience, 'Rudolf Nureyev will replace Erik Burke [!] at this performance.' The bloomer sent us into a collapsible heap, giving us only seconds to get our heavy legs in shape.

Erik Bruhn was not quite so convulsed.

On the return flight to London – our first together – we were coddled in first class. Yes, I would like a glass of champagne. Mr Nureyev would like a vodka-on-the-rocks with a twist. Rudi downed his drink, then curled up on the floor in a foetal position.

'Rudi! What are you doing?'

His face was hidden. 'I'm terrified of flying. The take-off, Lil. The landing. *Horrible*.' He was trembling in the most alarming manner.

Our stewardess said that safety regulations would not permit him to remain on the floor. 'Mr Nureyev,' I said, stressing his name, 'is not feeling at all well, and he always takes off in this position.'

She fetched the co-pilot who sauntered to our seats with a hearty John Wayne what-seems-to-be-the-trouble grin. Rudi remained curled on the floor. He was not budging. I suggested he bring a bottle of vodka to numb Rudi's anxieties. 'This is a primal reaction and no amount of modern technology will get him into a sitting position. I'll hold him tightly; you might as well take off.' Once we were airborne, Rudi bounced into his seat. 'Lil, you're marvellous. Even when you're not dancing.' That's just how I feel about Rudi.

When the Berlin venture began to crumble Rudi said, 'Remember, Lil, if you ever need anything, you telephone.' I promised that I would. And then, one day, Berlin lay in rubble. I was an unemployed dancer with a family and no immediate job on the horizon. Eike was about to start studying graphic design. We were not starving. We limped along each month, barely making ends meet. The sleepless nights of insecurity, which recalled my first days in London, returned to haunt me. I wrote to the Royal Ballet. My letter went unanswered. I telephoned Johnny Cranko in Stuttgart. Cranko's ballerina was Marcia Haydée, but I wanted to let him know that I was available for guest stints. 'You're Kenneth's dancer, I don't want to offend him,' Cranko said, 'and, anyway, your fees are too high for me.' I had heard *that* before. It was quite untrue but I had too much pride to argue with Johnny. I had the paranoid feeling that I was being black-balled. My decision was to stay in Berlin, an affordable centrally located city, until Eike finished his studies and my own plummeting career was firmly rebuilt. So I rang up Rudi, explained my plight, and he rescued me from the black slime, as I call the abyss into which I was rapidly sinking. Straightaway Rudi invited me to partner him for some *Giselle* performances in Barcelona. Then, hearing that Roland Petit was searching for a dancer with supple plasticity, Rudi recommended me to the French choreographer. Petit was completing a new ballet called *Kraanerg* which would open the National Arts Centre in Ottawa. 'Creating new ballets is what I like best,' I assured

Petit, drawing the theatrical parallel of premièring a new play by Beckett or Pinter or Osborne, as opposed to always performing Shakespeare. However, getting a chance to create new ballets does not come that often. I have been fortunate to create new works by Kenneth MacMillan, Frederick Ashton, Alvin Ailey, Glen Tetley, Roland Petit and Andrée Howard. A new ballet is created for your body. In the classics individualism must be restrained.

Roland Petit's most successful ballets are his 'story-dramas', such as *Carmen*, an international success with his wife Renée (Zizi) Jeanmaire as the sultry cigarette girl. He had created a Pop Art version of *Paradise Lost* for Rudi and Margot at the Royal Ballet. Petit's sensibility is *très chic*. He is influenced by the latest in music, art and high fashion. Roland Petit has a solid niche in French ballet. Many historians consider him the most outstanding French choreographer since Marius Petipa, the greatest master of 19th-century ballet.

I was pleased by his offer, sight unseen, to create the lead in *Kraanerg*, and, although it meant a separation from my family, there was no choice. Mum had to earn a living. Petit's new ballet was a plotless piece with kinetic, callisthenic movement – somersaults, knee-bends, free-form wrestling, acrobatic pyramids – all performed to electronic music by Iannis Xenakis. Petit's ballet was a glimpse into a futuristic society. The amplified music, carrying the shrill sound of a street drill, was a musical example of technology careening into the future. In the past Petit's sets had been designed by such artists as Nikki de Saint Phalle and Jean Tinguely. Victor Vaserely designed *Kraanerg*'s undulating black-and-white Op Art sets which created optical confusion and illusion. Calculatingly avant-garde, the ballet divided audiences and critics who were either fascinated or put off by the evening's dissonance. A few months later it was performed in Toronto and I found myself an international dance commuter. Within ten months I made seven trips between Berlin and Canada performing in *Giselle* and *La Sylphide*. Gone were the days of dreary digs. I stayed in hotels. But I was a dancer without a company. Without family. Without mates. My life was quite unreal: one month with the children, then off to the airport and another city and another ballet for three weeks or longer. I would lie awake most of the night wondering about Jers and Ads, feeling lonely and resentful about our separation. Nothing goads you on more than the precariousness of your bank account and career. Eike was becoming increasingly resentful of my necessary absences.

'I have a beautiful life,' I told a Canadian reporter, lying through my teeth. To keep money in the till I enacted the dancing Anna, who goes on a search for money to build a home, in Kurt Weill's *The Seven Deadly Sins*. This time my destination was Marseilles, where I performed before a French audience drinking wine and eating sausages. Anna's limbo reminded me of my own. A young French producer who had worked with Roland Petit asked me to dance in Paris. He was organizing a small dance company for a series of late matinée performances at the Théâtre de la Ville. It was not a de luxe booking, but it was interesting. I would be working with yet another choreographer on some new pieces. I was never certain when the next offer might come and loathed inactivity. So I accepted. Eike urged me to cancel. 'I can't . . .' I agonized inwardly; it was not *my* choice to be dancing in Paris. I was being ignored by the two obvious companies, the Royal Ballet and Stuttgart.

'The Royal Ballet's best dramatic dancer', in order to stay alive, in body and spirit, went through with the Paris engagement. I settled into a hotel near the Place de l'Odéon. The guests were tourists with guidebooks. The loo was down the hall.

I met two charming brothers, Gérard and Philippe, both

in their late twenties, who lived with their mother, Elizabeth de Wrangel, next to the hotel. Elizabeth was an eccentric Englishwoman who taught at a lycée. Her deceased husband had been a White Russian general. Gérard was an artist. Philippe was a Russian translator. The brothers had been to every performance and enthusiastically made it their business to make my lonely Parisian sojourn as pleasant as possible. They escorted me to-and-from rehearsals. We dined out most evenings with their mother, a tiny blossom of a lady who awaited us in turbans and shoulder-padded suits that she had worn since the war. Elizabeth de Wrangel went through a French ritual of studying the menu for some minutes and then consistently ordered the same thing: *steak haché*. 'Tonight,' she would trill in French, as if making the decision for the first time, 'I will have a hamburger.' The brothers liked to smoke and chat in my room. Gérard and I were in the midst of a discussion when the French producer knocked on the door. He was coming to see me on the pretext of discussing programme changes. He had a possessive pash for me, but I did not want to encourage *or* aggravate him. '*Un moment*,' I called out, hiding Gérard in the step-in armoire. The producer sniffed suspiciously at the unusual amount of cigarette smoke. Then he kissed my hand, declaring that he really wanted to discuss *l'amour*. That was not what I had in mind. The situation was saved by the arrival of Philippe. Grabbing the producer I dragged them both out of the hotel room and we strolled to a sidewalk café. The producer left in a huff. He assumed Philippe and I were up to some mischief and I purposely let him draw the wrong conclusions. I saw very little of him after that.

Elizabeth spotted me sitting in the café. I needed a quiet lull. 'What is bothering you, sweetie?' Elizabeth asked.

'Life,' I answered cryptically.

'*La vie?* It bothers everyone. You must not think about it.'

Her attitude for an Englishwoman was much too French, but then she had lived in Paris thirty years bringing up her sons alone. She said meditatively, 'You need "the waters". "The waters" cure all my ills. I do "the waters" every day.' Marvellous. But what waters, where? She heaved an indignant sigh. Positioning a Gitane in her mouth she painstakingly explained the benefits derived from spending ten minutes a day bathing on the bidet, that white porcelain fixture with hot and cold running water which sits on the floor in most French hotel bathrooms. I had thus far only used the bidet to wash my hair. Her mixture of hot to cold water, with soap and so on, was more complicated than preparing a dry American martini. I thanked her for the advice and started washing my hair in the sink. My Paris sojourn taught me quite a bit about *esprit* and *politesse*, and good common sense. 'If you do not expect too much from life, you will never be hurt,' Elizabeth de Wrangel counselled. Good advice, but so difficult to accept.

I returned to Berlin for guest appearances at the opera house, wondering when, if ever, I would dance again in London. And then, unexpectedly, on two days notice, I was asked to replace an ailing dancer for one performance of *Sleeping Beauty* with the Festival Ballet at the Coliseum. It was never a ballet in which I had excelled, but I was in fairly good shape and so prepared myself to face the caustic eyes of friends and foes. London was the city to which I was emotionally tied, where my friends lived, where I had achieved my reputation; and I was guesting for one performance – a fill-in slot for another performer. Once again, a displaced person. It was impossible to go anywhere without seeing ghostly settings from my past – an Indian restaurant, boutiques, pubs in Soho and Covent Garden. I shut my eyes and concentrated on the ballet. I was far removed from the London that had once been mine.

Rudi and Margot were the lustrous partners at the

Garden, but while I was in Berlin another Royal Ballet couple, Antoinette Sibley and Anthony Dowell, had won an affectionate public. I had no knowledge of my partner in *Sleeping Beauty*. I needed someone fresh, with no past associations. I found such a person at the first rehearsal and felt in my bones that this *Beauty* could be a dazzler: my partner was Peter Martins of the New York City Ballet. He was tall, blond and masculine with a cunning sense of humour. After the first minutes of rehearsal he put me at my ease in a role I had never considered 'me'. We were in tremendous rapport. He made light of the difficulties as we prepared for the performance the next evening. When the rehearsal was over we took each other out to dinner. Peter was divorced and had a son. We talked about our children, our marriages and affairs.

Peter observed wryly that most men were not interested in changing *their* standards of virtue. If a woman did not have affairs, she was a bore. And if she did have affairs, she was morally loose. I answered that I certainly did not ever want to be a bore – or loose.

'You know what I like about you?' Peter said the next morning while I brought a tray of tea and buttered toast to the bed where he lay propped against pillows. 'You don't have what I call "the ballerina mentality". You don't stare at yourself. You don't dance *to* the audience as if you were making a grand presentation. And you treat your partner as an equal.'

Sitting on my bed in my flannels I said, 'You know what I like about you?' He watched me with wary eyes, expecting a sassy remark. 'You're so divinely *sane*, Peter.' He choked, spilling some tea.

The interlude had a restorative effect. The sense of a thwarted career, the illnesses and awkward episodes of Berlin were temporarily calmed by Peter's lively companionship. He made me feel happy and confident.

The *Sleeping Beauty* reviews gave our parting a touch of glamour. I danced, they said, with complete assurance, as if the role had just been created for me. The critics pelted me with glorious phrases, calling it a 'triumphant performance' from 'a unique artist', and concluding that dancers of 'Seymour's stature, like Fonteyn ... come but once in a lifetime'. How long, they demanded, must we wait *before she returns permanently to London*? I said to Peter, 'It just shows you what you can do when there's an incentive.'

'What was the incentive?' Peter asked.

'Well, there was you, partner. And I want to come back to London,' I said in a whisper. 'But I'm not ... exactly wanted ...' I refused to admit aloud that I was the dance world's principal gypsy whose life was spinning round and round in meaningless circles and that I often pondered what might have happened to Kenneth and Christopher and myself – during the last three years – if we had stayed at the Royal Ballet.

My international dance commuting lasted one and a half years.

That winter we went to Holland for the New Year to visit Glen Tetley and Scott Douglas, ballet-master for the Netherlands Dance Theatre. They had rented a massive house by the sea. I spent many blustery afternoons tramping in the sand, listening to the crashing waves, silver-grey in the frosty winter sunlight like the sky itself. One grey Sunday when bitter winds whipped the ocean to menacing heights I set out for the beach wearing a woollen cap and a long Edwardian coat. Eike and the twins were romping with Glen's two dachshunds in front of a crackling fire. Scott was making a fish stew for dinner. Glen had already been out walking for hours. The cold salty air and the vastness of the turbulent sea evoked memories of my childhood in Vancouver with my isolated reveries and secret dances on the sand. Glen Tetley, a big, gentle man, hailed me, his cheeks merrily flushed from the wind. I had been waiting for the opportunity to talk to Glen privately. A breaker thundered on to the sand, almost sopping my feet, and I dashed on to higher ground, falling into Glen's arms. The stubborn pride had gone out of my face. I held on to Glen, pleadingly. 'I love you and Scott so much,' I said. 'Couldn't you find a place for me in the Netherlands company? I need a company, Glen, I need a home. I'm so tired . . .'

There was a brief, throbbing silence, punctuated by the music of the waves. 'I know how you feel, Lynn. You're a great dancer. You should be in a big company with a big repertoire. You wouldn't be happy here. After one season, your frustration would be worse than ever. You have to think of your future. We're a small company. With no soloists, no stars.'

I clutched his hand feverishly. Glen spoke the truth. *I had to think of my future.* What future? We resumed our long tramp along the beach, my head pressed against his arm. Glen Tetley was reading a book of Isadora Duncan's letters. He said that at one period in her life, when she was distraught, she moved to Holland and wandered up and down this very same beach with her two children. I stared at the coastline, imagining Isadora, in bare feet, flinging open her soul to the sea. Isadora, whose special life was as distinctly individual as her dancing. 'You remind me so much of Isadora,' said Glen. 'It would be an ideal role for you.' I smiled at him with a lighter heart and replied that it was something lovely to think about, but, meantime, my life was in a treacherous topsy-turvy state.

Kenneth MacMillan succeeded Sir Frederick Ashton as co-director of the Royal Ballet with John Field, in September 1970. Some months later, after further reorganization, Kenneth became director. He asked me back to the Royal

Ballet to dance an expanded version of *Anastasia*. 'You'll prove your greatness again,' Glen said when I gave him the news. Eike and I packed for London. A fresh start. A new life in London, again.

Vergie Derman had married a television producer and was living in Buckinghamshire. She said we could stay with her until I arranged a loan to buy a house. The Seymours descended on Vergie, a most patient and tolerant hostess. Eike was enrolled at the London College of Printing and I began classes at the Royal Ballet. For weeks Vergie's inquisitive neighbours could not sort out the characters in her house. After settling into Buckinghamshire her husband went off on a two-month assignment. Kenneth spent the odd night with Vergie. Then Eike and I arrived with the twins. A lady across the road accosted Vergie. 'I've just been wondering – which gentleman is your husband?' Vergie answered nonchalantly, 'You haven't seen him yet.'

As I opened the suitcases and boxes of dresses, slacks, boots, coats, shoes, shirts and flannelettes for a family of four, I said brightly, 'Aren't you lucky? Georgina got Kenneth, but you get us!' Vergie smiled stoically, like someone who has just lost the national lottery.

I hired a nanny, a teenage girl named Fiona, who moved into a spare bedroom. Vergie's husband finished his assignment in Ireland and there were seven of us in the house. Vergie's tolerance never wore thin but it was imperative to find a house and settle down. In the interim I rented an apartment at an exorbitant price on Gloucester Road.

By that time I was rehearsing *Romeo* with David Wall – and house-hunting. Each night I would return to Gloucester Road exhausted. One night the twins were crying for their supper. Fiona wasn't her usual self. My relationship with nannies has been informal like my household. I preferred to think of nannies as chums who got paid for helping out. The nannies called me Lynn. 'Miss Seymour' was too uppity, too grand. 'Oh, Lynn . . .' Fiona apologized, 'I'm preggers.' Her fiancé was a merchant seaman whose last letter was postmarked Panama. Oh dear, how was I to cope with a pregnant nanny? I tucked her into bed with a hot water bottle and some aspirin. Then I fed the twins, did the laundry and cooked the dinner.

It was now a do-or-die effort to finance the purchase of a house. Heeding Bobby Helpmann's advice about 'dressing for the occasion', I slipped into a black dress, donned a black hat and set it at a rakish tilt. I looked well-heeled, stable and smart. At last, a break: this bank officer was a balletomane. 'Lynn Seymour,' he said, shaking my hand, 'why haven't you been dancing in London?' I offered an edited capsulization of the last years and, fingering the brim of my hat, allowed that the performances he so admired were likely to be hampered if I did not have a house of my own *immediately*. I sincerely meant every word. But the costuming, as Helpmann would have approved, beautifully dramatized my seriousness. 'I foresee no difficulties,' he said at the end of an hour in which he recalled *The Invitation, Baiser de la Fée* and *Romeo*.

I bought my house in the Bedford Park area of Chiswick. Bedford Park was once known as the first garden suburb. Early residents were the poet William Butler Yeats and the playwright Arthur Wing Pinero. I selected Chiswick, landscaped with huge trees and flowers, because it is five minutes by tube to the Royal Ballet's rehearsal studios in Barons Court, twenty minutes by taxi to Heathrow Airport and twenty-five minutes by tube to Covent Garden. At the time of my purchase, Bedford Park was a forgotten grassy corner of London. Actors and writers sought Hampstead Heath, on the other side of London. My Chiswick neighbours now include artists and dancers and actors who appreciate its convenience and anonymity. We moved into Woodstock Road when the builders were still there. The house, chopped into three small apartments and two bed-sits, had to be reconstructed.

We lived in a desert of dust and bathed in a friend's house while the builders knocked down walls and restored long-covered floors and balustrades. The twins were scrubbed in a plastic bowl in the kitchen. It was my first home in London, my roots in the world, with a garden of rose bushes, sunflowers, lilac trees and sprigs of mint, rosemary and marjoram. 'Someone loved this garden very much,' I said to Rudi as I cut yellow roses and honeysuckle vines for a shelf in the completed kitchen. I had given Rudi a tour of the property and was beaming like a schoolgirl from sheer happiness. We stood side by side a little wistfully on the grass.

'I can hardly believe it, Rudi.'

His hand rested on my shoulder. 'It should have happened sooner.'

Jerome Robbins was staging his *Dances at a Gathering*, generally acclaimed as his masterpiece. The ballet had first been performed in New York. Among the dancers Jerry wanted were Rudi, Antoinette Sibley, Anthony Dowell and myself. Jerry is ruthless, brilliant, temperamental – a terrifying perfectionist. If Jerry does not approve of what you're doing, he will chuck you without a second thought. Kenneth MacMillan's directional signals are low-key, reticently expressed and observed. Fred Ashton never fails to exude a relaxed drawing-room charm. Jerry's tense quicksilver personality has the non-stop drive of New York, where he grew up. Devastatingly aware of everything going on around him, Jerry directs at crack speed with crackling commands.

When he was a dancer performing with Ballet Theatre in London after the war, one critic described him as 'monstrously talented'. He is also monstrously talented as a choreographer. And to dancers who shrivel before Jerry's curt advisories, he is simply a *monstre sacré*. Jerry has directed plays and choreographed for the opera. He is a great classical choreographer and has staged dances for dozens of Broadway shows. Agnes de Mille effectively integrated dances into musical comedy in the early forties. With *West Side Story* in 1955, Jerry subordinated the libretto to dance. His choreography 'told' the story. Jerry's show was a revolutionary dance event. For my money *West Side Story* is where American musical comedy stops, historically. Dividing his time between the ballet and Broadway, Jerry added more than thirty works to the rep of the New York City Ballet.

An outburst of vigorous dance (mazurkas, études, waltzes, a scherzo and a nocturne, set to Chopin piano music), *Dances at a Gathering* rhapsodically celebrates life and the irresistibility of all dance. Occasionally critics, enamoured by the sheer brio of ten dancers performing on a bare stage, look for a story within the lilting choreography, a loving merger of folk and classic dance. Is the ballet about lost youth and love, or Chopin's longing for Poland and the Old World? Jerry vociferously stated at an early rehearsal, 'There's no story. You're just dancing in that space. Dancing, dancing. That's all you have to think about.' All? Jerry gave us plenty to think about: intricate lifts, leaps, glides, slides, somersaults that required tremendous muscular control so that the effect seemed as light and feathery as a meringue. But, as any chef knows, a delicate meringue is most difficult to make.

Kenneth MacMillan brought him to the Garden. Jerry made us work harder than we believed possible, pushing us into mental outrage and physical anguish. He was challenging the Royal Ballet to equal – or surpass – the incandescent performance *Dances* had received from the New York City Ballet, and we were bloody well going to meet that challenge. He had us learn all the parts, women's and men's roles respectively, and would not reveal what we were dancing until a day or two before the opening. It was frantic and exciting. It was deadly. Jerry had us on tenterhooks.

Jerry arranged a costume fitting for *Dances* on the same day as my 'return' *Romeo* performance. The costumes for *Dances* are quite simple: flimsy dresses for the girls; blouses, tights and calf-high boots for the chaps. Nonetheless both Jerry and I wanted my flimsy little nothing to look like a flimsy little something. The problem was the hour of the fitting. Normally I would spend the morning in class, melding myself into Juliet, and the afternoon rehearsing with my partner, followed by a leisurely preparation at the Garden. 'Jerry, can't we postpone the costume fitting one day? I'm on tonight. Juliet.' I wanted to put my total concentration on Juliet. The role was fully mine. But I was jittery: it was several years since I had danced it and I would have to transcend past performances – for the critics, audiences, myself and, most significantly, Kenneth, the Royal Ballet's artistic director. Jerry was puzzled by my request to reschedule the fitting. It would take an hour; what was the big deal? Anyway, that morning at eleven was the only hour *he* had free.

Gritting my teeth over the interruption of *my* pre-performance routine I dutifully went to the fitting. I did not wish to argue with Jerry. I was overjoyed to be chosen for his ballet and I arrived promptly for the fitting as the clock struck eleven. At eleven-thirty, no Jerry. I was given a telephone message. A lighting crisis, or some such thing, had detained him and he would have to find a new date for the fitting.

The following day I dared to send up the incorrigible Jerome Robbins. I presented myself at a stage rehearsal minus make-up with a loud, tired sigh. I might have just removed the twins from their potty-chairs. In the full glare of luciferous stage lights I appeared on stage, a weary Russian peasant woman. Rudi and Anthony Dowell had difficulty containing their giggles while the cast paraded back and forth for Jerry who inspected us from the fifth row of the stalls.

Jerry coughed. 'What about your make-up, Lynn?' He coughed again, nervously. 'And your hair. It's a little . . . uh, skimpy.'

'Oh,' I said, batting surprised eyes. 'Do you want something *more*?'

'I think so,' Jerry muttered through stiff lips.

Excusing myself I went to my dressing room and painted my face. Crimson heart-shaped mouth. Lots of rouge. Ski-jump eyelashes. Then I took an unruly wiglet and tacked it to my head. A green scarf, tied into a giant bow, kept the overflowing hair from capsizing. I burst breathlessly on-stage, one arm akimbo. My dancing chums, doubled up with laughter, fled to the wings. From the stalls there was only a curious rustle of papers.

'*Jerrrrry*,' I called in a gingersnappy tone, '*okay*?'

'What's that for?' he asked, springing from his seat and coming down the aisle, a stricken look on his face. One of us, he assumed, had gone quite mad.

Wagging my hips like a burlesque queen I said in a clear amicable voice, '*That's* for insisting big ballerina have fitting on day of big Garden performance and big choreographer cannot keep appointment.'

Jerry's lean, unsmiling face, taut with nervous tension, dissolved into a mirthful grin. He became as soft as a marshmallow. Finger to his lips, he managed to get out, 'I like the bow.'

In *Dances* I had a whimsical waltz in which I flirted with three chaps who ignored me. At its conclusion I tilted my head, arched a shoulder in an aloof, carefree gesture, and flitted offstage with some dainty-débutante footwork.

Richard Buckle wrote in the *Sunday Times*: 'Seymour was such a miracle of Mozartian comedy in that waltz I was sure she had sprung it on them.' Jerry thought I had too. Next day he said: 'We didn't know she was going to do that.' But I was just following his directions the best way I knew.

While the house on Woodstock Road was being rebuilt, so was my professional career. The American choreographer Alvin Ailey, then in London with his company, asked me to be a guest artist in New York. He was eager to work with a trained ballet dancer but had no particular project in mind. 'I'lll come up with an idea just right for you,' he said. Alvin has an intuitive sense of theatre. He has acted on and off Broadway. His choreography, a blend of jazz, blues, and spirituals, flows from hurtful memories of growing up black and poor during the Depression in a rinky-dink Texas town. A powerfully proportioned chap, he played football in high school. His performance on the field won him respect, but his innermost fantasies were lived at the movies, watching Gene Kelly in the classic musicals (*On the Town, Cover Girl, Singin' in the Rain*). The Hollywood dream merchants affected us all, in one way or another.

When I arrived in New York, Alvin told me that the piece, entitled *Flowers*, was about famous victims: Judy Garland, Marilyn Monroe, Bessie Smith and Janis Joplin. Joplin had just died from an overdose of drugs. He was using a lot of her music as well as that of other rock groups. In Ailey's ballet, I danced for the first time to hard rock in high heels and quickly changed into pointe shoes for a hallucinatory dream sequence which culminates when the pathetic Joplin-type performer, driven to drink and drugs by her pimp-lover, writhes on the floor in stoned despair, begging for a 'fix'. I also pretended to puff on marijuana and snort cocaine. The ballet was rehearsed and lit within ten minutes of the première. A backstage error nearly unnerved me. The curtain went up and I sauntered out smoking an outrageous 'pretend' joint. With an extravagant gesture I cued the canned music. Instead of Janis Joplin, however, the stage manager put on Bessie Smith. I held my position – a foolish mummified object. The tape screeched to a halt after fifteen horrendous seconds. Then Joplin began singing and I had to hop into character, knowing the show was finished before it had started. I promised myself that if a similar mistake ever happened again in any theatre, I would walk offstage, forcing the stage manager to bring down the curtain and start afresh.

More theatrical than balletic, *Flowers* was a formidable acting role. Ailey's piece was very successful at the box office in New York and London. To some it was a smashing ballet, to others a shoddy descent into the lower depths. Alvin was an excellent collaborator. We explored the full breadth of the piece – free gestures, actions, postures, expressions – with the boldest of strokes. 'Just remember to keep that child real heavy,' Alvin said. 'She's got a lot of *baaad* habits.' I was the only woman in the cast. Some of the members of Ailey's company resented that his portrait of an American victim was created on a 'vaguely English' ballerina, so I extended myself at every rehearsal until my body was covered in bruises. The resentment disappeared. The critics commented that 'Miss Seymour's star quality . . . gives the work an emotional dignity . . .' The nicest accolade came from Alvin Ailey himself. 'Baby, stop worrying. I can't see anyone else in the role.'

A season later I worked with another American choreographer at Covent Garden. Seeking to expand the repertoire with modern ballets, Kenneth brought in Glen Tetley. Choreographers are rare, sensitive birds. Ashton starts with the music, Kenneth with a pas de deux, and a story. Glen Tetley tends to start with movement and then measures how the movement emerges from the music. How the ballet finally evolves, Tetley has stressed, depends on what happens in rehearsals. Glen studied and danced with Martha Graham. His cool intellectuality makes you forget that he was once a chorus boy in two Cole Porter shows – *Kiss Me Kate* and *Out of This World*.

Glen's ballet, *Laborintus*, with a score by Luciano Berio, focused on three couples on a journey through Dante's Hell, a labyrinthine underworld defined by ramps and mirrors which angled the dancers into fantasy figures inhabiting a Gothic twilight. Rudi and I, wearing flesh-coloured tights, slowly and sinuously spiralled into a setting that had the distorting quality of a painting by Hieronymus Bosch, master of the obsessive, haunted and terrifying fantasy. Tetley's inferno was a metaphor of our tormented contemporary society and I was a mother-figure who clasped two sleeping 'angels' to her bosom before leaving them to awaken in the distorting mirrored web – that is, the world around them. When our first performances were over Glen said, 'You're the perfect instrument for a choreographer. You bring to rehearsals so many of your ideas. Some day you must create your own ballets.'

The ballet which was responsible for stopping my helter-skelter dance commuting was Kenneth's full-length *Anastasia*. Giving Kenneth a triumph would, I thought, bury any personal rubble left over from Berlin. In showbiz, there is nothing like a hit to make everyone happy and kissy again, despite old grievances. If *Anastasia* were received with the enthusiasm of *Romeo*, his directorship of the Royal Ballet would be auspiciously launched.

Out of the Anastasia mystery, Kenneth devised an epic work of the doomed Romanov empire. He interwove a fragile mood of Chekhovian nostalgia with violent Russian history, all leading to the climax in a mental hospital. This sequence, originally the one-act ballet in Berlin, became the third act. The first two acts showed Anastasia on a summer picnic with the Imperial family and as an onlooker – and victim – of court life. In the first scene Anastasia is only thirteen. To establish her youth and rebellious streak, I decided that she should make her entrance on roller-skates. I had long hair and skates. Now, how else could I establish her character? Costuming is just as important as hair styles. I suggested that she first appear in a sailor suit. Anastasia was a bit of a tomboy and had a weight problem. The sailor suit separated her from the other members of the exquisitely attired family. The costume contrasted with her ball gown and the institutional smock. In three acts she developed from a capricious teenager into a shattered woman.

Kenneth assembled an all-star Royal cast. Svetlana Beriosova was the glacially beautiful Tsarina. Vergie Derman was a beloved elder sister. Derek Rencher was the handsomely distracted Tsar. Antoinette Sibley was the Tsar's favourite ballerina and Anthony Dowell her partner in a performance for the Tsar. The entire company was superlative. *Anastasia* stayed in the Royal Ballet repertoire through the seventies and increasingly won public acceptance. But there were boos on opening night when Kenneth took a curtain call. The critics zigzagged all over the place, faulting the use of three full symphonies (Tchaikovsky and Martinů), of naturalism and expressionism, of fact and fiction. Some hailed it as a glorious ballet – 'one of those rare and precious works of art'. Ballet buffs enjoyed arguing over *Anastasia*. It was respected. But the initial response was disappointing.

It was not a galloping triumph.

I believe *Anastasia* is a daring work because Kenneth broke rules – stylistically and musically. Film directors, from Luis Buñuel to Alain Resnais, throw viewers off balance by deliberately confusing styles (realism and surrealism with a splash of fantasy) but ballet audiences are less adventurous than hip filmgoers. They generally feel safer with a coherent unified drama. The *New Yorker*'s Arlene Croce later called it Kenneth's best full-length ballet to date, 'not so much because of what it achieves as because of what it attempts'. At the time of the London première in July 1971, Kenneth felt dejected and unappreciated. The praise I received for the portrayal of this complex role seemed to produce further resentment. Kenneth and I missed a shared victory.

The clock ticked on for two people whose lives had evolved. We stayed distantly friendly, and I never ceased to admire his amazing talent, but our rapport had been ruptured in Berlin. 'Kenneth depended on you in Berlin,' said a member of the original Diners' Club. 'Your illnesses – your love affairs – your pregnancy – how could you be the star *he* needed . . . ?'

One evening Lord Drogheda, the chairman of the opera house, gave a party. Lord Drogheda is a polished gentleman of considerable wit, the ultra-civilized courtier. Princess Margaret, Margot Fonteyn and Rudolf Nureyev mingled easily at his parties with board members, other dancers and names you would find in *Burke's Peerage*. These were not stuffy affairs but as eloquently relaxed as the host himself. I was reaching for an almond from a glass bowl on the sideboard when I heard a famous woman guest murmur to a dance critic, 'I can't understand why ballerinas have children. It is almost unacceptable.' Kenneth was standing across the room. As I slowly turned, dropping the almond on the carpet, our eyes met for an instant. Had he heard the remark? No, it was impossible, but for a few seconds I lost my equilibrium and quickly sank into the nearest chair. My children, my love for them, enriched my dancing and added a fresh dimension to my life which was, on the personal side, becoming sadly, shabbily grey. Eike and I were drifting farther and farther apart. We both knew the end was in sight. It was just a question of when.

Despite my unhappy personal life, I felt I was proving wrong the chi-chi rascals who claimed that dancers should not have children. In fact the crises in my life were never a result of my children. Nonetheless I was under psychological pressure – the constantly inferred shady track record – as demonstrated by the comment at Lord Drogheda's party: '*I can't understand why ballerinas have children. It is almost unacceptable.*'

Dad saw the twins in Vancouver before his death and he loved them dearly. I cried when he died, for my childhood died with him, along with my dream of bringing Mom and him to London, but Mom came by herself and lived on Woodstock Road for five months. She saw me dance at Covent Garden. Mom knew I was troubled about my status at the Garden and the associated undercurrents of my life. It was an uncertain and tense period.

That spring the company went to New York with *Anastasia*. Kenneth's ballet had received some unfriendly notices in the *New York Times* even before its première. This was the Royal's first American visit under Kenneth's artistic direction and balletomanes shouted, 'Ashton! Ashton!' at the stage door. Sir Fred had a devoted following in New York. He still symbolized the Royal Ballet. As a public figure Kenneth was too aloof for outgoing Americans. The first performance of *Anastasia* was a muddle, caused by backstage inefficiency, a replay of *Flowers*. The last act begins with her sitting on the hospital bed hearing sounds (on tape) from Anna-Anastasia's past. When the curtain went up, I realized with a sinking heart that the tape had not been properly rewound. We were in the middle of the sequence and would be losing a chunk of the ballet. Someone will correct it, I thought. But no one did. It was up to me. I stepped off the bed and strode towards the wings, shouting, 'Bring down the fucking curtain!'

'Awright, awright! Don't get excited, lady,' a stagehand said.

'Bring down the goddamn curtain!' I repeated again.

Staff members from the Metropolitan Opera House came running. They thought I had gone on a tangent – or something. Using sulphurous language reserved for arrogant conductors who do not keep time I explained that the tape was quite wrong. The gold curtains closed for what seemed hours while I explained the problem and then the ballet resumed, with the tape rewound. I learned during *Flowers* there comes a time when you simply have to ring down the curtain and start all over again. The same could be said of my personal life. I could no more acquiesce to piddling compromises. I needed to be completely free, independent and understood.

The company returned to London exceedingly depressed after the New York engagement. I was withdrawn and tense. Eike and I talked briefly one night after dinner and agreed that it would be better to live apart. He woke the twins and kissed them goodbye, saying that he would never be far away.

The break with Eike came as a great relief. But the tension involved in the severance took its toll. There were no new ballets involving me at the Garden and performances were few and far between. Inactivity made me nervous and fretful.

I was cast in Balanchine's *Serenade* and had a dress rehearsal on the same day as an evening performance of *Anastasia*. The *Serenade* costume was designed for a twig. I bubbled and bulged, and flushed beet-red throughout a rehearsal. I was asked to see Kenneth. 'I know what he's going to say . . . but don't tell me now. Wait until I've finished tonight's performance.' Glen Tetley, who was choreographing at the Garden, awaited me on Bow Street. We walked through the market without speaking. Then Glen said, 'Well . . . You have gained . . .'

I kicked a crate of potatoes. 'This is no life. And I don't know how to do anything else . . .'

Kenneth replaced me in the Balanchine for my 'own good'. I was too fat. Sitting with me in the kitchen on Woodstock Road after I heard the news, Glen saw me fragment into a dozen hysterical pieces. I was angry with myself. With my hateful body. With the undiminished indignities a dancer endures. Lighting and camera angles can hide a film actor's imperfections; a theatre audience, absorbed in faces and words, doesn't even notice a slight weight increase of a stage actor. But dancers must remain as firm – and unchanging – as a stick of furniture. 'Dancers have no rights,' I cried. 'We're just bits and bobs of furniture – polished, gleaming surfaces, always willing to be pushed and pummelled by the authoritarian furniture factory . . .' Glen placed a hand on my shoulder. I knocked it off with such force that he stumbled against a kitchen chair. 'You're going to tell me to calm down because this tension just makes me puff up. Step right up, folks, you can see the Waddler of Woodstock Road.' I giggled until the tears ran down my cheeks. Glen poured me a shot of whisky. Utterly deserted by self-possession, I rushed on, 'I hate the gossip – the backbiting . . .'

I took three sleeping pills and crawled into bed, hoping that I would awaken in Vancouver as a small child, lying on the living-room sofa on a Sunday afternoon, with Mom and Dad, all of us reading the papers. But my childhood was over. And my dad was dead. I awoke at eight in the morning with Addie and Jerszy on either side of me, a lovely habit of theirs, keeping very still until I had stirred and they would run and tell their Nanny that Mum was up and she would bring me a cup of black tea, my gluttonous breakfast before the inevitable daily dance class, come rain or shine, flood or famine, death or disaster. In less than two hours my thighbones would be moving round and round in my hipsockets; I would be stretching calf muscles and tendons so they remained elastic straps of steel wire. Exercises, exercises that I had been doing for years.

I had no desire to go to class, but if you miss one day the company knows, and if you miss two days the management knows.

I lay in bed brushing the twins' hair. My tea was untouched. The bath water was running. And the minutes passed. The ticking of the bedside clock gave my heart nervous flutters. I dreaded coming face to face with anyone that day, including my overweight and unwanted self.

The telephone rang.

'Lil!' exclaimed the buoyantly bemused voice of Rudi.

I sat up in bed, instantly alive, and asked the twins to turn off the bath tap. Rudi knew that Eike and I had separated, that the New York reaction to *Anastasia* had winded me and that I wondered what the Royal Ballet planned to do with me in the future. I wearily informed Rudi that my Garden schedule was thin because I was fat. He had already heard of the *Serenade* cancellation.

'Lil, I want you to do something for me,' Rudi said. 'I need you.' Nureyev needed me? A movie was being made about him, and he wanted me to perform a pas de deux from *Sleeping Beauty* with him.

'You'd best ask someone else. You'll get a hernia trying to lift me.'

'You'll do it, Lil,' he protested, with a laugh.

Then he rang off, observing that a prolonged discussion would make us both late for class.

I leaped out of bed, kissing the lads. 'Mum's going to make a movie! And your Nanny will bring you to the studio.' I flung myself into the tub, dressed quickly and dashed up the road to the tube station.

Nureyev saved me from financial and professional disaster in Berlin. Now he had gone out of his way to save my self-respect. Throughout the filming he treated me as if I were a presence for whom movies had been invented.

A very special chap who kowtows to no one, Rudolf Nureyev has a shrewd insight into character and a remarkable understanding of tangled loyalties. He is never judgemental. His knowledge of people is honest, his sympathy deeply human.

Once again Rudi gave me the inner strength to confront the cruel brightness of an uncertain dawn.

CHAPTER 14

Opera Bouffe

The sky in the Cotswolds on a fine summer day is like a Persian carpet with rich warm blues and oranges, faded reds and delicate golds. I delight in the fresh greenery, the sloping hillsides and streams, the wild flowers which fill the air with soft fragrance, the chiming of distant bells, and farmhouses built of honey-coloured limestone. In this idyllic setting I was visiting my second husband Philip Pace and his third wife Ellie, an astute and attractive woman, a writer who deftly sums up people with a phrase or shrewd observation. Philip Pace and I are fast friends – our marriage was high-flying fun, in a manic sort of way. After parting we were both too busy to get a divorce until Philip decided he wanted to marry Ellie and have a child by her. My solicitors made a bundle out of an amicable divorce, where no property or money was involved.

Whenever London seems a bit stifling I ring up Ellie. 'I must get away. Can I spend a Saturday in the Cotswolds?' This time Ellie telephoned me. Philip had been flat on his back with glandular fever and she was worried. I told Ellie that I would come out to see them and bring a bottle of good cheer. Philip is not allowed to drink, Ellie said, but I reminded her that *we* didn't have glandular fever.

Never certain as to what you should wear in the English countryside, I selected my 'Empire-builder' army shorts, a chiffon blouse and runners. I had a charmingly undisturbed train ride to the Cotswolds. Ellie met me at the station. 'Philip is very depressed. He wants to do a midnight flit.'

'A midnight flit? Oh, he wanted *us* to do that. Just pack up and disappear to some Eldorado.'

'He has an actual destination in mind,' Ellie said as we zipped up and down valleys, past grassy farmland. '*Ceylon.*'

'Dear Philip. He must be reading Somerset Maugham again.'

Ellie shook her head. 'He says we can live there for a year on what it costs a month in England.'

I patted Ellie's hand. 'It sounds lovely. Is it possible?'

Philip has a great sense of theatre. Our life became a play-within-different-plays. We were never synchronized. He would be doing an antic turn while I was writhing in harsh realism, or I would be moving towards sophisticated comedy when he was tragically dying from too much hemlock. If there is a budding actor in the family, it is Demian, Philip's son. Demian can cry on cue – and tear your heart out.

Ellie and Philip live in a spacious converted barn that has been featured in the glossies. They rent the barn furnished: Philip, in his maddest moment, would never cover the bedroom walls in paisley or install a toilet that resembles the king's throne in *Sleeping Beauty*. The barn 'parlour', with baroque tables, Victorian sofas, velvet armchairs and an immense easel holding Philip's latest painting, is a resplendent stage set itself. Philip has a penchant for luxury. When he has money he believes that it should be spent and not moulder away in banks.

Philip is not in the barn. He is in the thickly overgrown garden, lying on an iron bed under a pear tree. A boater is cocked on his shaggy sandy head and he is clad in a cotton caftan, his favourite lounging garment. He swings a fly swatter in his hand. I settled beside him on a wicker chair thinking how bizarre we must appear to the neighbours – Philip in his airy caftan, me in my army shorts.

'Lynsey, I am so weak. I haven't been to the studio in weeks. Don't believe I can photograph another fruit salad or veal cutlet again.' Philip is a master photographer of food

for advertising agencies. His colour photographs of beautifully arranged salads and vegetables have the quality of
dreamlike still-life paintings. In fact, he adores to paint in
his spare time. Philip comes from north-east England – 'the
arse end of the world', he says – and took a job as a
photographer's assistant in 'Swinging London' of the early
sixties when he was twenty-two. There were plenty of
fashion photographers around London; Philip found a tasty
niche for himself with food. I once visited his studio in Bow
Street, just steps away from Covent Garden, and a secretary
asked haughtily, 'Whom shall I announce?' I blanched at
her fancy airs and stated my name in a mumble. She picked
up the phone. 'Miss Moore is here.' Philip, on the other
end, shouted, '*WHO?*' 'Miss Lynsey Moore,' she repeated
while I crumbled in laughter. From that day on, Philip
called me Lynsey.

'You can't go to Ceylon, Philip. It's a long way away and
I suspect it's fraught with political unrest and tropical
tension. Besides, it is so pretty here.'

'I'd like to see palm trees and have a beachhouse with a
hammock on the veranda,' he answered, swatting a fly
buzzing near his ear. 'I'm almost forty, Lynsey. You made a
dramatic change in your life.'

'I've defected from the Royal Ballet again. I did not load
the family on a steamer for Pago Pago.'

'The bloody ballet. I hardly knew it existed until we
connected and it's just about all you ever knew. Narrow
bitchy lot, they were, not my kind, never were, except for
Rudi. Now there's a man of quality.' He removed the boater
and spun it around his fingers, studying it with an inscrut-
able smile. 'The problem is you tried to fit in.'

Ellie has appeared with a pitcher of lemonade and
glasses. She pours drinks for us and sits on the grass. '*Fit
in?*' I cried, sipping the lemonade and pulling a face. 'I
never fit – Ellie, is there any vodka in this?'

'*I know you never fitted in, but you wanted to, Lynsey.*' He smacked my knee with the fly swatter.

'Do that again, Philip, and I'll hurl you out of the bed.'

'You touch my bed and I'll throttle you. Of course then you'll say it was attempted murder.' Philip pointed the swatter at Ellie. 'Wife. Ex-wife would like some vodka. The only dancer at Covent Garden who could stay up till dawn *before* a performance and still outdance the technical cunts.' Ellie drifted to the barn, presumably in search of something stronger than lemonade.

Philip replaced the boater on his head and contentedly drank his lemonade. 'Glad you came to see me, Lynsey. Give us a kiss.' I obliged with a peck-peck on each cheek. Philip leaned against a pillow and stared into the sky. 'How's Kenneth?' he asked absently. I did not reply. 'Keeeeennneeeeth,' he repeated languidly, exaggerating Kenneth's voice.

'I do not know why every time I see someone from the past, they inquire about Kenneth. Why doesn't anyone ask about *me*?'

'We know about you, Lynsey. You're always in the press. Don't want to get emotional but I wish to bloody hell John Gale were here. Another man of quality. If John Gale were here, he'd be asking about you, Lynsey. Only you. He always worried about you. John Gale. Miss him, I do.'

I gulped down some vodka and lemonade lightheartedly, listening to the hum of tiny insects, the whispering of the trees caressed by a breeze. A mask of sociability crosses my face. Lynn Seymour, the dancer Sol Hurok said was 'a great actress', lights a cigarette in a snug outdoor setting, outwardly poised.

'John Gale suggested I was the wrong man for Lynsey,' Philip is telling Ellie. 'That was just after we met. Kenneth influenced her but Gale – he was special.' He sighed deeply. 'Glad to see you, Lynsey. Or did I already say that.'

I only knew John Gale for a short time yet he affected me very much. I still grieve for him. Philip understands because our three lives intersected.

Taking each feature separately, you might not have said she was beautiful, yet she was beautiful and, on occasions, extraordinary . . . The dark eyes were sad and funny, and the lashes real; the nose was almost straight, with expressive nostrils . . . She had made an impression on him from the very first; there was always, strongly, *something there*: It was not only bravery, wildness, a tendency to self-destruction: It was a quality deep and untouchable . . . She didn't care who anyone was: Her friends and lovers were often nobodies, at least to the world and this was attractive: If she was Thetis, mortals were indeed her fate . . . She took refuge in a small and self-effacing Canadian accent, which was extremely misleading. Belinda was a great actress on and off stage.

Belinda Skewczik, a dancer and mother of triplets, is a central character in John Gale's novel *Camera Man*. The hero is a photojournalist, married with children, who meets Belinda on assignment and does not see her again for several years when she is nearly thirty. They make no commitments but do sleep together once and then their relationship ends. For all mystery is gone. Lying in bed with his wife, the hero reflects: 'They used to say Belinda was the greatest artist dancing and he hoped, for her and her children, that she would always be for as long as she had to dance.'

John Gale's narrative is accurate about our friendship, except for one detail. We never slept together. I assume John thought readers would never buy the real conclusion. But he once told me, as we sat listening to Vivaldi, that the French called these intimacies with heterosexual men 'very rare, very exquisite'.

I met John Gale when he came to do a profile on me for the *Observer*. I was living in Charleyville Mansions with Colin Jones. John and Colin had been on assignment together and Colin said he was an absolutely smashing man. John was one of the paper's top journalists. 'John and Kenneth Tynan could mesmerize readers with 800 words,' said the *Observer*'s Nigel Gosling. 'Today, in some publications, it's the fashion to blather on. Gale and Tynan were the lean, spare aristocrats of journalism. No flab anywhere.' Very amusing and eccentric in his enthusiasms, John Gale was a person you do not forget. I was charmed by the solid chap in his late thirties, with scornful good looks, who spoke in a calm, precise public school voice. His wife, Jill, was a former dancer, so when I confided that exposing myself onstage was terrifying he listened attentively, appreciatively. I was rehearsing *Images of Love* with Rudi and Christopher. He came to a rehearsal and saw me throw myself into any shape Kenneth wanted – a twisted pretzel or a sinewy snake. I told John that I wanted to inspire the choreographer and be part of the creation – not just a lump with two legs sticking out.

He did not take notes. He remembered everything with ferocious accuracy. But how do you remember? I asked. By concentrating, he replied, just as you concentrate on your steps. Occasionally he jotted down a code word for an anecdote or statement. Over drinks in a pub John startled me with one question. Did I ever get depressed? My fingers clenched the red-and-white checked cloth. How did he know? How had I given myself away? He stared at the tablecloth caught between my nails. 'It's such a precarious profession, so very authoritarian . . .' he said slowly. 'Do you ever feel . . . unbalanced . . . ?' I dropped my hands in my lap, oddly comforted – not upset by the question. I did not know then that he had incarcerated himself in a bin after a breakdown – or that a bin awaited me in the future.

I opened my voluminous bag and fished out a cigarette, my eyes fixed on his sensitively lined face. 'I become detached. Egotistical. Completely unconscious of anyone around me when I'm creating a ballet. That's unbalanced, I guess.' He lit the cigarette. 'When I'm holding myself together, to succeed in these stage fantasies,' I said, 'nothing else matters.' I did not see John Gale again for six years.

Colin, *Romeo*, Berlin were past. I had rejoined the Royal Ballet. He dropped a note at the Garden asking if he might see me. He was doing a magazine article on death, he said, and how people reacted to it. We met in a pub. I showed up in a beige leather coat with an ocelot collar. John sat at a table, his wavy brown hair slightly rumpled, in corduroy and a conservative tie. We started talking as if there had been no interval in our lives. There was no conversation relating to his magazine piece. He asked penetrating questions about my life and I replied that after *Romeo* I simply ran away, searching for personal and artistic freedom.

'Will you ever find the freedom you need?' he asked, tauntingly.

I laughed a little too quickly, too loudly. '*Freedom?* Yes. It comes and it goes.'

He said I made it sound like a headache or rheumatism. He was making fun of me, but in the nicest way. He was a very cosy man to be with. After an hour he helped me into my coat, saying with forceful familiarity that a change would come, it had to come; he wanted to see me happy and he wanted someday to meet the twins.

That winter when Eike and I were only tolerating one another, I sent hundreds of Christmas cards. John Gale was on my list. But he was away on assignment and did not receive the card until summer when I was a single-parent on Woodstock Road. The company had just returned from its New York (*Anastasia*) booking, and I felt generally gloomy and disliked. I was gaining weight. There was little work for me at the Garden. I was not sleeping – or eating. Life seemed purposeless. And then, one evening, John Gale rang up thanking me belatedly for the Christmas card and inviting me to Sunday lunch at his home.

It was a super all-day party, with no ballet people whatsoever. John's friends were a hubble-bubble of writers, poets, painters and film directors. Wine flowed. A buffet was laden with an enormous roast, vegetables, salads and sweets. I adored his wife Jill, an incredibly sympathetic woman with dark hair and the dreamy quality of a wild flower that could outlast any thunderstorms on a jagged mountain. I met John's teenage daughters – his son was abroad. I was affected by the warmth of his family and friends, and the glowing atmosphere of the day. Sunlight dissolved into twilight. I did not want to leave. I did not want to return to the emptiness on Woodstock Road. The twins and I were the last to depart. Jerszy leaned out the window of a mini-cab, calling to John, 'Touch my hand! Touch my hand!' John was terribly moved and years later I included this gesture in a ballet of mine called *Intimate Letters*. The ballet was dedicated to the memory of John Gale. John had given me a copy of his autobiography, *Clean Young Englishman*. I seldom ask prying personal questions. He said the book would 'fill in the gaps'. It vividly captured a cricket-playing lad at prep school who became a young adventurer and ultimately a journalist who wrote eye-witness accounts of atrocities in Algiers during the French-Algerian war. The articles were not appreciated by the French government. The slaughter affected him and he had a breakdown which he discussed with remarkable candour. No wonder his eyes seemed to penetrate into your soul.

There were many Sunday lunches with the Gales and then, with no performances at the Garden, I went to Vancouver for two months. I carried on a correspondence

with John. His postcard replies were always provocative:
'Great dancers are not good dancers.' Or: 'The archduchess
marches to a different tune.' I wrote that I loved him. But I
misaddressed the envelope. When I returned to London he
came to Woodstock Road immediately. I was quite nervous, assuming he had received the note. While I bathed
the twins, John told them a story about typhoons. 'They go
clockwise in the northern hemisphere and anti-clockwise in
the southern hemisphere. It's the same as water running
down the plughole.' Suddenly he doubted himself. We
found a golfball, pulled the bath plug and to his relief, and
the lads' yelps, the water went spinning down the drain,
clockwise. After they were in bed I asked him about a
'certain letter'. He was bewildered. What letter? Well, I
faltered . . . an intimate letter. I recounted, a trifle awkwardly, what I had written, but adding that I refused to
intrude on his marriage and that given my own sensitive
state I had a horror of confronting another emotional crisis
of any sort.

John came to Woodstock Road often and when he did not
come he sent postcards with enigmatic messages or quotes:
'There's no use in knocking. I'm on the same side of the
door as you.' He telephoned one night and demanded, 'Are
you really honest?' I was taken aback. 'As honest as I can
be.' He thanked me for the reply and hung up. We were
both honest – as much as we could be. It was a tremorous
time. When he turned up unannounced with a bottle of
Mouton-Cadet, he removed any hint of sentiment from the
purchase by saying, 'It's a cheap bottle really – on sale.'
The twins and I were trying to dig a path in the garden and
they said we needed bricks. Two days later he stood at the
front door with a huge sack – bricks for the garden. The
twins screamed with delight. John was a worrier. He
repeated over and over again that he wanted the boys and
me to be happy. He was concerned about people's rights

and privacies and natural feelings. He did not want his children to grow up with sexual guilt. He did not want them to fret about social pressures from the Establishment. He would light a fire and we would sit on the couch talking about our children, and music and books. I listened and learned, keeping all feelings at bay. Sometimes I took comfort in the safety of the status quo. At other times, when a fire filled the room with a shadowy radiance and we smoked silently to the music of Chopin or Schubert, I was disturbed by his closeness. I resented what he was putting me through. 'I never want to hurt you,' he said, 'it's too risky, for you and for me.' If he was still on Woodstock Road past midnight he telephoned Jill and said, 'I'll be leaving in half an hour or so . . .' Jill was extremely tolerant and she trusted me. 'You always want your freedom,' he chided, 'but, remember, *obligations* destroy freedom.' That was a typical John Gale reflection.

One night he said carefully, 'I've found a solution.' He had just lit the fire. John could light kindling with one match. I stared at him blankly: solution? He proposed the idea of sharing his wife and me, without lies or deceit. He wanted to hear my reaction; he had not discussed it with Jill.

I replied that it sounded like a plot in a book. 'If you didn't love Jill and I didn't love you, it might be diverting. But you're a writer. You've devised a writer's solution, one that only works on paper.' Our relationship was unsettling in its restraint. He took me to lunch after dance class at a restaurant on the Thames and then we walked along the riverbank and sat in a grassy park. Stretched out on his back, he unbuttoned his checked shirt. 'Look at this – a middle-aged torso. It can't be as nice as what you see on your beautiful ballet boys.' He exposed a very nice chest, but I answered irritably that I was not seduced by a man's pectoral muscles, or any other limbs, having seen every rippling formation for so many years that a blemish was more arousing than monotonous perfection. We had touched forbidden ground. I went no further. I could not play the role of the seductress. Not with John Gale. We returned to Chiswick. The twins were playing in their room with the nanny when we entered the house. It was one of those sultry autumn nights when the air is thick and you wait for a cloudburst, for something dramatic to happen, and feel oddly despondent that nothing does. John's mood was aggressive from the luncheon wine. 'I should go home now. I'm sure you're getting bored with me.' The twins begged for a story and while he concocted a fable about a pirate who wore a black patch over one eye, I washed my practice clothes and permitted myself an idle moment with a cigarette, pondering my dilemma at the Garden – the dilemma of so few performances which daily eroded my confidence. This angered him. 'You're being ignored deliberately,' he said, and I burst into tears. The Garden, too, became a forbidden subject.

I glanced at my wrist-watch and slowly rose from the couch. The simple movement took all my strength. 'I think you should go home now.'

A little curve of amusement played around his lips. He said that I was 'the most determined waif' he had ever known. He brushed his fingers against my mouth. 'Take it easy, Lynn,' he said, opening the door to the night. 'I'll call you soon. Take it easy . . .'

During the next two weeks I decided to paint the parlour a chocolate-brown, and needing a helper and soulmate, someone from the past to whom I could spill out my thoughts, who would lift me from the gloom with his own solidifying brightness, I telephoned Christopher Gable. He was between film projects and came round. We tested a series of colours in egg cups – brown-black, brown-orange, brown-grey – until dozens of egg cups littered the kitchen floor and we were holding our sides with laughter. I selected a colour that Christopher called mush and then was unable to remember the combination of paints. 'No, Lynnie, *no . . .*' Christopher gasped, and our laughter echoed through the house. We flopped on the kitchen floor gazing in dismay at the chaos of cups. We started over again, found another colour – oatmeal brown – and, for one week, painted and painted and painted. There was scarcely time to think of anything else.

A Canadian dancer named Anne Ditchburn came to London to choreograph. She was a lively creature and needed a place to stay, so she settled into a bedroom on the third floor. Her company was invigorating and my lads liked her carrot cake. So did the chaps in the corps de ballet. Her ballet contained a duet between a lesbian older woman and a nymphet. Annie was dancing the nymphet. She wanted me to play the lesbian. The workshop was something to do after mixing paints. 'I don't know too much about lesbianism,' I allowed. 'In France, they're beautiful models with no tits and in New York they have uncombed hair and big bums.' Annie wickedly suggested that I find a mid-Atlantic interpretation. She needed a cowboy for another section of the ballet. Periodically I received letters from a dancer in Germany named Frank Frey. He had been my partner in Kenneth's production of *Swan Lake*. Frank was a rough diamond. Extremely tall, with huge shoulders and long arms, he startled everyone with his undisciplined muscularity. Dancers called him the Neanderthal Man. His quirky dance qualities appealed to Kenneth who always sought anti-cliché dancers. He thought we were the most strikingly odd couple he had ever seen in *Swan Lake*. Frank wrote that he had left the Berlin ballet. He was free. I invited him to London. He would make an excellent cowboy, with what we in the business call 'an mag' (animal magnetism).

Frank Frey arrived late one afternoon with a duffel bag. He had hitchhiked from Munich. He was clad in an anorak, baggy trousers, a thick polo-neck sweater and an endless woolly scarf. Annie looked at me. I looked at her. Annie was thrilled. Frank sat down at the table and leant back in his chair, smiling broadly at us both.

Later that week John Gale appeared unexpectedly one midnight. Frank, Annie and I had spent the day rehearsing her ballet. We were lolling on my bed watching the telly when the nanny ushered him into the room. John was, as usual, conservatively dressed. We were in our most at-home attire. I bounced off the bed, pleased to see him, and went through the usual social amenities: '. . . this is Frank . . . Annie . . .' He stared at me, his face grave, in polite discomfort. Excusing myself from the group I guided him down the stairs into the parlour.

He squinted at the painted walls.

'I've been quite occupied.'

'I see . . .'

I explained who everyone was and that we were working furiously on Annie's ballet which was about 'all sorts of different relationships'. I invited him and Jill to a performance at the Collegiate Theatre. John spoke with measured words. 'I'm glad you've been – *occupied*.' His tone indicated confusion.

We chatted for an hour over tumblers of Scotch. I asked after his family. He asked after the twins. He really loved the chaps. Then he departed and I very slowly, sadly mounted the stairs.

Rudi phoned, inquiring if an American friend who worked at Sotheby's might rent a bedroom. He advised me that she was a quiet, sensitive, responsible girl. Quiet, sensitive, responsible girls, I replied, paid ten pounds a week. So, besides the nanny and Annie and Frank, I acquired Bonnie as a paying guest.

We had a break-in one night. The thieves stole a radio and some jewellery. I dutifully reported the incident to the police. The following afternoon, while Annie and Frank were entertaining two lads from the Royal Ballet in the parlour, and the twins were playing hide and seek with the reluctant nanny, a policeman arrived in response to our call. 'Is this some kind of a commune?' he asked, pinching a walrus moustache. Bonnie arrived from Sotheby's with her friends, and a woman from the Royal Ballet who had a violent crush on Annie burst in with a bouquet of carnations for her. Terrified yelps emanated from the kitchen. The nanny, hiding from the twins, had climbed into a wicker basket and the twins were sitting on the basket, holding her captive.

'How many people live here?' the policeman asked. 'Where's the owner of the house?' Responsible Bonnie fetched me from the bedroom where I was doing tummy exercises. Not wishing to be disturbed I said, 'Tell him I have the vapours.'

'He's a policeman. I'm afraid he won't know what the vapours are.'

I sashed a kimono over my leotard and descended the stairs holding my neck and shoulders, as Winifred Edwards advised, as if I were dripping in diamonds. My Sarah Bernhardt entrance was spoiled by the nanny. 'Help! Help!' she cried, running past us, out the open front door, tailed by the twins who were pointing plastic pistols at her. The policeman's nostrils quivered. He fired a series of questions designed to put me on the defensive. When I realized he was present to investigate the robbery and not charge us with squatting, I denounced his attitude and threatened to telephone my solicitors. He scribbled a note on a pad with a shaking hand. I thrust Annie's bouquet into his arms and suggested that he give them to his wife. The house became a further topic of curiosity to neighbours and tradesmen when two dancers from the Alvin Ailey Company bedded down in the parlour for a week. Decorum always prevailed. The tasks were evenly distributed. The nanny cleaned, and looked after the twins. Frank did the shopping. Annie baked. I presided over the laundry machines. There were no tantrums or jealousies because there were no emotional involvements.

Three days before Annie's workshop performances, Frank Frey announced that he needed a massage. His muscles were tired and stiff. A hearty rubdown, he said, would also be just the thing for Annie and me. He rang up a Russian masseur who made house calls. The unresolved question was where the body pounding should occur. The beds were too low and too soft. The planked floor, Frank said, was impossible. The only place then was the dining-room table, a massive piece of furniture seven feet long and three feet wide. The dining-room windows face my neighbour who was then a retired opera singer from Trieste. She could have considered us her television set when she sat by her kitchen window a few feet away and watched our theatricks without having to switch on.

At this time I had not got round to curtains or blinds. The windows were bare – just as Annie, Frank and I were bare for our massage. The twins sat at their little table while the masseur arranged his oils and creams and flexed his alarming fingers. Bonnie had bolted herself in her room. We three dancers awaited our turn on the table, semi-covered in bath towels. Frank was first. He stretched out on the table, towel flung aside – oblivious to our operatic neighbour. The nanny plunged a saucepan of ravioli – the children's favourite dish – into a sink of soapy water.

'Mum, she's *washing* our dinner,' the twins shouted.

The nanny was gaping at Frank.

'*Mein Gott*,' Frank groaned pleasurably as the masseur kneaded his thighs.

'Darling, I think you need a massage, too,' I told the nanny. 'You're much too nervous. Find yourself a towel . . .'

The nanny darted out of the room. 'There are some things I won't do,' she howled.

I followed her into the hallway. 'Well, one thing you must do is make the boys scrambled eggs. You've ruined their meal.'

Annie looked up from her crossword puzzle. 'Why don't you hire a real nanny? That girl's a bit twee.'

Annie was next on the table and Frank fell into a chair with a slap-happy grin. As the masseur applied his hands to Annie's curvy form we heard a crash from next door.

'Your neighbour, she sees too much,' said Frank.

'Heavens! I do hope she's okay!'

The twins were rattling their plates, wanting something more to eat. 'Tell nanny it's safe to come in now, lads.' While Annie was slapped and pummelled we planned our dinner menu: a vegetable salad with iceberg lettuce seasoned with a big glug of olive oil. Frank offered to scramble the children's eggs. He really was sweet.

My neighbour's windows were flooded with illumination. We waved to each other. In a coloratura, she started the 'Sempre Libera' from *La Traviata*. 'Isn't she dreamy? I was once invited to a musical soirée at her house. It was a Monteverdi evening.'

Annie's workshop was quite a success. We were quite chuffed. John and Jill Gale attended. Kenneth was there and so was Leonide Massine with whom I had worked briefly ten years earlier at the Royal Ballet. Frank went back to Germany and performed in some interesting fringe films. Our paths crossed briefly in Los Angeles. That tender big lug is now settled in Hawaii. Annie did break into films. She starred in *Slow Dancing in the Big City*, the story of a dancer with a congenital muscle defect in one leg. It was one of Hollywood's love-and-disease movies. Pure bosh. But, as they say, a hard-earned gig is a gig.

I had a few performances at Covent Garden, but nothing new or exciting on the horizon. The house was menacingly quiet. Even Bonnie was renting her own flat. Lack of work pitched me into an awesome depression. The frivolity and mateyness of Annie and Frank had distracted me from brooding. It also put distance – and therefore perspective – to my relationship with John Gale.

I cut myself off from the Sunday lunches with John and Jill Gale and their friends. I was cut off from Kenneth who was having a serious romance with the Australian he later married. The matchmaker was Jeffrey Solomons, who remained Kenneth's faithful confidant. Kenneth had found his 'belongingness'. He was no longer an 'I' person. He could say 'we'. Kenneth gradually, smoothly put his life in order. Mine was in disarray. My spirits were five thousand feet below sea level. My friends were seeing psychoanalysts. I decided to track one down and rang up Vergie and Georgina. Did they have any suggestions?

During a performance at the Garden I found myself sobbing in the middle of a pas de deux. At home I was unequipped to perform the simplest of chores. I felt stifled, locked into past personal griefs. I had to throw myself on a loving shoulder, someone who wouldn't snap: 'Pull yourself together. Stop snivelling.' And it had to be someone I trusted, who would not repeat my confidences as amusing dinner party prattle. The only friend I could think of *and* dared to call was Clement Crisp. An intensely perceptive man, Clem would understand my dark confusion without uttering wretched platitudes and stern admonishments.

I held the telephone for some minutes without dialling, staring into the garden, damp and drippy after rain. The sun had just emerged, sweeping the sky clean of clouds. 'Clem, it's me . . .' My voice was strangulated. 'It's very bad . . .' I did not have the nerve to say anything else. I didn't have to. Clem said he would be at the house in twenty minutes. I waited for him, shivering under two blankets on the couch, listlessly smoking cigarettes. Clem appeared, a guardian angel, with a bottle of Valium in one hand and a blank cheque in another. If anyone was in trouble, he said, it was either of the mind or to do with money, or both. I leaned on him, finding it impossible to articulate the value of his affection. He consoled me for some hours and gave me the name of an analyst, the same one, it so happened, that Kenneth was seeing. I made an appointment and also checked myself into the slimming clinic that had worked miracles on me before Berlin. The diet doctor said that the most likely reason for my weight gain was a tendency for water retention. Stress, he pointed out, brings on depression and there is a relation between depression and water retention. He prescribed pills and put me on a no-calorie diet: salads without oil, green-leaf vegetables and mushrooms. The offending fat melted away during a three-week stay and when I left the clinic I was, again, Thinnie Lynnie, eager to return to the stage. The dance and fashion photographer Anthony Crickmay, another kindred soul, brought to the clinic a swashbuckling chum named Philip Pace whose hazel-green eyes beamed with impudence and rebellion. He was a reckless extrovert with a racy sense of humour. 'Lynn looks good in bed,' said Crickmay as the two charged into the room. 'She looks even better on the stage.' Philip replied saucily that *he* would be the judge of that. Our introduction was a put-up job: Crickmay knew that I'd be cheered by Philip's patter and style. Philip had long russet-coloured hair and a devilish smile. He wore jeans, an embroidered Indian shirt and clogs.

Lying in the hospital bed I mentioned that my feet were cold. 'Cold feet?' asked Philip Pace, grinning dangerously.

'Can't allow that, can we?' He was warming my feet with his hands, a terribly *nice* gesture, I thought, when John Gale walked in. Gale gave Philip a most penetrating stare. Philip nattered away, describing a lunatic conference with executives of an advertising agency for whom he had photographed Eggplant Supreme. One executive thought there was too much red in the eggplant; another thought there was too much yellow. Philip said he would shoot it again, highlighting the black olives. 'They think I'm a bloody genius,' said Philip, squeezing my toes. When Philip Pace and Tony Crickmay bowed out in a sort of goofy clog dance, John Gale sat on the bed and folded his arms across his chest.

'Are you going to get yourself into a state over that one?' he asked. Young hippy photographers who looked a bit like David Hemmings in *Blow-Up*, he said, 'were arty bohemians who would upset the Garden and your peculiar system'. Scold, scold, scold. He was beginning to sound like Kenneth in Berlin.

'I hope to see lots of Philip. Everybody is falling in love – even Kenneth.'

I held John's hand. 'Sometimes grand passions turn to friendship, but friendship, as you once said, has more depth than passion.' John Gale became very matey with Philip and they had long drinking sessions together. That was before John left England on a foreign assignment and after he sent a note, which I showed to Philip, suggesting that I was with the wrong man. I was then living with Philip and John had no intention of leaving Jill, so the letter was our last 'safe' romantic communiqué, a final fragrant corsage which made both the sender and the recipient feel subversively virtuous.

During my second week at the clinic Philip urged me to play hooky one night and go to his flat. He was tired of warming my feet. He wanted to warm the rest of my anatomy. I fibbed to the head nurse, saying one of my twins was in bed with fever and needed his mum for the night. I received an exit permit but my destination did not fool her. The staff were aware of Philip's daily visits. You couldn't miss him: his clumping clogs and Indian shirts – orange, fuchsia, purple, pomegranate red – gave him clear visibility.

Philip's flat was trendily arranged with piles of soft, sinkable velvety cushions and pillows. Candles glowed on little tables and footstools. Velvet draperies enclosed the room, muffling outside sounds. I reclined on a bed of cushions and Philip set a tray of blue-glass cups brimming over with lemon tea.

When Philip moved into the house on Woodstock Road the twins willingly accepted his expansive, slightly madcap presence. Philip did not know much about ballet. He did not particularly like dancers or go out of his way to get along with them. We saw his friends – photographers, pop musicians, graphic designers and several secretive chaps who dealt in rare books one week, antique furniture the next and 18th-century prints after that. We met Crazy Charlie, an accident-prone Hell's Angel who constantly suffered motorbike crashes. The first time I met him his jaw was wired together. The next time his head was stitched together. The time after that he was in plaster up to the knee. Crazy Charlie was a good egg. He was also unpredictable. He drove up one afternoon in a white Bentley and strode into the house with a German shepherd dog five feet tall.

'What are you doing with a Bentley?'

'Looking after it for some bloke. You said Demi's bike was broken? I'll see to it.'

'Maybe you could leave the dog in the car?'

'He wouldn't like that.'

'The bloke?'

'No. The dog.'

Philip had once chummed with the Rolling Stones at a villa in the south of France. He was an inventive cook. 'The kids only eat that bloody ravioli. We have to make them something special,' he said. When I would be in class or rehearsal and the nannies asked the twins what they wanted their reply was the same: ravioli. The nannies did not argue; the request simplified meal preparation. I assisted Philip in the kitchen. He would pass me sliced tomatoes, watercress, and cheese thingies, muttering, 'Throw that rubbish in the big bowl and mix. Here's cider and oil. Knock it together, Lynsey.' Philip had the twins eating artichoke vinaigrette, beef bourguignon, couscous and brandied duck with cherries. He conducted his culinary forays barefoot, in a caftan. Philip is masculine enough not to look absurd in that floor-length garment. To be specific, Philip, who often imitated the danseurs of the Royal Ballet — 'Lynsey! Did you see my *Swan Lake* leap? Now, for an arabesque!' — was dancing in his clogs atop parked cars on Woodstock Road. The twins watched his derring-do, hooting and clapping. A Philip Pace *jeté* dented the roof of a Volkswagen. Feat achieved, he retired upstairs for a nap. An hour later I answered a rappity-rap-rap at the front door.

A portly man with two pendulous chins and an aquiline nose was breathing heavily.

'Hello . . .' I said in a musical voice.

The man glared at me. 'Is there a geezer here who wears a yellow frock?'

'*Frock*? You mean a flowing, rather grand . . . biblical robe, with exquisite tulips embroidered in turquoise thread imported from Bombay?'

The breathing became heavier. 'Can I speak to him, please?'

'My dear fellow,' I said, 'the chap is asleep. What seems to be the trouble?'

He scratched one of his chins. I too was wearing a caftan and clogs. 'He danced a hole through the roof of my car.'

The music faded from my voice. I found it dreadfully unpropitious to be gazing at a strange mountain of adiposity. I approached his car, removed my own clog, opened the car door and hammered and hammered at the offending spot until the dent disappeared. More or less. He stood on the sidewalk, staring in wide-eyed astonishment. Stepping from the car, I curtsied in my caftan and marched back into the house. Next door my operatic neighbour launched into 'Un bel di' from *Madame Butterfly*.

We never saw the affronted gentleman again, but the Volkswagen remained parked on the street, in the same spot, for about five months.

When Philip was good, he was very, very good – and when he was bad, he was naughty. The Garden gossips said that he was a bad influence. He said *they* were a bad influence. We seldom attended the theatre or films for entertainment. We co-starred in our own. When a new nanny commented that it must be glamorous being married to a dancer, Philip thundered: '*Glamorous?* Do you call what you see here glamorous? Ballerinas were once collected by princes and dukes. This thing . . .' he grabbed me around the neck, '. . . travels on the Piccadilly Line.' I do not like being called 'a thing'. I removed his hands and gave him a light push. Like many dancers I am not aware of my strength. Caught off-guard, Philip took a spin and landed on his bum.

'Glamorous!' I repeated loudly, stalking the shrinking violet of a nanny. 'Do you think it's glamorous to come home after slogging all day and find your old man pissed? Dancing on cars, on the coffee table, on the stairs, on the bed, thinking he's Nureyev?'

Then to Philip: 'How's your bum, my darling? Shall I give it a kiss?'

The nanny was so distressed that she burnt the ravioli and tried to correct the accident with an excess of salt, cheese and nuts. The twins turned up their noses. 'I thought she was going to be a problem,' mulled Philip, 'but she has cured them of ravioli.'

Philip adored fine wine. On his thirty-second birthday he bought two bottles and said we must visit some musicians in Hammersmith. It was past midnight. I was in lounging attire. Philip was in a flowing caftan. We trundled into his car, without changing clothes, and roared off in the direction of Hammersmith.

'Lynsey, we may not see this very lovely wine once we get there. Let's have a nip now.'

I popped open the bottle and we passed it back and forth.

'What's the address, Lynsey?'

'Haven't a clue, my darling.'

At four in the morning we were close to finishing the second bottle when a police car stopped us. I opened the door and began pouring the evidence down the drain.

'Don't do that, love,' said a policeman. 'I'll give you a glass at the station house.' When the constable saw us he chortled. 'Coming from a masquerade party?'

Philip blurted out, rather audaciously, that it was *my* birthday and he thought we should go on the toot. Some explanation! There followed a puzzled silence. The constable and his cohorts awaited a reasonable conclusion that would excuse, or at least explain, our attire and behaviour. But Philip, having run out of conversational gas, smiled appealingly and shuffled his bare feet on the floor. I feared a Terpsichorean demonstration.

When we got to the station the constable was surprisingly gentle, particularly after he heard my name. Five sets of eyes turned with renewed interest in my direction. I smiled weakly. 'Happy birthday, Miss Seymour,' said the constable pouring a glass of the offending wine. 'What will I have the pleasure of seeing you in next?' Expecting to be sentenced to thirty days of penal servitude for cheekiness I replied, with compelling candour, *The Seven Deadly Sins*. Kenneth had staged a new production and I was cast in a small role as the tartsy Queen of the Cabaret. I wore a strawberry blond wig and wiggled sequined tassels on my tits. Philip lost his driving licence. Two officers drove us home in a squad car. Four hours later I was at the barre in Barons Court.

I was pleased that Philip was around to galvanize my home with his mad extravagances. Nothing remarkable was in store for me at the Garden. Everyone knew that I was living with 'that mad photographer', so flip and frivolous, it was said, and eager to tell the assemblage at Barons Court to piss off. Assuming that my dance career was over already I thought, well, to hell with it, and *them*. I had fallen out of favour with the powers and although my personal life never once affected me onstage, the reason given for the fall-out was my excess. If people hear something often enough, it is accepted as fact. The excess that kept me awake for six hours after a performance, incapable of swallowing anything but two boiled potatoes, was the ballet, not my beaux. In the early sixties, a pleased smile from Kenneth stabilized me. But this was now the early seventies and we were both pursuing and asserting independent lives. Those thoughts occupied my mind as I lumbered wearily down the road after class and rehearsal, thoughts that were interrupted by Philip running towards me.

'Murder, Lynsey!' he shouted. I was too frightened, too bewildered to move. My heart constricted. Had I been selfishly thinking about other things while someone was dying? He reached me, gasping: 'The nanny . . .'

His cheeks were flushed. 'It was horrible, Lynsey.' Looking for a snug corner Catty, the house kitten, it seems had crawled into the electric dryer: our nanny seldom closed the port-hole door. Catty fell asleep and the nanny loaded the machine. When the nanny removed the dried laundry she let out a piercing scream. The remains of Catty tumbled on the floor. Fortunately Philip had just returned home from his studio. He forced two slugs of brandy upon the nanny who passed out, and cleaned up the last flattened furry bone of the ill-fated cat. The laundry, he said, wasn't such a pretty sight either. We would have to buy new sheets and towels. The lads still did not know why Catty was missing. I was despairing with the nanny.

'I'm going to sack her.'

'I wanted her sacked last month,' Philip said, 'when she poisoned the twins.'

'I can't sack nannies every month.'

'Well, *I* can.'

'You didn't want them eating ravioli anyway.'

'We've gone far beyond ravioli, Lynsey.'

'The discussion is closed. It's not easy to find nannies. Her heart's in the right place.'

'If the nanny stays, *I* go.'

'Philip, don't start a dramatic incident. Let's just have a nice funeral for Catty and then go out to dinner.'

'*Funeral?* I'm attending no funeral. I'm thinking of the lads.'

'That's the whole point. The funeral is for them. Can't you stage a nice funeral? Oh, please, Philip. Catty should be laid to rest with dignity.'

We told the lads the awful truth and Philip, who grew up with a hymn book in hand, conducted a memorial service in the garden. He sang 'Rock of Ages' while I cradled the weeping twins, imploring them to be brave little soldiers, and we heaped the tiny mound of earth with roses and lilacs and had a Chinese meal in Hammersmith. The next day I sacked the nanny.

* * *

While new roles were being created at Covent Garden, I created a role of my own: the mother of Philip's child.

The most peaceful moments of my life occurred during my pregnancy. Dance was consolation. Dance was Power. Dance was Success. But with each passing month I needed a greater incentive to keep myself doing the daily exercises in class. I had spent over five thousand mornings at the barre. Perhaps putting my life in order meant giving up the ballet. It seemed to have given up me. I confided this to my analyst, adding ruefully that no one would miss me at the Royal Ballet, certainly not Kenneth. Who is Kenneth? my analyst asked. He had injected me with a drug, a sort of truth serum that unlocks the subconscious. I was lying on a red velour sofa in his darkened office. The injection made me very languid and talkative. Kenneth? I asked, lighting a cigarette, but you know Kenneth, and we both know you, *doctor*, so don't diddle me. Again he asked in his guttural Prussian accent, who is Kenneth? Philip insisted that my analyst was deaf. 'Do you realize how much rot an analyst has to hear?' I answered coldly. 'If he's deaf, it must be a distinct professional advantage.'

My analyst, a small man from Silesia with huge Peter Lorre eyes, was not deaf. He had peculiar ways and means of luring a patient into revealing buried emotion. His patients were a Who's Who in the arts. Still insisting that he did not understand my reference to Kenneth, I snapped that one of his longstanding patients was Kenneth MacMillan, the dominant masculine figure in my flight from philistia. Ah, yes, he conceded. He knew MacMillan. But MacMillan never mentioned my name. 'He never mentioned me . . . at all? *But that's impossible . . .*' His eyes glittered behind his spectacles. He revealed nothing. But later he scheduled our appointments back-to-back, so we would run into each other and have brief nostalgic chats. I left the chambers on Upper Brook Street that day quite shaken. Kenneth must have mentioned my name . . . *once*.

I happily told my friends at the Garden that I was pregnant, and so withdrew from a new ballet in which I was to play Charlotte Brontë. The press department, forgetting that I was not married, released an item explaining the reasons for my withdrawal. The item went unnoticed. Meanwhile Philip and I decided to marry. Society reporters who made a living checking the registry offices for the licences of Lords and Ladies spied Seymour-Pace, and one clever journalist, having seen the Brontë release from the Royal Ballet, put two and two together. Lynn Seymour, pregnant. Lynn Seymour, to be married. The Establishment concept of morality is rigid. It does not change overnight. News that receives a yawn today made front pages in 1974. My telephone began ringing. I told the reporter to direct his questions to the Royal Ballet. He rang back: 'The press department says it's your baby, not theirs.' Within hours reporters and photographers assembled outside the front door like vultures from a 'spaghetti Western'.

I rang Philip at his studio. 'It's like Number 10 Downing Street. What am I supposed to do?'

'Put on a gaudy caftan and hold a press conference. But don't let them into the house.' Highly amused by the soup in which I found myself, Philip quipped that I made better copy than most British film stars – 'except for Vanessa Redgrave and her political soapboxing.'

MOTHER-TO-BE BALLET STAR NAMES THE DAY shouted one headline.

The press said that I was expecting a baby in seven months and was 'thrilled to be marrying the father in four days'. Readers were reminded of my previous marriage to Colin Jones and my relationship with Eike. I was seething inside: if the *Brontë* press release had gone out one week later I would have been married. There would have been no 'story', no scandal about the pregnancy. When a woman reporter asked about my disregard for convention and whether it might harm my career, I replied between huffs and puffs of a cigarette: 'One just goes ahead and *lives*. Other people make scandal . . . not oneself. They must be people who are intensely bored with their own lives.'

Philip and I were married in the Kensington Registry Office. Philip wore a shocking white suit and an ivory-coloured silk shirt with pale yellow embroidery. I selected a brown silk chiffon dress from the twenties and a Victorian hat with ostrich feathers. Philip's errant cronies, the Diners' Club and friends from the Royal Ballet flocked to the reception. The party hummed late into the night as Philip expertly staged the warm-hearted affair.

Our son Demian was born in July 1974. Philip selected the name. He was reading *Demian* by Hermann Hesse and had grown fond of the sensitive, inquiring young hero. We were now a family of five. The twins were entranced by their baby brother. Unfortunately Philip and Eike, the twins' father, did not get along very well. Philip is ruled by his heart and Eike by his head. Philip punished one of the twins for a household offence. The lad was bawling his eyes out when Eike telephoned. 'I have some books that I suggest you read on child care,' Eike said to Philip. Suddenly we were plunged into a tempestuous Italian opera, directed with flamboyant élan by Philip, in a La Scala mood. He threatened Eike with deportation if he did not mind his own business. I did not take this libretto seriously. But I joined their emotional duet with an impassioned aria of my own. The action reached a mighty fortissimo in a closed courtroom scene. However we managed to keep that spectacle out of the newspapers. The argument was between Philip and Eike. But I was cast in my first unsympathetic role.

Kenneth was on the telephone, his voice soft and languid,

the voice I associated with my youth, the voice I reacted to with childlike happiness. He heard that I planned to stop dancing – at least for a while – but he wanted to discuss his ballet *Anastasia*. Neither of us had forgotten its tepid reception and yet we strongly believed in the piece. He had various ideas for revising and rearranging sections. Would I be willing – or even ready, after Demian's birth – to have another go at the Russian Revolution? How could I reject his creative proposal? Under the most strained circumstances in Berlin we stimulated each other. 'It is like having a conversation with an old friend,' Kenneth has said. 'We are so attuned that I do not have to explain anything to her.'

Naturally my response to an altered *Anastasia* was yes.

Soon after Demian's birth I was doing exercises. Philip looked on bemusedly. During my pregnancy our bank account had dwindled constantly. 'I must do this ballet,' I said. 'We need the money.' Philip grew morose. I promised not to tour. I would only dance in London. I had forgotten what Philip never realized: the amount of time dance extracts from your life. To be ready for a seven-thirty curtain, an actor does not have to be in class every morning, rehearse every afternoon and warm up hours before the show. Dancers have to live dangerously with exhaustion. 'You give up your bloody soul for two hours onstage,' Philip said when I began a spartan regime. 'It's not much fun any more, Lynsey. I never see you . . .'

Once again I was feeling supremely confident. After Demian's birth I emerged astonishingly slim and lithe. I proceeded to confound the ballet world by dancing with greater strength and expressiveness. I had toppled the rules and tossed them into a topsy-turvy heap. My coach was Terry Westmoreland whose boundless sympathy for dancers had been recognized by Erik Bruhn, who urged him to teach. We had danced together at the Garden and on tour.

He appreciated the eccentricities of my body and had me stretching muscles daily until, he said, 'you're a breathtaking windmill of legs and arms'. He made light of my difficulties and urged me faithfully on. When the revised *Anastasia* opened the winter season of 1975, critics and teachers, friends and fans bubbled that I was the only ballerina who danced her best at the age of thirty-six, having had three children. It was a mystery to them and it seemed I could do no wrong. Maybe I just felt wanted . . . *The Times* reported that I was welcomed back at the Garden 'with the longest ovation for a ballerina since the great days of Fonteyn'. Struck by some perverse magical wand, my earthbound career was taking off, up up up, into the sky. And to Philip's dismay I wanted to stay suspended in mid-air, dancing at Covent Garden.

Jerome Robbins returned to stage his hilarious romp *The Concert*. He chose me for a zany role. I was so chuffed that I turned a cartwheel in the parlour for my three young sons. There were lyrical ballets and anguished ballets and cerebral ballets, but few comedic ones. If not performed with absolute precision, this rare genre veers into parody. Comedy is never as fully appreciated as drama but it is twenty times harder to perform. Jerry's ballet explored the fantasies of a motley group attending a Chopin piano concert. 'Your mind wanders at a concert, doesn't it? Well, mine does,' said Jerry. 'And your daydreams listening to Chopin are different from listening to Bach – or Wagner.' Jerry designed his epigrammatic choreography as a series of James Thurberesque sketches. For example, Georgina Parkinson played a matron in pearls whose husband fantasized stabbing her. I was a dippy lady who became aroused by the pianist and also had reveries about trying on flowery, feathery hats. Robbins deftly spoofed lovers of music and dance. When Philip saw me in costume – a skin-tight leotard – he gasped: 'Bloody hell, Lynsey. I can see all the way up Newcastle.'

As usual with Jerry, we were abnormally nervous during rehearsals, fearful of being banished. We had, in fact, more rehearsals for *The Concert* than you usually get for any ballet. Jerry insisted on them and he was right. 'It has to look easy. No strain. No sweat.' We sweated and strained for days on timing, gesture and attitude. 'Panache. You gotta have panache,' Jerry said. In one scene a dancer named Michael Coleman had to hurl a goblet. Jerry was not pleased with the movement. Jerry wanted more vigour! More anger! More force! He took the goblet and pitched it across the rehearsal room with such vigour, anger and force that it cracked one of the huge mirrors. Uncharacteristically he blushed, as the cast exploded with laughter.

I invited Jerry to an 'English Sunday Breakfast' on Woodstock Road. Jerry had never been to Chiswick. 'It's where Becky Sharp went to school in *Vanity Fair*,' I said. (The famous little Becky Puppet who was 'pronounced to be uncommonly flexible in the joints, and lively on the wire'.) Jerry had never been to my house. He had never seen the chaps. Stroking his salt-and-pepper beard he accepted enthusiastically. Outside the theatre, Jerry is a love, although he would loathe having that known. He feels more secure with his monster image. Our Sunday breakfast should have had eggs and sausages and muffins and ham and bacon and toast and tea and coffee and fresh cream. Everything went woefully wrong. The nanny had the weekend off, and Philip and I had a row. We were not arguing about the moon. We argued until the wee hours about my hours in rehearsal, long, long hours away from home. Awaking late I found only four eggs in the fridge and a loaf of dry bread. Looking like an unkempt housewife I was feeding Demian while Philip padded around in a caftan and bare feet, trying to get the kitchen in order and demanding why I hadn't told him that Jerome Robbins was coming.

'I did tell you.'

'You haven't been *home* to tell me.'

Jers and Addie were having a pillow fight in the front hall. 'Chaps! Up the wooden hill. Get dressed. We're having company,' I called.

'He'll want coffee,' Philip said. 'We don't have any coffee.'

'Make very strong tea. Typically English tea.'

'Three strips of bacon, Lynsey. That's all we've got.'

'I'll dash off to the store. You finish with Demian.'

There was a rap on the front door. Jerry entered amid flying pillows.

'Take Demi. I have to change clothes, Philip.' I gave Jerry a hug and hurried upstairs, suggesting that he either play with the twins or feed Demian because Philip was preparing one of his scrumptious omelettes. The telephone began its steady ring. 'We're running a little behind schedule, Jerry, but it's just a lazy Sunday . . .' When I reappeared, Jerry was sitting at the table showing the twins how to draw outlines of their hands on sheets of white paper. Demi needed a nappy change. There was a commotion at the front door. Two friends of Philip's were delivering a new mattress for the guest room. I helped them manoeuvre it up the stairs, forgetting to buy more eggs and fresh bread. The twins chanted that they were hungry and wanted breakfast. Philip stared at the eggs. 'Do *something* with them, darling,' I whispered. I gave the twins bowls of cold cereal and set the table. Would Jerry like some orange juice? Of course. There was just enough to fill one glass. But we did have plenty of jam: strawberry, apricot, peach and blueberry. I put out all the jars and then hustled Demian off to his crib. Philip whipped up a plump omelette. I brewed the tea. The twins dragged Jerry into the hall for a tussle of ear-pulling and arm-twisting. Philip turned on some music and turned off the stove. Breakfast was ready.

Jerry was having a good time, I think. He said: 'Quite a carnival.'

Jerry was wonderful with the children and we got into a discussion of their names – Adrian, Jerszy and Demian. Jerry confessed that he always wanted to be called Jason. He did not like the name Jerome. When I write to Jerry, I always begin: 'Dear Jason'.

Dear Philip, meanwhile, was moving into a severe depression, wishing he had more time to concentrate on his own painting. And the more I danced the more *that* depressed him. The non-speak silences were cutting. We met when I was the Garden's unwanted butterball. It was a bit jolting for him to wake up one day and read that his wife was, according to one critic, 'the greatest universal artist of the Royal Ballet'.

That June I was given several new roles and returned to many old ones during the Royal Ballet's 'Big Top' tent season in Battersea Park. It was a divinely busy time for me, dancing with both companies and enjoying the hot summer and the under-canvas activities. I also agreed to dance with a young American named Robert North in a gala by the London Contemporary Dance Theatre, which meant criss-crossing the city for rehearsals and even for performances in both theatres on the same night. Admittedly my moods were often as inconsistent as Philip's. Months earlier I had said, yes, I probably would retire. Now I was telling Nureyev that dancing was the only thing that kept me alive. Having been tacitly barred from the Garden stage because of my weight, I wanted everyone to see the new svelte Seymour – mother of three. This was balletic justice. The one person I saw very little of was Philip who waited up nights for me, tapping his foot, and I resented being watched. When I went on tour with the Royal Ballet to Greece, Philip felt deceived. 'You're dancing around the bloody world and I want to know what the

hell is going on. You promised *not* to dance out of England.'
Indeed I had. But I changed my mind. The reasons were
financial and personal. We needed the money and I needed
to dance. Our rows were not tongue-in-cheek spats any
more, but fiercely real. On my return from Greece, Philip
and I communicated through the nanny. I immediately
started rehearsing a refurbished production of *Romeo*. I
would leave the house around eight in the morning and
come home exhausted twelve hours later.

One night Philip went on the toot with his cronies. He
swaggered in towards dawn. I was not asleep. I was fretting
about the opposite directions in which our lives were
rapidly moving. But I was not in a conciliatory mood either,
so pretended to be asleep. 'Lynsey, I know you're awake,
you bloody insomniac,' Philip said, smothering me with a
pillow.

I did a fast roll. Philip crashed to the floor. I leapt from
the bed, ran barefoot down the stairs and out of the house to
some friends who live up the road. I woke them at four-
thirty in the morning. 'Please, don't ask any questions. I
just need some help, there's trouble at home.' A little later I
rang up the house. Addie answered the phone.

'Are you all right, Mum? I heard a bit of noise.'

'Yes, darling. Where's Philip?'

'Asleep.'

It was just past eight when I walked into our bedroom in
a borrowed raincoat and slippers. I took my dance gear and
tiptoed from the room. I left Philip a note: 'Please be gone
before I get back.' And Philip, a proud and gallant man, did
not linger.

The day's rehearsals were achieved in a curious state of
suspension.

The nanny fixed the twins their evening meal and ate
with them. Sensing distress they slipped quietly to their
rooms. The nanny handled Demian. I sat for hours on the

black leather couch in the parlour smoking one cigarette after another. I was numb – physically and emotionally. I thought of John Gale. Had he foreseen this ending with Philip? I wondered. 'You're dangerously emotional,' John Gale had said. So was he. At least I had not botched my relationship with John, I reflected. I handled it with a maturity not generally credited to me and its memory was protected like a precious gem under glass that no one could touch. John Gale also said: 'You like risky relationships.'

John Gale never fully recovered from his breakdown. After my marriage to Philip he disappeared into other misty worlds and then, one day, his wife telephoned with the news that he had killed himself. I was stunned into utter silence. Stunned beyond tears. Thereafter when I performed Juliet and sat quietly on the bed during that dramatic passage of music I did not think of the next scene or the next movement, but of John Gale who had crept away from us all in the night.

When Philip moved into the house I told John that I was hopelessly in love with the idea of love. A look I wrongly interpreted as scorn flashed across his face. He said nothing. Pressing for a response I said: 'You think I'm trite – a superficial person.'

He seized my hand, poised against my chin, and twisted it in his. 'Those who only love once in their lives are the superficial people. What they call fidelity, I call a lack of imagination.'

I asked if that was his latest maxim to be inscribed on a postcard. He shook his head and said that he was only paraphrasing a gifted Irish writer who died penniless in Paris after a scandal in London.

The Cotswolds. A sweet scent of flowers and grass. Frogs in a distant millpond are croaking fussily.

'When I first met Lynsey, I thought the big competition

was John Gale,' Philip is telling his wife Ellie. 'But the competition was the ballet. I couldn't pirouette. I couldn't do a complete turn.' Philip laughed boisterously. He is still lying on the bed under the pear tree. We have finished a perfect lunch of steak tartare and salad. Ellie has gathered our forks and plates, loaded everything on to a tray and carried the remnants into the converted barn.

'Do you really want to do a midnight flit?' I asked him. 'You only want to do that when you're depressed, Philip, or feeling sick. Give yourself a chance. You have all the gifts.'

Philip's gaze unsettles me. I know he, too, is thinking of our operatic marriage.

'Thank you, Lynsey.' Philip settled against a cushion and closed his eyes.

Ellie joined us holding their year-old daughter. 'Do you want to spend the night? We'd love to have you.'

I replied that the chaps awaited me on Woodstock Road, but I would come for a weekend when I returned from New York. Philip removed his boater and tossed it on the bed. 'Last time you spent the night – when was it? Two years ago? More than that?'

He whistled sharply and looked away.

CHAPTER 15

The Old Girl Shows Her Mettle

The twins, having seen Superman flying through the air on the telly, called me Supermum. And for three extraordinary years I flew with the greatest of ease through the classics, new and old ballets by Kenneth, Sir Fred and Antony Tudor. When I appeared in *Romeo* and *The Invitation* the critics remarked that I looked younger as I grew older. I performed with the confidence of youth. I was in top form. It was a kind of miracle, said the critics, 'a belated summit'. I was also choreographing my own projects for the stage and television. Reflected in the Victorian mirror above my fireplace I saw a slender yet attractively ripe figure with cheekbones. The image was not displeasing. The house on Woodstock Road was well organized. A serious live-in married couple became part of the family. Even the snippiest cynic was silenced by my disciplined schedule, although, naturally, I heard that 'Lynn's emotions adapt to the man she's living with.' Which certainly put a dreadful onus on the fellas. In this case the onus was on dancer-choreographer Robert North, a rugged American from Charleston, South Carolina. North was studying theatre design in London when he decided to take up dance. He was then nineteen. He spent four seasons with Martha Graham and danced solo roles. A few people fluttered over the fact that he was seven years my junior. If a man has an affair with a woman twenty or thirty years younger, he is an admirable, sexy rogue who clearly has *quelque chose*. But let a woman start seeing a younger chap and she is lambasted. This is just another form of discrimination. Robert North's manners were flawless. He was ambitious and dedicated to the ballet. He understood pre-performance panic and the round-the-clock concentration that went into being a dancer.

On an early date I was impressed by his ingenuity. After a party he was escorting me home in a taxi. Passing the Kensington Gardens Hotel, I suggested that we stop and have champagne. It was after licensing hours but I thought we could foil the law. We looked quite glamorous – I was in a yellow gown and my red fox fur; Robert was in black tie. We plumped ourselves down in the lobby. Robert ordered the champagne. A waiter motioned him aside.

'Excuse me, sir. Are either of you residents here?'

'The lady is a resident,' said Robert adroitly.

The waiter fingered his pencil. 'What is her room number?'

Robert flashed a candid all-American smile. 'I don't know her number *yet*. It would be rude to ask. That's why I'm ordering the champagne here.' The waiter emitted a conspiratorial giggle and fetched a chilled bottle.

Dating and dancing were shortly interrupted. I had been feeling queasy for weeks. I assumed my menstrual cycle had been disturbed – a concern to all women dancers. A visit to the gynaecologist revealed, one year after Demian's birth, a womb tear increasing in size. I was back in the hospital for surgery. I could not do any partnering for three months. Robert North encouraged me to use this time to mull over choreographic ideas. He inspired me with confidence. I flippantly remarked that I should use the time to write the medical history of a dancer, but who would believe a dossier that includes an abortion, glandular fever, a thrombosis, the birth of twins, a third child and a womb tear – not to mention a strained Achilles tendon, weak feet, knee surgery and a nervous breakdown.

Have I left anything out?

Undoubtedly.

When Robert went on tour with the London Contemporary Dance Theatre I earnestly pondered projects, made scads of notes for him to peruse and then joined him in Scotland. I had been doing something quite irregular with the telegraph office – sending naughty limericks in code. All in all, six telegrams with such phrases as 'the front is mending, the back is bending' to reveal 'dark enclosures of new exposures' were received at His Majesty's Theatre in Aberdeen. During this limericky lark I proposed *Gladly, Sadly, Badly, Madly* as the title for a collaborative work – a series of duets matching the moods, the ups and downs, of my life. You can scramble that title any way you like and it still comes out right. The ballet, performed by the London Contemporary Dance Theatre to a pop score, was a nifty success.

The only thing we disagreed on was my analyst. Robert thought he was a bit weird. No matter. I liked him and my visits allowed an opportunity to bump into Kenneth. Some of our old camaraderie was restored. Kenneth's eyes gleamed: I was dancing with joy *and* things were going well. I had been dancing *Giselle* and *Raymonda* with Nureyev in Edinburgh and, before that, *Spectre of the Rose* with Baryshnikov in Hamburg.

Kenneth cast me, fittingly enough, as a pregnant woman in *Rituals*, a new piece that explored the grandeur of the Japanese theatre, and I did my Kabuki Lil number to the music of Bartok. 'There's a chance for you to do *Manon* once on New Year's Day,' Kenneth murmured, 'and you won't do it again until May. Are you interested?' Oh, yes, I replied casually, hiding my excitement at playing the courtesan who trades her favours for jewels, is arrested as a prostitute and dies in a Louisiana swamp. The splendid first cast had featured Antoinette Sibley as the feckless Parisienne; Anthony Dowell as her corrupted lover; and David Wall as her conniving brother. I would be the fifth

Manon. I had four weeks to learn the full-length ballet for two performances, five months apart. It is impossible to imagine actors doing the same with *Hamlet* or any other play. In three years I danced *Manon* six times at the Garden.

Having seen the four other characterizations I was determined to bring my own interpretation to the role. (Visually *Manon* is quite a spectacle with courtesans and bluebloods, pimps and convicts, jailers and beggars, cavaliers and trollops. The ballet is framed against a backdrop of mud-coloured rags because Kenneth wanted to contrast the flurry of the demi-monde with the inescapable poverty of the working class.) The rehearsal period was highly creative. I approached *Manon* as an entirely new ballet never before seen. Kenneth, as usual, trusted me. He permitted me to experiment and develop Manon's character through movement and acting and what *I* instinctively felt about Manon. Very few choreographers allow this freedom, but Kenneth and I possessed an innate understanding. Our minds ticked together. The victim, I decided, was not Manon but her lover, an idealistic divinity student until he falls under the spell of the passionate Manon. She is not amoral. Her idea of sin is to be poor. Taking a rich lover for financial gain was not evil. To the rapacious girl, the only evil was poverty. Jumping into bed with an old coot was what you did – now and then – in order to survive. She depended on her debauched brother to sell her to the highest bidder. I kept harking back to the relationship between Manon and her brother. Two of a very special kind. When I said, 'I want to build up the sister-brother relationship – there's something curiously incestuous there,' Kenneth was pleased as punch. The veiled hint of sexuality between the two took on an unexpected fleshy decadence: Anthony Dowell and David Wall swapped roles so that Dowell played the dissolute brother, and gave one of his finest performances.

The dramatic movement and character delineation in

Kenneth's ballets emerge from the various pas de deux and he created four beautiful duets for Manon and her lover, which David Wall and I spent hours rehearsing, eliminating anything that smacked of melodrama and extending ourselves, or so we hoped, into the realm of tragedy. We concentrated on the psychological reality of each pas de deux – the promise of love; passion fulfilled and then corrupted; the embrace before death. We were two rococo hothouse flowers, exuding the most erotic perfumes.

The effort paid off.

Manon (after only one stage-call the morning of the performance) was mine, a creation, said the critics, that convinced them I was that person. The critical consensus was that the ballet now made more dramatic sense. Even those who previously found it a 'gift-wrapped package of protracted boredom' were exhilarated by the new characterizations. The three of us raised the roof of the Garden. We were a smash hit. Removing my wig after the performance (sewn into my hair that afternoon and glued to my forehead so it would not fall off), my fingers trembled like a leaf; a cigarette hung limply from my lips: I remembered with a painful shock that eighteen Christmas holidays had passed since I made my debut on the Garden stage in *The Burrow*. For a moment I saw myself sitting alone in the corps dressing room while all the other kids were embraced by friends and family, and thinking with absolute certainty that I had failed. Odd, I thought in an impersonal sort of way, that I should suddenly be struck with that memory. A quick glance backward in time to an evening that still affected me: *The Burrow* and Christmas past.

Off with the wig. The mascara. The paint and powder. Off with Manon's dying rags, and, with the practice bag slung over my shoulder, I sauntered into the misty drizzle of Bow Street. Taxis and limousines and cars jostled together with the hurrying Garden crowd, a standing room house which had just celebrated the first day of 1976 at *Manon*. In jeans, a turtleneck and raincoat I waited for the lift at the Covent Garden tube station. Nobody in the throng clutching programmes and chattering excitedly about the performance stirred in recognition. Which suited me just fine.

The lads and I officially welcomed the New Year the following morning with Robert North. I prepared a gala breakfast – the breakfast Jerome Robbins missed – of pancakes and sausages, kippers and scrambled eggs, cinnamon toast and fresh orange juice, coffee and champagne. Robert opened the champagne and proposed a toast to Supermum.

'How'd it go last night?' Jerszy asked.

'Oh, all right, I guess. Now, let's dig in while everything's still hot . . .'

My last major collaboration with Kenneth MacMillan, though I did not know it at the time, was his production of *Mayerling* two years later. This was another full-length ballet, a difficult form to pull off but which increasingly captured Kenneth's choreographic imagination. Kenneth told an interviewer: 'I suppose this may be partly due to the influence of George Balanchine in the United States who believes in dance as abstract form, as making shapes. You can't have that kind of non-narrative ballet lasting for much longer than one act.' His biographical dance-drama centred on the love affair between Crown Prince Rudolph of Austria-Hungary and his mistress, Baroness Mary Vetsera. The two died in a double-suicide pact at the Prince's hunting lodge near Vienna in 1889. The story of the sado-masochistic Prince unfolds with a series of duets and bravura solos against the intrigues of the sealed Habsburg court. The role of the Prince may well be the longest and most strenuous ever created for a male dancer and it was danced stupendously by David Wall. Mary Vetsera is a dicey part to establish because she does not appear until the ballet is half over, yet she becomes a catalyst for the dumb tragedy. She must instantly convey that she knows what the Prince likes, wants and fantasizes sexually. She is a willing plaything. She is also a social-climbing bitch.

David and I slithered and twisted in rehearsals, practising Kenneth's pas de deux for the depraved couple. After finishing the duet for Kenneth, who observed approvingly from a folding chair – long legs crossed and fingers gently rubbing a moustache – David and I kept going – dizzily, wildly, madly, evolving lightning turns and cyclonic bends of a rather explicit nature. Some people do not want to believe that the characters in a ballet have sex. Of course, a chap can't have sex with a sylph or a silver moth. But Kenneth likes characters of flesh and blood. We fell on the floor in a fit of laughter, stuck together by our own sweat. Kenneth ambled over and stared down at us. 'Mmmm . . . yes,' he said, slowly, languidly, 'that last bit is nice . . .' When *Mayerling* was filmed I was labelled 'television's first lady of sex'. I was demonstrating a theory that in bygone days Kenneth and I had often discussed: ballet is the most total theatre you can see, for the body can say something far more expressively than words. Kenneth wanted to make ballet 'real'. I have always been attuned to the 'reality' he wants, which was the basis of our collaboration. 'Lynn is as real as anyone can be onstage when wearing point shoes,' Kenneth said. 'Although she is on point, which is artificial, she makes the audience forget this convention and see only the reality of the character.'

At one performance of *Mayerling*, an unsuspecting audience almost saw the Austro-Hungarian Empire suffer its decline and fall not from gunshots but from strangulation. Nico had designed a splendidly danceable costume – a négligé of silk chiffon – for the erotic pas de deux. But the dance itself is incredibly acrobatic. I seldom touched the stage and seemed to be whirling in the air most of the time or hanging upside down with my arms searching for my partner's extremities. On cue, David gripped me tightly and we took off with an explosive burst of energy. The delicate fabric tore at the waist and the skirt, very, very slowly began to come apart. The full skirt was adorned with yards and yards of lace. David tried ripping away the torn part of the skirt. This only succeeded in loosening *all the lace*. With each whirl we were wrapped in an embroidered nine-foot-long umbilical cord. The music accompanied us, faster and faster like a great rushing wind. The skirt, attached to me by half a dozen threads, was ready to give, but not the lace. David swung me round and round, faster and faster. On each frenzied movement the lace threatened to encompass our bodies. Before the final lift there was a long diagonal run after which I had to hurl myself around David's neck. Terrified of the result, I made a final effort to rend the lace and adopted a stance like a weight-lifter's. But I strained in vain.

'Oh well, here we go.'

I hurled myself at him. We clenched our eyes tight. When our spinning, wrapping movement was over we opened our eyes to find that we had been miraculously spared. My stage death came as a relief to us both.

Slim, secure and elflike, without make-up, I was at my peak and, on one occasion, over-extended myself. I had finished a season with the Royal Ballet and danced with Nureyev in his own summer season at the Coliseum. Margot Fonteyn and Natalia Makarova also performed in his starry summer seasons. I then guested with American Ballet Theatre in New York. Too few performances and a dancer loses confidence. Too many and a dancer is knocked out. Performances must be evenly spaced, but guest artists are slotted into company schedules. At the State Theatre, performing *Swan Lake* for the first time in seven years, I could not complete the thirty-two fouettés – despite constant coaching from Rudi the weeks before. I was furious with myself and for the first time ever behaved completely out of character: I stalked sulkily up to a papier-mâché column and leant against it while the orchestra concluded the hideous movement. Standing in the wings, Robert North and the stage crew heard me gasp, 'Shit!' like someone awakening from a bad dream and expecting an even worse day. I held the weepies until the end of the performance. I was knackered because a few nights earlier I had danced Antony Tudor's *Pillar of Fire*, perhaps the first modern ballet to thrust lust, despair and promiscuity at prim and proper audiences in 1942. Since I had to compete with memories of Nora Kaye's original performance, I depleted myself during rehearsals. And Antony Tudor, an English-born choreographer who had moved from the Ballet Rambert in London to Ballet Theatre in New York before the war, is a strange rather icy individual who can be cruel, especially to the young. Fortunately I was experienced enough not to let his temperament affect me. (Fred Ashton and Kenneth MacMillan do not belong to the school of choreographers who shriek at dancers. I could never have developed with a screamer.) Tudor had taught the ballet so many times that he was less interested in my first getting to know the steps than delving into the torment of the sexually repressed woman in a small town. When I learn an existing ballet, as opposed to creating a new one, I must know the music, the steps, where I'm going to be onstage, and with whom – at the same time as developing the character. Rehearsals were not enjoyable. Tudor was cantankerous and impatient. 'You're not getting the inter-relationship of the characters,' he stormed. 'You're not getting into the soul of the woman.' Robert North was in New York with the Seymour circus – Jers, Addie and Demian. I would meet him after rehearsal, pour myself a glass of chilled white wine, light a cigarette, and angrily hiss: '*He* wants inter-relationship! Inter-relationship, inter-relationship,' I muttered, 'I'll *give* him inter-relationship.' I then performed with blazing commitment – as did the equally aroused new cast of principal dancers. Tudor was effusive in his praise. 'You naughty girl. I heard you were full of surprises. Why didn't you let me know?' I replied, 'Why didn't you trust me?'

'Press onward and upward and never say die,' concluded one of my code limericks. Pressing onward I continued with the classics at Nureyev's insistence. I tended to resist them because whenever I donned a tutu and tiara one or two critics gleefully pounced on my 'technical deficiencies', which did not arouse my eagerness to portray swans and sylphs. It is rather crushing, after slogging for weeks, to be slugged repeatedly with the same criticism. 'You dance like a Russian, that is your technique,' Rudi often said. 'Your sensuality disturbs the effete.' With Rudi as partner in *Swan Lake* I completed the thirty-two fouettés. Pressed onward by Rudi, I telephoned the management at the Garden for the first time in my life, some seasons later, to say that I wanted to dance *Sleeping Beauty* with him. His Aurora, Natasha Makarova, had cancelled the engagement because she was expecting a baby. I was then dancing the evil fairy in a new *Beauty* production by Madam. I portrayed the fairy as a licentious exile from the court. Dicky Buckle said that I looked like a crazed Italian countess who had just gone mad on a mountain of cocaine.

Rudi and I were paired in *Beauty* for three performances and rehearsed on the Garden stage between acts of other ballets. When he was not available I rehearsed afternoons and evenings by myself at Barons Court. At the first performance Nureyev stood in the wings watching me in the exacting 'Rose Adagio' sequence, when the Princess accepts a rose from each of her four suitors. He became so immersed that he unwittingly wandered on to the stage for a closer look – an uninvited member of the palace festivities, in riding habit and feathered hat. The prince was having a peck at his future bride one act too early! 'You can do the classics, Lil,' Rudi said. 'You can do anything in the classics.'

Two works by Frederick Ashton, in the mid-seventies, made the decade significant for me and secured my reputation in dance history as a dramatic ballerina. These were Ashton's *Homage to Isadora* and *A Month in the Country*.

Margot Fonteyn says that Sir Fred's 'ear for music, his eye for movement and his perception of human nature make him to ballet as Shakespeare is to drama.' Margot is a woman of superior knowledge and solid judgement who first worked with Ashton in the early thirties when she was a mere slip of a girl with a slightly oriental face. The Ashton-Fonteyn collaboration, which extended over thirty years, formed the 'dance-style' of the Royal Ballet. Ashton has choreographed about sixty ballets, from the snowy skating party in *Les Patineurs* (Margot and Bobby Helpmann on 'skates') to his version of the *Dáphnis and Chloë* legend (Margot, an innocent maiden kidnapped by pirates but reunited with her lover, Michael Somes), to *Ondine* (Margot, the water nymph who claims her mortal lover with a fatal kiss). One of Ashton's most charming productions was *La Fille Mal Gardée*, first performed in France in the late 18th century. Pavlova and Karsavina had both danced in revivals of *La Fille*, and Ashton, a man strongly influenced by ballet history, and whose signature is beautiful dancing in a poetic atmosphere, invented – out of an old work – a modern classic of pure 'Ashtonia'. The pastoral romance is a humorous account of a prosperous country bumpkin who discovers that the girl he pines for, when not churning butter, is having a jolly good time with the husky farmboy of her heart. I never danced the girl. I am not the butter-churning type. But my darling Christopher Gable gave many ingratiating performances as the farmboy. Ashton's picturesque rustics engaged in maypole and clog dances, a duet at harvest and a stave dance. Ashton is not interested in the dark side of life. Sir Fred's view of the world is highly romantic.

Ashton grew up in Lima, Peru, where his father was 'a sort of honorary consul'. He attended public school in England: 'Ghastly cold. Ghastly beatings.' Harnessed to a clerical job in the city, he was unhappy. His pleasure was attending the Diaghilev company and taking dance lessons with Leonide Massine. He danced in the commercial theatre and on Brighton pier, but he was too slim, too frail to succeed as a dancer. He began choreographing for the Camargo Society (the elite membership included such founders of British ballet as Ninette de Valois and Marie Rambert). His comic ballet *Façade*, produced by the Society in 1931, is probably the oldest 'modern' ballet in any rep. Ashton was then twenty-seven. He danced in *Façade* with Alicia Markova and Maude Lloyd (the future Mrs Nigel Gosling). His apprenticeship was served at the Ballet Rambert. Dame Ninette appointed him official choreographer of what became the Royal Ballet.

There is some irony to the Ashton-Seymour collaboration. I left the Royal Ballet and went to Berlin because I did not think I had the ghost of a chance when Ashton was named artistic director. I was Kenneth's 'muse'. We were a twosome. We worked and played together. We shared private jokes and a private language. Kenneth MacMillan was the commander, warden, chieftain, caliph and sun king of a worshipful clique, and I was Kenneth's property. Ashton frowned on some of my unladylike attitudes – strolling down Bow Street in ragged jeans, smoking countless cigarettes, muttering, 'Oh, *fart*', during rehearsals, and telling the press I always had a Guinness for lunch. Choreographers, like theatre directors, art dealers, editors and photographers, favour their personal discoveries. I had not been snatched from the corps by Ashton. Yet it was the retired Sir Fred who created two works that let me burst into bloom, wrote Clive Barnes in the *New York Times*, as 'one of the great ballerinas of the world'.

The Isadora homage was not a calculated 'event'. I was just becoming acquainted with Robert North when I flew off to Hamburg to partner Baryshnikov in *Spectre of the Rose* as part of the Nijinsky gala. I couldn't find anyone to teach me the part and phoned Margot, who was on tour in America. She sent me an endearing letter from an anonymous hotel in the mid-West, explaining in detail the choreography. She also lent me her costume. The performance went down well but the programme's startling surprise was one dance 'in the manner of Isadora Duncan' that I winkled out of Sir Fred, with a little push from Hamburg's valiant artistic director John Neumeier.

Encouraged by Clement Crisp I had performed an Isadora 'dance' that I devised myself for a lecture-demonstration weeks earlier. I have never 'identified' with Isadora Duncan, but her daring and questioning of tradition inspire me and one shelf in my bedroom is devoted to books on the revolutionary who liberated dance – and women. Isadora Duncan, the freewheeling spirit from San Francisco who defied society at the turn of the century, was the first 'star' of modern dance. She stripped it of all artificiality – scenery, point shoes and tutus. She did not view dance as an ornate pageant or elaborate diversion but rather as a 'religion of beauty' for the free expression of emotion and passion. Performing barefoot in diaphanous draperies to the music of Chopin, Gluck and Beethoven, she demonstrated an ideal form of woman – freed from all conventions – by assuming the running, jumping and flitting movements that she admired on Greek vases. But her solo concerts in New York, Paris, Berlin, London and St Petersburg were not celebrations of ancient Greece. Her melodic abandon revealed the perfection of human grace, of poetry in motion. To achieve complete naturalness onstage, she unbound her hair and bared her breasts. Fiercely independent, her 'religion of beauty' extended not only to her art but also to her body. She belonged to no one but had many fervent affairs. Her two children, born out of wedlock, tragically drowned in a freak accident. A third died shortly after birth. She tippled heavily with simpering parasites on the Riviera during the twenties and was strangled by her own scarf when it became entangled in the rear wheel of a Bugatti. Most biographers contend that she was forty-eight when she died. She influenced Pavlova, Fokine, Nijinsky, Balanchine and Martha Graham. I read my first Isadora biography on the Australian tour when I made my début in *Swan Lake*. That was when I decided that I too was sole guardian of my body.

Ashton has total recall. He had seen Isadora dance three times in London when he was sixteen. His recreation of one dance for the gala in Hamburg was not conceived as significant. It was just 'a little something' that we tried. Nothing more. Sir Fred had me draped in peach-coloured chiffon. My single undergarment was a pair of knickers. Ashton belted long string around my waist and furiously cut and brushed my Titian-coloured wig. Ashton recollected, 'People talk about Isadora's strength. They forget her consummate delicacy – her magnetism – oh, plenty there! She was in her early forties and getting a bit fleshy, but the force of her personality was something you could never forget. Her head . . . shoulders . . . arms . . . expressed her emotions . . .' Remembering that an onstage pianist once played a Brahms waltz while Isadora ran forward, scattering rose petals, Sir Fred staged, as he put it, his 'memory' of that movement. 'Now, keep your fingers crossed. You know, it might look terribly silly today, that sort of leaping around.' Neither Sir Fred nor I expected the tumultuous reception. 'You made me believe I was a youth again, watching Isadora at the Prince of Wales Theatre,' he said.

One year later, in the summer of 1976, Ashton recreated four more Isadora dances for a London gala celebrating the fiftieth anniversary of the Ballet Rambert. Isadora had been one of Dame Marie Rambert's idols and 'Mim' had urged the young Fred Ashton to have a go at choreography. Ashton said that the two highlights of his life had been seeing Pavlova and Isadora. He saw Pavlova dance in Peru when he was about thirteen. He also saw her last matinée in Golders Green. 'Pavlova injected the poison into me. Like Isadora, she had enormous personality. Audiences reacted to her. There are some excellent dancers who don't stir audiences at all . . .' Comparing Pavlova and Isadora, he observed: 'Pavlova was a spirit and a flame. Isadora was a spirit and a fury.' Isadora could be quite dramatic or marvellously still, he said. She had a prodigious leap and terrific speed; she could alter her attitudes very quickly. During a performance to Chopin or Liszt she would casually remove sections of her costume and hang the filmy material on the piano. Then, at the conclusion, standing in a scanty wraparound, she would chat with the audience like a nightclub performer. 'Oh, Bernard Shaw is here,' she might announce, waving to him. Ashton transported me into the past. I saw Isadora in white gauze lifting her bare feet, arching her back and swaying her arms, a plastique figure with a fantastic yielding quality.

The dances for the Rambert anniversary were variations of Isadora's moods and moves: Isadora, in reverie by the sea. Isadora, a statuesque martyr carved out of marble. Isadora, dashing and leaping with a billowing silk scarf. Isadora, a mountain shepherdess reaching towards the sky with clenched fists. Isadora, natural and unaffected, sprinkling rose petals in a Delphic grove. The work, originally called *Five Brahms Waltzes in the Style of Isadora Duncan*, lasted about eight or nine minutes. Fred said I must perform the dances for 'Mim' before the gala, so we had a private performance for her at Sadler's Wells. Mim was in tears. She dabbed her eyes with a handkerchief. 'That's exactly what I remember, Fred, it's quite amazing.' Then she congratulated me. 'You were Isadora, with her mystery and heart. Mysteriousness on its own isn't very interesting unless there is an emotional quality.'

Mim's expression of genuine admiration touched me beyond words. 'It's Fred,' I said quietly. 'He brought her to life.' By the time the five dances were performed in New York and later filmed the homage had a cult following. They acquired an historical importance that was never intended. The critic Arlene Croce wrote: 'Seymour's rightness for the part isn't measured only by her magnetism. If there had been a poll in the dance world on the question of whom to cast in the movie of Duncan's life, the choice would have been Lynn Seymour – Seymour the actress, the performer of epic daring, but most of all Seymour the dancer. She has always possessed the roundness and fullness of contour, the plastic vigour, and the coherent rhythm to express the sculptural depth that Isadora's dancing must have had . . . Ashton's and Seymour's Isadora is a virtuoso.'

I was ready to perform one of the Isadora dances a few years ago, but the show didn't go on. Nureyev and I had been invited by Jacob Rothschild to a house party at his villa in Corfu. Jacob is a tall, imposing man, deceptively shy, with a subtle warmth under a cool, judicious manner. Jacob, Rudi and I once got the giggles at a buffet party when Rudi, a wonderful cut-up, recounted how he had once heard a heart-rending cry from the wings, 'It's no use, it's no use.' I had just exited from the second-worst solo performed in living memory of Giselle's first act. (The first worst had been danced the night before.) Vocal extravaganzas are no part of 19th-century ballet.

At our next encounter on stage Rudi muttered, giggling, 'Feel better?'

'You bet!'

Jacob understood the strain and became a lasting friend of ours whose advice I respected – and sometimes heeded. Hence the invitation to Corfu. The first days it rained and rained. Rudi is miserable in the rain. He stayed in bed, smothered in layers of clothes, listening to Tchaikovsky. When the sun came out we did 'class' in a studio, swam and sailed and nibbled wild strawberries. The guests wanted Rudi or me to dance. Reluctantly I agreed to evoke one of the Isadora dances. Rudi stage-managed the event: he rigged up the lighting on a terrace – 'You must dance in the moonlight, Lil' – and selected the music. The sheer beauty of the mountains and the sea and the moon rising in the sky presented an outdoor setting that would have staggered Isadora.

Rudi dimmed the lights. To the strains of a Brahms waltz I floated on to the terrace, red and yellow poppy petals in my hands. Suddenly Demian began crying. He would not be soothed or petted. Weeping buckets he ran on to 'the stage' and grabbed my leg, forcing me to stop. Demi had seen me in class, at rehearsal and on the telly. But his mum's 'live' performance apparently frightened him. 'What were you afraid of, my darling?' I asked later.

He buried his head in my lap. 'I knew it was you, Mum, but I had to be sure.' He grinned sheepishly.

I stifled a laugh, thinking, Why, the little rascal! He deliberately upstaged his mum.

Nureyev politely informed everyone: 'Performance cancelled.'

Secretly I heaved a sigh of relief. Ad-lib performances were not my forte.

Long before this unauthorized performance, Sir Fred's Isadora dances prompted critics and admirers to insist that the old master come out of retirement and choreograph a work for the Royal. Ashton had wanted to choreograph a ballet of Turgenev's play, *A Month in the Country*, for forty years. As a young man, he had first seen the play performed very melodramatically by a noisy cast. Turgenev, he knew, required the delicate handling of crystal goblets; the aristocratic Russian was not a playwright of kitchen crockery. Over the years Ashton not only re-read the play but also Turgenev's novels and a biography of the expatriate landowner who leisurely and lyrically recalled a childhood amidst social change in Russia. Turgenev's characters are astonished by their own emotions. And since Sir Fred is a creator of romantic moods it was only natural that he should be drawn to Turgenev's compassionate play of a bored wife who falls in love with her son's comely tutor while enduring another lethargic summer on her husband's estate. The spoiled Natalia Petrovna lives in a hermetic world. Her passion, boredom and anguish are carried deep within her. Tender meetings, hushed partings, and silent farewells. Perfect material for Fred Ashton.

'It is always the music that starts me off,' Ashton explained, and, never finding the right music, he postponed the ballet. The play has a cast of twelve and he thought that was too many for an intimate chamber work. Natalia Petrovna was not a role for Fonteyn, so whenever the play 'danced' through his head, he considered Svetlana Beriosova. By 1975, when he finally solved the musical and adaptation problems, Beriosova had retired. One day Sir Fred telephoned asking me to tea. I had heard rumours about *A Month in the Country*: at seventy-one, Ashton was planning his first major ballet for the Royal Ballet in six years. Was it possible . . . ? I dressed with extreme care. I hoped to look a little grand with a hint of Russian.

Seated opposite Sir Fred in his drawing room, which I think of as being delightfully pinkish, though it isn't pink at all, I felt a sentimental kinship for the man who auditioned a shy child in Vancouver so many years ago. Ashton smiled contentedly. Perhaps he was feeling a wee bit sentimental, too. We had just done the first Isadora dance in Hamburg. We chatted the entire afternoon and grazed, for the first and only time, some personal topics. Fred said that it was difficult for a dancer to have an outside life as 'one's emotions do get in the way of one's dancing', and I was a person of 'great feeling'. He was sorry I had gone to Berlin but he appreciated that I was a creative dancer who found more satisfaction in creating roles than being the 250th Swan Queen. He repeated that he originally fell in love with my feet: 'I love glorious insteps. You have them.' And he again complimented my musicality, which allows a dancer, when necessary, to take liberties with the score and never lose the proper beat.

Fondling some stalks of daffodils he disclosed *his* Turgenev project. He did not want to produce another ballet with the most obvious musical choice – Tchaikovsky. When a friend suggested Chopin he replied, 'Oh, please – don't say Chopin! Jerome Robbins has already picked him over.' But after hearing a record of Chopin's orchestral suites the ballet took shape, and, by concentrating on Natalia and her volatile passions, he reduced the number of characters to eight, thereby tightening the atmosphere of *ennui* and unrequited love in a forty-minute adaptation. The role of Natalia Petrovna was a gift from Sir Fred. In ballet women are never allowed to grow old. We must be perpetually young. We must dance teenage virgins and fairies and childlike courtesans. I think it's foolish for a forty-year-old to dance Juliet, but there is no other choice if you want to keep working. Fred gave me the exceptional opportunity to portray a mature woman just a few years younger than myself. Although Turgenev lived well into his sixties, he once said that his life was over at thirty-five. Natalia Petrovna's life was also finished, suffocated by the hazy desolation of provincial Russia. Her lassitude heightens her panic – endless hot summers await her as the years hopelessly pass and she verges on becoming a spiteful woman. But Ashton stressed her romantic illusions which fade away, leaving her alone and sad.

A Month in the Country with Sir Fred, and Anthony Dowell as the tutor, was a completely happy experience. Ashton creates the steps – those small, quick killing movements that require tremendous energy – in rehearsal, but he knows, in advance, precisely what kind of movement he wants and how long each dance will last. Natalia's opening allegro dance with dainty knitting steps and her melancholy sarabande just before she finds a rose dropped at her feet by the departing tutor were executed within the first days. The tightly constructed ballet, designed in blues and beige, is a satiny example of brevity. I was a bit heavy for Anthony Dowell whose ideal partner is Antoinette Sibley. She is light as thistledown. But Ashton did not put in any huge lifts. Our duets were exuberant and airy, though you can never bend or stretch enough in an Ashton ballet. Anthony Dowell and I meshed musically. Our bodies yielded to Chopin's music as Natalia progressed from infatuation to ecstasy over the tutor.

The opening scene worried me. Natalia is seen on a chaise reading a book and holding a fan. Stiff as a ramrod, tense. That is not a very bored position. And she *is* supposed to be bored, with nothing to look forward to. I realized that instead of playing Natalia Petrovna and *lazily* fanning away the tedium of a summer day, I was Lynn Seymour, anticipating, with some dread, the first moment when I would begin Ashton's whizzy allegro solo; all intricate footwork – one misstep and that's it. Stanislavsky wrote that the lacework of Turgenev's psychology of love demanded a special sort of playing. 'One needed to suggest unseen radiations of will, emotion, yearning; one needed looks . . . pantomime, psychological pauses . . .' And so, in the first moments of the opening scene, I suggested, through pantomime, radiations of laziness . . . and yearning. Once I stopped fretting about the first solo, Natalia's lethargy became visible and her character real for me.

I almost missed the première in February 1976. The morning of the big night I awoke with a temperature of 104 degrees. It was more difficult to breathe than move. The company doctor believed I had pleurisy. The fever subsided and he allowed me to perform the première on condition that I cancelled the following performances. The opera house agreed to this and at six-thirty that evening the stage manager phoned Sir Fred: 'She's in the house. She's going on.'

A Month in the Country had London absolutely potty over Sir Fred and his chosen Natalia Petrovna. The dizzying unequivocal success was repeated in America, and, for the first time, I was interviewed by the New York press, which, in the past, only ran features on Rudi and Margot. 'Lil, you're an international star,' Rudi shouted rapturously. And I thought, well, maybe I am, maybe . . . I wondered what it would be like to feel like *A Star* for a while. Margot had retired. Antoinette Sibley and Beriosova had withdrawn to private life. I was waiting, waiting for the Royal Ballet to take advantage of my stardom, as such.

But nothing happened.

The Royal Ballet did not fancy me doing the classics, and important new roles were not being offered. I was utterly frustrated. My energies were submerged by an engulfing panic: why am I being held back? I asked myself.

Kenneth resigned as artistic director in 1977 and was replaced by Norman Morrice, former director of the Ballet

Rambert. He is sweet and offends no one. But the Royal Ballet, as Rudi and I have said, truly needs a director with the shake-'em-up attitude of Dame Ninette.

'Look, my best years are *now*,' I announced desperately to the management. 'I'm drifting into inactivity. I know you have to bring up the young dancers, but they've got years ahead of them. You've only got me for about four or five years. Make use of those years. Make use of me.'

But nothing happened.

Nervously I waited again for something to turn up. When I quit the Royal Ballet a second time, it was, ironically enough, to go to Germany again. And once again my life was irrevocably changed.

Time: Present. Place: Woodstock Road. To-ings and fro-ings in the kitchen, the all-purpose rumpus room, salon, wine cellar, conference chamber, massage parlour, laundro-mat, Indian restaurant, and scenes of noisy discourse until dawn; of tearful hellos and tight-lipped farewells (very Natalia Petrovna). Decisions are carried out with cool, unsentimental dispatch in the kitchen. The kitchen is where Robert North and I said farewell in 1977 when I was rehearsing *Mayerling*. I am waiting for the kettle to boil, so I can offer Robert a cup of tea.

It is just past six. The lads were surprised and pleased to discover Robert North as a 'mystery guest'. Robert is now director of Ballet Rambert and the chaps have not seen him in years. Addie is sitting on the staircase and Robert is chatting with him. I overhear Ads reporting about his school, a camping expedition on the Isle of Wight and his collection of shells and rocks. We all spent a vacation in Key West after my last exhausting engagement with Antony Tudor and the American Ballet Theatre. Robert and the chaps passed happy hours on the beach gathering shells which we brought back to Woodstock Road. In Key

West I found a funny straw hat from Haiti at an outdoor stall that I wore to Buckingham Palace when I was invested as a Commander of the British Empire. Our nanny's little farter of a car followed the graceful line of Daimlers, Rolls-Royces, Bentleys and Rovers through the Palace gates, gasping like a steam engine, but we held our heads high nonetheless. The twins were bored stiff by the ceremony, but vied for the medal on the way home. For several days they called me Commander.

Addie was wanting to show Robert his new disco routine and perhaps pick up a few tips.

'You should drop in and see me, Addie,' Robert is saying. 'It's really been a long time. I'd like to see Jers, too.' The Rambert offices are a short distance from the house. 'Come round and say hello.' He explained that if he wasn't in his office Addie should ask for his wife.

Matches, matches. Where are the bloody matches? Why are there never any matches when I need them? I remembered that emergency matches are hidden on a shelf with decanters and vases. My cigarette was lit when Robert seated himself at the table with a calm reflectiveness. I asked Robert over to hear his opinion about some changes in my ballet *Rashomon* which will be produced in the States. Based on Kurosawa's classic Japanese film, *Rashomon* is a tale of murder and rape, involving a nobleman, his wife and a bandit who enact contradictory accounts of what happened in a woodland long ago. Some of the duets are lyrical, others violent. Each character dramatizes a different point of view, illustrating the subjective nature of reality in a kind of psychological guessing game. The ballet for three dancers was first seen at Sadler's Wells. Robert, who danced the bandit, recalls with a droll sigh that one critic said I had choreographed some positions you might not find in the *Kama Sutra*. Movies and plays are sexually candid today, but many ballets are still choreographed for an audience of

Aunt Ednas. Stirring his tea, Robert grinned. 'You're a rebel, Lynn. And you believe in freedom. But you're a much *straighter* person than most people would believe.'

Our last days – I was working on *Mayerling* and choreographing a short ballet for television. Besides three children and a nanny, the house swarmed with producers, agents, designers, dancers. Robert said he was going nutty from lack of privacy. He planned to rent a flat of his own, but we would continue our relationship. I wanted to hear the old clichés: I can't endure being apart from you for even a moment; you are the only person in the world who matters to me. And so forth. Not hearing these clichés, we came to an impasse and I pulled one out of the bag, the old 'it's all-or-nothing' cliché. Since it was not going to be all, we parted. Guess I am pretty straight.

'It's almost seven, Lynn. I have to be on my way.'

Seven? I must be en route, too. And I am frightened. 'Are you taking the tube?' He nodded yes. 'I'll go with you as far as Hammersmith. Then I have to change to the Piccadilly line.'

'Where are you off to?'

'The Garden.' And I cannot be late. I have not attended a performance at the Garden since I quit the Royal. I cannot tell Robert how apprehensive I am. The entire management will be there, their eyes upon me, the defector. And yet I must not panic. I know exactly how long the trip takes, down to the last second.

'I forgot to ask, what's on at the Garden tonight?'

The front door closed behind us and we were greeted by a cool, cloudless evening. 'I produced *Rashomon* in Munich and I am hoping the Munich opera house will send the set to America . . .' I blither furiously, changing the subject. There are no further references to Covent Garden.

CHAPTER 16

Ballettdirektorin

The Glockenspiel sounds in Munich's town hall every morning at eleven o'clock. Two miniature knights appear, raise their lances and perform a jousting tournament in the open archways high up on the building's façade. This little dollhouse scene in Marienplatz charms tourists. It also charmed my lads on their first visit to Munich. The twins raced to the town hall with cameras to take snaps back to London.

In the fall of 1978, after being named artistic director of the Bavarian State Ballet, I moved to Munich with Demian. The Big Boys continued their education in London. The Munich appointment seemed quite *gemütlich*. The general director of the Munich opera house, August Everding, offered a two-year contract that challenged every creative impulse: I would choreograph new ballets, perform as prima ballerina in whatever I chose and run the fourth largest dance company, numbering over sixty, in Germany. Here was a dream come true.

Here was a dream too true to be good.

By the late seventies I had become restless from inactivity at the Royal Ballet. The management was lackadaisical about capitalizing on my recent successes. The younger kids were not receiving much encouragement either. The company did not appear to be leaping ahead with *any* definite artistic thrust. The Garden failed to perceive that with 'the dance explosion' around the world, the Royal Ballet faced severe competition, particularly from American dance companies. Living on its illustrious past, the Royal Ballet was growing dusty. I told the new director exactly what I thought and then tuned my ears to the Glockenspiel in Marienplatz.

I was not the first choice for Munich. There were reports that the American director-choreographer John Neumeier, who energized the Hamburg ballet, had declined the Bavarian bid. Unbeknownst to me, the reputation of the opera house was one of such grisly intrigue and treachery that it would bollox the Borgias. Munich itself suffers from Bavarian-Catholic piety and provincialism. But it is also a city of carnivals and art treasures and fairy-tale palaces near snowy forests and tranquil purple lakes. Historically it has a rich musical tradition: Wagner's *Die Meistersinger* and *Tristan and Isolde* were first performed in Munich.

The Royal Ballet was winding up an American tour and we were in Houston, Texas, when I heard from August Everding. I hastily glanced at the telegram and recognized the name. Everding had staged operas at the Garden and the Met in New York where he is known as 'the German Ben Franklin'. A kindly, bespectacled man, he is rather stocky and baldish with a fringe of long hair not unlike the American inventor-scientist. There was not time to decipher his message. I was hurrying to a performance of *Mayerling* and in a grump because the bigwigs of Houston were giving a dreaded post-performance party for us. These obligatory affairs are a nightmare: your face is red like a beetroot; your hair is soggy; you can't stop sweating and you are so exhausted that you can't swallow any food. The hostess said I had to attend; she was seating me next to Michael York. 'You'll have so much to talk about. He was in the film version of *Romeo* and you were in the ballet.'

Michael York was quite dreamy, but I was still in a lather, as usual, after a very heavy show. I tried to make conversation. I genuinely admired his acting achievements. Perhaps I was gushing. He stared at me oddly. I am sure he considered me an eccentric dinner partner. I was wearing my Mary Vetsera wig to save time 'twixt curtain down and reception.

Returning to my hotel I read again the telegram from Munich but it did not make sense. The message was garbled. I decided not to pursue the matter until the tour ended. When I rang Everding he reminded me that we had met in Hamburg at the Nijinsky gala: 'You left a vivid impression.' Then he came to the point quickly. He wanted a director-choreographer for the Munich ballet company. 'You would bring us the discipline and tradition of Covent Garden.' The assignment, although awesome under the very best of circumstances, made my toes wriggle. I was thirty-nine years old, and, nervously mulling my future, doing more choreography. A second ballet of mine, *Intimate Letters*, set to Janáček's Second String Quartet, was in rehearsal. If I planned to ease myself from dancing into choreography, Munich was a golden opportunity not to be missed.

During negotiations with Everding, I sought the advice of two close friends, both former dancers with the Munich company, who lived there and knew the dance scene. 'Stay away,' said Kenneth Barlow. 'It's a Byzantine opera house badly managed by petty bureaucrats.' Albrecht Widmann warned, 'The dancers claw each other like cats. There's one big pussy. Don't come unless you're prepared for trouble.' *Well.*

Surely the chaps were alarmists? The tactful and most gracious August Everding did not preside over a chamber of horrors. I have a stubborn, fighting spirit. My old pioneer ancestry. The monumental task of cleaning up a muddled dance company and giving it a polished glaze stimulated my imagination. With Everding's blessing I would rebuild and reshape the Bavarian State Ballet. Acceptance of his contract meant that for three months, from September through November, I would be commuting between

London and Munich as I had dance commitments at the Garden (*Mayerling*, *A Month in the Country*, *The Concert*). My own ballet was opening at Sadler's Wells. But I am happiest when overworked. I become frustrated and get into mischief with little to do.

My appointment was announced and I flew to Munich to look over the opera house and the company. The departing artistic director – a former corps dancer – refused to let me observe the morning class. When I reported this rudeness to Everding, the director simply cancelled the class. Not very nice. I had not unpacked a suitcase before it was evident that the Munich press and opera house factotums did not want Lynn Seymour, *Direktorin*, in Munich. Antagonistic jabs appeared in the newspapers. The staff greeted me with condescending politeness. They found me unacceptable for two reasons: I was a woman and a foreigner. One powerful clique was hell-bent on proving that Everding had made a regrettable mistake, no matter what I did.

An optimistic innocent, I busily began contacting guest artists and planning the winter season and opening night programme. For that November event I selected three ballets: a new work by a choreographer-dancer in the company; *Etudes*, a piece of pure dance, with showy roles for three women soloists; and, since my contract requested new ballets from me, *Intimate Letters*. It was receiving final touches in London for an October première. The vaguely autobiographical ballet centres on a married woman who drops a clandestine note, an 'intimate letter', to her lover at a musical soirée. Her husband and their two sons as well as a worshipful admirer and his wife are also at the party. The heroine is dismayed when she sees her lover drawn to a younger woman, and the ballet concludes with the host stepping forward to lead her in a duet signalling the beginning of a new romance. The musicians perform ons- tage, within the context of the piece, exactly as they would at a soirée. Bits of taped conversation, spoken by such actors as Albert Finney, Diana Quick and Sarah Kestelman, theatrically bridge the musical movements.

The scenario was based on an outline of mine by Gillian Freeman, a skilful novelist who worked with Kenneth on *Mayerling*. 'Does Kenneth know you're using Gillian?' asked John Tooley, general administrator of the Royal Opera House. 'One writer working for two choreographers can create misunderstandings.' I told Kenneth about my collaboration and he was a darling. Kenneth was most positive about my choreography, though he said I would never develop into a great choreographer until I gave up dancing: 'I don't think, except in very rare cases, you can be both.' The London première, to be followed one month later in Munich, was fancy and festive, symbolizing all sorts of personal and professional changes in my life. I hardly noticed two visitors: Konstanze Vernon, who considered herself the 'prima ballerina' of Munich, and her sidekick Von Karsten Peters, the critic of Munich's boulevard newspaper, *Abend Zeitung*. Vernon is a big, tough, intelligent lady. Peters is just big. We exchanged hellos and I thought how terribly sweet of them to fly in for my première; the tales I've heard about 'the intriguer Vernon' and the 'bitchy dance criticism' of Peters are without foundation. I was in a lovely mood. When I read the London reviews my heart went pitty-pat. The ballet had flaws, said the critics, but I was commended for producing a serious work, 'a distinguished addition to the Sadler's Wells repertoire'. All in all, it was an affectionate send-off.

The only sour note was heard in Munich. Von Karsten Peters knocked the ballet in an advance review. But I still did not feel threatened.

Taking up residence in Munich I plumped myself down in a hotel with Demian until a suitable apartment was found, and, in a state of exhilaration, tackled the coming

Munich première and my job as artistic director. The company was ragged but had tremendous potential if the dancers committed themselves to rigorous daily slogging. I tried out one girl for the lead in *Letters* and found her so unsuitable that I took her out and invited Galina Samsova as a guest. Samsova created the role in London. There was no one in the Munich company with her radiant expressiveness. Her dancing, I hoped, would inspire the whole cast.

Konstanze Vernon was not happy. She scorned a part in *Etudes*. We had a meeting and, to filch a line, butter would not melt in her mouth – or anywhere else. She wanted the lead in *Letters*. 'I'm not fond of your ballet, but the role is perfect for me. If you let me do *Intimate Letters* . . . it will help us . . . both.' I swallowed hard. Again I proposed *Etudes*. Again she refused.

'I'm too old for *Etudes*.'

'If you feel that strongly, I respect your feelings, but it does mean you won't be dancing on the opening night and I ever so much wanted you.'

I discussed Vernon with my two confidants, Kenneth Barlow and Albrecht Widmann.

'Lynnie, do be careful,' said Barlow. 'If you want to have peace, best get rid of her.'

'I can't do that yet, darling. I just got here.'

'She will run to Karsten Peters and tell him everything. They are very thick,' said Albi.

'I will not give in to that salted radish,' I said stubbornly.

Barlow and Albi were the only people in Munich I trusted. However, I had not trusted them enough when they urged me to stay away from the 'Byzantine opera house'. We first met when I was pregnant with the twins. I was visiting friends in Munich. Albi was a member of the company but not dancing. He was limping around with a broken foot and doing a lot of self-examination. Very young and a good dancer, he was a bit short and I reminded him that there are not many parts for smallish male dancers. He quit and got a teaching credential. Barlow is a Brit who buys and sells Art Nouveau objects. He attended the Royal Ballet School and was with the Royal Ballet for six years. A teacher had taken a dislike to Barlow because he refused to wash the chap's car. For a while he feared for his future. But the lanky youth from Manchester caught the eye of Madam who scrupulously inspected all the classes. 'Why have you been hiding that lad?' Madam chastised the teacher. 'He has spirit. I like him.' Barlow, adoring Dame Ninette, graduated into the Garden Corps. He then joined Cranko's group in Stuttgart, distinguishing himself as Tybalt in *Romeo* when I was dancing Juliet. Ballet politics in Stuttgart sent him to the Munich company. How did I respond, he once asked, when the casting-couch question reared its little head? The question stumped me for I have never been put in the position of having to go to bed with someone for a part. 'Aw, shucks, I wish I had,' I replied facetiously. 'It would have done wonders for my ego to think that anyone wanted me *that* badly.' I maintained a healthy social distance from the Munich company, which strikes me as conduct most becoming a director-choreographer. The drawbridge was up – and needed to be.

Especially after the première.

Friends flew in from New York and London, including two chaps I wanted Everding to meet as I desperately required an assistant. The five-tiered opera house overflowed with two thousand first-nighters. Many, it seems, were dressed to kill. Outwardly I was poised; fortunately no one could hear my thumping heart. At the very last minute dancers had to be juggled around, along with the order of the programme. The male lead in *Etudes* developed an 'injury' and could not perform. Seconds before the house lights dimmed Konstanze Vernon made a grandstand entrance upholstered in furs and jewels. She halted in the aisle, blowing kisses and waving to her reverential claque. Von Karsten Peters beamed with pleasure. Knowing the opera house and its various vibrations, Barlow and Albi sniffed the air and detected an atmosphere of malicious glee. 'Oh, kkkkerrist, we're in for it tonight,' Barlow said.

Vernon's fans were predisposed to dislike my ballet after reading the review a few weeks earlier by Von Karsten Peters. August Everding would hear what Munich thought of his choice of an artistic director! *Intimate Letters* was disrupted by boos, obscene giggles and piercing whistles. I had to take a bow with the cast. Galina gripped my hand, willing me strength. We kept our dignity despite shouts and cat-calls. It was a set-up but the hysteria was frightening nevertheless. Albi's ballet teacher, who sat next to him, broke down and wept. 'I have never – never heard anything like this,' she sobbed. A stunned correspondent from Frankfurt said the emotional outburst exceeded 'the laws of hospitality and fair play'. In a second blistering review Von Karsten Peters went beyond Seymour, the choreographer, and took a personal poisonous stab at Seymour, the dancer. The programme stated that I was a prima ballerina. Implying that the good citizens of Munich were being culturally swindled Peters demanded proof of this description. The opening was duly reported in the London press as a 'disastrous début' for Lynn Seymour. If anyone in London carried a grudge, such as a sacked nanny or two, here, at last, was cause for private jubilation.

Following the première I had to attend a reception in the opera house. My friends were in shock and very concerned about me. The old chin might have wobbled but there was no question of tears. I was simply livid. Seated at a table between Everding and Leonard Bernstein, who had been conducting a Mahler concert in another auditorium, I lit a cigarette with trembling hands and turned to 'Lenny', the world-famous conductor and composer. A kindred spirit, a man of compassion and humanity, I assumed *he* will sympathize with what I have just endured; *he* will offer comforting words. 'We had a catastrophe tonight,' I said quietly. 'You wouldn't believe it.'

Bernstein gave me a disdainful glance, the kind you give a hapless parlour maid whose tiny thumb-print has smudged a corner of the master's morning paper. 'Oh . . . really . . . ?' he said indifferently. '*I* just conducted one of the most successful concerts of my life.' I was incapable of an answer. He began speaking animatedly about himself with someone else and the agony of the last two hours hit me. Out-of-town friends, dispersed at other tables, noticed my visible distress and smiled lovingly. I acknowledged them with a wet wink and drank ice-water, making chit-chat with Everding. I did not engage Leonard Bernstein in further conversation. There was no point in ruining his evening.

The next day, bright and early, I sent Everding a lengthy memo stressing that my confidence was in no way shaken, but that an assistant must be hired immediately, and implored him to hire an American named Charles France who had flown to Munich for an interview. Everding resisted the strong opinions of France, now assistant to Baryshnikov at American Ballet Theatre. What about Rodney Fisher, a young man who directed plays and managed theatre companies in England and Australia, also in Munich for an interview. Fisher was quickly dismissed. He did not speak German. I again repeated my need of a bilingual secretary who could handle appointments, con-tracts, correspondence and telephone calls. The only secre-tary available was a retired dancer who could not type or take shorthand in English *or* German. '*Please, please help me out!*' my memo ended. I was never given a bilingual secretary and was forced to run the company alone until spring when the management reluctantly conceded to the hiring of Albi Widmann. He was German, a former dancer and his personality could not be faulted. 'He knows the opera house *too* well, he will have favourites,' the management petulantly argued, but I got Albi – seven months later.

Wherever I turned for the resolution of a problem that would be rectified instantly in any other dance company, I stumbled up against a brick wall – and more memos, memos, memos. Everything had to be written out in memo form and I had to write them myself. I was in my office until eleven at night . . . composing memos. 'To become excellent and international we have to start *now* on every detail,' a memo pleaded.

The company had one rehearsal pianist. He could not sight read. A pianist is crucial for class and rehearsal. Obviously, I wanted to hire a second pianist. But I had no control over who was hired or fired. On the day of a performance I discovered that the one pianist was not available. I steamed into the office of the music director and demanded: 'How can this happen . . . ?' He said I was just being difficult.

The lighting plots were ancient and unrehearsed. The stage was lit by spots from behind the proscenium arch. I sat with the lighting man for hours during performances, trying to explain what we needed. They said I was just being difficult.

The sets for some of the productions were peeling. I wanted them repainted or completely redone. The set designers said I was just being difficult.

Many senior dancers were lazy and out of shape. They would not be allowed to perform in the tattiest provincial company. But they had a nice, easy life in Munich. When I called for more rehearsals they complained to their union. The union said I was just being difficult.

The younger dancers being given new roles didn't want

to work after lunch. They too complained to their union. Again, the union said I was just being difficult.

Stories of the 'difficult' Lynn Seymour were leaked to the Munich press which smugly reported my every move. Casting changes, negotiations with guest artists and choreographers were also leaked. The only person with access to the files was the 'secretary' who viewed herself as the rightful artistic director. The previous director had allotted her vast responsibility. Then I turned up and she was in a snit. I was fearful of making a phone call to Demian: I might read that the *Ballettdirecktorin* wasted her days chatting with her son.

The situation was pathetic. It was also ugly.

After the removal of an impacted wisdom tooth I took a prescribed painkiller in my office. Within hours the staff whispered that I was a drug addict. Wayne Eagling of the Royal Ballet came for a guest stint. We were to fly back to London together as I was scheduled to dance *Manon* at the Garden. Snowy weather played havoc with our departure. The airport was closed, then open, then closed again. We kept dashing back and forth between the airport and opera house. When we arrived breathless at the stage door a third time, the dancers laughed, 'Are you back *again*?' Wayne composed a ribald verse about the struggles of air travel, likening it to the old in-and-out, and we pinned it on a call board. His text was interpreted as a smutty swipe at German efficiency. The music director groused to Everding who hauled me into his suite clamouring for an explanation. This transgression of Bavarian morality popped up in the press, the essence being 'Dirty Ditties by *Direktorin*'.

And so the days passed.

The Glockenspiel sounded every morning at eleven o'clock.

* * *

The younger dancers who refused to be aroused by the irrational campaign against me appreciated that if we all worked together with support from *the top*, I could bring the Munich troupe a bit of status in the dance world. Negotiating by phone late into the night and writing all the contractual letters myself when the secretary had flown home on her broomstick, I succeeded in obtaining Nureyev and Makarova for two performances of *Swan Lake*. Even after Rudi and Natasha said yes I had no authority to hire them. I had no budget. Approval had to come from Everding. More memos. He approved. The dancers leaped with joy.

The needling Munich press was momentarily silenced.

Having seen the company perform *Swan Lake* I stressed to Everding that the production had to be relit. I warned that our glamorous guests would be appalled at the harsh lighting and might not dance for us again. More memos, always ending, '*Please help!*' It became horrifyingly clear that I could not alter a button on a costume unless Everding gave written permission. General directors of opera houses usually do not concern themselves with such production details. I had to go to Everding because the staff would not budge without his consent. The twelve hundred employees at the opera house – the committees within committees, the department and sub-department heads – thrived on bureaucratic red tape. And my staff, particularly, did not like taking orders from a foreigner and a woman. Like? They adamantly refused.

The presence of Rudi and Natasha, two beautiful friends, revived my rapidly ageing heart, and their divine dancing won me some grudging respect among Munich's balletgoers. After *Swan Lake* it was my turn to face the same crowd from the other side of the footlights. Since I was being pressured to dance, which was part of my contract, I scheduled Cranko's *Romeo*. Given my hectic daily pace I felt it would be best to lump together three Juliet performances instead of scattering them over several weeks. Everding called on me, always tactful, always gracious. *He* had a problem. Her name was Konstanze Vernon. 'She's very upset. Could you appease her with one performance?'

'Gladly, Professor Everding.' I had to bite my cheek to keep from laughing. 'I would be quite happy to give her all three performances.' He said that would not be necessary.

I had danced starring roles in London, New York, Paris, Berlin, Vienna, Hamburg, Toronto, etc., before the most knowledgeable dance critics. The local expert Von Karsten Peters had questioned my ballerina status; I now had to verify my credentials in Munich. I had only danced Cranko's *Romeo* once, years ago. Not wishing to be pelted with tomatoes I carefully arranged the rehearsals. In a four-page memo to Everding I explained why I required more than three rehearsal hours – on three separate days. I further requested as 'essential and sensible' one stage-call. His underlings had rejected the stage-call. 'I have never danced with a company that would not expect to do this *comme il faut*,' the memo stated. A memo came back: 'Approved.' Marcia Haydée arrived from Stuttgart to give me and the company special coaching. Richard Cragun, also of the Stuttgart Ballet, was my partner. Successful partnering is what dancing is all about. He was familiar with the ballet and we were friends. There were complaints that my partner was an 'outsider'. I ignored them. Far more difficult to brush aside were two dozen letters and several anonymous phone calls promising trouble if I appeared.

'It's rather creepy,' I confided to Barlow and Albi. 'The letters are not just evil. They're evil *evil*.'

'Deliberately organized,' said Barlow, 'to drive you out of Munich.'

'No one is driving me. I'll have to be carried.' Prophetic words.

Seeking a rapprochement with Vernon, who was dancing Juliet at the third performance, I had talked to her about my plan to develop a ballet school that would foster a 'company style' and feed young choreographic and dancing talent into our company, which is how the Royal Ballet established its strength under Ninette de Valois. Madam had said she would contribute her invaluable ideas. Vernon ran a government-supported dancing academy and I wanted to draw her into this long-range project from the start. The school and her academy could be melded into one vigorous unit attached to the opera house. On parting it was kiss-kiss and *wunderbar*. The threatening letters, however, disturbed me. I suspected that her followers were responsible. Publicly I dismissed them. But they did give me sleepless nights . . .

Von Karsten Peters had already declared himself an enemy, allied with Vernon, in many printed and spoken words. His editors shunted him aside for one performance. The *Romeo* assignment went to a guest critic. The night of our first performance, when Richard Cragun was doing warm-ups, I said, 'Are you feeling strong tonight, Ricky? I hope so. I'm planning to live up to my "dramatic" reputation.' I threw myself to the 'lions', defiantly and splendidly supported by Cragun. Neither tomatoes nor Molotov cocktails were hurled at the stage. *Romeo* was a conspicuous success. The *Daily Mail* reported to the London dance world that, 'The jeers have turned to cheers.' The humility with which I took my bows was acting at its finest hour.

With the nervous relief of a prisoner on parole I flew to London for Christmas 1978. Demian had preceded me with his nanny. I fell upon the Big Boys with great hugs and kisses. But no tears, certainly not when we were together. Our life for many years had been a series of reunions and farewells. They understood that I had to fly hither and thither to earn a living, and they would be spending their

Easter holidays with me in Munich. At ten they were dutiful, responsible gentlemen – going on thirty. We had a snowy sugar-plum Christmas. The lads unpacked boxes of Christmas ornaments – silver stars, red and gold balls, tinsel, stuffed angels and reindeer – and 'decked' a giant tree. And I gave my annual Christmas party. During my first years in London, when I was without friends, I dreaded the aloneness of Christmas, never knowing until the last minute how I might be spending the day. After I bought my house, I initiated the annual party, frequently inviting foreign students from the ballet school and other strays. Now I was so grateful to be in London that I even invited my cheery-pip of a cabbie who brought me from the airport, but he declined. He was taking his son to see Santa Claus.

I returned to Munich with hope for the New Year. The nonsense and nastiness at the opera house would surely melt away with the snow. Nureyev-Makarova in *Swan Lake*, Seymour-Cragun in *Romeo* had demonstrated, at least to Everding, that he had not erred in his choice of an artistic director. I looked forward to guest appearances by Cynthia Gregory and Fernando Bujones of the American Ballet Theatre, a new ballet by Kenneth MacMillan, a programme devoted to Bournonville, featuring his classic *La Sylphide*, in which I would dance the wicked witch, new works by emerging international choreographers, and the Munich première of *Anastasia*. Cooperating to the fullest, the Royal Ballet had agreed to lend its sets and costumes. Yes, the New Year would be good and when I rented a flat that comfortably accommodated my family and the flow of visitors I longed to entertain, I was assured that we were off to a fresh, happy season. I filled the flat with white and yellow roses and had it painted and carpeted in pearl-grey.

But grey, dark grey, blobby grey clouds gathered over the office of the *Ballettdirektorin*.

The Germans are fond of dramatic ballets and I believed *Anastasia* would be popular. It would also please Konstanze Vernon. I intended to cast her as the Tsarina, a role created by Beriosova. The management rejected *Anastasia*. Everding had never seen the ballet, but he heard that the revolution scene was not very good. MacMillan, he said, was too English. 'We're lucky to get any ballet by Kenneth,' I replied. Kenneth, meanwhile, said he was too busy to choreograph a new work for me. I was disappointed, but definitely wanting MacMillan in the rep I staged his *Las Hermanas*. Lar Lubovitch came from New York to stage two ballets. Knowing the problems I had with Vernon, he cast her in one role. Naturally she spurned the part – and wanted another 'that is more appropriate'. During rehearsals the financial commandant began nit-picking with Lubovitch over some *Pfennigs* in his expense account. I was hideously embarrassed. 'Lynn, I love you, but I cannot produce in this atmosphere,' Lar Lubovitch groaned.

He confronted the keeper of the purse, who refused to yield. Lubovitch became so rightfully angry that, in trying to talk sense, he slammed his fist down on the stubborn man's desk with such force that he cracked it. He only staged one piece instead of two and then jumped on the first plane leaving Munich. He didn't care where it was going. He just wanted *out*. The management resisted the Bournonville evening. I fought until I was hoarse and succeeded in getting it accepted. Now, Bournonville created the signature style of the Royal Danish Ballet for which he choreographed more than sixty works in the 19th century. He is respected throughout the world. Predictably the local-yokel critics said that Bournonville was schmaltzy.

The opposition and stupidity did not drive me to pick every flower in the Englischer Garten. I was too occupied writing memos and business letters. The other dancers and I were suffering an inordinate amount of injury and muscular stress because of the extreme hardness of the rehearsal room floor, which was set directly on to concrete. Both this and the stage lacked the necessary spring or resilience necessary for dancing. Also there were gaps and cracks in the surface of the stage caused by heavy scenery being dragged across it. This was pointed out at the start, but our memos were flung aside. Albi Widmann, finally hired as my assistant in May, joined the battle arguing in German for new floors. The argument was presented to deaf ears.

The Munich Ballet Week is much looked forward to by dancers and public alike. It takes place in late spring, with old and new ballets. Teetering psychologically and physically from seven months of hostility, I somehow scheduled the programme, securing guest artists and choreographers. Unable to find a reputable name to create a piece for Konstanze Vernon, I choreographed a short work to music by Kurt Weill.

She refused to perform it. Everding insisted I did it instead.

Unwisely I let the management persuade me into dancing one performance of *Romeo*, again with guest Richard Cragun. Instinctively I knew this was wrong. I was too tired, too strung out to perform a full-length ballet, and I had a foot injury still healing. Your head has to be 'centred' on those countless movements and if you want to bring something more to a role than robot-like steps – if you want to become that character – you must forget everything else. Such roles demand total concentration. The outside world vanishes. You forget your name, your children, your mate and the day of the week, so that for two hours onstage you are a possessed being. In twenty-five years of dancing, I have cancelled about five performances. But one incident at Covent Garden started the legend that Seymour was unreliable, that she might-or-might-not perform, you never could tell. Sir John Tooley of the Royal Opera House says that my 'jolly few cancellations have been exaggerated . . . I would never associate the word "unreliable" with you.'

That legend-making incident: Nureyev and I were paired for a performance of *Romeo*. Rudi hurt his foot and could not dance. I had not performed for over three months and my confidence was at its lowest ebb. I was not prepared to face a new partner. The morning of the performance I informed the Garden that I was not 'up' to going on. I was mentally whacked. I told the stage manager, the ballet-master and the artistic director, who was then Kenneth. I deliberately told everyone. And everyone said pull up the old socks, dearie, don't let us down. So I dropped my practice bag in a dressing room and began sewing on the Juliet wig. A twenty- to thirty-minute operation. Then I applied the Juliet make-up. Another thirty minutes. In practice tights, for the costume would be donned prior to curtain, I proceeded to the stage to do the warm-up. The set had not been hung. A prop man said the curtain would be half an hour late because of some mechanical problem. I panicked. It was wrong for me to be dancing and the delayed curtain confirmed my fears. I organized for a replacement and advised Kenneth that I was shaking and had to go home. I asked the stage doorman to call a taxi.

Then I slowly unstitched and unglued my wig and got into my street clothes – a sweat shirt and pants. Rivulets of tears washed away the rouge and eye shadow. The back-stage intercom suddenly warned: 'Five minutes, ladies and gentlemen.' I threw all my stuff into the practice bag. Then, to my horror, I heard on the intercom: 'Miss Seymour, your taxi is here.' Dumbo at the stage door. The entire *Romeo* cast, scattered backstage and unaware of my departure, went into baffled convulsions: Juliet was leaving Verona by mini-cab! My exit provided talk'n'titters for days. Those who call me 'unreliable' conveniently forget that I rushed to the Garden one night to replace Svetlana Beriosova in the second act of *Giselle* when that gorgeous woman was in the midst of a personal crisis – which nobody cared about, they never do – and unable to complete the ballet. The irony is that, given my 'bad odour' at the time, I was not the first replacement the management called. Two other dancers, I learned, hearing that Beriosova was a bit wobbly, did not answer their phones.

On the day of my *Romeo* performance during Munich's festival week, with the house sold-out, I did not have the stamina or ability to dance that night. I hadn't performed in three months. And I had just produced the festival programme which included *Eugene Onegin*, *La Sylphide*, *La Fille Mal Gardée* – and commissioned four new ballets and choreographed two myself. Though I knew that the Munich press would be warming their critical ovens for me and the ballet week as a whole, I scribbled a note for Albi: 'I'm not dancing tonight.' I remembered Rudi's phone call after my 'five-minute' exodus: 'Lil, how are you? I wish I had your courage.'

Then I walked through the rain to the Alte Pinakothek, to clear my brain with a few Rembrandts, Raphaels and Rubens. Later that evening I appeared at the performance I could not dance in to apologize to Richard Cragun and to thank the ballerina for stepping in. The whole incident quickly became another 'Did-you-hear-what-Seymour-did-this-time . . . ?' story.

The company longed to tour, which – because of its opera duties – it was rarely able to do. A potential morale-raiser, a glimmer of blue in the darkening sky, came from London. Lord Grade wanted to televise a production of *Giselle*, starring Nureyev, that would also be sold, across the counter, as a video-cassette. Would I dance his Giselle and would the Munich company provide the corps? No problem. I hoped that this might be the boost the company was waiting for. The opera house was not really interested but grudgingly agreed. We would be in London five days, returning on a Saturday. This was a tight schedule, but we could squeak by. Hotel rooms were booked for the Munich dancers and plane tickets were in hand. Lord Grade beckoned.

The day before our London flight I was called into an administrator's office. Wetting his lips with a long, moist, maroon tongue, he announced with a smirk: 'You can't go to London.'

Albi opened a bulky envelope. 'Everything's in order. Here are the plane tickets. The contracts. What seems to be *your* problem?'

'The opera company has to give a special performance on Saturday,' he said curtly. 'We need some of the dancers for the opera. You can't go.'

'In that case we'll be back Friday night,' I replied calmly.

'The plane might be late, bad weather . . .'

'It's spring. You expect a blizzard?' I interrupted.

'. . . and the opera performance would be in jeopardy.'

He was talking rubbish. He knew it and I knew it. He had his job to do but was being brutally punctilious. The entire ballet corps was not going to London, I reminded him. There would still be enough dancers in Munich for the demo. Did he not appreciate the prestige of a television production with Nureyev? He twirled his hand contemptuously. 'It is impossible. Besides, Nureyev is not in such good form. You cannot jeopardize the opera.' Our interview, he indicated, was over.

I blocked his path, absolutely enraged. 'This is not the way dance companies are run in civilized houses of the world.' I waved the plane tickets under his nose. 'Take these plane tickets. Roll them up. And then you know where you stick them?' He collapsed in his chair. I bowed politely. My voice was pure honey: 'Now don't fret. *You'll like it.*'

Albi and I swept out. We went into an emergency

huddle. If we returned to Munich one day early, on Friday, the opera performance could not be used as an excuse to quash *Giselle*. I telephoned Nureyev, who was co-directing the film, and explained that the management hoped to stop the production. He was appalled. Can we finish the shoot in three days? I asked. The schedule would have to be reorganized and we might have to work overtime, he said, but, yes, somehow we'd get it done. And we did. It was a bitter victory, and, ultimately, an unimportant one. With each passing day my spirits sagged lower and lower. The management had no commitment to me. The opera house did not seem to want any artistic director or direction. Outside recognition only increased resentment towards me.

Rashomon closed my first season in Munich. The management had heard that it was distressingly erotic. Everding and two assistants attended a dress rehearsal to inspect the amount of exposed flesh. The wardrobe assistants did not sit quietly and observe, but gabbled loudly in German as if they were in a beer garden disputing the nutritional worth of a pork knuckle. I expected them to censor *Rashomon*, but they filed out of the rehearsal in sanctimonious silence. Nothing was ever said to me. Von Karsten Peters telephoned. 'We have had differences,' he simpered. 'We should be friends. I'd like to do a feature on you and your new ballet.' The press department encouraged the interview as a diplomatic manoeuvre. Not wanting to give up, not wanting to be accused of cowardliness, I consented to the interview, stupidly believing in his sincerity. We spent two hours discussing style and technique, the classics, psychological ballets and non-story ballets of pure dance. I praised the company's growth and spoke optimistically of its future. He asked about *Rashomon*. I explained that it was a highly stylized ballet on a universal theme: the elusive nature of truth. He smiled and made flattering noises. The session concluded with a handshake and laughter.

The split between appearance and reality was soon made brutally clear. His review of *Rashomon* was a sneering, belittling indictment of me. He turned everything I had said into a tasteless joke. I gnashed my teeth after reading the review, then simply caved in. I could not take Munich seriously any more. I lay in bed, staring at the ceiling, with terrified eyes, wondering why they were determined to destroy me. The struggle was not over, but I wished I could die, and there was no one to save me, and I hardly cared. I dozed off in a feverish state and awoke lying upside down in bed. Now, with a steady hand, I sought the telephone and rang Albi. 'I have to get out, darling. I must leave *today*. Please come.'

Albi drove Demian and me to the airport, a silent and forbidding drive. I was a waxen passenger. If I can just reach London, I thought, I can stay alive. My balance was gone, my vision blurred. Albi supported me silently on to the plane. I kissed him goodbye. When I last glimpsed him tears were streaming down his face.

I was not in Munich very much the second and final year. I underwent surgery in London and later injured my Achilles tendon studying and rehearsing *Onegin* with the Stuttgart company. But I am proud of my accomplishments as artistic director. Besides the numerous guest artists I brought to Munich, I introduced over fifteen new ballets. Twelve of these were world premières. The most exciting were two by the young American choreographer William Forsythe, who was with the Stuttgart company at the time. Billy is a controversial odd-man-out whose tense, jagged imagery is not to everyone's liking. He belongs to the new generation of choreographers. Dance critic Anna Kisselgoff of the *New York Times* said, 'He is a major talent – a radical new force to be reckoned with. He opens up new possibilities for ballet itself, reflecting, as ballet once did more overtly, the society in which we live.'

When the movers were packing my belongings in Munich I had a farewell appointment with August Everding. It was a brief meeting. I stated that the attitude towards ballet in Munich was impoverished, scandalous and selfish in the extreme. Friends have said to me, 'How did you ever expect to manage as artistic director, choreographer and ballerina?' Granted, this was a bit heavy. In time I would have concentrated on running the company. Yet, without any authority or budget, without an assistant for months or proper secretary, I almost pulled off the Herculean task while maintaining two households. With a supportive management I would have succeeded completely.

The rehearsal studio eventually got its new floor – a milestone in the company's development.

Carefully folded in an envelope and placed in the drawer of my bedside table is my only fond memento of Munich, an opening night telegram from Nureyev:

TO LYNN SEYMOUR DIRECTRICE DISTINGUEE CHOREO-
GRAPHISTE EXTRAORDINAIRE GRANDE MERDE AVEC
BEAUCOUP DE SUCCES QUAND MEME WISH YOU SURVIVE
AND DETERMINATION TO OUTLIVE LOTS OF LOVE
RUDOLF PIZDOF

CHAPTER 17

The Lost Isadora

The crush-bar at Covent Garden blazes with light, the musical hum of voices and the tinkle of glass as balletgoers order wines, champagnes and whiskies during the twenty-minute interval of Kenneth MacMillan's *Isadora*. This is Kenneth's biography of the American dancer whose life and art freely expressed her emotions. Ashton made his 'statement' on Isadora Duncan with the dances he recreated from memory. Intrigued by the richness of her personality, Kenneth used her life as the basis of his fifth full-length ballet. *Isadora* was created for the Royal Ballet's fiftieth anniversary in 1981.

But this is not the opening night. I was not invited.

This is many months and many performances later, and Kenneth, a perfectionist, is still making changes in the work, a fascinating contribution to any dance season. The Royal Ballet press office, at my request, set aside tickets for me at the stage door and I arrived by tube with plenty of time to spare. Even with the vagaries of the underground and waiting for the lift at Covent Garden station I know the precise length of the trip from Turnham Green to Bow Street, and I was never late. But then I have usually been on the other side of the crimson curtains. The press office reserved excellent seats in the stalls. The seventh row centre was not my favourite vantage-point, however. I left my date, with both seats (an extra for his coat), and stood in a shadowy corner of the grand tier.

I have not been to Covent Garden in a long time, not since I left the Royal Ballet. I wanted to see the ballet I was once promised to do.

'Would you fetch me a glass of white wine?' I asked my date. 'Just push through the mob, don't be timid, darling. The bar can serve eight hundred drinks during an interval.' I pretended to read my programme, thereby avoiding the faces swirling around me, promenaders in twos and threes, so lively and graceful, their fine clothes displayed to advantage by the glittering chandeliers in what is fondly called the Crush Bar. Two young women slowly pass, and I hear one remark, 'It's Lynn Seymour . . . in the black tunic and velvet pants . . .' They move away in a tide of people. 'They say she . . .' Other voices grow louder, drowning them out. *They say she what?* That she's a boozer? That she's letting herself go to hell like Mother Goddamn? That she's keeping a young man, a rock musician? If the truth be known, he was keeping *her* – alive. Thrice-told tales. And partial truths. I have already firmly resolved in the days ahead to alter the unpleasant truths.

'Lynn. How nice to see you.' I gazed into the hale and hearty face of Sir John Tooley, the general director of the opera house. 'You're looking very lovely.' Do I really look lovely? Well, the old girl still tries, even at forty-two. We are blocking the entry into the crush bar and the throng is tremendous. Surrounded by staff members who wave to me, he steps aside and is immediately swept into the crowd.

My date approaches with two glasses. 'The occasion calls for champagne, don't you think?'

'Oh, my darling. Thank you so much.' I take a sip. 'What occasion?'

'Kenneth is here.'

Of course Kenneth would be here. The press department said he had just made some cuts in the ballet. I have not seen Kenneth for a long time.

'Hello . . . Lynn . . .' That languid musical voice . . . He does not appear displeased by what he sees. Introductions are made. Curious onlookers stare at us. They always did.

Kenneth quietly discussed some of the bits he eliminated from the ballet, and then murmured, 'The cast would be so pleased to see you . . . Do come backstage afterwards and say hello.'

'No. I don't think I can.' The words, almost inaudible. Thinking, thinking rapidly I rushed on with the smile of a too-eager soubrette, 'Kenneth, I'm planning to have dinner with Nico and Becky next week. We just want to sit around and talk about the old days. The Diners' Club. With Poffer . . . and Puss. Becky says there's a deliciously awful Indian restaurant in Chelsea.'

'Becky?' he repeated vaguely, slowly backing into the mob, now surging towards the auditorium. The interval is over.

'I mean Jeff. Jeffrey Solomons. Do come.'

'I'm leaving for New York this weekend and will be there a while.' A mass of people have come between us.

'Oh! But I'm going to be in New York, too.'

'We'll have dinner there . . .' And he is gone.

I finished the glass of champagne, feeling excessively warm, excessively young and hopeful. My date declared rather coolly: 'Well, I always wanted to see the two of you together.'

'And what did you see?'

'The historic team. It's still there, you know.'

Before I could reply he dashed down the grand staircase to the stalls. The lights dimmed. I returned to my niche.

The last act is about to begin!

Around the time I accepted the Munich appointment Kenneth revealed that he planned a ballet on the life of Isadora Duncan. 'Keep yourself in shape because I want you to do it.' I promised to make myself available. We would just have to synchronize our schedules. Isadora Duncan would be the pinnacle of my dance career. I had missed 'international stardom' fifteen years earlier when circumstances prevented Kenneth from letting me première his Juliet. But a new ballet by Kenneth centred on the most provocative woman in contemporary dance presented a 'second chance' which comes so rarely in life, if ever. It might completely anaesthetize the *Romeo* experience.

Lack of new parts in London was one of the reasons why I found the Munich offer so enticing. I was not content repeating the same roles over and over again. I was not enthused at the prospect of dancing Juliet when I was forty-five. There is little satisfaction in hearing fans say, 'Amazing! And do you know how *old* she is . . . ?' To stay artistically alert as a dancer, I needed, like an actress, the stimulus of new roles. A versatile actress moves, with age, from Eliza Doolittle to Hedda Gabler. There are no character leads, no Lady Catherine Champion-Cheneys, in the ballet. Dancers cannot grow old onstage: we must constantly 'sell' youth and beauty. The critics shrewdly noted that Natalia Petrovna was that balletic rarity, a mature woman. Isadora Duncan was more complex, more theatrical than Natalia Petrovna. She was an over-ripe woman whose body and temperament were not unlike mine. Isadora could become a classical role for ballerinas past the first blush of youth; and since there were not many dancing years ahead of me, Isadora would be the great firecracking sparkler of my partnership with Kenneth MacMillan and my career with the Royal Ballet.

We would make it a positively brilliant ballet. *How could we miss?* Throughout the grey, grey months in Munich, despite the almost unbearable antagonism, I trained daily, sometimes alone at eight A.M., remembering the light – the sparkler – which shone for me in London.

Isadora. An incentive to live. To dance.

I was utterly downcast when Kenneth said he did not have the time to choreograph a new ballet for the Munich company. I had hoped the dancers would have the privilege of working with him; and, selfishly, I had looked forward to having him all to myself for a few weeks in Munich. It would have been a giggle, a marvellous giggle, just like the old days. I would have done my imitation of Konstanze Vernon and Von Karsten Peters. We would have shrieked with laughter until dawn. And we would have discussed *Isadora*. But Kenneth could not get away from London. By phone and letter he mentioned that he was committed to produce *Isadora* for the Royal Ballet's fiftieth anniversary but that was two years hence. I was not troubled. As the months passed in Munich I knew that, by mutual consent with the management, I would be free from my two-year contract as soon as I said that's enough. The moment fast approached. When Kenneth creates a ballet, especially a full-length work which takes months, he likes his principals within easy let's-meet-for-coffee reach. Kenneth, Christopher Gable and I were inseparable when Kenneth created *Romeo*. If he worried about the possibility of my prolonged absence in Munich, I would calm him down: the possibility did not exist.

Once he said, 'I need you . . .' I would make myself available night and day.

The subject never came up.

Weeks passed. I began to squirm.

I flew to London in June for a spree with the Big Boys. I missed them terribly. A nice cosy weekend was in order before I started choreographing *Rashomon* in Munich. Kenneth and his wife had invited me to dinner. Lovely. In London the name of Lynn Seymour was associated with hard cheese and tattles of my *Romeo* walk-out. I would explain to Kenneth what was really going down in Munich. And Kenneth would give me the details on *Isadora*. A real shoes-off evening. I phoned Kenneth on my arrival.

'What I really want to talk about, Kenneth, even though the production is two years away,' I said gaily, 'are your rehearsal dates for *Isadora*. When do you think you'll need me?' There followed a stiff silence, the silence you hear when you tell someone you'll see them at a party which they haven't been invited to.

Kenneth coughed a bit and finally said that he wasn't quite sure. 'Well, I'll see you at dinner tomorrow night. We'll talk then.' I hung up, gazing distractedly at the telephone. My hand gripped the receiver. An alarm bell went off in my head: Seymour, you're bloody well blinkered. You didn't get the message. He doesn't *want* you to do the ballet. I instantly called him back. 'Kenneth. It's me. Lynn, again. Are you saying, in your way – that you don't want me, is that it?'

His voice became cordially apologetic. I imagined him in his study, coiled in a chair, his eyes gloomy, the colour rising in his cheeks. 'I've sent you a letter . . . about various things. I'm afraid I can't do *Isadora* with you as I don't know your plans. I don't know where you'll be . . .' He cleared his throat. 'I assumed you . . . just understand. I'm doing the ballet with another dancer.' Pause. 'She already knows. It's arranged.'

I could not continue the conversation. I was shivering. My eyes were stinging. 'Oh. I see. Well, yes . . . in two years . . . I must fly now. I'm off to the theatre.' Once again I hung up. I found myself sitting at my desk, frozen, without a tremor, staring at a bouquet of violets, the snooker table, the windows into the garden where a soft languorous breeze caressed the trees in the bright spring sunlight. Jers and Ads dropped their bicycles on the grass and bounded through the door into my arms.

'What's the matter, Mum, you look so *peculiar*,' Jers said.

My fingers rumpled his blond hair. Another arm went around Addie. 'Hold me, my darlings. You're the Big Boys, the big chaps of the house, aren't you?' We laughed and they held me tightly, instinctively knowing that something was dreadfully wrong yet instinctively knowing, sophisticates that they are, not to ask questions. I remembered the phone call from my mom years ago, telling me that Dad had died, a man I loved very much, and I held the twins, just babies then, touched by their warmth. Subconsciously they knew that something tragic had taken place, but I never talked of Dad's death, even after they grew up. I mechanically disconnected myself from that event. I refused to dwell on that lost part of my life.

Unflinching detachment. That is how I deal with breathless shock. Abnormally cool I now told the twins that we would go out for hamburgers and chips. They routed Demian from his room and the four of us set out, bantering amiably, a cheerful-looking lot, for a restaurant in the Chiswick High Road. On the way home I bought some Guinness. My diet doctor advised that one Guinness was calorically equal to a chunk of chocolate cake, but this thick, beery drink calmed the agitation of my heart and gave me an extra shot of vitality. For absurdly enough I was, in fact, going to the theatre. I had tickets to a production of *Measure for Measure* at the Riverside Studios in Hammersmith. The last play I wanted to see was a dark comedy about tyranny, corruption and the rewards of chastity. But I could not disappoint two friends who were going with me and so I sat pensively through the performance, half-hearing such lines as: '*To whom should I complain? Did I tell this, who would believe me?*' I was starting to simmer.

The house was quiet. The boys were in bed and their nanny was in bed, with her boyfriend. I flung my coat and purse on a wicker laundry basket, and stalked noisily across the floorboards in my heels, trying to decide whether I wanted to scream with rage or cry. Self-possession, utter detachment – the abnormal cool I prided myself on were gone.

Swiftly, angrily I stomped into the parlour and dialled Kenneth. It was only eleven-thirty. His line was engaged. I removed my shoes and hurled them across the parlour. I lit a cigarette, then dialled again. He answered on the second ring.

Omitting trivial politeness I said, coldly, rapidly: 'Kenneth, I want you to know – before you hear it from anyone else – that I really hate you. *You've betrayed me.*' He started to give me as good as he got. Then I slammed down the phone. I began trembling. Forgetting that one cigarette was already burning, I was lighting a second when the telephone rang. I grabbed the receiver.

'Lynn, I want you to know – before you hear it from anyone else,' said Kenneth in a liquid drawl, 'that you're not invited to dinner tomorrow night.' Then *he* hung up.

I stared at my two burning cigarettes and screamed in frustration. Kenneth was always quick with a funny turn of phrase, much funnier and faster than anyone else in the Diners' Club, but we weren't lolling any more in Poffer's apartment playing Sunday afternoon games and eating Nipples. The Lesbos Ensemble had disbanded. For one mad moment I wondered if Kenneth was teasing, if the Isadora Game was a new amusement. Good Christ, no. This was horribly, revoltingly serious. Kenneth was not teasing. We had goaded and provoked each other like unruly children in Berlin and now he had issued the final sentence: you cannot have my fabulous new Isadora puppet.

My mouth twitched idiotically. Fifteen years ago Kenneth had been a diffident young man, too fragile to fight the management for the dancers he wanted to première *Romeo*. He even had no control over the performing sequence of the five Juliets. But now he had The Power to select. He had

The Power to make demands. Months later Sir John Tooley said, 'Kenneth is not someone who discusses his decisions, or explains his reasons or motives. Unquestionably the ballet would have turned out quite differently with Lynn, but the decision was totally his. I asked, "Are you sure this is right?" And Kenneth answered, "I can't make it work with Lynn." Kenneth was the creator. We abided by his decision.'

As an artistic director-choreographer *I* fully respect Kenneth's decision. I would also argue on his behalf: the choreographer should cast the dancers of his choice without outside interference. But as the dancer who had just lost that coveted role I split at the seams. I had asserted my personal independence from Kenneth years ago. Now, with a star vehicle, for the Royal Ballet's fiftieth anniversary, he fully asserted his professional independence from me.

That night, sitting at my desk, I tried calling Rudi in Paris and La Turbie. Fortunately he was in another corner of the world. After all, what could I say: 'Oh, Rudi . . . Kenneth won't let me do Isadora'? Nonsense. The ballet was Kenneth's, not mine. I opened a fresh pack of cigarettes, thinking, should I go to Kenneth's house, throw myself on my knees and beg forgiveness? 'Forgive me for being sick in Berlin. Forgive me for having husbands and having children. For cancelling performances. Forgive me for wounding you in some way which my dumb egocentric head does not understand. Forgive me for not always being available, I am here, now, available . . .'

Gathering myself together, I put on my glasses and flipped through the Talmud. I needed to talk to someone, someone who had nothing to do with the dance world. Philip Pace and Ellie. Being far removed from the dance world, they could perhaps put things in perspective. It was past midnight when I rang them, asking if I could spend the night. Wrapped in an overcoat and scarf I arrived on their doorstep. Two friendly faces appeared in the dark, moon-less night and spirited me away. An hour later Ellie made a cosy bed for me piled high with cushions, and Philip urged me not to talk until I had knocked back a strong vodka. I stretched out on the bed, with Philip and Ellie beside me on cushions, and poured out my woes. 'Fonteyn, Beriosova, Sibley, Makarova – all the stars you used to talk about are gone,' Philip exclaimed. 'There's no one at the Garden any more. If this were a film it would never get financed, not without a star.' *Isadora* was a very expensive production.

'It's illogical, but your absence probably worries Ken-neth,' said Ellie. 'That's all I can think of, unless he really *doesn't* want you . . .'

Two days later I was in Munich rehearsing *Rashomon*. Kenneth's letter was at the opera house. A most difficult letter to write, he said, but he did not know any other way to soften the blow: he was creating *Isadora* on a dancer named Merle Park. 'Please don't think too badly of me,' he concluded. 'I miss you. Much love, Kenneth.'

The day came when I barely managed to hobble out of Munich. Something ghastly was going on inside my body, leaving me enfeebled and sickly. I struggled on to the plane with Albi's help and, upon reaching Woodstock Road, locked myself into the sanctuary of my bedroom. An enormous carbuncle seemed to be oozing poison into my system. If I shut out the world and stayed in bed the poison would drain itself away . . . But the physical pain did not cease. I saw my gynaecologist. The examination did not take long.

He solemnly advised a hysterectomy. 'I stress the word "advise". If you have an important role I can "fix" you up – temporarily – without an operation . . .'

I jabbed my eyes with a tissue. 'There *is* no role . . .'

'You won't have to stop dancing long. The recovery, for you, should be about four months.'

Four months, three months away from class? I would be in some unsightly shape. I laughed uncontrollably. 'Sorry, doctor, you don't know what a funny year it has been. Especially the last weeks. Go ahead. What must be done, must be done.'

Only two or three friends were initially aware of the operation. I decided that the first person I see when I wake up . . . will be someone who truly cares for me . . . I remember luminous eyes. A heart-shaped face. Black hair and olive skin. Margot Fonteyn stood at the bedside table arranging a vase of white orchids. Her sweetness and warmth haunted me for the rest of my hospital stay. Margot is a woman without affectation. Her beauty and grace are effortless. There is nothing at all grand about Fonteyn. She is a woman of humour and human understanding. At an hour when I longed to disengage the mysterious bubbling tubes attached to my veins, she clasped my hand, giving me tremendous courage. The light in her eyes filled my heart with love. Quite a woman, that Margot.

A hysterectomy, I discovered, is rather more complicated than having a baby. The recovery is slow and the aftermath, for me, was psychologically depressing. Nonetheless my first day home I hosted a garden party for the Dance Theatre of Harlem. I sat in a straw chair, wearing a large hat and a pink flowing dress and played the disabled Grand Duchess.

However, I had to get back into practice. Gloomily and with faint heart, I put on the ballet slippers and was bending and twisting and stretching, slogging away harder than ever to get my squishy stomach muscles tight. A handful of faithful fans, led by Rudi, refused to let me give up. It was an agonizing year. After I injured my Achilles tendon rehearsing Cranko's *Eugene Onegin* in Stuttgart, I reasoned it was useless trying to pump fresh air into a worn-out old balloon. But I persisted. With a stiff upper lip and a quivering lower one.

The *Evening Standard*, which had given me its annual dance award some years earlier, announced that 'Lynn Seymour, probably our greatest ballerina, will be back at the Royal Opera House Covent Garden . . .' The announcement was premature. When my Munich contract was amicably and mercifully terminated, the Royal Ballet actually told me that I was not needed at Covent Garden. The press speculated it was because I had been having problems keeping my weight down – a problem 'which had not been helped by a recent operation'. I seemed to have no future anywhere. With a minimum of fuss I resettled on Woodstock Road, delighted that the family was united again, and, not giving up, doggedly resumed daily class at Barons Court. 'SEYMOUR IN THE DOGHOUSE', hooted one headline. I did not discuss *Isadora* with anyone. Throughout the balmy summer nights of 1980 I lay awake reading and listening to music, and smoking non-stop. The daily classes were purgatory, and my mind was full of questions: 'What does the future hold? What's the point? What am I doing? Why, why, why?'

I had been advised to wear clogs to protect my dodgy Achilles and rest an arthritic toe-joint. One afternoon I stepped into the garden to have a chat with Jers. A clog jammed between two flagstones and I badly sprained my ankle. This was the last straw. Seeing the 'black abyss' looming and knowing that I was on the verge of cracking from mental fatigue, I asked my psychiatrist to find a haven where I could stop the descent into hell. He recommended one in north London.

'Have you ever been in the bin?' I asked Stevie Harmsworth, a young American woman with a droll sense of humour. We used to go on the toot before I divorced Philip

Pace and she married Guy Harmsworth, the scion of the British publishing family. I mentioned a private clinic called Greenways. It sounded so restful and soothing.

'*Greenways?*' Stevie exclaimed. 'Oh, Lynsey, it's wonderful. I've romped through there. Greenways is the Grand Hotel of Great London Bins. You'll meet everyone you know at Greenways.' Her eyes scanned my yellowish complexion and an unsightly rash on my arms. I wanted to sleep peacefully, to cleanse my mind of collected débris and my body of tensions. 'You really should go . . .' Stevie said. I decided to hold myself together for another week until the twins boarded a plane for their Canadian vacation. I refused to disappear, leaving the lads in the lurch. Demian would stay with Philip and Ellie.

The dancer Gelsey Kirkland, a dark, lithe, affecting person, small-boned and delicate, appeared in class. Gelsey had grown up in a theatrical environment. Her father Jack Kirkland dramatized the novel *Tobacco Road* which ran for eight years on Broadway. Gelsey was only sixteen when she began dancing leads with the New York City Ballet. Her lightning fouettés and impeccable timing, her 'slim curves like a Brancusi', made her an instant star in New York. I liked her very much. She too struggled against performing fears and personal crises that seemed at times far beyond the reach of normal buck-you-uppo remedies. Gelsey was a guest that summer with the Royal Ballet in *Romeo* and had asked Georgina Parkinson to coach her. Georgina is now ballet-mistress for American Ballet Theatre, Gelsey's 'home' company. Gelsey indicated that without the sympathetic guidance of Georgina, she would not perform. 'I won't be seeing you any more,' I said to Gelsey as we removed leg-warmers and shoes after class. 'I'm incarcerating myself in the bin.'

Gelsey gave a little start. 'Have a good time,' she said with a secret smile. When I showed up in class the following day, Gelsey said, 'What are you doing here? I thought you were in the bin.'

With one hand on the barre, I bent my knees up and down. My limbs were a quivering mass of jelly. 'I decided to wait one more day.'

'Well, it's much better out than in, isn't it?'

'I really don't know,' I answered.

Finally the twins were organized on to the plane for Canada and Demi was packed off to Philip and Ellie. The next morning, too distressed to swallow hot lemonade, I telephoned Stevie Harmsworth and asked her to drive me to Greenways. She calmed my anxiety by turning it into a larky venture. We dickered over my arrival clothes: a chiffon dress or a dark suit? Would I need a hat? I fretted like Manon over her jewels. Stevie was comfortably attired in pink sweat pants and shirt. We sailed across London in her bashed-up Volkswagen singing 'A-binning we will go, a-binning we will go . . . heigh-ho, heigh-ho, if love were all . . .'

Greenways looks like a smart London house where there is always a general air of repose. There are about a dozen patients in spacious rooms, many of which open on to a garden. I had a garden suite. On entering Greenways I suddenly felt terribly frightened. Stevie merrily called to a matron: 'Sister Peacock! You remember me? How are you?'

Sister Peacock said, 'Hello, dear. Are you checking in?'

'No, no. I'm fine. It's my friend here.' She gestured towards me. 'Lynsey! Come on, mate. Don't be afraid . . .'

The first thing I did, after signing various forms, was to check escape routes in case of the need for an emergency bolt. Sister Peacock assured me that I would not have to leap over the wall. I was free to walk out the front door whenever I chose. That, I thought, was probably easier said than done.

Psychologically I was in deep *schreck*, a condition which

lasted for months. Munich, Isadora, 'my return', and the condition of my body at forty-one after a hysterectomy gave me the heebie-jeebies. The effect of the relaxing drugs I was given was not entirely euphoric. My vision blurred. I could not watch the telly, read or write letters. So I spent five weeks there taking bubble baths, painting my face a variety of colours ('Ah, fuchsia cheeks today') and curling my hair. I plucked roses and hydrangeas from the garden and created floral coiffures. Stevie brought a bouquet of carnations, not knowing my dislike of them. 'Oh, Stevie, I hate carnations. They smell like death. Get the buggers out of here!' Stevie gave them to a rheumatic marquise down the hall who designed floral collages. Her accent was so utterly-upper that I had trouble, in my tranquillized state, understanding her. When she confided that she was rheumatic, I replied dopily, 'How lovely. I'm romantic too. There are so few of us left.'

I had lots of visitors. Stevie, Philip and Ellie with Demian, and Crazy Charlie, who discovered quite accidentally that I was in the bin. Charles France of American Ballet Theatre was guesting on Woodstock Road. He was padding around the kitchen one morning, in my robe and slippers, minding his own omelette, when Crazy Charlie sauntered in the front door, zipped from head to foot in shiny black leather adorned with silver studs. Charles France dashed upstairs where Stevie was doing a sweep. 'A guy in leather, with stitches in his head, just walked in and I don't know *who* the hell it is,' he panted breathlessly.

'Not to worry. That's Crazy Charlie,' muttered Stevie. 'If he brought his Harley-Davidson he can give you a spin to the bin.'

Finally I said goodbye to Sister Peacock and checked out of Greenways. The hour had come to face the music – or rather the inevitable dance. With a mouthful of humble pie I asked the management to take me back. 'I think I can behave like everyone else,' I said with desperate cheerfulness. 'I'll even go on a normal salary – not my usual per performance payment. In that way I'll be all yours. I'll be your normal ballerina.' And I believed my words at the time. The Royal Ballet rehired me. But I had to deliver the dancing goods: no whoring: nothing cheap, the real McCoy. For I have always said that if you can't deliver one hundred per cent, you don't go on the bloody stage. I candidly told the press that the Munich years had been absolutely awful and that after a lengthy illness I was back in training. I did not add that 'my return' frightened me or that I feared I would not make it or that my heart was not in it.

The Royal Ballet considerately gave me what seemed plenty of time to prepare for my 'return'. The scheduled date was 29 January 1981, in *A Month in the Country*. My rep included *Romeo*, *Manon* and *Mayerling*. When Erik Bruhn returned to the stage after a premature retirement he refused to dance old roles. He would not compete with his past image. That precise ordeal confronted me and increased my panic. New ballets with roles designed for your plastique and personality are as scarce as precious gems. Kenneth's *Isadora* was created on a dancer quite different from me. I was informed, however, that I would be one of the Isadoras. Third-cast. 'It's unthinkable not to create the ballet on Lynnie,' said Svetlana Beriosova. 'It's a Seymour role,' Fred Ashton commented.

Staring into a glass of wine I saw my life being replayed: the fifth Juliet, the third Isadora. An American confidant, Alan Groh, a private art dealer known for having one of the best art 'eyes' in New York, said, 'You may be the last to dance Isadora, but you'll knock the critics flat.'

Who is *that*? I asked silently, gazing in the mirror one day at class. There was no vitality in the face or form. I plodded without incentive. Not wanting to think about 'the return', Isadora or anything else, I filled my house with people and assured everyone that I really was not disturbed or fretful. And everyone believed me. It was Kenneth who first discerned: 'Lynn is a great actress.'

The last time beloved Nigel Gosling invited me to tea, some months after I left the Royal Ballet, I revealed both the turmoil I experienced over losing Isadora and the cool 'let's-see-if-she-can-do-it' atmosphere surrounding my attempted comeback. 'It's the herd instinct,' he said quietly. 'The herd instinct is cohesive, but it can also be very damaging. You know the story about the elephant? He got sick and hid in the jungle. When he came back, the others were furious. They wanted to kill him.'

I had indeed gone away twice. My loyalty to 'the team' was questioned. A few dancers could have been worried or jealous that I was now back at the Royal Ballet – for a third time. Eyes, critical eyes, observed every exercise in class as sweat poured off my body like water from a wet towel. I wanted to telephone Madam: 'Come to class for an hour . . . watch me . . . what do you think . . . *can I make it again?*' Pride held me back. I would succeed or fail on my own. There was no one I dared lean on.

From the days of breastfeeding Demian I have generally had nothing but a Guinness for lunch, to keep me energized during a long hard day. Of course it leaves a beery odour on your breath. Kenneth phoned me, 'People are saying you're on the booze, Lynn. That's what I've heard.' Fighting tears I thought, 'Bloody hell, everyone knows Guinness is a tonic.' In the Seymour 'can-do-no-wrong' period, a four-pack would be part of my equipment for long rehearsals – along with endless point shoes and woollies. No one batted an eyelid.

One day I became angry with myself for being so bloody blinkered: you're not really wanted, ducky; why are you slogging? '*You don't fit in.*' I must have known then that I would never again dance with the Royal Ballet.

Each day seemed worse than the preceding one. As the weeks flew by the frustration of daily class – when it went badly – and the general doubts gnawed away like some hideous incurable disease. How could I articulate this unabating ache?

In late November Anya Linden and Anthony Dowell sponsored a benefit for single-parent families at the Palladium. Many old friends were performing – Dowell himself, Christopher Gable, Robert North, Antoinette Sibley. There would be music by Handel and Elgar. John Gielgud would read Shakespeare's sonnets. Anya Linden asked me to participate, a welcome-back-to-London appearance. Christopher said, 'You *are* the most famous single parent in London.' I asked Billy Forsythe to create a three-minute solo. The ballets he created in Munich were my special pride. He understood my predicament and I wanted to introduce him to London. He devised a diary-of-a-mad-housewife number. I strutted onstage to a far-out rendering of 'Money' and performed jarring, frenetic steps, in a tacky leather coat, sunglasses and hat, while pointing a gun at my head and spraying myself with an aerosol can. Billy called it 'Famous Mother's Club' – 'Famous *Single* Mother's' in private. The nihilistic piece was not taken the right way on that particular occasion. People, to our surprise, were offended. After the gala I was seen as a woman whose judgement was highly questionable. The unmanageable misfit would be tolerated as long as she behaved and no one expected her to behave. Trudging home with flu one icy January afternoon I decided:

I do not want to dance any more.

That part of my life is over.

Finished.

Three weeks before 'my return' in *A Month in the Country* I telephoned Sir John Tooley at the Royal Opera House and Sir Fred at his home in Chelsea. Begging their understanding, I explained gravely that I could not fulfil my contract. I had no choice but to resign from the Royal Ballet.

Sir John was sweet and kind and gentle. Ashton said affectionately, 'You may leave us now, but you'll be back on the boards again, someday.'

CHAPTER 18

Finale

Some months ago, when the sky was streaked with purple with spots of blue, an enormous rabbit pressed his nose against the glass windows. Emotionally expressive, he possessed an intimidating *esprit* that disquieted me. When I informed Christopher Gable he said the rabbit was most certainly a hare and the hare was probably a momentary visual aberration of mine. I forgot the incident and mentally locked it away.

And then the creature reappeared again one evening as I hurried to the tube station, on my way to Sadler's Wells Theatre. It was twilight and I walked along Woodstock Road admiring the flowers and shrubs and trees in the cool breezy evening.

I came to a dead halt.

Loping across the road, tossing me a casual, careless wink, was my rabbit. But seeing him in full size, on the street, I realized that Christopher was right. The animal was a hare. Rabbit, hare — what the hell. It was not a row of pink elephants. I was not hallucinating. I was frightfully sober and even more frightfully sane. At the top of the road I paused at the greengrocer's and said in a puzzled rush, 'I do believe I've been seeing a hare lately,' expecting to hear derisive guffaws. The greengrocer, who was closing for the night, assured me that I did not require another incarceration in the bin. A new neighbour, who lived almost directly behind me, he said, raised the robust mammal as a pet. So. I had not passed through the looking-glass into a land of Mad Hatters, Mock Turtles and White Rabbits. This knowledge was a positive sign.

My perception was not distorted. I was seeing on the 'right' side of the glass.

'A lot has happened lately, eh?' the greengrocer asked in a bemused voice.

'Yes. A lot has happened.'

The Sadler's Wells Theatre on Rosebery Avenue is where I made my London stage début in the corps of the opera ballet with Christopher and Betty Anderton. Our ballet-master then was Peter Wright whose ballet *A Blue Rose* had its première on our first provincial tour. He had been John Cranko's right-arm man in Stuttgart during the early stages of this now famous company's creation. I danced in his production of *Giselle* in Canada a decade later and he was a much-respected guest choreographer for me in Munich. He is now artistic director of the Sadler's Wells Royal Ballet, and the *Evening Standard* was presenting its annual dance award to him. He specifically invited me to attend the performance when he would be presented with this honour.

I was reluctant to attend the performance at the theatre where my professional life had started, but eager to be with Peter to celebrate his triumph. The evening included Kenneth's ballet *Solitaire* which I was very interested to see (it was a new production which I had danced in but had never seen from the front) and a work-in-progress of Kenneth's with a stunning cast which included my lovely Galina Samsova.

Peter's reception at the end of the evening took place in a small private room near the dress circle. The room was a lively scene of laughter, chatter, exclamations and hugs among London's balletomanes. Peter and I hugged and Dame Ninette warmly shook my hand. I talked with critics and dancers. In the deliciously convivial atmosphere, amidst the friendly touching of hands, comradely embraces and clinking of glasses I chatted amiably with Kenneth about *Solitaire* and how Barry Kaye's imaginative sets and costumes had helped highlight certain aspects of the ballet. I congratulated him on the work-in-progress. And how did I like the costumes? he asked. I admitted that I did not really care for them. They neither added nor detracted . . .

We slowly drifted apart, merging into conversations with other people. Galina and I were going out to dinner, and I was on the point of leaving when I saw Kenneth coming towards me, cutting past Madam and Peter Wright. A deep flush crossed his face.

I waited, cheerfully puffing on the nub of a cigarette.

Suddenly Kenneth was beside me, breathing heavily. 'You didn't like the costumes because my wife designed them,' he said, in a voice quivering with rage, 'and you only said it because you're pissed.'

I gasped.

Then – in full view of the throng – he slapped me.

The slap did not hurt, but I was astounded – and angry. How petty! I thought. How dare he ruin Peter's evening? But that slap severed the umbilical cord to everything that had been important to me in the past. I was overjoyed to find that it no longer mattered.

'You were a tremendous influence on me, your approach to dance – your dare-devil spirit.' I am still flattered by a compliment, but this one particularly impressed me. It was made by Peter Martins, who, with Jerome Robbins, co-directs the New York City Ballet. Peter is the first man who ever said I influenced him. I never thought I influenced *anybody*, least of all a man. Peter and I had a quiet supper in New York when I was on a personal odyssey, a period of reflection and rebirth. For my life indeed was beginning anew; I was mistress of my future, free to move in any field of my choice. 'And the choices,' I said to Peter, 'are overwhelming.' I formed a company called The Famous Mothers and merged ballet with pop-rock music, our contemporary equivalent of chamber music. There was a lot of interest from the public but not from the financiers, conservative types all, who resisted this mixture of styles. I did choreograph a rock ballet, performed by members of the Royal Ballet, which gave two sell-out performances. 'Seymour and her crazy ideas,' some people glowered. Not so crazy. I must always explore the new and I must always find the answers for myself.

I became a young woman again, out in the world for the first time, and the emotional security and fulfilment that had eluded me were attained with a very special chap. 'Seymour in love – again?' No. Free at last to love as a mature woman without projecting my feelings on to an authority-figure. It took a long time, mates, but I've always been a late-starter. We were married early in 1983. My third, his second. 'Seymour married – again?' My attitude towards marriage has changed over the years. It is more of a statement today than it was thirty years ago, I have concluded, because the stigma of being a woman alone, of being unmarried with children, does not exist. When marriage is not forced upon you it is a statement of trust.

The name of my special chap, with a frightfully agile mind – I hesitate to say brilliant – is Vanya Hackel. His mother is of Irish descent, his father Russian. He is not just anybody, as friends have quickly perceived, he is definitely somebody.

Vanya studied the philosophy of religion at the University of London and took a graduate course in management sponsored by the Arts Council. Co-director of his own talent-production company, Vanya conceived and produced with the Duke Ellington estate a concert of Ellington's sacred music in St Paul's Cathedral. He brought tap and modern dancers, jazz singers and a full-scale band into the historic church for the first time. We have two dance projects and a dance film in preparation. Vanya is a

Renaissance man. He belongs to a new generation of arts administrators who finance, structure and produce festivals and concerts. On our bedside table you will find Huysmans, *Lautréamont* and a copy of *Variety*. He is that rarity: a scholar in showbiz.

Vanya is some years younger than old Seymour, but then who isn't nowadays? Actually, he is considerably older – a wise owl who can see in the dark. Earnest and funny, boyishly handsome and devastatingly worldly. He was introduced to my friends, the old and new members of the continuing Diners' Club, at our champagne reception on Woodstock Road. We arranged the party at the last minute. The house was decked out in daffodils, as usual. Kenneth accepted an invitation. I thought it was elegant of us to invite him and elegant of him to come. He appeared at twilight with his wife and daughter. Kenneth greeted me with outstretched hands and a smile more eloquent than words. There was a brief contemplative silence and he moved his head in approval at my glow of undisturbed happiness.

He kissed my cheek.

'I'm so pleased for you, Lynn.' His voice was soft and tender. He raised his eyebrows, carefully scrutinizing my face. 'You're very beautiful.'

My throat was choked, my eyes misty. 'But, Kenneth, I always was.'

A neighbour girl slowly pirouetted through the hall in my old Giselle costume, a white tutu with a velvet vest. Kenneth's daughter was tantalized by the dress. Her fingers reached out, delicately touching the costume. I asked if she would like to try it on. She hesitated, clearly longing to. But her small hands withdrew from the tutu and she shook her head. Her world is safely removed from the fairyland of tutus and tiaras, just like that of my sons.

Kenneth's eyes caught mine in complete understanding.

Simultaneously we burst into helpless, passionate laughter. Silently, on winged feet, Vanya was beside me. With one deft loving movement he encircled me in his arms. I leaned my head against his with a sigh of delectable satisfaction. He asked what we were laughing about and I murmured ambiguously, 'Our childish dreams – of yesterday.' The youngster in the white tutu continued her dance. We wandered amongst the guests, clinking champagne glasses. Darkness fell and candles were lit as we remained clasped together in the blue shadows of night. I remembered most meaningfully, from a reading of Shakespeare, Portia's speech to her husband Bassanio:

> *One half of me is yours, the other half yours,*
> *Mine own, I would say; but if mine, then yours,*
> *And so all yours.*

I have taken flight into a sweet and expectant new life, but I am not a creature of the sky any more. I am of this earth. I press on now, with a joyous difference.

For at last my house is in order.

APPENDIX A

Teachers and Coaches

(in no particular order)

Jean Jepson	Raymond Franchetti
Nikolai Svetlanoff	Milko Sparemblek
Mara McBirney	Ramon Segarra
Winifred Edwards	Sir Frederick Ashton
Ailne Philips	Hector Zaraspé
Barbara Fewster	Terry Westmoreland
Pamela May	Stanley Williams
Katherine Crofton	Poul Gnatt
Errol Addison	Kirsten Ralov
Peggy van Praagh	Bill Griffith
Harijs Plucis	Peter Appel
Patricia Wilde	Victor Gsovsky
Pauline Koner	Svetlana Beriosova
Valentina Pereyaslavec	Gerd Larsen
Tamara Karsavina	Brian Shaw
Leonide Massine	Michael Somes
Sergei Grigoriev	Galina Samsova
Liubov Tchernicheva	Scott Douglas
Sir Robert Helpmann	Hal Lehrman
Erik Bruhn	Sarah Neece
Rosella Hightower	Alan Beale
José Ferran	Peter Wright

APPENDIX B

The original MacMillan *Romeo and Juliet* cast list

WHEREFORE CASTMANSHIP . . . *(see pages 246–56)*

	JULIETS	ROMEOS
1)	Margot Fonteyn	Rudolf Nureyev
2)	Annette Page	Christopher Gable
3)	Antoinette Sibley	Anthony Dowell
4)	Merle Park	Donald MacLeary
5)	Lynn Seymour	Christopher Gable

DANCE CHRONOLOGY

by John Percival

Abbreviations: m. = music by; arr. = arranged by; ch. = choreography by; prod. = produced by; f.p. = first performance.

1945–54

Dance classes in British Columbia with Florence Clough, Victoria; Grace Goddard, Vancouver; and at the Rosemary Deveson Studio, Vancouver; principal teachers Jean Jepson and Nicolai Svetlanov.

1951, 1952 and 1953

First prize in solo dance competition organized by the Ballet Society of Vancouver.

1953

April: Member of British Columbia Ballet Company specially formed to take part in Fifth Canadian Ballet Festival in Ottawa.

Created roles:

A Faun in *Daphnis and Chloe* (m. Ravel; ch. Heino Heiden).

Winter solo in *Cinderella* (m. Brahms – Variations on a Theme by Haydn; ch. Mara McBirney).

November: Auditioned and accepted for Sadler's Wells Ballet School.

1954–6

Student at Sadler's Wells Ballet School; principal teacher Winifred Edwards, and Pamela May, Peggy van Praagh, Barbara Fewster, and Harijs Plucis.

Appeared 22.1.56 in *Spectroscope* (m. Lennox Berkeley – Divertimento; ch. Terry Gilbert) for Sadler's Wells Choreographic Group.

1956–7

Member of Sadler's Wells Opera Ballet.

Created role:

Pas de deux with Christopher Gable (ch. Peter Wright) in production by Cambridge University students of Gluck's *Orpheus*.

Other new roles:

Pas de deux from *Les Sylphides* (m. Chopin; ch. Fokine) for Cecchetti Society demonstration.

Also in opera-ballets in *Hansel and Gretel*, *The Pearl Fishers*, *Rigoletto*, *The Bartered Bride*, *Eugene Onegin*.

Walked on in *Romeo and Juliet* for the Bolshoi Ballet at Covent Garden.

Took part with Pamela Moncur in RAD development of the present Advanced Syllabus, coached by Tamara Karsavina with solos created by Frederick Ashton (m. specially written by Leighton Lucas).

1957–8

Member of Royal Ballet Touring Company, in British regional theatres and at Covent Garden.

Created roles:

An Adolescent in *The Burrow* (m. Frank Martin – Concerto for seven wind instruments, kettledrum, percussion and strings; ch. Kenneth MacMillan; f.p. 2.1.58).

Pas de deux with Donald MacLeary in *First Impressions* (m. Kenneth Leighton; ch. Alan Beale) for Sunday Ballet Club. Wyndham's Theatre, 23.3.58.

Also in corps de ballet of *A Blue Rose* (m. Samuel Barber – *Souvenirs*; ch. Wright; f.p. 26.12.57), *The Angels* (m.

Richard Arnell, specially written; ch. John Cranko; f.p. 26.12.57).

Other new roles:

Dawn in *Coppélia* (m. Delibes; ch. after Cecchetti, prod. Ninette de Valois).

A Tarantella Dancer in *Veneziana* (m. from the operas of Donizetti, arr. Denis ApIvor; ch. Andrée Howard).

Pas de trois in *La Féte étrange* (m. Fauré, selected by Ronald Crichton; ch. Howard).

Pas de trois in *Swan Lake* (m. Tchaikovsky; ch. after Petipa, prod. de Valois).

Also in corps de ballet in *Pineapple Poll* (m. Sullivan, arr. Mackerras; ch. Cranko), *Giselle* (m. Adam; ch. after Coralli and Perrot), *Les Sylphides*, *Swan Lake*, etc.

1958–9

Soloist with Royal Ballet Touring Company, in Australia and New Zealand and British regional theatres. Also appeared with Royal Ballet at Covent Garden.

New roles:

Don Quixote pas de deux, (m. Minkus; ch. after Petipa).

Odette and Odile in *Swan Lake* (ch. after Ivanov and Petipa), coached by Robert Helpmann.

Polka in *Façade* (m. William Walton; ch. Frederick Ashton).

1959–60

Principal dancer with Royal Ballet Touring Company at Covent Garden and in British regions and Dublin. Also appeared with Royal Ballet at Covent Garden and for Vancouver Ballet Society (June 1960) with Christopher Gable.

Created role:

The Fiancée in *Le Baiser de la Fée* (m. Stravinsky; ch. Macmillan; f.p. 12.4.60).

Other new roles:

Giselle in *Giselle*.

La Belle Dame in *La Belle Dame sans Merci* (m. Alexander Goehr after madrigals by Clément Jannequin and Claude le Jeune; ch. Howard).

Pas de deux in *Les Patineurs* (m. Meyerbeer, arr. Lambert; ch. Ashton).

The Girl in *Solitaire* (m. Malcolm Arnold; ch. MacMillan).

Solo first danced by Svetlana Beriosova in *Birthday Offering* (m. Glazunov; ch. Ashton).

Princess Aurora in *The Sleeping Beauty* (m. Tchaikovsky; ch. after Petipa), coached by Ashton.

La Favorita in *Veneziana*.

January 1960: Seymour and Antoinette Sibley named 'Dancers of the Year' by *Dance and Dancers*.

1960–61

Principal dancer with Royal Ballet Touring Company in British regional theatres, at Covent Garden, and in Tokyo, Osaka, Hong Kong and Manila. Also with Royal Ballet at Metropolitan Opera House, New York, and at Covent Garden.

Created roles:

The Girl in *The Invitation* (m. Matyas Seiber, specially written; ch. MacMillan; f.p. 10.11.60).

The Girl in *The Two Pigeons* (m. Messager; ch. Ashton; f.p. 14.2.61).

Other new roles:

Cinderella in *Cinderella* (m. Prokofiev; ch. Ashton).

Pas de deux in *Danses Concertantes* (m. Stravinsky; ch. MacMillan).

1961–2

Principal dancer with the Royal Ballet Touring Company

in Baalbek, Damascus and Athens, and in British regional theatres.

From January 1962, principal dancer with the Royal Ballet at Covent Garden.

New roles:

Mazurka and pas de deux in *Les Sylphides* (coached by Tchernicheva and Grigoriev).

Solo in *Napoli Divertissement* (m. Edvard Helsted and Holger Paulli; ch. August Bournonville; prod. Erik Bruhn).

Dorotea in *The Good-Humoured Ladies* (m. Scarlatti, arr. Tomassini; ch. Leonide Massine).

1962–3

Principal dancer with the Royal Ballet at Covent Garden and on tour of USA and Canada.

Also with Royal Ballet Touring Company on tour of Germany and Scandinavia; and danced for Vancouver Ballet Society with Desmond Doyle.

Created role:

Leading part in *Symphony* (m. Shostakovich; ch. MacMillan) but did not dance f.p. 15.2.63 because of illness.

Other new roles:

Mariuccia in *The Good-Humoured Ladies*.

Tango in *Façade*.

Pas de deux from *Flower Festival at Genzano* (m. Helsted and Paulli; ch. Bournonville).

Crystal Fountain Fairy, Woodland Glades Fairy, and Florestan's Sister in *The Sleeping Beauty*.

1963–4

Principal dancer with Royal Ballet at Covent Garden and at Theatre Royal, Drury Lane, and with Royal Ballet Touring Company in Germany and Holland. Guest star with the Stuttgart Ballet, the Marseilles Ballet and with Western Theatre Ballet in Bath.

Television documentary *Telescope* directed by Allan King for Canadian Broadcasting Company.

Created roles:

Duet, 'If you love her', and Trio, 'Two loves I have', in *Images of Love* (texts by Shakespeare; m. Peter Tranchell, specially written; ch. MacMillan; f.p. 2.4.64).

Other new roles:

Solo in *La Bayadère* ('Kingdom of Shades' scene) (m. Minkus; ch. Petipa; prod. Nureyev).

The Bride in *La Fête étrange*.

Ophelia in *Hamlet* (m. Tchaikovsky; ch. Robert Helpmann).

Juliet in *Romeo and Juliet* (m. Prokofiev; ch. Cranko).

The Lilac Fairy in *The Sleeping Beauty*.

Can-can dancer in *La Boutique fantasque* (m. Rossini, arr. Respighi; ch. Leonide Massine), coached by Moira Shearer.

La Sylphide in Divertissement from *La Sylphide* Act 2 (m. Herman Løvenskiold; ch. Bournonville; prod. Bruhn).

1964–5

Principal dancer with Royal Ballet at Covent Garden and on tour of USA and Canada.

Guest star with National Ballet of Canada in Toronto and Washington. Studied extensively with Valentina Pereyaslavec.

Created role:

Juliet in *Romeo and Juliet* (m. Prokofiev; ch. MacMillan) f.p. 'Balcony' pas de deux with Christopher Gable in television programme for CBC, September 1964. Full role in Royal Ballet production created on Seymour but first danced by Margot Fonteyn.

Other new role:

La Sylphide in *La Sylphide* with National Ballet of Canada, coached by Bruhn and Nureyev.

1965–6

Principal dancer with Royal Ballet at Covent Garden and in Italy, also with Royal Ballet Touring Company in Oslo, Stockholm, Hamburg, and Copenhagen. Guest star with Ballet of the Vienna State Opera, and with the Stuttgart Ballet.

Created role:

Albertine in *Albertine* (ch. MacMillan) directed by Peter Wright for BBC television.

Other new roles:

Two of Diamonds in *Card Game* (m. Stravinsky; ch. Cranko).

Second and Sixth songs in *Song of the Earth* (m. Mahler; ch. MacMillan).

Odette and Odile in *Swan Lake* (ch. Nureyev after Petipa and Ivanov) with Nureyev in Vienna, coached by Plucis.

1966–7

Principal dancer of Ballet of the German Opera House, Berlin. Studied with Victor Gsovsky.

Created roles:

Second movement in *Concerto* (m. Shostakovich; ch. Mac-Millan; f.p. 30.11.66).

The Woman who thinks herself Anastasia in *Anastasia* (m. Martinů – Fantaisies symphoniques – and electronic music by Fritz Winkel and Rüdiger Rüfer; ch. MacMillan; f.p. 25.6.67).

Other new roles:

Giselle in *Giselle* (prod. Antony Tudor) with Jean-Pierre Bonnefous.

Russian Ballerina in *Gala Performance* (m. Prokofiev; ch. Tudor).

1967–8

Principal dancer with Ballet of the German Opera House,

Berlin, including tour of Germany. Studied with and helped
by Ramon Segarra and Peter Appel.

Created role:

In *Olympiade*, (m. Stravinsky – Symphony in Three Movements; ch. MacMillan; f.p. 11.3.68).

Other new roles:

Aurora in *The Sleeping Beauty*, prod. with some new ch. by
MacMillan.

Eldest sister in *Las Hermanas* (m. Frank Martin – Concerto
for harpsichord and small orchestra; ch. MacMillan).

1968–9

Principal dancer with Ballet of the German Opera House,
Berlin, including tour to Vienna. Guest star with Dutch
National Ballet in Barcelona with Rudolf Nureyev, with
National Ballet of Canada, and with London Festival
Ballet. Studied with Hector Zaraspé.

Created role:

In *Kraanerg* (m. Iannis Xenakis, specially written; ch.
Roland Petit; f.p. 2.6.69).

Other new roles:

Odette and Odile in *Swan Lake*, prod. with some new ch. by
MacMillan.

Princess Aurora in *The Sleeping Beauty*, prod. by Ben
Stevenson and Beryl Grey with some new ch. by
Stevenson, with Peter Martins.

Terpsichore and Polyhymnia in *Apollo* (m. Stravinsky; ch.
and prod. Balanchine).

Second Movement in *Symphony in C* (m. Bizet; ch. and prod.
Balanchine).

1969–70

Freelance ballerina, dancing with National Ballet of
Canada; Les Ballets de Félix Blaska; Western Dance
Theatre, Vancouver; London Festival Ballet; and Ballet

of the German Opera, Berlin. Studied with Raymond Franchetti.

Created roles:

In *Ballet pour tam-tam et percussion* (m. J. P. Drouet; ch. Blaska).

In *Pas d'action* (m. Schumann; ch. Blaska).

Other new roles:

In *Poème* (m. Samuel Barber; ch. Pauline Koner).

Pas de deux from *Walpurgisnacht* (m. Gounod, from *Faust*; ch. after N. Sergeyev; prod. Galina Samsova).

Giselle in *Giselle* (prod. Peter Wright) with Egon Madsen for National Ballet of Canada.

Anna in *The Seven Deadly Sins* (m. Kurt Weill; ch. and prod. Milko Sparemblek) in Marseilles.

1970–71

Principal dancer with the Royal Ballet at Covent Garden and in British regional theatres, and with the Sadler's Wells Royal Ballet.

Guest star with Alvin Ailey American Dance Theatre at the ANTA Theatre in New York, with National Ballet of Canada and Ballet of the German Opera, Berlin. Studied with Valentina Pereyaslavec and Ramon Segarra.

Created roles:

The Artist in *Flowers* (m. rock by Janis Joplin and Big Brother and the Holding Company, Pink Floyd, Blind Faith; ch. Alvin Ailey; f.p. 15.1.71).

The Grand Duchess Anastasia and Anna Anderson in *Anastasia* (three-act version, m. Tchaikovsky – First and Third symphonies – Martinů and electronic tape; ch. MacMillan; f.p. 22.7.71).

Other new roles:

Mazurka, Op. 6 No 2; Waltz, Op. 70 No 2 in *Dances at a Gathering* (m. Chopin; ch. Robbins).

Raymonda in *Raymonda Act III* (m. Glazunov; ch. Nureyev
   after Petipa).

1971–2

Principal dancer with the Royal Ballet at Covent Garden,
at Metropolitan Opera House, New York. In USA, studied
with Valentina Pereyaslavec and Patricia Wilde. Also guest
star with the Belgrade Ballet and in film with Nureyev, *I Am
a Dancer*.

Created roles:

Pas de deux in *Side Show* with Nureyev (m. Stravinsky; ch.
   MacMillan; f.p. 1.4.72).

In *Laborintus* (m. Luciano Berio; ch. Glen Tetley; f.p.
   26.7.72).

Other new role:

Waltz and Elegy in *Serenade* (m. Tchaikovsky; ch. George
   Balanchine).

1972–3

Principal dancer with the Royal Ballet at Covent Garden
and at the London Coliseum; also with Royal Ballet
Choreographic Group. Guest star with Alvin Ailey American Dance Theatre in London.

Created roles:

In *Kisses* (m. Satie, Ibert, Laura Nyro and Ossibisa; ch.
   Ann Ditchburn; f.p. 18.1.73).

The Queen of the Cabaret in *The Seven Deadly Sins* (text by
   Berthold Brecht; m. Kurt Weill; ch. MacMillan; f.p.
   19.7.73).

1973–4

Principal dancer with the Royal Ballet at Covent Garden
and in New York, Washington and British regional theatres, also with Royal Ballet Touring Company in Israel.
While in US, studied with Valentina Pereyaslavec.

Choreography:

Solo in homage to Isadora Duncan – for herself (m. Scriabin).

Night Ride (m. Michael Finnissy, specially written; dancers June Highwood and Nicholas Johnson; f.p. Royal Ballet Choreographic Group, 20.11.73).

New roles:

The Siren in *Prodigal Son* (m. Prokofiev; ch. Balanchine).

1974–5

Principal dancer with the Royal Ballet at Covent Garden and in the Big Top, Battersea Park, also with Royal Ballet Touring Company in Athens. Guest star with London Contemporary Dance Theatre and Ballet of the Hamburg State Opera. Studied with and helped by Terry Westmoreland.

Choreography:

Breakthrough (m. Michael Finnissy, specially written; principal dancers June Highwood and Andrew Moore with students of Rambert School; Royal Ballet Choreographic Group, with London Sinfonietta).

Created roles:

Brahms Waltz in the Manner of Isadora Duncan (ch. Ashton; f.p. 22.6.75).

Other new roles:

In *Corsair pas de trois* (m. Minkus and Drigo; ch. Nureyev after Petipa; f.p. 4.3.75).

Leading role in *The Concert* (m. Chopin; ch. Robbins).

Summer in *The Four Seasons* (m. Verdi, from *I Vespri Siciliani*; ch. MacMillan).

The Girl in *Le Spectre de la Rose* (with Baryshnikov at Hamburg), coached by Anton Dolin with written advice from Margot Fonteyn.

The Lady in *Shukumei* (m. Stomu Yamash'ta, specially written; ch. Jack Carter).

Pas de deux by Bernd Berg with Wayne Eagling for the
Royal Ballet Choreographic Group and with Robert
North for London Contemporary Dance Theatre gala
(m. Scriabin).

1975–6

Principal dancer with the Royal Ballet at Covent Garden,
in British regional theatres and on tour of USA. Guest star
with American Ballet Theatre, and in Nureyev season at
the London Coliseum; also with London Contemporary
Dance Theatre and Ballet Rambert. 'An Evening with
Margot Fonteyn' in British regional theatres. Studied with
and helped by Stanley Williams in USA.
Awarded CBE, June 1976.
Evening Standard Award for ballet, April 1976.
Choreography:
Gladly, Sadly, Badly, Madly (m. Carl Davis; ch. Seymour and
Robert North; dancers Seymour and North; f.p. 28.11.75
with London Contemporary Dance Theatre).
Created roles:
The Mother in *Rituals* (m. Bartók – Sonata for two pianos
and percussion; ch. MacMillan; f.p. 11.12.75).
Natalia Petrovna in *A Month in the Country* (m. Chopin; ch.
Ashton; f.p. 12.2.76). Filmed by BBC TV (dir. Colin
Nears).
Four Brahms Waltzes in the Manner of Isadora Duncan (later
called Five Brahms Waltzes to take account of one played
as introduction; ch. Ashton – extended version of earlier
solo; f.p. 15.6.76). Filmed for *Trailblazers* (Thirteen, PBS)
and live satellite broadcast by BBC TV.
Other new roles;
Manon in *Manon* (m. Massenet; ch. MacMillan).
In *Twilight* (m. John Cage – *The Perilous Night*; ch. Hans
van Manen).

Juliet in *Romeo and Juliet* (m. Delius; ch. Antony Tudor; with Fernando Bujones for American Ballet Theatre).

Corsair pas de deux (m. Drigo; ch. Nureyev after Petipa) with Nureyev for Nureyev and Friends.

Pas de deux in *Aureole* (m. Handel; ch. Paul Taylor) with Nureyev for Nureyev and Friends.

The Wife in *The Moor's Pavane* (m. Purcell; ch. José Limón) for Nureyev and Friends.

Hagar in *Pillar of Fire* (m. Schoenberg – *Verklaerte Nacht*; ch. Tudor) with American Ballet Theatre.

Odette and Odile in *Swan Lake* (prod. David Blair) with Ivan Nagy for American Ballet Theatre, coached by Nureyev.

1976–7

Principal dancer with the Royal Ballet at Covent Garden, in British regional theatres and in the Big Top, Battersea Park, and with Royal Ballet Touring Company at Sadler's Wells. Also in the Nureyev season at the Coliseum. Guest star with American Ballet Theatre, and with the Scottish Ballet for Nureyev season at Palais des Sports, Paris. Studied with Stanley Williams in USA and Copenhagen.

Choreography:

Rashomon (m. Bob Downes, specially written; designed by Pamela Marre; lighting designer David Hersey; dancers Robert North, Desmond Kelly and June Highwood; for Royal Ballet Touring Company; f.p. 19.10.76).

The Court of Love (m. Howard Blake, specially written; designed by Demitra Maraslis; lighting designer David Hersey; principal dancers Suzanne Fitzgerald, later known as Siobhan Stanley, Carl Myers, Susan Lucas, Bernd Berg, Vyvyan Lorrayne, Derek Purnell; for Sadler's Wells Royal Ballet, formerly known as Royal Ballet Touring Company; f.p. 21.4.77).

Created roles:

In *Fourth Symphony* (m. Mahler; ch. John Neumeier; f.p. 31.3.77).

In *Gloriana* (m. Britten; ch. MacMillan; f.p. 30.5.77).

Other new roles:

Leading part in *Voluntaries* (m. Poulenc; ch. Tetley).

Katherina in *The Taming of the Shrew* (m. Kurt-Heinz Stolze after Scarlatti; ch. Cranko).

The Wife in *The Invitation* (m. Seiber; ch. MacMillan).

Scriabin Solos (ch. Lar Lubovich).

1977–8

Principal dancer with the Royal Ballet at Covent Garden and in Liverpool and on tour to USA, also with Sadler's Wells Royal Ballet to Tehran and Salonika. Guest star with Chicago Ballet and at Commonwealth Dance Gala, Alberta. Also in Gala Nights of Ballet at Royal Festival Hall, London, with Fonteyn, Makarova and others. Television documentary on the making of *Mayerling* for LWT, directed by Derek Bailey.

Choreography:

Mac and Polly (m. Kurt Weill, from *The Threepenny Opera*; designer Ian Spurling; for Commonwealth Dance Gala and Gala Nights. Dancers Seymour and Stephen Jefferies; f.p. 7.8.78).

Leda and the Swan (text by W. B. Yeats, spoken by Christopher Gable; m. Howard Blake, specially written; designed by Michael Anderson and Spyros Coskinas; dancers, Rashna Homji and Ashley Page, for BBC Television's Dance Month 1978).

Created role:

Mary Vetsera in *Mayerling* (m. Liszt, arr. John Lanchbery; ch. MacMillan, f.p. 14.2.78).

Other new role:

Carabosse in *The Sleeping Beauty* (new prod. de Valois; also danced Princess Aurora with Nureyev).

1978–9

Principal dancer (part season) with the Royal Ballet at Covent Garden and Sadler's Wells Royal Ballet. Ballet director and principal dancer, Ballet of the Bavarian State Opera, Munich. Guest teacher Peter Appel. *Giselle* filmed for video-disc and television with Nureyev and the Munich Ballet.

Choreography:

Intimate Letters (Scenario by Gillian Freeman, text spoken by Albert Finney, Sara Kestelman and Diana Quick; m. Janeček; designer Nicholas Georgiadis; principal dancers Galina Samsova, David Ashmole, Alain Dubreuil, Desmond Kelly, Siobhan Stanley; for Sadler's Wells Royal Ballet; f.p. 10.10.78).

Intime Briefe (new production of *Intimate Letters*: principal dancers Samsova, Conrad Bukes, Ferenc Bárbay, Hella Schönbrunn; Munich; f.p. 25.11.78).

Tattoo (m. Weill, from *The Threepenny Opera*; dancers Seymour, Peter Marcus, Werner Dittrich, Ulrich Busse; Munich; f.p. 5.5.79).

Boreas (m. Herbert Blendinger; dancer, Bárbay; Munich; f.p. 5.5.79).

Rashomon (new production, dancers Louise Lester, Dinko Bogdanić, Frank Perra; Munich; f.p. 16.7.79)

Tattooed Lady (new production of *Tattoo*; principal dancer Martine Van Hamel; Gala Season of Ballet, Royal Festival Hall, London; f.p. 31.7.79).

Created role:

Leading part in *Take Five* (m. Dave Brubeck; ch. David Bintley; f.p. 26.9.78).

Other new role:
Madge in *La Sylphide* (m. Løvenskiold; ch. Bournonville), coached by Poul Gnatt and Kirsten Ralov.

1979–80
Ballet director and principal dancer, Ballet of the Bavarian State Opera, Munich. Studied with and helped by Bill Griffith in USA and London, Sarah Neece and Alan Beale in Germany.

1980–present
Freelance.
Choreography:
Love of Life (m. Marc Goodings and Bruce Irwin; principal dancers Sandra Conley, Michael Coleman, Ashley Page; Royal Ballet Choreographic Group; f.p. 2.11.80).
Rashomon (new prod. for Miami World Festival of Arts 1982; dancers Naomi Sorkin, Zane Wilson and James Sutton; fight sequences Hal Lehrman).
Created roles:
Famous Mothers Club (solo m. 'Money' arr. Flying Lizards; ch. William Forsythe; for Single Parents' Gala; 30.11.80), and filmed for *Omnibus*, BBC TV, directed by Vanya Kewley.
Salome in *Salome* (Herod played by Vladek Scheybel, with text by Oscar Wilde, m. Marc Goodings and Bruce Irwin; ch. Geoffrey Cauley; designer Bill Gibb) at Fishmongers Hall, 1981.

Index

Note: Lynn Seymour is abbreviated to LS